WOMEN PLAYWRIGHTS

The Best Plays
of 1999

SMITH AND KRAUS PUBLISHERS
Contemporary Playwrights / Collections

Act One Festival '95
Act One Festival '95

EST Marathon '94: The One-Act Plays
EST Marathon '95: The One-Act Plays
EST Marathon '96: The One-Act Plays
EST Marathon '97: The One-Act Plays
EST Marathon '98: The One-Act Plays

Humana Festival: 20 One-Acts Plays 1976–1996
Humana Festival '93: The Complete Plays
Humana Festival '94: The Complete Plays
Humana Festival '95: The Complete Plays
Humana Festival '96: The Complete Plays
Humana Festival '97: The Complete Plays
Humana Festival '98: The Complete Plays
Humana Festival '99: The Complete Plays

Women Playwrights: The Best Plays of 1992
Women Playwrights: The Best Plays of 1993
Women Playwrights: The Best Plays of 1994
Women Playwrights: The Best Plays of 1995
Women Playwrights: The Best Plays of 1996
Women Playwrights: The Best Plays of 1997
Women Playwrights: The Best Plays of 1998

If you require prepublication information about forthcoming Smith and Kraus books, you may receive our semiannual catalogue, free of charge, by sending your name and address to *Smith and Kraus Catalogue, PO Box 127, Lyme, NH 03768.* Or call us at (800) 895-4331, fax (603) 643-1831. www.SmithKraus.com.

WOMEN PLAYWRIGHTS

The Best Plays
of 1999

Edited by Marisa Smith

CONTEMPORARY PLAYWRIGHTS
SERIES

SK
A Smith and Kraus Book

A Smith and Kraus Book
Published by Smith and Kraus, Inc.
177 Lyme Road, Hanover, NH 03755
www.SmithKraus.com

Copyright © 2001 by Smith and Kraus, Inc.
All rights reserved
Manufactured in the United States of America
Cover and text design by Julia Hill Gignoux, Freedom Hill Design
Photo Credit: Theresa Rebeck photo by Eileen O'Meara

First Edition: August 2001
10 9 8 7 6 5 4 3 2 1

The Library of Congress Cataloging-In-Publication Data
Women playwrights : the best plays of 1999 / edited by Marisa Smith
p. cm. — (Contemporary playwrights series)
ISBN 1-57525-274-0
1. American drama—women authors. 2. American drama—20th century. 3. Women—drama.
I. Smith, Marisa. II. Series: Contemporary playwrights series.
PS628.W6W668   1994
812'.540809287—dc20
94-10071
CIP

CONTENTS

INTRODUCTION

I realized with amazement that this summer I'm celebrating my fortieth year in the American theater. During these years changes for women have been profound. Forty years ago there were few women directors, artistic directors, and writers. Now women are a formidable force in all those areas. If women are nurturers and if theater needs some nurturing, women are indeed working in the right area. The women of theater art show us what is really important in our existence. They are working with pride, strength, and great intelligence. The play in this volume are varied and marvelous and beg to be produced because of their vitality.

Theresa Rebeck's *Abstract Expression* deals with a powerful father/daughter relationship. The play examines whether the value of art lies in the process or the product. Rebeck's jaundiced view of critics delighted me.

I have a fondness for writing from the American South. And I fear that the homogenization of culture in the United States will eventually destroy unique voices such as Joan Vail Thorne's. *The Exact Center of the Universe* looks with sympathy at the shifting values in the old and new South. Again, the vehicle in this play is a child/parent relationship, in this case mother and son. The "Tree House Gang" of that play now lives on in my memory.

A Small Delegation by Janet Neipris looks at the cultural gap between artists and educators from this country and China. Throw in some repression and some cross-cultural friendship, and you've got a riveting piece of personal and political theater.

Art offers the possibility of a journey into the unknown. Such a journey can provide exhilarating and terrifying insights. In *Lobster Alice*, Kira Obelensky gives us such a roller coaster ride, as Walt Disney Studios meets Salvador Dali.

Some plays rely on dialogue while others use visuals—props, movement, and lighting. *Fall,* by Bridget Carpenter, uses swing dancing as a metaphor in this terrific coming-of-age play. In *Last Train to Nibroc,* Arlene Hutton makes subtle use of dialogue to, as she says, show us that "stories of love and forgiveness are universal to all ages."

A superb group of plays to read, enjoy, and *produce!* I am proud to be a small part of this presentation.

Elizabeth Huddle
Writer/Director, Former Artistic Director
Intiman Theatre Company and Portland Center Stage

ABSTRACT EXPRESSION
by Theresa Rebeck

ORIGINAL PRODUCTION

Abstract Expression had its world Premiere at Long Wharf Theater, November–December 1998.

CHARLIE . . . . .David Wolos-Fonteno
SYLVIA . . . . .Beth Dixon
LILLIAN . . . . .Kristine Nielsen
EUGENE . . . . .Bray Poor
LUCAS/RAY . . . . .Larry Gilliard, Jr.
PHILLIP/JORDY . . . . .Glenn Fleshler
JENNY . . . . .Angie Phillips
KIDMAN . . . . .Jack Willis
WILLIE . . . . .Mark Nelson

DIRECTOR . . . . .Greg Leaming
SET . . . . .Neil Patel
COSTUMES . . . . .David Zinn
LIGHTING . . . . .Dan Kotlowitz
ORIGINAL MUSIC . . . . .Fabian Obispo
SOUND . . . . .Matthew Mezick
WIGS BY . . . . .Paul Huntley
PRODUCTION STAGE MANAGER . . . . .Kevin E. Thompson

BIOGRAPHY

Theresa Rebeck's plays have been seen in London, Brazil, Finland, and Scotland, as well as Boston, Chicago, Los Angeles, Philadelphia, New York, and many other American cities. Her newest play, *Dollhouse,* a contemporary retelling of Henrik Ibsen's masterpiece, just finished a run at Hartford Stage. Also recently her play *The Butterfly Collection* was produced by Playwrights Horizons, after summer workshops at both South Coast Rep and New York Stage and Film. *Abstract Expression* was produced in a world premiere at the Longwharf Theatre of New Haven in November 1998. In 1996, her political satire *View of the Dome* opened the season at New York Theatre Workshop in New York while her adaptation of Ionesco's *Rhinoceros* was playing across town at the Valient Theatre Company. Reception to *View of the Dome* was critically mixed (some reviewers thought it was too "extreme") until a subsequent production of *View of the Dome* at Victory Gardens Theatre in Chicago opened in February 1998, four weeks after the Monica Lewinsky scandal broke. As the play is about a sex scandal involving a low-level campaign worker, it was suddenly hailed as a prescient spot-on assessment of Washington politics.

Previous plays include *The Family of Mann, Loose Knit,* and *Spike Heels,* all of which were produced by Second Stage Theatre in New York, in 1992, 1993, and 1994. *The Family of Mann* won the National Theatre Conference Award for playwriting and was a finalist for the Susan Smith Blackburn Prize in 1994. *Loose Knit* was also seen in productions at New York Stage and Film, the Source Theatre in Washington, and the Long Wharf Theatre. *Spike Heels* is Ms Rebeck's most widely produced play, having been produced at E.S.T., New York Stage and Film, The Philadelphia Theatre Guild, and opened in New York in 1992 with Kevin Bacon, Tony Goldwin, Saundra Sauntiago, and Julie White. Subsequently, the play has been seen all over the world, including at the Edinburgh Fringe Festival.

Other plays includes *Sunday on the Rocks,* written in 1989, and performed to wide acclaim in Boston and as part of The International Women in Theatre Festival that same year. It was later produced by the Long Wharf Theatre and is often performed in colleges. In 1994, Ms. Rebeck worked with Bill Irwin on fragments of an adaptation of *The Twelve Dancing Princesses* at the Seattle Rep. She is currently working on a musical melodrama adaptation of *The Two Orphans.* Ms. Rebeck is a member of Naked Angels as well as New York Theatre Workshops' Usual Suspects.

Ms Rebeck's one-acts have been produced by Alice's Fourth Floor, the Westbank Café, Manhattan Punchline, Double Image Theatre, New Georges, Naked Angels, Actors Theatre of Louisville, and HB Playwrights Theatre. A collection of the one-acts, *Rebeck Revisited* ran for nine months at Theatre Neo in LA, making the LA weeklies' ten best list as one of the ten best plays of 1999.

View of the Dome, Sunday on the Rocks, The Family of Mann, Loose Knit, Spike Heels, and *Does This Woman Have a Name?* have all been published by Samuel French. *View of the Dome, The Family of Mann,* and *Spike Heels* have also been published as part of the annual Women Playwrights: Best Plays of the Year series, put out by Smith and Kraus. Her collected plays have been published by Smith and Kraus.

In television, Ms. Rebeck has written for the HBO series *Dream On, Brooklyn Bridge, L.A. Law, Maximum Bob, First Wave, Third Watch* and *NYPD Blue,* where she also worked as a producer. She is currently consulting producer on *Law and Order: Criminal Intent,* starring Vincent D'Onofrio. In film, she has written the screenplay for *Kalamazoo,* an independent short starring Wallace Shawn and Adrienne Shelley. Her produced features include *Harriet the Spy* and *Gossip,* scheduled for release in March 2000. She is currently writing *Catwoman* for di Novi Pictures/Warner Brothers, *The Richest Girl in the*

World for 20th Century Fox/RKO Pictures, and *War Crimes* for Francis Ford Coppola.

Awards include the Mystery Writers of America's Edgar Award, the Writer's Guild of America Award for Episodic Drama, the Hispanic Images Imagen Award, and the Peabody, all for her work on *NYPD Blue.*

Rebeck earned her M.F.A. in Dramatic Writing and her Ph.D. in Victorian Literature at Brandeis University, where she met her husband, the stage manager Jess Lynn. They have a six-year-old son, Cooper.

CHARACTERS
CHARLIE: Black, mid-fifties.
SYLVIA: White, early sixties.
LILLIAN: White, late thirties.
EUGENE: White, forty.
JENNY: White, twenty-eight.
KIDMAN: White, early fifties.
RAY/LUCAS: Black, late twenties.
PHILLIP/JORDY: White, late twenties.
WILLIE: White, thirty.

SET
The locations vary between Charlie's apartment, quite small and meager, on the Lower East Side; Sylvia's elegant apartment on the Upper East Side; the kitchen of Kidman's artist's loft; and the office of Lillian's gallery.

ABSTRACT EXPRESSION

ACT ONE
Scene One

Lights up on a man at a table. He is unloading a bag of groceries and talking to a small bird in a cage on top of a very small television set.

CHARLIE: Who needs money? Long as we can eat and watch a little television now and then we be okay, hey Sweetpea. Look at this, dollar ninety-nine for toilet paper, you believe that? Plus they raised the coffee again. I don't really care long as I don't have to drink that stuff tastes like nuts and berries. Four ninety-nine a can. That's a crime. If I was making the rules, I'd keep down the coffee, that's what I say. Only sure way to stave off the revolution. Yeah, don't look at me like that, I got your peanut butter.
(He pulls it out of the bag and looks at it.)
Reduced fat. They charge the same and take things out, that's the way the world, huh. Everything just shrinking down, well, we don't mind. You and me and a good cup of coffee, little television, who needs money. Like a kingdom in here.
(He looks at his mail and stops at a letter. Considers it, then goes back to the can of coffee.)
Make me some coffee.
(He studies the can. Blackout.)

Scene Two

Lights up on a dinner party. Eugene, Sylvia, Lillian, Lucas, and Philip are finishing their dessert and coffee.

SYLVIA: I just think the whole thing is much ado about nothing. I mean, the city has been going to hell as long as I can remember, I just think it should go there in style and I'm not going to apologize about that.
EUGENE: Don't be ridiculous, Mother.
SYLVIA: I'm not being ridiculous, it's absolutely everywhere in the news again. The gaps between the rich and poor, as if this were a noteworthy situation, or an actual social condition or something. When it's really noth-

ing more than a *definition*. I mean, it's just what the words mean, isn't it? Some people are rich, and some are poor, and the poor ones don't have as much *money*. How is this news? This is some idiot's idea of news.

LILLIAN: Sylvia. You're just trying to be controversial.

SYLVIA: But I'm not! This isn't even original, what I'm saying. I mean god, people have been — who was it who said that thing about poor people being around all the time —

PHILLIP: The poor will be with you always?

EUGENE: That was Jesus Christ, actually.

SYLVIA: There, that's what I mean. Even he was saying it and he *liked* them.
(Jenny enters and starts clearing plates.)

LUCAS: Your point being what, Sylvia? I mean, I'm not saying I disagree with you, but this is starting to make me uncomfortable. I am a person of color after all —

SYLVIA: Oh don't start that. That's not what I'm talking about and you know it. I'm just saying how bad is it really, being poor? Don't you think they're exaggerating, at least a little, the source of all our social problems et cetera, et cetera; well I know plenty of rich people who have social problems. And if the rich are as bad as the poor, socially I mean, or any other way for that matter, well. Then all this fuss is really over nothing.

EUGENE: All what fuss? I don't even know what you're talking about.

SYLVIA: You do too, and don't use that tone with me, young man.

EUGENE: I'm not using a tone, Mother, you're just rattling on about nothing as usual —

SYLVIA: *(Overlap.)* Oh really, and may I say your manners are lovely, at your own engagement party which *I* am paying for I might add —

EUGENE: Oh for god's sake —

SYLVIA: Well, honestly, you're turning into one of those people who hate their own money and I don't have anyone else to leave it to —

EUGENE: Mother —

LILLIAN: Eugene does not hate money. I won't let him.
(She kisses his hand.)

EUGENE: *(Good natured.)* Of course I don't hate money, that's ridiculous. I'm just uncomfortable with the assumption that just because you have it that means you know something about social conditions.

PHILLIP: Well why shouldn't it mean that? Look at Donald Trump, he thinks he knows everything.

EUGENE: When in fact I happen to know that she personally has never *spoken* to anyone whose trust fund is smaller than two mil on a good day in the market.

SYLVIA: Oh that's not real money —

LILLIAN: *(Laughing.)* Sylvia —

EUGENE: *(Animated.)* Meanwhile we live in a city where people are starving, literally starving, if the newspapers are to be trusted at all —

PHILLIP: Which they're not —

SYLVIA: Oh, nobody starves on Manhattan. Manhattan is thirty-four square miles of room service, my father used to say that.

(They all laugh.)

EUGENE: Not that I care, I don't care. I just don't know why you keep going on about it.

SYLVIA: Oh, now you're upset.

EUGENE: I'm not upset.

LILLIAN: What about you, are you poor?

(She looks at Jenny. Jenny stops her cleaning for a moment and looks up, surprised.)

PHILLIP: *(Amused.)* Oh really, Lillian.

LILLIAN: What's it like?

EUGENE: Lillian.

SYLVIA: Oh no, that's not what I meant at all. I don't want to know to know what it's like, that's not the point.

LUCAS: No, I think it is.

(Jenny starts for the door, carrying plates.)

LILLIAN: Where are you going? I asked you a question.

JENNY: *(Surprised.)* Oh.

LUCAS: You're serious.

LILLIAN: Eugene has a point. I don't see how we can talk about this, consider ourselves informed on any level, if we're not willing to confront the reality of poverty in the city.

(To Jenny.) So what's it like? Can you tell us?

SYLVIA: Yes, but she's not poor. Look at her, she's clearly educated. You're educated, aren't you, you're an actress or something.

LUCAS: Actresses are poor.

JENNY: I'm not an actress.

SYLVIA: But you're educated.

(There is an awkward pause at this.)

JENNY: I've been to high school.

SYLVIA: Not college?

JENNY: No.

LILLIAN: But you graduated high school.

JENNY: *(A slight beat.)* I haven't, actually. Excuse me.

(*She heads for the door, with the plates.*)

SYLVIA: Oh, you dropped out, is that it? To be an actress, or something?

EUGENE: She already said she's not an actress, Mother.

(*To Jenny.*) I'm sorry. You need to finish up, and we're keeping you.

SYLVIA: All of a sudden you're so sensitive; well, she can just answer the question before she goes. What is it like to be poor?

(*They stare at Jenny. She considers this.*)

JENNY: It's like not having enough money.

SYLVIA: This is my point. . . .

JENNY: You worry a lot.

SYLVIA: You worry? Well I worry.

EUGENE: You worry about your nails, and whether or not you can get theater tickets.

JENNY: Did you need anything else?

LILLIAN: Stop trying to run off, this is interesting.

JENNY: It's not interesting. It's not. It's just, you don't have enough money. That's all it is. You skip breakfast. You buy cheap shoes. You stand in the drug store and try to figure out how much it costs per aspirin if you buy the big bottle instead of the little one, and all you can think is of course it's better to just spend the money and have the big bottle because then you've paid less per aspirin, but if you do that, there won't be enough left to go to a movie and sometimes you just want to go to a movie. You'd be amazed at how long you can think about that. Then you think about other cities where movies don't cost eight dollars and you get mad, 'cause eight dollars is a *lot*, for a movie, it's . . . it's boring, really. A lot of boring things stick in your head for a long time. You just, you think about money all the time.

EUGENE: *(Dry.)* So in one way at least, it *is* like being rich.

SYLVIA: Don't your parents help you?

JENNY: My mother's dead.

PHILLIP: What about your father, doesn't he work?

JENNY: No, he does work, he works very hard. But he's, actually, he's an artist.

LILLIAN: An artist? You mean a painter?

JENNY: Yes.

SYLVIA: Oh, that's different. Her father's an artist. So she's poor, but it doesn't count.

EUGENE: Why not?

SYLVIA: Artists are supposed to be poor. It helps their art. And don't argue with me about this, I'm right about this.

LILLIAN: *(Interested.)* What's his name?

JENNY: Walter Kidman.

LILLIAN: Mac Kidman?

(There is a surprised stir at this. Jenny is clearly startled.)

LUCAS: *(Amused.)* My god, Lillian. You know this man?

LILLIAN: Is it him?

JENNY: *(Now truly uncomfortable.)* Yes, actually.

LILLIAN: No one's heard from him in years. He's still painting?

JENNY: Of course he's still painting. That's what he is, he's a painter.

PHILLIP: *(To Lillian.)* Is he any good?

LILLIAN: There was some debate about it, but he had something of a career, what, fifteen or twenty years ago. My uncle reviewed one of his shows. He didn't much like that particular batch, but he always felt he had talent.

JENNY: Your uncle?

LILLIAN: Yes, he was the art critic for the *Times*. You must've been a child, I'm sure you don't remember.

JENNY: Of course I remember. It was his last show.

LILLIAN: Was it?

JENNY: I have to go.

(She suddenly turns and heads for the door.)

LILLIAN: *(Calling.)* But your father's still painting?

JENNY: *(Tense.)* Yes. He is.

LILLIAN: I'd love to see what he's doing these days. I have a gallery. Lillian Paul. My uncle had terrific respect for your father. He just thought he was going down the wrong track, I think.

(A beat. Jenny doesn't respond. She finally turns and goes.)

SYLVIA: Well, that was rude.

EUGENE: For god's sake. You were examining her like she was some kind of bug!

SYLVIA: We were expressing interest. How is that a bad thing?

PHILLIP: This Kidman was good, you say?

LILLIAN: Not likely, but for god's sake, you can't say that to the man's *daughter*. What kind of a bitch do you think I am?

(They laugh. Blackout.)

Scene Three

Kidman's loft. Kidman and Charlie sit at a table, getting drunk on Jack Daniels. They are looking at a painting.

CHARLIE: I like it.

(Kidman goes to the painting and turns it so that it now stands horizontal, which is the correct way to look at it.)

KIDMAN: It's shit.

CHARLIE: No, it's good.

KIDMAN: No, I mean, yeah, it's good shit. But Jesus, this bullshit —

CHARLIE: That part, looks like a duck?

KIDMAN: What?

CHARLIE: It looks like a little duck in a lake, or one of those birds with the legs. And the things over there . . .

KIDMAN: What things?

CHARLIE: You know, those things grow out of the water. Bullrushes.

KIDMAN: *(Annoyed.)* Those aren't — this is not a duck, all right?

CHARLIE: Then what is it?

KIDMAN: It's abstract. It's not anything.

CHARLIE: If it's not anything, it can be a duck.

KIDMAN: No it can't.

CHARLIE: That's what you said before. Before, you said —

KIDMAN: It's *abstract.*

CHARLIE: So, it's an abstract duck.

KIDMAN: It's nonrepresentational!

CHARLIE: *(Overlap.)* I'm just pulling your leg. You get all worked up and start using words, I'm just having a conversation here. Good lord.

KIDMAN: *(Overlap.)* I'm having a conversation. Am I not having a conversation? I'm just saying it's not a duck.

CHARLIE: Yeah, okay. . . .

KIDMAN: This line is shit. Look at this, it's like some giant worm.

(He looks for a brush.)

CHARLIE: Leave it alone, I like it.

KIDMAN: You think it looks like a duck! I mean Jesus, you're like some fucking German expressionist, why don't I just put a woman and a tree in there, that would really make it good —

CHARLIE: Oh, cut it out.

KIDMAN: Those idiot Germans acting like they invented the moon, when they didn't even —

(He starts to smudge something.)

Fucking philosophical shitheads. Look at this. Aw, shit.

CHARLIE: Leave it alone!

KIDMAN: Hey, who's the painter, you or me?

CHARLIE: I'm just saying —

KIDMAN: Who's the painter?

CHARLIE: Don't pull that shit on me. You want to fuck that up, be my guest, but all I'm saying you should calm down, stop being such an asshole, and just accept the fact, that's a damn duck.

(Kidman sits and stares at it.)

KIDMAN: Fuck, I'm fucked. It's a fucking duck.

(He laughs. Charlie laughs, too. Kidman pours another round of drinks and stands to put the painting away.)

CHARLIE: Well, I like it.

KIDMAN: You want it?

CHARLIE: You mean to have? You throwing that away?

KIDMAN: I'm not throwing it away. I'm giving it to you.

CHARLIE: Don't you throw that away. That's good, I'm telling you.

KIDMAN: I'm not throwing it away, I'm giving it to you.

CHARLIE: 'Cause a lot of people might like a picture like that.

KIDMAN: You don't want it?

CHARLIE: I didn't say that. I been saying I like it.

KIDMAN: But you don't want it.

CHARLIE: I'm just saying you could sell that for a lot of money.

KIDMAN: What are you, nuts?

CHARLIE: They sell pictures, people make a lot of money off pictures like this.

KIDMAN: Really? No, really?

CHARLIE: Yeah I know you being smart with me. All I'm saying, one day, we'll be singing and dancing 'cause you gonna be *rich*.

KIDMAN: 'Cause the market for paintings of ducks is about to take off.

CHARLIE: That's what I said.

KIDMAN: Too bad it's not painted on velvet, that would make it really good.

(They laugh. Jenny enters, still in her catering outfit, carrying a large paper bag of leftover food.)

JENNY: Hey, Charlie. Hi, Daddy.

(Charlie whisks the bottle off the table and holds it between his legs on the floor. Happily involved in her own news, Jenny doesn't notice it at first.)

CHARLIE: Hey, honey.

KIDMAN: Hey, where'd you go? I turned around and you were gone.

JENNY: I took this catering gig at the last minute, I *so* did not want to do it, but they were begging, and I thought, well maybe I can work this into a favor from Bernie sometime, so I went and I was the only one working, right, and these people are kind of a nightmare, but they could not care *less* about the leftovers, which is like, I mean, excuse me. Chicken with mustard tarragon sauce.

CHARLIE: Oh my goodness, how 'bout that.

JENNY: Stuffed acorn squash.

KIDMAN: Oh, this is fantastic.

JENNY: *Crème* brûlée. I love even just saying that, *crème* brûlée. Crème brûlée. I got all of it, most of these people are, they're all so worried about getting *fat* they've completely forgotten how to eat. Crème brû —

(She sees the bottle of whiskey on the floor. The mood changes. Charlie looks embarrassed. Kidman becomes immediately defiant, openly picking up the bottle. He takes a mug full of paint brushes off the table, knocks the brushes out, and makes a show of pouring a large drink.)

CHARLIE: I guess we gonna have a feast, huh?

(Beat.) Just come up to watch the game. My TV busted.

JENNY: *(Still trying to recover.)* Oh, huh?

CHARLIE: *(Tap dancing now.)* Picture don't even come in, just scramble, you know. So I came up here, saying I'll just watch on your set, then Mac, he can't even find it. Put it away somewhere, he don't even know.

KIDMAN: It's here somewhere.

JENNY: So you couldn't find the TV, so you decided to get trashed.

(A beat. Charlie is embarrassed. Kidman is not.)

CHARLIE: Oh now.

KIDMAN: That's right, we took your hard-earned money and said what's the surest way to piss that girl off? What's gonna really tie her up? How can I make my long-suffering daughter suffer even more?

JENNY: Daddy. You promised.

KIDMAN: "Daddy, you promised."

JENNY: *(Patient.)* Yes, you promised, and I don't know why you'd, it's been months, and everything's fine, you were doing, we're —

KIDMAN: Oh now I have to justify myself to my daughter? Is that where we're at? I'm such a sorry hack I have to lie to everybody when I want a drink or you're what, you're gonna cut off my allowance —

JENNY: You told me —

CHARLIE: We was just having one drink, Jenny.

JENNY: Charlie, half the damn bottle is — I'm not — no.

    (She dumps the food and heads for the next room, trying not to lose it.)

KIDMAN: *(Yelling after her.)* You're an old woman!

JENNY: You're a drunk!

KIDMAN: Oh you really cut me. That's a hit. Oh *my* —

JENNY: I can't believe this. I've been working like an animal, serving eight courses
    to assholes so we can pay for some heat in this — I can't even — I'm beg-
    ging scraps of food and you're back here killing yourself! You know that
    stuff will kill you, and —

KIDMAN: Christ you need to get laid.

JENNY: *(Losing it.)* I WOULD get laid if I had a *life* instead of —
    (Beat.)
    I'm such an idiot. I'm just a complete fucking idiot.

KIDMAN: That's my girl.

JENNY: Fuck you.

KIDMAN: Yeah, fuck you too.

CHARLIE: No, now, Jenny! You know, we was just having a nip.

    *(There is a terrible pause while Kidman glares at her. She doesn't know what
    to do. She sits, finally. Kidman prowls. Charlie looks at them both, nervous.)*

CHARLIE: *(Continuing; tap dancing again.)* Did I tell you? Got a letter from
    my sister's boy, Ray. He's finally gettin' out of the joint. I say that's a good
    thing, you know, but he been in there upwards four years, so who knows.
    Wants to come stay with me, I'm thinking, well, I don't know about that.
    Ain't exactly a palace down there. Don't have the kind of room you all
    got. Plus the TV's on the blink. Well I told you that.

    *(He stops, unhappy, wondering what the others will do. Jenny wipes her eyes
    and finally looks up, resigned.)*

JENNY: Ray? Did I meet him once?

CHARLIE: Well maybe you did. You remember that, you got a good head on
    your shoulders, 'cause that would be a long time ago. Course you got a
    good head, we know that.
    (Jenny sobs, briefly.)
    Oh now honey. You're okay.
    (Kidman prowls, restless.)

KIDMAN: I don't ask for this. You want to take off, take off. No one's begging
    you to prostrate yourself on the altar of filial devotion. Your brother had
    the balls to leave. You want a life, go get one.

JENNY: I'm going to bed.

KIDMAN: Just don't come home expecting people to genuflect, you're so holy, you're so good. Your life is your own.

CHARLIE: You're going to bed? I thought we was gonna have a party. All this nice food.

JENNY: You eat it.

CHARLIE: Oh now Jenny.

JENNY: I just don't know why I even — these people were hideous, they — and you think that's nothing? That I have to stand there and take it, the whole time I'm just thinking, pay me. I'm doing the job, why can't you just pay me, you sons of bitches, why do I have to be humiliated to just get the damn MONEY.

(Beat.)

Fuck it.

(She heads for her room, speaking as she goes.)

Oh. By the way. One of them knew who you were. Her uncle was that critic who said your sense of color was pre-adolescent.

KIDMAN: Asshole.

JENNY: She wants to see your work. She has a gallery, Lillian something.

KIDMAN: You didn't even get her damn name?

JENNY: Lillian Paul, all right —

KIDMAN: Yeah, Lillian Paul, and I'm supposed to jump, is that it? They're coming crawling now, I'm supposed to go pay obeisance to some cunt wouldn't know a real painting unless she pissed on it —

JENNY: Never mind.

KIDMAN: Did you tell her she can go fuck herself? Did you tell her that?

(There is a short beat while Jenny looks at her father.)

JENNY: No. I didn't.

(Blackout.)

Scene Four

It is the middle of the night. Kidman sits at the table, totally drunk, surrounded by half-open boxes of leftovers and the now near-empty bottle of Jack. Jenny enters, in a T-shirt and old pajama bottoms. She looks at him, in the half-light.

JENNY: It's three in the morning. You should go to bed.

KIDMAN: All this food. I was gonna . . .

JENNY: Just go to bed.

(She starts to put away the food.)

KIDMAN: That stuff is shit. It's shit anyway. I was in Pisa, with your mother, we had crème brûlée, that was the real stuff. Got in a fight with some asshole on the street, he's screaming at me in Italian, right? I did something, who knows, your mom gets so embarrassed, she starts screaming back at him in German. He's yelling Privato! Privato! And your mom is, she was embarrassed, so she starts talking German, so this guy doesn't know we're American idiots. Ich ben Deutch something, wasser bitte, shit like this.

JENNY: And then you had crème brûlée.

KIDMAN: She did. I ordered . . . pear tart with avocado sauce. She hated pears. Only ever had two in her life that she liked. One was in France. The other. . . . Spent years, trying to get her to eat another pear. Big thing with her. The search for pear number three.

(Beat.)

You got that from her. This thing for food. The woman would take a bite of something and swoon. Thought a corn dog was a gift from god.

JENNY: Well. Corn dogs.

KIDMAN: She was like that. Skinny as a twig. Loved food. Any food. Except pears.

(Beat.)

JENNY: How was it?

KIDMAN: Huh?

JENNY: The pear tart with avocado sauce.

KIDMAN: It was Italy. Pear number three.

JENNY: *(After a beat.)* You should go to bed.

KIDMAN: I was gonna paint. You went to bed and I was, but I can't. . . .

JENNY: It'll be okay tomorrow.

KIDMAN: *(An apology.)* This is — I didn't — It's just, the painting is shit right now —

JENNY: It's not, Daddy.

KIDMAN: You don't know.

JENNY: I *do* know. There's no light now. You can't, you're drunk, and —

KIDMAN: Don't you fucking throw that at me —

JENNY: Daddy, there's no light! It's three in the morning. There's *no light*.

(The force of this argument actually gets through to him. He nods.)

KIDMAN: That fucking prick. Preadolescent.

JENNY: *(Patient.)* He was an asshole.

KIDMAN: Dead now, you know. That's the only good thing you can say about critics. Eventually, they're gonna die, just like everyone else. They come up with these words, preadolescent, it's *primitive,* we're *doing* something, but ever since Picasso, you can't use that word as an insult so they come up with something else because they don't want to spend half a brain cell thinking what someone's trying to do.

JENNY: Daddy, your paintings are beautiful. It doesn't matter what he said.

KIDMAN: That's what I'm saying.

JENNY: They didn't stop you. You still did it. And they're beautiful.

KIDMAN: They tried to stop me.

JENNY: They lost.

(*Beat.*)

KIDMAN: I'm murdering you.

JENNY: No.

KIDMAN: There's such light in you.

JENNY: There's light in you, Daddy. There's light in you.

(*He cannot look at her. Blackout.*)

Scene Five

The office of Lillian Paul. Lillian sits at her desk. Charlie stands before her, holding a painting.

LILLIAN: Where did you get this?

CHARLIE: My friend give it to me. Walter Kidman, he's a friend of mine.

LILLIAN: Really.

CHARLIE: See I know him and his girl Jenny, who said she met you and you said, you wanted to see what kind of painting Walter was making, 'cause you remembered him from before.

LILLIAN: And he sent you as his emissary.

CHARLIE: He don't know I'm here.

LILLIAN: Such a surprise.

CHARLIE: 'Scuse me?

LILLIAN: No, continue.

CHARLIE: Well, he's a little contentious on account that's just how he is, but he give me this painting, and when Jenny said you remembered Walter I thought maybe I could sell it.

LILLIAN: This is yours to sell?

CHARLIE: Yeah, he give it to me. It's a present.

LILLIAN: He gave you a present, and now you're selling it? That's not very nice.

CHARLIE: Well, I'm way out of cash, and that's a fact. My nephew's coming to stay with me, my TV's busted, and now they's these cuts the goverment keeps talking about. I don't know. Spent two years in Vietnam, that don't seem to mean much to people, but can't change the world, I guess.

LILLIAN: I guess not.

(She looks at the painting. Charlie watchers her, nervous.)

CHARLIE: 'Cause see, I really like it. Don't get me wrong about that. That's how come I'm here, Jenny said you expressed interest, and I thought, she don't even know, on account nobody's been seeing what all Walter can do for how long. This is a fine piece of work. I think it looks like a duck. *(A beat, then, as she doesn't respond.)*

'Cause you can see him, swimming on the lake, with those things, look like bullrushes to me. I know, you're not supposed to do that. Decide what it looks like.

LILLIAN: Why not?

CHARLIE: I don't know. Walter, he just gets worked up sometimes, when you suggest stuff like that.

LILLIAN: And how much are you asking?

CHARLIE: 'Scuse me?

LILLIAN: Your price. How much would you like me to pay for it?

(There is a bit of a pause at this, as Charlie never quite expected to get this far.)

CHARLIE: Oh, I don't, you know. You'd know more about that.

(She shrugs. He looks about, uncomfortable, then decides to go for it.)

CHARLIE: *(Continuing.)* It's art and all, so that's worth something. That's all I'm saying.

(Beat. She waits.)

CHARLIE: *(Continuing.)* I was thinking six hundred dollars. Maybe seven, even.

LILLIAN: Which, six or seven?

CHARLIE: Seven.

LILLIAN: Six.

CHARLIE: Whoa, really? Okay. Six.

LILLIAN: Sold.

(Charlie grins, having hit the jackpot, and even laughs a little. His laughter becomes uncomfortable. Blackout.)

Scene Six

Sylvia's apartment. Lillian is laughing. Eugene is looking at the painting. Sylvia bustles about, serving tea.

SYLVIA: Well, I just don't know what you're saying.

LILLIAN: I'm saying I bought a painting, a very good painting.

SYLVIA: From that girl's father? That cater-person who told us what it's like to be poor, and then went on and on —

LILLIAN: *(Overlap.)* Oh god, I feel terrible about that. I was drunk —

SYLVIA: Why do you feel terrible? She was very well paid. And she took all the leftovers. I think we treated her very well.

LILLIAN: *(To Eugene.)* Yes, but what do you think?

EUGENE: I . . .

LILLIAN: You don't like it?

EUGENE: No, I do, I just . . .

LILLIAN: Because I love it. Look what he's doing with perspective, it's like the whole thing *moves,* look —

EUGENE: This isn't my forte, Lillian. I mean, you never show this stuff.

SYLVIA: No one's interested in abstract expressionism, because you can never tell if it's any good. That's the problem with it

LILLIAN: You *can* tell. This is good.

EUGENE: He actually showed up, then? The father?

LILLIAN: No, God no. This is fabulous. This old black man showed up, dressed like you wouldn't — I mean, I almost called *security,* this guy looks like he's living on the street, but he's carrying this *painting.* Turns out they're friends, and he needs cash.

EUGENE: How much did you give him?

LILLIAN: Six hundred dollars.

SYLVIA: For that? No. Really? You paid six hundred dollars for that?

LILLIAN: I'm telling you, Sylvia, I love it. And not only that, I think it's going to be worth something.

(She goes up behind Eugene and hugs him, enthusiastic. He looks at her, bemused.)

EUGENE: I haven't seen you like this, ever.

LILLIAN: *(Laughing.)* I know! I'm just so . . . you get so sick of this damn bull-shit, putting together group shows, schmoozing the fucking critics, just to get them into an opening once in a while, following who's showing what in some stupid gallery in Minneapolis for god's sake, forcing a sale out of a friend so that you can generate some little bit of heat for someone who's really good, it's all just, nothing is a bit of fun since Black Thursday. When the hell are we going to recover from that, that's what I want to know. And then to have something *different* happen, something really different. You should have seen this guy. And what did that girl say, this guy's been out there for *years,* painting, he's been painting for fifteen years in some garret, probably, and not showing anywhere. Abject poverty, blah blah blah —

SYLVIA: *(Interested.)* You mean like Van Gogh?

EUGENE: Not Van Gogh again, when are we going to —

LILLIAN: Come on, this is a *story,* Gene. I can do something with this.

EUGENE: A story. And here I am, thinking you liked the painting.

LILLIAN: I *love* the painting. The painting is fantastic, that's what makes the story so good. If the painting's no good, the story is just pathetic. But the painting is fantastic.

SYLVIA: How can you know that? It's abstract. Who can tell if those things are any good?

(Lillian is now looking for pen and paper.)

LILLIAN: We have to find Kidman. Sylvia, that catering company, what's the phone number. We have to track that girl down.

EUGENE: I already did.

(Lillian looks at him, surprised.)

EUGENE: *(Continuing.)* I felt bad. Forgot to give her her tip.

(He hands a card to Lillian. She considers this, and him, as Sylvia speaks.)

SYLVIA: *(Preoccupied, looking at painting.)* Don't be ridiculous. I tipped her the way I always do.

EUGENE: Exactly.

SYLVIA: *(Rattling on.)* Plus I let her take all that food, she did very well by us. Well, I just don't see it, Lillian. I'm glad you're excited, but I have to say, if I'm going to hang something on the wall, it should look like something. Well, I suppose you could say that's a bird, or a duck over there. I suppose you could say that.

(Blackout.)

Scene Seven

Kidman's loft. Eugene stands at one side, casually disinterested. Jenny waits, nervous.

EUGENE: They've been in there for a while.

JENNY: Yes.

EUGENE: She was very enthusiastic. About the one painting. She doesn't get this way.

(Beat.)

How many does he have? I mean, I just got a glimpse. Looked like quite a few.

JENNY: Yes.

(She paces.)

EUGENE: Hundreds, even. Fifteen years worth, I guess.

JENNY: Look, why are you here?

EUGENE: She liked his work. It's not unusual for gallery owners. Visiting an artist in his studio, that's —

JENNY: No one has been interested in him for *years*.

EUGENE: So this is a good thing. Right? Which is why you're so cheerful.

JENNY: I just think you should go. I mean, I didn't say anything, at that dinner party, but, this isn't, you don't know what —

EUGENE: Look. I wanted to apologize about that. The way people spoke to you was inappropriate, and —

JENNY: No. I'm not —

EUGENE: Well, I wanted to apologize.

JENNY: I'm not —

(Beat.)

You know, does your girlfriend know you were hitting on me at your own engagement party?

EUGENE: I was what?

JENNY: Oh, you weren't hitting on me. In the kitchen.

EUGENE: No.

JENNY: "What's that perfume you're wearing?"

EUGENE: I wanted to —

JENNY: I wasn't wearing —

EUGENE: So you said. I asked a question, you answered it. That's hardly —

JENNY: "Do you want to go have a drink sometime." That's not —

EUGENE: It was an honest —

JENNY: *(Starting to laugh.)* Oh my god. It was your own *engagement* party and you were, and now —

EUGENE: Lillian wanted to see your father's paintings, and I came along. I admit I find you interesting. That's not a crime.

JENNY: Interesting? What? I'm what?

EUGENE: Interesting. You seem —

JENNY: Interesting?

EUGENE: Yes. Interesting.

JENNY: *(Matter-of-fact, confrontational.)* Don't you mean pretty? That I seem pretty?

EUGENE: I mean what I said. You seemed interesting.

JENNY: Then I'm not pretty.

EUGENE: Of course you're pretty. That's not what I was talking about.

JENNY: *(Finally defiant.)* So you would find me just as interesting if I weren't pretty? If I were some sort of huge fat person? Or some little nerdy boy with greasy hair and glasses, but the same person, I'd be just as interesting to you?

EUGENE: If you were those things, you wouldn't be the same person.

JENNY: Funny, somehow I knew you were going to say that.

EUGENE: Do you think I'm hitting on you?

JENNY: No. I think you find me "interesting."

EUGENE: *(Growing amusement.)* Yes, you grow more interesting by the second.

JENNY: Oh, good.

EUGENE: You weren't like this at all the other night. I mean, you're very —

JENNY: *(Frustrated finally.)* What?

EUGENE: Nothing. Interesting.

(Lillian and Kidman reenter the room. Kidman and Lillian are deep into it. Lillian is happily enthralled.)

KIDMAN: Yeah, it's possible he wasn't a complete vegetable, I'm just saying, people admit he didn't even paint —

LILLIAN: Unquestionably, his assistants were doing some of the work. But there's plenty of critical discussion about —

KIDMAN: Don't you fucking talk to me about critical discussion. I'll kick you out of my fucking studio, you —

LILLIAN: But that's not what we're talking about. We're talking about what *you* think.

KIDMAN: About de Kooning.

LILLIAN: Yes.

KIDMAN: Yeah, see, I don't think that's what we're talking about.

(He looks at her. She gives him a slight nod of acknowledgement.)

LILLIAN: I think that many things inform an artist's work, and many things taint it. Your work is untainted but not uninformed. I would say it's a tragedy that you haven't been showing all these years, but I don't think you could've done this otherwise. The sense of privacy and turbulent isolation, it's absolutely stunning. My future mother-in-law says the problem with abstract expressionism is that no one understands it, but it's impossible to misunderstand the greatness of your paintings. Really, I haven't any words.

EUGENE: And yet.

LILLIAN: *(Excited, oblivious.)* Yes, and yet I could go on! But I won't. I'm going to show these paintings, Walter. And I'm not talking about next year; I'm talking about now. Next month. This is absolutely the right time, no one's seen anything like this in years. It's going to be huge, I can't even — in one year, I am going to have you in the Whitney Biennial, and in five you'll be in MOCA. Along the way I don't know, I wouldn't be surprised if we got you in the Modern, what with your pedigree, this is like a resurrection for god's sake! Fuck de Kooning, we've got Walter Kidman back from the dead! These paintings make the post postmodernists I've been showing look like pure bullshit —

KIDMAN: They look like that anyway, Lillian.

LILLIAN: *(Laughing.)* Oh, Walter. This is going to be *fun.*
(She takes his hand and smiles at him. He doesn't quite know what to make of this.)

JENNY: Well, that's just —

LILLIAN: What?

JENNY: Crazy. I mean, this is just — crazy.

LILLIAN: I don't think so.

JENNY: Well, but, so are we supposed to clap? No one's even spoken to him in fifteen years and now we're supposed to jump up and down because you like his paintings?

KIDMAN: What's your problem?

JENNY: Dad, they're not even — they didn't even come over here because — oh, shit.

LILLIAN: Oh.

JENNY: I mean it's . . .

KIDMAN: *(Offended.)* What? It's what?

JENNY: *(Defiant.)* It's crazy.

KIDMAN: Since you know so much about it.

JENNY: Dad.

KIDMAN: I mean, I thought *I* was the one painting my guts out for fifteen years. I didn't realize —

JENNY: Oh, for — you're the one who said it! All this time —

KIDMAN: *(Overlap.)* You were the great genius behind the throne. Last I checked, I was in there by myself, mixing the paint, picking up the damn brush, day after day, I didn't realize you were running in there every night like some little magic pixie after I'm asleep —

JENNY: *(Overlap.)* You've been doing this for fifteen years without them!

KIDMAN: Don't you fucking talk to me like an idiot —

JENNY: You're the one who, you keep saying, what do you need them for?

KIDMAN: It's not a question of needing them. I don't need them.

JENNY: Exactly. You did that, before, and they treated you — You did what she's talking about, the galleries, and the critics, and it almost killed you!

KIDMAN: Oh no no.

LILLIAN: The critical environment is very different now, if you're concerned about —

KIDMAN: We're not concerned.

EUGENE: We should go.

KIDMAN: No. She's nuts. She's got like no life, she's a nun in training, it's made her —

JENNY: No one would take your damn phone calls! Sending slides out into the void, galleries couldn't even be bothered to send a rejection letter! All because one asshole in the *New York Times* —

LILLIAN: It's a little more complicated than —

JENNY: It wasn't more complicated to us. My mother died. We had no health insurance, we had no heat —

KIDMAN: *(Cutting her off.)* She had cancer!

LILLIAN: *(Alert.)* Your wife died of cancer?

EUGENE: We can come back.

JENNY: Don't. This doesn't have anything to do with you. All those years, you left us alone, and it almost killed him, but then it didn't, and that's what he did. Now all a sudden, you show up, and he's supposed to jump? You can forget it. He doesn't need you. He doesn't need anything you can offer. He doesn't need it.

(There is a silence at this. Lillian looks at Kidman, who looks down. She nods.)

LILLIAN: All right, look. This was very sudden. I'm a little, I can't say I'm enthusiastic by nature, because I'm not, so maybe I got carried away. Why don't you think about it for a few days.

(She waits a beat, then looks at Eugene and turns to go.)

KIDMAN: *(To Jenny.)* Yeah, we're not thinking about this, 'cause I'm gonna do it. I mean, what are you, insane? Are you completely insane?

(Beat.)

LILLIAN: Is there someplace we can go and talk?

KIDMAN: Let's go get a drink. *(To Lillian, as he goes.)* My friends call me Mac.

LILLIAN: Well, Mac, how about some champagne?

(She laughs and they go, leaving Jenny alone. Eugene stops for a moment, wanting to say something. She looks at him. Blackout.)

Scene Eight

Charlie's apartment. Ray, energetic and edgy, looks around the small room.

RAY: This is great, Uncle Charlie. Fantastic.

CHARLIE: *(Cautious.)* It ain't big or nothin'. I mean, you gonna have to maybe sleep in the couch.

RAY: Kitchen floor do for me. Hey, you got a bird. What's your name, bird?

CHARLIE: That's Swee'pea.

RAY: Swee'pea. That's nice.

CHARLIE: *(Lecturing.)* And I know you're gonna work hard and meet your obligations. It's not easy comin' out of the slammer, and I told Charlotte I'd give you a hand, but you gonna have to work. She says that's part of the parole. You want to rest your coat?

RAY: No, I'm okay. And Uncle Charlie, trust me, you don't have to worry 'bout that other stuff, 'cause I am not going back. I'm a reformed person. Look at this, a new TV.

CHARLIE: *(Uncomfortable making small talk.)* Yeah, the other one it just finally busted. My friend Mac give me a picture he painted, and I had to sell it for the money. Woman give me six hundred dollars for it.

RAY: Six hundred dollars? For a picture of what?

CHARLIE: It's not that kind of picture.

RAY: What kind of picture is it?

CHARLIE: It kinda looks like a duck.

RAY: Six hundred dollars for a picture of a duck. And probably she woulda paid a lot more, that's how those things work. White woman, right?

CHARLIE: *(Uncomfortable.)* She was white, sure, but she didn't seem like she was taking advantage. I mean, I wouldn't say that.

RAY: That picture was probably worth two or three thousand dollars. You think she gonna pay you what it's worth? I don't think so. Black man comes to her with something she wants, she ain't gonna say let's do the right thing for this black man. She gonna say, how much can I steal this for. 'Cause that's what they like to do. It ain't worth it to them 'less they rob you.

CHARLIE: I don't think that's what it was. 'Cause she give the whole six hundred. Paid for the whole television out of that. Plus a toaster oven and a microwave.

RAY: If she give you six right out, that's 'cause she don't want you thinking about it! You got that money in your pocket, you ain't thinking about nothin', that's what they like! She don't want you thinkin', how come she's trying to get rid of me so fast? Maybe six hundred isn't such a good deal now. White women, that's how they work. Lookin' to make you a fool, that's how they work.

CHARLIE: Well, I don't know about that.

RAY: You got peanut butter? 'Cause all I'm saying, you got to be aware of what the white man's tryin' to do to you. I spent four years in prison for a robbery I didn't even do, and I regret none of it, you know why? 'Cause it taught me 'bout the world. Now I see what's comin', cause of what the white man and the black man mean to each other. There is going to be a racial explosion and that's just a fact. Other than that, the only solution is a complete separation between the black race and the white race.

CHARLIE: Some of them okay, now.

RAY: They's some tarantulas okay too, only I don't want 'em sleepin' in my bed. Look at this place, all you got's four walls and a bird, that white woman won't even let you buy a decent TV. That's all I'm saying. You went to Vietnam.

(There is a pause at this, as Ray eats peanut butter.)

CHARLIE: *(Finally.)* Little more money, I coulda got cable, I guess.

RAY: That's what I'm sayin'. That's all I'm sayin'.

(He continues eating peanut butter. Blackout.)

Scene Nine

Sylvia's apartment. Another dinner party is in full swing. This time, Kidman is one of the guests. They are looking at a painting.

SYLVIA: Do you like it?

KIDMAN: Like? I don't know. It's hard to talk about paintings that way.

SYLVIA: How would you talk about it?

KIDMAN: Well, I wouldn't go so far as to say that it's bad. For instance, it's not that I wouldn't piss on it if it was burning. But that's sort of the general area I'd use in discussing it.

SYLVIA: Oh, really.

KIDMAN: It's just not my kind of thing.

PHILLIP: Why don't you like it?

KIDMAN: You mean, besides the fact that it's ugly?

LILLIAN: It's never been my favorite, either, Sylvia —

SYLVIA: What do you mean, you never told me that.

EUGENE: I think —

SYLVIA: You stay out of this. Well I don't care. I like it very much. This artist is very successful.

KIDMAN: Oh yeah, well then, what do I know.

PHILLIP: Not only that, but this particular piece has been especially well reviewed.

KIDMAN: Oh, the asshole critics like it, there you go. That means it's art.

SYLVIA: No, it's not just that, although they're professionals. I don't see why I shouldn't take their recommendations. I do take their recommendations, and besides that, I like it a great deal.

LILLIAN: That's what matters.

KIDMAN: No it's not. I mean, this is — can I have more of this?
(He holds up his glass. Eugene refills it.)

SYLVIA: It doesn't matter that I like it?

KIDMAN: No, because you don't know anything.

SYLVIA: Lillian!

LILLIAN: *(Trying to save this.)* Maybe we should eat.
(She steers them to the table, where they sit.)

SYLVIA: Well, *I* don't like abstract paintings. So clearly, there are just different opinions on this matter.

KIDMAN: Yeah. Right ones, and wrong ones.

LUCAS: You've hurt her feelings, she doesn't mean it. You like some abstract paintings, Sylvia. I took you to the de Kooning retrospective, you loved it.

SYLVIA: I was being polite. Oh some of it was all right, I like the colors. I just don't like it when I can't tell what a picture's about.

LILLIAN: It's about whatever you want it to be about. However it makes you feel.

SYLVIA: I know, I know, but I don't like that.

KIDMAN: *(Fed up.)* Then don't look at it.

SYLVIA: Well, that's no answer.

KIDMAN: Yes it is.

SYLVIA: Well, I have to look at it. If I don't I won't ever know if I *can* like it.

KIDMAN: You just said you didn't.

SYLVIA: Maybe I'll change my mind.

KIDMAN: *(Getting fed up with this.)* Who cares if you change your mind? You're a moron!

SYLVIA: Oh, really!

LILLIAN: *(Again trying to save this.)* I think what Mac means is he doesn't particularly feel the need to defend his idiom. Nor should he. It's like a Frenchman defending the fact that he speaks French.

SYLVIA: If he were speaking French, I'd like him much better.

PHILLIP: Well, I think that Sylvia might have a point.

SYLVIA: Thank you.

PHILLIP: That's not to say that I object to abstract expressionism per se. But if the subject of American art is in fact "The New," as Hughes posits, then how do you justify its return, a mere thirty years after its flowering?

LILLIAN: It's American Neo-classicism. The only significant movement that was absolutely defined by American artists is, after all, abstract expressionism —

PHILLIP: Oh Lillian. Andy Warhol is spinning —

LILLIAN: I don't care; Pop Art was a dead end. The whole scene just turned into one huge disgusting crowd of poseurs and hypocrites, and I ought to know. People are hungry for art again, real art, beauty, truth, and everything else holy and good that got tossed out in the eighties. That's what we're going to give them.

LUCAS: You are so good.

LILLIAN: Thank you, and I've barely even begun. Mac and I are planning on making a ton of money, aren't we, Mac?

KIDMAN: A ton of money. That sounds about right.

LUCAS: Careful, Mr. Kidman. You're very close to admitting that you very much care if people like your paintings after all.

KIDMAN: I only care if they buy them. The only one who has to like them is me.

LUCAS: Ah. A romantic distinction.

PHILLIP: Really, well, forgive me, but I think you'll care if the critics like them.

KIDMAN: *(Starting to lose it.)* Yeah, okay —

PHILLIP: Am I wrong? Because from what we heard you stopped showing because of one or two bad reviews —

KIDMAN: You don't know dick about it, asshole.

PHILLIP: Have I touched a nerve?

KIDMAN: *(To Lillian.)* Who are these people?

LILLIAN: Leave the critics to me.

SYLVIA: You see, I was right. You care if the critics like you.

KIDMAN: Hey, I didn't ask to come here. I mean, this is horseshit —

LILLIAN: All right, Mac, thank you —

KIDMAN: This fucking homo trying to tell me something about my work. I mean —

PHILLIP: *(Outraged.)* Excuse me? What did you call me?

LILLIAN: All right, that's enough! No more talk about art or artists or critics. Let's talk about something else. Eugene —

EUGENE: *(Awakening from an ironic stupor.)* Yes —

LILLIAN: Another topic, any topic.

LUCAS: Except poverty.

LILLIAN: Yes, except that.

EUGENE: Oh, all right. I was reading the other day about serial killers —
(All react.)
— Yes, and how psychologists have observed that these killers have actually driven themselves mad with self-loathing, and so the only time they're not in pain is when they're inflicting pain on others. The pleasure of murdering another human being is the only thing that makes life livable to them. And when I read this, I thought, my god, serial killers are just — critics. It's exactly the same thing.
(There is a terrible silence at this. Kidman suddenly roars with laughter.)

LILLIAN: *(Dry.)* Thank you, Eugene.

EUGENE: You're welcome.
(Blackout.)

Scene Ten

Kidman's loft. Jenny sits at the table, trying to do homework for her GED class. Willie, her brother, is there bothering her. He is an entertaining jerk.

WILLIE: So he's gonna do it? He's really gonna show? And you're gonna let him?

JENNY: Oh, like he listens to me.

WILLIE: This is insane. It's suicide. Do you remember what happened the last time?

JENNY: Of course I remember —

WILLIE: Jesus, Mom ended up in jail.

JENNY: It wasn't her fault.

WILLIE: Of course it wasn't her fault. It was all his fault. I'm just saying, Jesus. It's going to be a bloodbath. He's gonna show? What moron decided to give him a show?

JENNY: Some woman.

WILLIE: Is he screwing her?

JENNY: No. I don't know.

WILLIE: Do women still like him even? He's always seemed so repulsive to me. Like some big disgusting cowboy. Why you stay with him, I will never understand.

JENNY: Somebody has to. He'll starve.

WILLIE: Good riddance. What a jerk. Remember when he got drunk and locked us in for three days? Remember that? What an asshole. Why do you stay here?

JENNY: It wasn't three days, it was one day.

WILLIE: It was one and a half days because Charlie came up and heard us yelling and picked the lock. As you'll recall, Mac didn't come back for three entire days. He didn't know Charlie had picked the lock. As far as he was concerned, which wasn't very far —

JENNY: Willie, could you — god. I mean, I'm glad to see you, I am, but do you have to —

WILLIE: I'm just saying, Jesus. Look at this, you're still studying for your GED, that's pathetic.

JENNY: Oh well, thank you, I appreciate the support.

WILLIE: I mean that in a good way. I mean, it's pathetic, he's feeding off you like some sort of giant bug, why don't you leave him? Come live with me. You're my sister, I love you, come live with me.

JENNY: You just want me to live with you because you hate him and you want him to starve.

WILLIE: Hey, if he starved, I'm not saying I wouldn't enjoy that. He's an asshole. He murdered mom.

JENNY: He didn't —

WILLIE: Why do you defend him?

JENNY: I'm not defending him. It's just, you know, I was there too. I was there more than you. And I know he made a lot of mistakes, but Mom died of cancer, and I just don't — why can't her death just be hers? Why does it have to be part of him?

WILLIE: You don't think he had anything to do with her getting sick, and when he was too drunk to take her in for chemo —

JENNY: Oh god, Willie. Let's just have a good time, huh? I hardly ever get to see you. It's so great, you came over, and I just — I just don't want everything to always be about him.

WILLIE: That's what I'm saying. You shouldn't let him do this show. He'll be insufferable. And drunk. And then he'll get so worked up, we'll have to listen to him go on about the critics ad infinitum, ai yi yi —

JENNY: He's already started.

WILLIE: See? See?

JENNY: Please, he never stopped. Drinking, sometimes I can get him to stop drinking. But obsessing about the critics, no way.

WILLIE: Why do you stay with him?

JENNY: He's a really good painter.

WILLIE: That's not a reason.

JENNY: Do you want a drink?

(He looks up at this, startled. She grins at him.)

WILLIE: A drink?

JENNY: A gin and tonic. Would you like a gin and tonic?

WILLIE: A gin and tonic?

JENNY: Have you ever had one?

WILLIE: Yes I've had a gin and tonic. You don't drink.

JENNY: I drink. I started drinking; I drink gin and tonics. Do you want one?

WILLIE: I'm stunned.

(She finds gin and tonic in the refrigerator and starts making a couple of drinks.)

JENNY: Oh why? Everybody in the world drinks. I got tired of not drinking. Everybody else just does whatever they want, I should be able to have a drink once in a while.

WILLIE: No, of course, you were just so against it. You're so good.

JENNY: I don't want to be good anymore.

WILLIE: I don't think it's optional with you.

JENNY: I'm not saying I'm going to go out and, and starting being *mean* to people.

WILLIE: Heaven forbid.

JENNY: I just want to relax a little. What's wrong with that?

WILLIE: Nothing. Does this mean you're going to start dating?

JENNY: Maybe.

(She hands him a drink.)

WILLIE: The entire west side just heaved a huge sigh of relief.

JENNY: *(Laughing.)* Yeah, here's to it.

(They toast. There is a knock on the door. Jenny goes to answer it.)

JENNY: *(Continuing.)* Who's that? Charlie?

(Eugene enters, carrying Mac. Both are drunk.)

EUGENE: It's me.

KIDMAN: *(Drunk.)* This is a great guy, Jenny. You need to talk to this guy. He's fantastic.

JENNY: Dad, would you — aww Jesus.

(She helps him sit, annoyed.)

EUGENE: Who are you?

WILLIE: Who are you?

JENNY: His name's Eugene. He's, his girlfriend is the woman who's giving Mac his show.

KIDMAN: What's that, gin? You're drinking gin? *(To Eugene.)* Let's have a drink.

WILLIE: Yes, have a drink. That's what you need. Because as usual you are nowhere near drunk enough.

KIDMAN: Shut up. You're never here, I don't have to listen to you.

JENNY: I'm here all the time. Will you listen to me?

KIDMAN: No. We saw the gallery, Jenny. It's amazing. It's amazing.

WILLIE: Yeah, I heard you were showing. What a great idea, Walter; that was so much fun for everyone when you were doing that.

KIDMAN: Fuck you.

WILLIE: Fuck you too.

EUGENE: Who are you? *(To Jenny.)* Who is this?

JENNY: This is my brother, Willie.

EUGENE: You have a brother?

JENNY: Of course I have a brother.

EUGENE: You never talk about him. *(To Willie.)* They never talk about you.

WILLIE: They both wish I was dead.

JENNY: That is so not true!

KIDMAN: I wish he was dead.

WILLIE: Yeah, see, Mac wishes I was dead, and Jenny wishes I didn't wish Mac was dead. It evens out.

KIDMAN: *(Again on his own track, making drinks.)* We went to the gallery. It's nice, it's not great —

EUGENE: But it's big. Bigger than it —

KIDMAN: *(Overlap, agreeing.)* Bigger than it looks.

EUGENE: *(Overlap.)* And we hung like six of them. It's — man, you should —

KIDMAN: *(Overlap.)* Drinking and hanging paintings, you should see it, Jenny.

EUGENE: They look amazing.

KIDMAN: Amazing, right?

EUGENE: They look *amazing*.

JENNY: Dad, don't drink anymore.

   (She tries to take the drink from him.)

KIDMAN: This was here! I didn't buy it!

JENNY: I bought it, I bought it for me, and —

KIDMAN: *(Amazed.)* You're drinking? You shouldn't drink.

JENNY: *You* shouldn't drink.

KIDMAN: No no, I drink all the time.

JENNY: Dad, give me the drink.

KIDMAN: You're so good.

JENNY: I am not good.

EUGENE: Yes you are.

JENNY: I am not good!

KIDMAN: *(To Willie.)* He thinks she's interesting.

WILLIE: I just bet he does.

EUGENE: *(Off Jenny, drunk.)* She's interesting. What's so wrong, all I said was she's interesting.

JENNY: *(To Eugene.)* Could you leave, please? I have to get him to bed.

KIDMAN: No, no! He came to see you.

EUGENE: *(To Kidman.)* I came to bring you home.

KIDMAN: Oh please. I been wandering this city drunk for more years than you were born. You shoulda seen it, Jenny. The gallery. They look great on those walls. You're gonna love it. I know you don't want me to do this, but they look great, the paintings look like, you know, fuck you! All of you, they look fucking amazing, and we are gonna make a ton of money, I'm gonna take you to Italy, Jenny — *(To Willie.)* — Not you because she's the one who stuck it out, and I'm gonna take you to Italy and I'm gonna feed you pear number three, you think you know food, but you don't know food because you've never been to Italy, and we're gonna — you — we — (His mood suddenly drops.) I'm a piece of shit.

WILLIE: Oh, there's a news flash.

JENNY: Willie.

KIDMAN: (Brightening suddenly.) No, he's right. So what, I'm a piece of shit. Those are great fucking paintings, and they look great and you can quit your fucking day job, because I am going to make a ton of money. Do they look great or what?

(He laughs, delighted. He throws his arm around Eugene, who laughs too at his sudden good humor. Mac takes Eugene's drink.)

EUGENE: They look fucking amazing.

JENNY: Don't give him that.

KIDMAN: You don't believe us? Believe me, darling, cause this time the truth will set you free. Those paintings are damn fucking good.

(He hugs her. She starts to laugh, finally infected by his mood.)

JENNY: I know, Dad, I've been telling you that for years —

KIDMAN: They're fucking great.

EUGENE: It's true. I've seen a ton of these shows, and this is a great show. It doesn't matter what the critics say.

KIDMAN: No, cause they're idiots. (Laughing.) They're serial killers, that's what we figured out.

(Eugene and Kidman are laughing.)

WILLIE: Well, then you should all get along fine. Killing mom, killing me, killing Jenny, you have much more in common than anyone thought.

JENNY: Willie —

WILLIE: I'm kidding! You have no sense of humor. You're too good.

JENNY: I'm not good!

KIDMAN: You are good, my sweetie pie. You're my good girl.

(He kisses her on the forehead and then slumps on her. She helps him in a chair and takes the bottle of gin from him.)

JENNY: Oh, Daddy.

EUGENE: He's all right.

JENNY: He's not all right. I mean, why do you think he's drinking like this? He's scared to death.

(She takes the glasses to the sink, annoyed now.)

EUGENE: No, you should have faith. It really is a great show. If he keeps his mouth shut and doesn't insult the wrong people, he'll be the next big thing.

WILLIE: So how much did he drink?

EUGENE: Not that much. Some, you know, wine with dinner, and some scotch, this gin here, then at the gallery people had, tequila, I think.

JENNY: Oh, that's really great.

EUGENE: He's the one who brought it.

JENNY: And you just let him drink as much as he wanted.

EUGENE: Oh, you try telling him what to do.

JENNY: I do.

EUGENE: Yes, and I see how successful it is.

JENNY: You should go. Could you just go? Willie give me a hand.

(She goes to Mac and tries to help him stand.)

JENNY: *(Continuing.)* Come on, Daddy.

(He slumps over.)

EUGENE: I'll help.

JENNY: It's fine.

EUGENE: Come on, let me help.

WILLIE: It's not fine, Jenny.

(He has picked up a cellophane packet that fell out of Mac's pocket. Jenny looks over, startled, as Willie looks in Mac's face.)

WILLIE: *(Continuing.)* Mac? Come on, Dad, what is this stuff?

JENNY: What is it?

WILLIE: I don't know. Come on, Mac, talk to me.

(But Mac is completely out. He slumps to the floor. Willie tries to hold him up. Jenny looks at the pills, horrified.)

JENNY: What is this? What is this?

EUGENE: *(Startled.)* I don't know. I didn't — I don't know where he got that.

JENNY: Call nine one one.

EUGENE: I didn't know.

JENNY: Call, would you call?

(Desperate, Willie looks for the phone.)

JENNY: *(Continuing to Mac.)* Dad? Come on, Dad. Talk to me, Dad. Daddy?

WILLIE: Where's the damn phone?

JENNY: Come on, Dad. Oh no. Daddy, come on. Please.

(She holds him. Blackout.)

END OF ACT ONE

ACT TWO
Scene Eleven

Charlie's apartment. One of Ray's friends is there, completely comatose from the crack they are both smoking. The microwave is gone. Ray takes a hit off the crack pipe.

RAY: If negroes were actually citizens, we wouldn't have a racial problem. There is going to be a racial explosion. The only solution now is complete separation between the black race and the white race. Just as the white man has the right to defend himself, we have the right to defend ourselves. We don't hate him. We love ourselves. For the white man to ask the black man why do you hate us, is like the wolf asking his victim, do you like me? The white man is in no moral position to ask us anything.

JORDY: *(Mumbling.)* Yeah, okay.

RAY: Look at you. Your sorry white ass wasted on crack, nobody in their right mind be smoking this shit no more, but here's you and me suckin' it down, what you think's gonna happen if we get busted on this? You get sent to rehab and I'm back on Rikers for selling it to you.

JORDY: *(Correcting him.)* I sold it to you.

RAY: I'm talking white man's logic, fool. White man goes down on an o.d., everybody talks what a tragedy, big fucking articles in the newspapers. This happened right here, I'm talking right in this building, piece of shit white man gets himself fucked up on pills and booze and everyone's all upset. Black man OD's, you think it's gonna show up in the papers? More like they try to arrest his dead ass. Dead white man, he's in the newspaper, meanwhile I'm still on parole for a job I didn't even *do*.

JORDY: You did that job.

RAY: That's not the point. I'm trying to tell you something.

JORDY: And I'm trying to tell you, you're full of shit, and you know why? Because O.J. walked.

RAY: You want to talk to me about O.J.?

JORDY: I don't want to talk about O.J.

RAY: You want to talk about O.J.?

JORDY: I don't want to talk about O.J.

RAY: 'Cause in case you failed to notice, O.J. was found innocent in a court of law. That man is a hero and I'm not saying he didn't do it, what I *am* sayin', he got himself a fair trial, which is something that has hitherto been denied to the black man. The only way the black man can earn respect in a white man's world is by having money, and that is what O.J. knew, and he stood up before this entire nation ard said, I'm not your nigger, I am a rich man and I am going to buy me some justice, just like you white men been doing for hundreds of years That is what O.J. did. And don't get me started on Nicole, 'cause that's not to say she wasn't asking for that shit —

JORDY: Aw come on, I don't want to talk about O.J.!

RAY: Yeah, white people don't want to talk about O.J. 'cause they don't like to hear the truth.

JORDY: Fuck the truth, Ray. Come on.

(Jordy offers him the pipe.)

RAY: There's gonna be a race war. Count on it. Now, gimmee that.

(Ray takes it and takes a hit.)

RAY: *(Continuing.)* This is good shit.

JORDY: It is indeed.

(They laugh. Blackout.)

Scene Twelve

Kidman's loft. Eugene is there, talking to Charlie.

EUGENE: How is she?

CHARLIE: Not so good. Well, you know. It's a shock for everybody. I don't know what I'm thinking half the day.

EUGENE: Yes.

CHARLIE: All those years he was just a wild man, this never happened. Don't seem right, things finally looking up. You were here, they said.

EUGENE: Yes.

CHARLIE: They said he went real fast.

EUGENE: Yes.

CHARLIE: Yeah, that's what they said.

EUGENE: I'm here . . . I have something for Jenny.

CHARLIE: *(Awkward.)* She said nobody but me and Willie. Plus she's sleeping, I don't . . .

EUGENE: Of course. *(Explaining, awkward.)* It's just, she's going to need money. Funerals, and the hospital, emergency rooms are expensive. Death is expensive. *(He holds out a check.)*

CHARLIE: I don't think she's gonna take that.

EUGENE: It's hers.

JENNY: Hey, Charlie, it's okay, I'll talk to him.

(She stands in the doorway, sleepy, looking at the men. She clutches a sweater, which she wears over a nightgown.)

JENNY: *(Continuing.)* What is that?

EUGENE: It's from the show. The paintings, some of them were presold. This is your money. I just thought, you'll probably need it.

(She steps forward and looks at the check, confused.)

JENNY: The show isn't until next week.

EUGENE: Tonight, actually, it's tonight.

(A beat, explaining again.)

But some of the paintings are sold already. It's something the galleries do sometimes; they let important collectors come before the opening when there's a sense that it's potentially a big show.

(He is increasingly embarrassed. Jenny is confused.)

JENNY: What do you mean, a big show? How would they know? No one knew who he was.

EUGENE: *(Apologetic.)* They know these things. There's a machinery. Publicists, you know.

JENNY: *(Ignoring him.)* Yeah, but this can't be right. Look at this, Charlie, this is a lot of money.

(She shows the check to Charlie.)

CHARLIE: They paid that for Mac's paintings?

EUGENE: Actually, that's only fifty percent. That's Mac's cut. It's your money.

JENNY: Well, I don't need that. I'd rather have the paintings back.

(She puts it on the table.)

EUGENE: The paintings are sold.

JENNY: So, give them their money back.

CHARLIE: Can I get my picture back?

EUGENE: I don't think you understand. This is an important event. What's happened? The show is an important show.

JENNY: Oh yeah, now he's important, now that he's dead.

(She sits, miserable.)

CHARLIE: You want anything, honey? How 'bout I fix you a sandwich?

JENNY: Maybe some water would be good. I don't know.

(She looks around, honestly perplexed.)

JENNY: Doesn't it seem weird, he's not here? It's like, I can't believe how much it looks like the same place. Look, the walls, they're the same walls, and the door is the same door. That night, when we came back from the hospital, I found a tube of paint behind the coffee machine. Burnt Umber. He dropped it there. Sometimes, he would get in the middle of something and then go for something else and lose his paint. You know, he did that. So his paint's still here. I can't quite figure it out.

EUGENE: Jenny. You're going to need somebody to help you.

JENNY: Help me what?

EUGENE: Things are going to start to happen.

JENNY: *(On a different track again.)* I don't understand why I can't get those paintings back. I mean, what's the point, he's not here, what's the point of having the show?

EUGENE: The paintings have been sold. People think he's important.

JENNY: Stop saying that. He wasn't important when he was alive. He's not allowed to be important now.

CHARLIE: Don't talk about it, sweetie.

JENNY: *(Starting to cry.)* Charlie.

CHARLIE: It's okay, sweetie.

(He goes to her. To Eugene.)

You want to help, go see if you can get those paintings back.

EUGENE: I don't think I can.

CHARLIE: Mine looks like a duck.

(They both look at him, miserable.)

EUGENE: *(Beat; defeated.)* I'll see what I can do.

(Blackout.)

Scene Thirteen

Lillian's office. She is on the phone. Eugene sits before her.

LILLIAN: *(To Eugene.)* Is she *insane? (On the phone.)* No, not you, Ivan. I know, that's — yes, I'll be there, I'LL BE THERE. I just have to take care of this. Do not let the *Times* go, I need to talk to that guy.
(Another line rings.)
Just a minute.

LILLIAN: *(Continues. She beeps it.)* Hello. Hi, Sy. Yes it's stunning, it's really an astonishing show. I told you he was major, you should have — of course I'll hold — *(To Eugene, hand over the phone.)* Sy Newhouse, now he wants in. He can just beg; the last three artists I told him about he — *(To phone.)* Yes, Sy, I'm here. Sorry, the place has gone completely insane, as you might imagine, it's such a tragedy what happened, the timing was just hideous, not that there's ever a good time to die, God, I sound so, but how can you ever talk about death without sounding like an idiot? I just, he was a personal friend and I really feel wretched. Yes, I know, Fred came by last week, and — I wish I could — yes, of course there are, he's been painting for years in obscurity, his loft is — I don't know, the daughter is desolate and it's just not clear what her plans are, much too soon, but as soon as I know I'll call you. Yes. This week. I'll —

(Three lines beep at once.)

Sy, I've got to go, the place is a zoo. Yes, this week.

(She hangs up, interjects to Eugene.)

Fuck him. I told him two weeks ago this was going to happen, it' not my fault he didn't — hello.

(She picks up another line.)

Ivan, I'll be there. Just give me three minutes. Look, we know it's a rave; that's not going to change if I make him wait for three minutes. Hello.

(She picks up another line.)

Yes, hello. Yes, I'm sorry you're not here, it's quite extraordinary. Thrilling but so sad, too; you know, his death has taken us all completely by surprise and it's just so hard to know what to feel. No, the reviews don't come out until later this week, of course, but we've heard from everyone that, well, there's really no question about the greatness of the work, so — utter obscurity, yes. Terrible story, the wife dying of ovarian cancer because they just didn't have the money; literally they were starving for all those years, and now, well, it's just a tragedy.

(Another line starts ringing.)

Tomorrow? I'm not sure, it's soon, but I'll — oh, you did. No, we're in direct contact. I'll speak to her about it. Absolutely. Thanks.

(She hangs up, grabs the other line.)

Ivan, I'll be there!

(She hangs up, continuing her rant to Eugene.)

Vanity Fair wants to do a major profile, they're talking to Dominick Dunne. Every major art critic is raving, Sy Newhouse is begging to see the rest of the collection, the value of those fucking paintings tripled overnight, and she wants them BACK? That is not a realistic position, and I know she's in pain, God knows we're all devastated, but this is no time for sentimentality! I have worked like a dog to see this through, *everyone* in town is here, Neal Costello is on the verge of offering him a retrospective at MOMA, which is astonishing given that the damn show hasn't even been reviewed yet, and in case you didn't notice, the fucking *New York Times* gave him a picture with an obit written by Robert Hughes *himself*, hasn't it even *occurred* to anybody that that didn't just *happen*? Mac isn't here to see this; well, he's going to get his moment in the sun just the same, and it's not like I'm just doing this for myself by the way, so you just stop glowering at me like —

EUGENE: *(Overlap.)* If I'm glowering, it's because you haven't given me a moment to get a word in edgewise!

(The phone suddenly rings again.)

(Angry.) Do you think you could put that thing on hold and talk to me for just one minute?

(She does. She looks at him.)

LILLIAN: I'm sorry. But as you can see, a lot is happening, very quickly, and if I don't take care of this, now, someone truly hideous is going to step in and exploit the whole thing.

EUGENE: That's hardly a reason for you to exploit it.

(Beat.)

LILLIAN: You find this grotesque.

EUGENE: Yes, I find it grotesque! You need to slow down. That poor girl is devastated —

LILLIAN: Well, that "poor girl" might try thinking about her father for once —

EUGENE: Don't start on her.

LILLIAN: Don't *you* start. I've been very patient about her, Eugene. After all. She's a cater-waiter who didn't even finish high school, and you tried to pick her up at our *engagement* party. And it's ridiculous, you thinking I didn't know.

(Beat.)

EUGENE: Nothing happened.

LILLIAN: I know nothing happened. I know.

(Upset, she reaches into her purse, searching for something, drops a prescription bottle.)

I have *such* a migraine. I'm only saying, this is exactly what he was eating himself up about all those years; this is it. This is what he wanted, and I'm the one who got it for him. And she is not going to fuck it up!

EUGENE: She just doesn't understand —

LILLIAN: Don't explain her to me. Please. I will take it from here. I will let her know that she's not getting her paintings back; the paintings that are here in the gallery are off the table. What is now in negotiation is the *rest* of the collection. She's sitting on millions, for God's sake, and I'm not talking a few millions. I'm talking many, many millions.

(Eugene starts to hand the bottle to her, then stops and looks at it.)

EUGENE: You just had this filled last week.

LILLIAN: And things have been a little tense since then, and now I have to have it filled again.

(She takes it back from him and shoves it into her purse. She kisses him.)

LILLIAN: *(Continuing.)* Now please, can you please go out and keep Ivan calm for just a few more minutes? That call is still holding.

(Eugene nods, considers her for a beat, and goes. She picks up the phone.)

LILLIAN: *(Continuing.)* Hello? Yes, hi, hi, I meant to call you back, but things are just crazy. I know. It's not clear what's going to happen, the daughter is very confused right now. No, I know, but I truly don't think it's going to be a problem. There's also a son.

(Blackout.)

Scene Fourteen

Kidman's loft. The light is on. Mac sits at the table, reading the newspaper and eating a donut. Jenny enters the room and sees him. He looks up.

KIDMAN: Did you see this? This guy compares me to Van Gogh. I'm an abstract expressionist, you fucking moron! Van Gogh painted flowers!

JENNY: Daddy.

KIDMAN: *(Reading.)* Christ, this stuff is unbelievable. I mean, it's like all of a sudden I invented painting. Schnabel's just shitting, you know he is. Trust me, he's eating his own liver out. Oh yeah, here we go, Basquiat. Yeah, our work is *so* similar.

JENNY: Daddy!

KIDMAN: What?

JENNY: I can't believe you came back from the dead to read your reviews.

KIDMAN: *(Of course.)* Good reviews?

JENNY: Am I the only person in this whole city who doesn't care about those things?

KIDMAN: I think you are, babe.

JENNY: Great.

KIDMAN: Hey, come on. Somebody writes about you in the newspaper — for instance let's say maybe The Biggest Newspaper In The World — it's a temptation to at least check it out. I'm not saying it's not fucking ironic. Christ, this stuff is tedious as shit. How come the most boring people on the planet get to write for the newspapers? I mean, I sat in this apartment for years making one pithy fucking brilliant observation after another, no one put *that* in the newspaper. And I'll tell you, if I were writing for the fucking *New York Times* it would be a shitload more fun to read. Listen to this —

JENNY: *(Cutting him off.)* Do you mind? I'm really not interested.

(Kidman sets the newspapers down, considers her.)

KIDMAN: So how's your lovely brother?

JENNY: Willie? He's fine. Busy. I haven't seen much of him since the funeral.

KIDMAN: Want to know why? He's out there, selling my paintings.

JENNY: *(Confused and surprised by this.)* He can't — he can't sell them without me.

KIDMAN: Hey, he's out there doing it! It's done. And I don't want him to get the money. I want you to get the money. You're the one who stuck it out. He doesn't get shit out of this. I don't care if he is your brother.

JENNY: Would you stop calling him "your brother" like I created him? He's your son.

KIDMAN: Don't remind me, he's a total piece of shit.

JENNY: He is not! He's, what do you expect, anyway, you were such a lousy father, what do you expect?

KIDMAN: *(A gentle rebuke.)* Jenny. Sell the paintings.

JENNY: No.

KIDMAN: I want you too.

JENNY: Well, I don't want to.

KIDMAN: Goddammit! That's my life in there —

JENNY: It's my life too, Dad. I am the only person, I kept you going, all those years everyone told you it was shit, and now it's like, oh big deal, that's your problem, Jenny, none of it was true, that it didn't matter what they all said; it mattered, it's the only thing that did. And now everyone just wants, but that's what I did, with my life, and I know it was stupid, everyone keeps telling me how stupid I've been, but what was I SUPPOSED TO DO, let you die? I told you not to drink, I told you so many times and I know, I'm too good, well, I'm the one who bought the damn — it's my fau — I bought that, you were drinking, that night, if I didn't have that here.

(Beat.)

KIDMAN: Oh, Jenny.

JENNY: *(Immediately defensive.)* No. It's not my fault. You killed yourself, you son of a bitch. You couldn't be bothered to try and live, for me, because I needed you, that didn't even occur to you. You just went right ahead and killed yourself. Well, you're dead now so you don't get everything you want anymore! I'm not selling those paintings.

KIDMAN: Whoa, wait a minute. You're trying to punish me?

JENNY: Why not? It's a good a reason. Maybe it's the best. You want to be famous after you're dead? Well, guess what, that's not gonna happen unless I feel like it, and I'm in a bad mood these days.

KIDMAN: You sell those paintings.

JENNY: No.

KIDMAN: You little bitch.

JENNY: Yeah, and you're an asshole.

KIDMAN: It won't make you happy.

JENNY: You don't care if I'm happy! You never cared. You just did what you wanted. You didn't give a shit about me.

KIDMAN: *(Simple.)* That is not true.

JENNY: Why don't you go away? Just go away. You're not here anyway. Are you? *(Beat.)*

KIDMAN: No.

JENNY: Then go away.

(She starts to sob. He leaves. As he goes, he picks up the newspapers. She sits alone at the table sobbing. She falls asleep. The lights change; it is morning. Charlie enters. He brings the bird and a coffee pot.)

CHARLIE: Rise and shine, Sweetpea. Jenny, sweetie. Brung you breakfast.

(He touches her on the shoulder. She sits up and looks around. After a moment, she looks at Charlie.)

JENNY: Charlie.

CHARLIE: You sleep out here? You hurt your neck, doing that.

JENNY: *(Sleepy, curious.)* You brought your bird.

CHARLIE: Thought you might like the company. Yeah, she's a real good bird.

JENNY: You can't give me your bird.

CHARLIE: Not to keep, just for a little while. I come up here, I can visit her, watch some TV with you, that's what I thought. Brought you some coffee, too.

(He turns on a light and bustles about. He offers her a bagel from a bag.)

JENNY: *(Taking it.)* Did something happen to your new TV?

CHARLIE: Oh no, it's fine. Real nice. Here you go.

JENNY: Then why do you want to come up here, our TV is terrible.

CHARLIE: Just for the company, sweetheart, that's what I meant.

JENNY: Charlie.

(He hesitates. She waits for his answer.)

CHARLIE: Ray took it, I guess.

JENNY: (Disappointed.) He sold your TV?

CHARLIE: Got the microwave, too. (A joke.) Now's he lookin' at Swee'pea funny, I didn't want to take any chances.

JENNY: Look, we have some money around here somewhere, they gave me that big check. Let's go buy you a TV set.

CHARLIE: No no.

(She finds the check.)

JENNY: Yeah, why not. I don't have anything to do with this, now that Mac's not here. Let's buy you another TV set. It would make me feel better.

CHARLIE: We could buy you a TV set.

JENNY: I don't watch TV.

CHARLIE: Everybody watches TV.

JENNY: I don't want a TV I want you to have a TV.

CHARLIE: Well, let's just wait, then. You buy me another TV, Ray's just gonna sell that one, too.

(She sighs, sets the check down and checks the bagel.)

JENNY: What is this, lox spread?

CHARLIE: Yeah, I know that's your favorite.

JENNY: (Starting to eat.) This is excellent.

CHARLIE: Only the best for you, honey.

JENNY: You shouldn't be spending your money on me. And you should kick Ray out. Selling your TV. It's not right.

CHARLIE: He's my sister's boy, Charlotte. She's a nice person, worked hard her whole life trying to keep him out of trouble. I hate to give up on him on account she's his mama. When I come back from the war, she used to just sit with me for days. Everybody else acting like you gotta get over this now, and here's this nine-year-old girl just willing to sit. It meant something, you know. I don't like to talk about the war now, but afterwards, you feel so beat down, like every one of us, not even that you don't have a soul, but if you do, it's a evil thing, and this world needs to spit us out. All that killing teaches you what a man's worth and that's the sad truth. Then there's this little girl, just sitting there, waiting for me to say something, day after day. Sometimes we'd take a walk. And I started thinking, there's another side to things. Can't put a price on a life. We're worth more than killing alone. That's what she give me. And now, she got so much hope sunk into that boy, I just hate to give up.

(He joins her, eating the bagel.)

JENNY: Well maybe if he got a job. That would help.

CHARLIE: It's hard, black man with a record. Least if he's gonna steal, he's only stealing from me, that's the way I look at it, 'cause honestly, he is not a very good thief. You know how they caught him? He's breaking and entering this dry cleaning operation after hours, climbs down a empty chimney they had there. Then he breaks open the cash register, takes what's there, which ain't much, looks around, can't find the safe, 'cause it's not even on the property, realizes this is all he's gonna get, seventy-two fifty, something like that, so he gets mad. Finds a crowbar and trashes the place for kicks, just 'cause he's in a bad mood now, right? So then he goes to the back door, looking to take off? It's locked. It's locked, of course it's locked! It's two in the morning! Front door's locked too! He can't get out! Tries to climb back out the chimney, gets stuck. He's stuck in the chimney! All night! He's in there so long he pees his pants! They find him in there, the next day, yelling help me, help me! People running the dry cleaner call the cops, and he tells this crazy story, how he just fell in the chimney and heard the robbers next door trashing the dry cleaner. Only his prints are all over that crowbar and he got seventy-two fifty in his pocket. Four years, breaking and entering. That boy is not bright.

(Jenny laughs. Charlie smiles at her.)

CHARLIE: *(Continuing.)* Four years. That does seem a lot, don't it? For a robbery he didn't even finish? 'Cause I think prison did something to that boy. I don't know. I do know, he didn't get that way by himself. So, I don't mind he took my television. I'm just back where I started, that's the way I figure it. Serves me right, selling Mac's painting like that. That's my only regret. Sure wish I still had that.

(Jenny reaches over and takes his hand, grateful.)

JENNY: You want one? I'll give you one.

CHARLIE: Oh no, sweetie.

JENNY: He would want you to have one.

CHARLIE: He already give me one, and I sold it to that woman, and if I didn't, he maybe would still be here. I know it's stupid to think things like that, but sometimes you can't help it.

(He smiles at her, a sad acknowledgement.)

JENNY: Take a painting. Please.

CHARLIE: Those things are worth something. You can't just be giving 'em away.

JENNY: Why not?

CHARLIE: Well, because it'd be nice to have a little money for once! All those years, you working so hard, keeping things together for Mac. Wouldn't you like a little rest?

JENNY: You just told me your only regret was selling Mac's painting, and now you're telling me that's what I should do? Charlie.

CHARLIE: Yeah, that don't make much sense, do it?

(They smile at each other. The door opens; Willie enters.)

WILLIE: Hey.

JENNY: Willie!

CHARLIE: Hey, Willie.

(She hugs him.)

JENNY: Where have you been? You're never here.

WILLIE: So, come live with me, you'll see me more. He's dead now. Come live with me.

JENNY: Do you want some coffee?

WILLIE: Yeah, okay. How have you been? Are you all right?

JENNY: I don't know, Willie, it's all been so — I think I'm making myself a little nuts, stuck in here. I'm so glad you came by. Can you stay? There's bagels, too. Here, you can have some of mine. Lox spread.

WILLIE: Jenny, we have to talk about the paintings.

(She stops at this, looks at him.)

JENNY: What about them?

WILLIE: We have to talk about who is the best person to handle them.

JENNY: What do you mean, handle?

WILLIE: Sell. Who we want to sell them for us.

(She looks away.)

WILLIE: *(Continuing.)* I've been down to the gallery, several times, and I've talked to a lot of different people, and I really think we should let Lillian continue to take care of this. She's clearly, she's absolutely as professional as anyone out there; she knew Mac, she loves the paintings —

JENNY: *(Bitter.)* None of this would have happened if she hadn't come along in the first place.

WILLIE: Look, Mac did what he wanted to do. This was what he wanted.

JENNY: *(Angry now.)* Yeah, I know. I know, okay? But I don't care. Nobody's gonna "handle" anything, because I'm not selling anything.

(Beat.)

WILLIE: Do you know how much they're worth now? Millions. Many millions.

CHARLIE: How much?

WILLIE: That's right. This is a good thing, and I'm not going to let you pretend that it's not. Our whole lives have changed. You can move out of this shithole, finish your GED and go to college. You can take a trip if you want. Mac wanted to take you to Italy? Go to Italy. He would want you to go to Italy!

JENNY: He doesn't get what he wants anymore. He's dead.

WILLIE: But you're not. And neither am I. I'm telling you, honestly, when all this started to happen, I admit I was not immediately thrilled. I mean, there's no point in my lying about it; I wasn't Mac's biggest fan. But you know what? I was wrong. All this hooha, Mac's suddenly a genius, you know what I decided? I can live with it. You always wanted me to forgive him, I can do that. You want me to be his son? I'll be his son. I'll tell everybody whacky stories about what a crazy nut he was. What a whacky genius. And you know what? They'll pay me for the stories. They'll pay you for the stories. And they'll pay us both for those goddamn paintings.

JENNY: I'm not selling the paintings, Willie! Are you listening to me? I'm not selling them! We are not selling them!

(They stare at each other.)

CHARLIE: Well, I guess I better . . .

JENNY: Charlie, no, stay here, this isn't anything. This discussion is over. Please. Go, take a painting. I want you to have one.

WILLIE: What?

JENNY: I told Charlie he could have a painting! Is that all right with you?

WILLIE: I'm standing here begging you to let go of the damn things and he gets to just walk off with one?

JENNY: You want to sell them!

WILLIE: Yes, I do! They're mine now, I —

JENNY: They're not yours!

WILLIE: They're half mine. I'll take half.

JENNY: You're not taking any.

WILLIE: So he gets one and I don't get any.

CHARLIE: I don't —

JENNY: Yes. Yes! He loved Mac. He loves those paintings. You don't.

WILLIE: I love you! Doesn't that count?

(There is a terrible pause at this. Jenny cannot answer for a moment. Willie turns away, shaking his head.)

JENNY: Of course it does. Of course. I'm sorry, I'm so confused. I don't mean to be like this. I'm sorry.

(He goes to her. Jenny embraces him.)

JENNY: *(Continuing.)* I'm sorry. It's so hard. It's *so* hard, to know how to be, and you haven't been here —

WILLIE: I'm sorry. I thought I was doing the right thing; I knew you wouldn't want to deal with all this — it's chaos; it is chaos, and I was trying to take care of it so you didn't —

JENNY: *(Overlap.)* I know. I know, you're right, it's just — maybe if you took one, Willie, just for now, just one.

WILLIE: *(Gentle.)* Jenny, one is not going to be enough. They want all of them —

JENNY: Well, they can't have all of them, they —. Okay, look. I'll give you one, and you can sell it, and it'll be worth a lot, Willie, they'll give you a lot for that, and, and —

WILLIE: You have to give me more than one, Jenny.

JENNY: *(Suddenly losing it.)* I don't have to give you any! You're just gonna sell it, it's just money to you, it's just MONEY.

(She turns away from him, at a loss. Both Charlie and Willie are stunned into silence at her outburst.)

CHARLIE: Willie, maybe now is not the best time.

WILLIE: Don't you tell me what to do here. This is not your business.

JENNY: It *is* his business. He is as much a part of this —

WILLIE: No, he's not! You and I were the ones who lived through it, every sorry, miserable sordid fucking moment of that man's misery, Mom's death, you and I were the end result —

JENNY: And the paintings.

WILLIE: They're not a person! They're nothing! He sat in that room and scribbled self-indulgent bullshit for thirty years, while he was also, by the way, ruining our lives, and now all of a sudden, people are saying that scribble is worth a zillion dollars, well, I want the money! Now, I'm sorry Mac's dead, not because I'm really sorry, but I'm sorry for you. Okay? I'm sorry because I know you loved him, and I know you're in pain, but I didn't get what you got from him. We all know that. He loved you, and he didn't love me, and he owes me now. And I'm taking those paintings.

(She doesn't answer. They stare at each other, immovable.)

CHARLIE: *(Trying to mediate.)* It's too soon, maybe. Hey, Willie? Maybe it's just too soon.

WILLIE: *(Near tears.)* Jenny. Let me have the paintings.

(She shakes her head. Charlie stands there, awkward.)

CHARLIE: Maybe in a little while. Hey, Willie. It's just too soon.

(After a moment, Willie turns and goes. Blackout.)

Scene Fifteen

Sylvia's apartment. Another dinner party. Eugene, Lillian, Lucas, and Philip are there. Lillian and Eugene are arguing.

LILLIAN: *(Heated.)* It's just that this situation with MOMA could not be more out of hand, and if you honestly think —

EUGENE: *(Overlap.)* I realize that, Lillian, but I have been as clear as I know how to be about this —

LILLIAN: *(Overlap.)* That I would be asking, although why I am not, in this situation, permitted to ask for a little bit of help.

EUGENE: *(Overlap.)* That I do not want to be involved. I simply do not want any part of this!

LILLIAN: *(Overlap.)* If not for me, then for Mac. You were fond of him. I just don't understand why you can't do this for Mac.

(This finally silences him. The others look back and forth, a little alarmed.)

SYLVIA: My goodness, a battle royale!

LILLIAN: I'm sorry. I'm sorry, Sylvia.

(She leaves the table momentarily, to collect herself. Philip and Lucas take this in.)

SYLVIA: Oh don't apologize, that was very exciting. And I have to say, I'm on your side. I think Eugene is being a cad about this.

EUGENE: A cad?

SYLVIA: Well, not very nice then. Why shouldn't you pitch in a little. She's working so hard, and all she's asking is that you make a few phone calls. Isn't that it?

LILLIAN: It's all right, Sylvia.

SYLVIA: It's not, oh. Look how unhappy she is. Your bride-to-be. Why won't you help her?

PHILLIP: It's money again.

EUGENE: It's not money.

SYLVIA: Well, what is it?

EUGENE: I don't know, mother, I don't —

SYLVIA: Well, she doesn't have time for you to be confused. She needs your help now.

LILLIAN: Eugene. Just because —

EUGENE: Could we not discuss this here?

LILLIAN: Just because people are now willing to pay for those paintings doesn't mean they've been corrupted. All it means is that people with money have come to recognize what I recognized months ago: The paintings are good. And I just don't think it's wise to get sucked into some impossibly romantic position, that they were somehow "better" when no one was willing to buy them. It's a ridiculous idea, Eugene. It just is. Mac would have tossed it back in your face.

EUGENE: I know he would have.

SYLVIA: Now wait a minute. Is he arguing that those paintings are worth more if no one will pay for them?

EUGENE: I'm not arguing anything.

LUCAS: Sooo . . . you're helping?

(They all stare at him.)

EUGENE: Yes, fine.

SYLVIA: Of course he'll help, we both will. Although I have a confession to make about those paintings. I still don't like them! Well, I'm not saying I don't like them. I don't like them, but it's not that I don't like them a lot. It's just that I don't love them. I like them a little. I just don't know what to think now. All right, I'm just going to say it. I don't care that everyone likes them so much. I still don't like them.

LUCAS: You just don't understand them, Sylvia. That's different.

SYLVIA: Are you sure? Because I think I don't like them.

PHILLIP: Abstract expressionism is a very intellectual taste. It's not for everybody.

SYLVIA: I'm intellectual. I hope you're not saying I'm not intellectual.

PHILLIP: No no, of course —

LUCAS: *(Overlap.)* No, that's not at all — I think you actually like them, you just don't know it.

EUGENE: Oh, for god's sake —

SYLVIA: Stay out of this, Eugene, please! I'm trying to understand, I want to share in everyone's — everyone's so excited, and I just, I'm sorry, but he was so — you didn't really like *him,* did you?

LUCAS: Who, Kidman? Well, he was difficult —

PHILLIP: He was a homophobe. There, I said it.

SYLVIA: Precisely. He insulted people.

LILLIAN: He had his demons, no one is denying that.

PHILLIP: Oh please, demons. If anyone else had acted like that you would just come out and call him a bigot.

LILLIAN: Yes, and Picasso was a misogynist, and Eliot was an antisemite, and D.W. Griffiths was a racist. But they were also gifted, and so we look the other way.

(Lillian's cell phone rings. She answers it.)

LILLIAN: *(Continuing; annoyed.)* Ivan — *(To the others.)* Sorry, I'm so sorry, really, I'll be right —

(She leaves the group as they continue their debate. Eugene watches her, worried.)

LUCAS: Well, I suppose the only thing to conclude is, you can enjoy an artist and appreciate his work and still not want to have dinner with him.

SYLVIA: There. That's what I mean. I mean, I feel terrible even, the man is dead after all —

PHILLIP: Sylvia, he was rude to you; he was, and no one expects you to forget that. But the paintings are a different matter.

SYLVIA: *(To Lucas.)* So you actually like them?

LUCAS: They're magnificent.

PHILLIP: They are, Sylvia. We both need to put our feelings about the man aside and just appreciate them apart.

SYLVIA: Apart from the painter, as if someone else painted them.

PHILLIP: Yes. Someone you like. Lucas. What if Lucas painted them?

SYLVIA: Well, if Lucas painted them I would like them because he painted them and he's my friend and I would think oh how wonderful, that I have such talented friends, and I'd throw a big party to celebrate your grand success.

LUCAS: Thank you.

SYLVIA: I wish Lucas had painted them, it would be so much easier on me. Or Eugene, if Eugene had painted them, I'd be the mother of the artist, wouldn't that be fun.

EUGENE: Oh my god.

SYLVIA: Well, why shouldn't I think that would be fun? All you do is sit around and mope about having so much money. At least if you were an artist, I'd have something to be proud of.

(There is an uncomfortable beat while everyone tries not to notice what she just said.)

LILLIAN: *(Snapping.)* Ivan, I cannot deal with this now!

(Beat; to the others.) I'm sorry, really. I'm so sorry.

(To phone.) Tell him he'll get it, and I'll call him in the morning.

(She hangs up.)

LILLIAN: *(Continuing.)* Sorry. Where were we?

EUGENE: We were talking about art.

LILLIAN: Of course we were. Sylvia, you do like those paintings. I won't let you not like them.

(She takes her hand, firm. Blackout.)

Scene Sixteen

Kidman's loft, night. Eugene is there with Jenny.

EUGENE: Thanks for seeing me.

JENNY: No, I was glad to get your note.

EUGENE: I tried calling.

JENNY: I unplugged the phone. People keep calling, newspapers . . . I just unplugged it.

EUGENE: I don't blame you.

JENNY: *(A little awkward.)* So, I was glad to get your note, and I'm glad you came. I've been meaning to thank you.

EUGENE: Thank me?

JENNY: For trying to get the paintings back. I mean, I know that was a crazy thing to ask for. And I never heard back from you. Well, of course, I did unplug the phone. But, thank you for trying.

EUGENE: I didn't —

JENNY: I know, but —

EUGENE: *(Abrupt, suddenly bitter.)* Look, don't thank me, okay? I mean, we all know, I haven't been — look. It wasn't exactly your lucky day when you met me. I know that. I came onto you at my own — and I'm not apologizing for that, that was — and everything else, let's face it. I hunted you down. They probably would have found you anyway, but I was the one, I brought Lillian here, you knew that, I brought her here because I wanted to see you, and then that night, we were drinking, he was, and I knew it was too much, and I knew it was a problem, and I didn't stop it because I was thinking about you, and how I wanted to see you and be his friend so I could come home with him, and see you. So don't thank me. Just don't thank me.

(Beat.)

JENNY: It wasn't your fault.

EUGENE: *(Erupting.)* I'm not asking for absolution!

(Beat.)

I'm sorry, but this is — do you know what you're doing? Do you have any idea?

JENNY: *(Confused now.)* No.

EUGENE: I told you, things were going to happen. I told you.

JENNY: What's happened?

EUGENE: They will not stop, do you understand that? You're being a fool! Just sitting here, like some sort of — if you *rot* in here with them, what will it prove? What will it prove?

(Beat. He looks at her.)

I'm sorry. I don't know what I'm . . .

JENNY: It's okay. It's not your fault.

(He shakes his head, at a loss, and prowls the apartment, looking about. She watches him, confused. He turns on her.)

EUGENE: *(Sudden.)* Would you have dinner with me?

JENNY: Dinner?

EUGENE: Yes, I would like to do something for you. I haven't been able to *do* anything, and I keep thinking about that first night, when we met — you were so sad, and we were so hideous — and you were *waiting* on us. Like a servant.

JENNY: I *was* a servant.

EUGENE: Yes, you were, and you behaved better than anyone else in the room, and I would like to take you to dinner. There are so many beautiful restaurants in this city, beautiful, where the food is like nothing you've ever tasted before, not even in your dreams —

JENNY: *(Smiling slightly.)* As good as Italy? Mac said the best food in the world is in Italy.

EUGENE: Oh, no no. I promise you, at this moment in history, food is taken very seriously in New York City, and Italy has been left in the dust. And I would like to take you to a restaurant, with chandeliers, flowers everywhere, staggeringly beautiful bouquets of — six people to wait on you alone. At your place setting, there will be twelve forks, and no one will know what any of them are good for — and there will be champagne, and sorbet, in between courses — to cleanse the palate, the flavors, one stranger than the next. Once, I had sorbet made out of parsley —

JENNY: *(Laughing.)* That sounds terrible.

EUGENE: It was delicious. We will have it between the appetizer and the fish course.

JENNY: What will the appetizer be?

EUGENE: *(Thinking.)* Oysters in a sauerkraut cream sauce topped with Beluga caviar.

(She laughs at this, delighted.)

JENNY: And dessert?

EUGENE: Chocolate crusted coconut sherbet, swimming in a lemongrass citrus soup.

JENNY: No.

EUGENE: And that's just one of them. We'll order four. The other ones, I can't even begin to describe. If I tried, you would never believe another word out of my mouth.

(They smile at each other. He reaches out for her. They kiss. The kiss becomes passionate. She pulls away.)

JENNY: This isn't right.

EUGENE: Jenny, maybe it's time you faced the fact that doing what's right hasn't gotten you anything that you wanted.

(He kisses her again. She pulls away. They consider each other for a moment.)

JENNY: Are you still engaged to that woman?

EUGENE: Yes.

JENNY: Why?

EUGENE: Why are you hanging onto those paintings?

JENNY: You don't know me well enough to ask that.

EUGENE: Please. I don't even know myself. Come with me.

JENNY: To dinner.

EUGENE: To dinner, and whatever else happens. Let me do this for you.

JENNY: Oh, for me?

EUGENE: For myself then, but frankly, I don't think the conversation would have gone this far if you were indifferent.

(She thinks about this.)

JENNY: You know, I did date once. For something like three weeks when I was fifteen. Mac was a nightmare. This guy, he could not have been more ridiculous, he had *side*burns for god's sake, and he wore *loafers*. He came by to pick me up, Mac was on a bender and I tried, I told him to wait on the street, but the lock on the front door was busted and he was so polite, this boy, I don't know where he came from. I think he was from Ohio or something, or Brooklyn.

EUGENE: And he came up.

JENNY: Yes. Mac went ballistic. He was screaming at this poor kid, what do you think you're doing, I can read your sorry little teenage mind, you think you're going to fuck my *daughter*, you little piece of shit? You thinking about boning this girl?

(Starting to laugh.)

It was *horrifying*. He was a complete raving *lunatic* and this poor kid from *Ohio* who I didn't even like — I mean, I liked him okay, but he was such a nerd. Sex was the *last* thing on his mind.

EUGENE: Teenage boys, sex is never the last thing.

JENNY: Well, that was the last of him. And I was so mortified, I, you know, I more or less realized I could never bring a real date over here. I made out with guys a couple times. At school, you know, behind the bleachers in the gym. It was real romantic.

(A beat.)

Mac liked you.

EUGENE: You are not doing this for him.

JENNY: Who cares why I'm doing it?

(She kisses him. It starts to get quite heated. She pulls away.)

JENNY: *(Continuing.)* We still have to make it through dinner.

EUGENE: Let's go.

(They do. Blackout.)

Scene Seventeen

Lillian's gallery. Lillian sits alone, by her desk, smoking a cigarette. She waits for a long moment. The phone rings. It rings again, and then again, and then again as she considers it. Finally, she reaches forward and picks it up.

LILLIAN: Hello?

(Blackout.)

Scene Eighteen

Kidman's loft. The lights are out. Willie sits there, alone, for a long moment. The door swings open. Jenny and Eugene enter, kissing. They do not see him at first.

WILLIE: Jenny.

(She turns, startled.)

JENNY: Willie — oh, man, what? You scared me.

WILLIE: We have to talk.

JENNY: What are you doing here?

WILLIE: We have to talk. He should go.

(He looks at Eugene. There is a terrible pause.)

JENNY: What happened? Something happened.

(She looks around, uneasy. She looks at the door of the studio.)

WILLIE: Jenny —

JENNY: What did you do, Willie?

WILLIE: I took the paintings. Okay? I took the paintings.

(She looks at him in horror, then goes to the studio. Willie looks at Eugene.)

EUGENE: You piece of shit.

WILLIE: Look, I'm not going to say anything about whatever it is you're doing here, but this is also none of your business, so —

JENNY: They're all gone. All of them, not one of them is —

(To Eugene.)

Did you know he was doing this?

WILLIE: I did it, Jenny. I did it myself.

JENNY: You couldn't, there were too many of them, you had to — they're all gone, not one, you couldn't leave me one?

WILLIE: I did it for your own good —

JENNY: *(Losing it.)* That is a FUCKING LIE, Willie, would you just — you took the paintings.

(A breath.) You took the paintings.

(She looks down, trying to stay somewhat on top of this.)

EUGENE: I'm calling the police.

WILLIE: That's not gonna do her any good, and you know it.

EUGENE: *(Pissed.)* Yeah, I don't know anything of the kind, asshole, so —

WILLIE: *(Overlap.)* I already talked to a lawyer, all right, and you know as well as I do, him dying intestate gives me a ton of rights in this situation. I mean, I didn't want to handle it like this. Jenny. You know I didn't. But you didn't leave me much choice.

JENNY: *(Trying to figure this out, upset.)* How did you know? How did you know I was going out tonight, even I didn't — he just came over and said dinner, I — you couldn't have known. And moving them all, they're all — where are they — he's gone. He's gone.

(She sobs for a moment, turns away. Willie goes to her, touches her shoulder.)

WILLIE: Jenny —

JENNY: Do not touch me! You are not allowed to touch me, Willie. No more. Don't ever try to touch me again.

(He looks at her, shattered.)

WILLIE: I did it for your own good.

JENNY: You did it because you're greedy.

WILLIE: Hanging onto those pictures is not going to bring him back.

JENNY: Don't talk to me about what I'm going through —

WILLIE: *(Overlap.)* He died. He's gone. He maimed your life, he maimed mine, and he's dead now, and you need to try and figure out how to live.

JENNY: *(Overlap.)* This isn't about me — you didn't do this for me!

WILLIE: Yeah, okay, fine, I did it for me. I admit it. I did it to get something back for me. I asked you, I *begged* you to come live with me. He got mom, and then he got you, and you have done nothing with your life. You're a cater-waiter for god's sake! And you're sitting here like this is some fucking holy sepulcher, some tomb, some — you're my family too! I mean, what was it supposed to be, forever, I get nothing? He gets everything, and I — *(He stops himself. She shakes her head.)*

WILLIE: *(Continuing.)* I had every right to do what I did.

JENNY: I just needed more time. Why couldn't you —

WILLIE: We did not have time. It was happening now. Time was the one thing I couldn't give you.

JENNY: You didn't even try. You took them *all,* all of them — that's not — that's mean, Willie. That's revenge.

WILLIE: That's not — I *tried.* God, I did nothing but — I begged you, and you wouldn't give me any, you wouldn't give me—why didn't I matter? Why — this is on you, Jenny. This is on you.
(He turns away, furious. She looks at his back, suddenly defeated.)

JENNY: I just couldn't do it. When it was just me and Mac, and the paintings, I just thought that was better. All those years, watching him paint, he was so — *big.* While he was painting? It was a sight to see. And they were so *beautiful.* I used to wonder where they came from; the color, and the light, it was such . . . a gift. From, I didn't know where, but they were a gift. And I was a part of them. Then when he left, I just wanted to hang on to that sense that I did something, I — my life wasn't about money. It was a gift. That's all I was trying to do.

WILLIE: A gift to him, but not to me.
(A beat. She closes down.)

JENNY: You need to get out of here. You got what you wanted. Take the paintings, and take the money, and get out of here, and don't ever come back.

EUGENE: Jenny—

JENNY: Both of you. Leave me alone.
(She goes to her bedroom. Blackout.)

Scene Nineteen

Charlie's apartment. It is dark. Ray and Jordy are counting money.

JORDY: No, come on, this ain't right.

RAY: That's right.

JORDY: You think I'm stupid?

RAY: I don't know you're some kind of genius, but that's not saying that ain't right.

JORDY: Hey Ray, you know what? You talk bullshit. And I'm six hundred short here.

RAY: Hey you want to count my split? 'Cause —

JORDY: Five thousand dollars, you said —

RAY: I said four —

JORDY: Fuck you, man. Don't you fuckin' talk to me like I'm a fuckin' moron!

RAY: It was my gig, I cut you in.

JORDY: I did all the fuckin' work.

RAY: Yeah, how you figure that? 'Cause my memory is I arranged the job, I got the truck —

JORDY: *(Overlap.)* I figure that 'cause you and the skinny guy stood around chatting up old times while I was movin' that shit —

RAY: Bullshit, you a half-brain crackhead, your fuckin' problem —

JORDY: Fuck you —

(He pulls a knife. Ray looks at him, shocked. Charlie enters.)

CHARLIE: Hey, how's it goin' — hey. Whoa. Shit.

(The two younger men look over, startled.)

RAY: Hey, uncle Charlie.

CHARLIE: What's goin' on?

JORDY: I want my six hundred dollars.

(To Charlie.) He took six hundred dollars off me.

RAY: I never did.

CHARLIE: Put that thing away. I'm telling you, we are not having any sort of conversation here, till you put that thing away.

(Jordy pockets the knife. Charlie considers them both.)

CHARLIE: *(Continuing.)* Okay, Ray. Now why don't you tell me what you did.

RAY: I didn't do nothin'.

CHARLIE: *(To Jordy.)* That right?

RAY: *(Reacting.)* You gonna believe him, over me? Your own nephew, that's real nice. Mama gonna be real happy to hear about that —

CHARLIE: *Don't you talk to me about your mama. (Beat, to Jordy.)* Now, you tell me what this is about.

JORDY: We did this job.

RAY: Whoa — that is not —

JORDY: Yeah, and you're a fuckin' liar, cause I heard you talking to that guy, agreement was five thousand dollars, and you stiffed me, man. I am six hundred short. Six hundred bucks. Short.

RAY: That is not —

JORDY: Yeah, it is —

CHARLIE: Tell your friend to shut up because I'm talkin' to you now, you little piece of *shit.*
(Charlie suddenly grabs Ray, shoves him against the couch, reaches into Ray's pocket, and takes out a wad of cash.)

CHARLIE: *(Continuing.)* Not enough you stealing from me, you doin' jobs now? You gonna break your mama's heart one more time, that what you're doing?
(He hurls him to the floor. Ray tries to crawl away.)

RAY: No way! It was a legit job! We moved those paintings! No stealing about it!
(Charlie stops, looks at him.)

CHARLIE: You stole Mac's paintings?
(They face off.)

RAY: I moved 'em. Willie told me about his sister goin' crazy, he needs to get them out of there. So that's what we did. I'm on the lookout, see when she takes off, give him a call, and we move 'em.

CHARLIE: *(Taking this in.)* You stole Mac's paintings.

RAY: *(Protesting.)* They ain't called the cops yet, and they ain't goin' to, Charlie. Them things half Willie's to begin with, and she ain't gonna want the trouble.
(Ray starts to pick up the money.)

CHARLIE: 'Cording to Willie.

RAY: That's right. Aside which, he gonna keep us out of it. Cops get involved, he did the whole thing himself. Better for him, better for us that way. I'm telling you, there is no downside here. Till this fool starts up with all his money negotiations.

CHARLIE: They catch you, how many years you back in for?

RAY: I told you, that ain't coming into it.

CHARLIE: Long as you can trust Willie. A white man. Any of it goes wrong, you really think he'll keep you out of it? 'Cause the way I see it, you put your freedom on the line for five thousand dollars.

RAY: Hey, don't you talk to me about money. A black man wants respect in this community, he got to have money, and I'm not *talking* minimum wage. You go get yourself shot up in Viet Nam, how much they give you for that, Charlie? Nine hundred dollars? Nine thirty-two a month? You can't even buy yourself a TV set! Only way a black man earns respect, he got to have the cash. Then they listen. And now they gonna start listening to me.

CHARLIE: That's fine, Ray. That's a fine way to think about it. 'Cause way it looks to me? White man bought and sold you like a slave.

RAY: *(Stung by this.)* Yeah, listen to you, tired old black man spends all his time running after some white girl. I mean, she's a nice piece of ass, but you honestly think she gonna be dishin' that honey your way? Then again, maybe you'll get lucky. 'Cording to Willie, she's a complete fuckin' nutjob. *(Beat.)*

CHARLIE: You get out of my house. You get out of this neighborhood. I ever see you again, I'm sending you away.

RAY: You mean I don't get to sleep on your shitty little couch no more? That really breaks my heart.
(Beat.)
See ya 'round.
(He goes. Blackout.)

Scene Twenty

Sylvia's apartment. Another dinner party, with Lucas, Willie, Lillian, Eugene, and Sylvia. Mac's painting is there.

LUCAS: You just — took the paintings? You took them! Is that legal?

SYLVIA: Oh, who cares if it was legal? It was bold, and daring, and we applaud you!

WILLIE: *(Answering the question.)* It was no more or less legal than her refusal to give them up. I had to do something.

PHILLIP: Is she going to sue?

WILLIE: I don't know. It's unlikely.

SYLVIA: Well, that's too bad, because if you ask me, the only thing further that we need, is a *trial*. Wouldn't that be fun?

WILLIE: Really, what I did, I did it for her own good. I think, with time, she'll realize that. I think she may know it already.
(But he doesn't seem too sure. Lillian pats his hand.)

LILLIAN: You didn't just do it for her. You did it for Mac.

WILLIE: Oh —

LILLIAN: Don't be modest. We had many many talks about this, and Willie
    realized that time was of the essence and his father's legacy, to the world,
    was the most important consideration. It's true, Willie. What you did was
    very brave.

SYLVIA: Well, I'm happy things have finally settled down, because you seem
    like a very nice young man, but I feel that I must be forthright. I was not
    your father's biggest fan.

WILLIE: No?

SYLVIA: Oh, I love the paintings, of course I love the paintings, but frankly, I
    found him — difficult.

WILLIE: *(Confiding.)* So did I.

SYLVIA: *(Relieved.)* You didn't like him either. Thank god. But we mustn't judge
    an artist by the way he behaves. Phillip taught me that.

LUCAS: Well, when your sister feels better about the whole thing, I think we
    should invite her to dinner. To make the picture complete.

SYLVIA: What? Invite her? But she waited on us!

PHILLIP: Oh my god, I just put it together. *That's* the girl? The girl who was
    here, who went on and on about being poor?

SYLVIA: Yes and she's not poor anymore, and you'd think she'd be grateful, instead
    of just giving everyone so much trouble.

EUGENE: Maybe she just decided some things were worse than poverty.

LUCAS: *(Good natured.)* Here we go again.

SYLVIA: Change the subject!

LILLIAN: Not at all. I'd like to hear what Eugene has to say.

EUGENE: Would you?

    *(There is a pause while they face each other from across the table. Their atti-
    tude toward each other is distinctly frosty.)*

LILLIAN: Yes. Mac's retrospective opens in two weeks, advance word is stun-
    ning, his work will be seen alongside every major expressionist in every
    major museum in the *world* in the years to come, and if you think things
    could have worked out better, I think we'd all be interested in hearing how.

EUGENE: Do you really want me to answer that?

LILLIAN: Why don't you just tell us what's bothering you.

EUGENE: I just think there are loose ends.

LILLIAN: What kind of loose ends?

EUGENE: Questions. You know, after something terrible has happened, a death,
    everyone sits around and wonders, if I had only done something a little
    different, maybe this wouldn't have happened. We all blame ourselves.

SYLVIA: It's no one's fault.

EUGENE: I was drinking with him. Someone gave him those pills.

LILLIAN: It wasn't the pills that killed him. It was the pills and the alcohol and the years of sheer, pointless excess that killed him. *(To Willie.)* Forgive me.

WILLIE: It's true. One way or another he was going to do himself in.

EUGENE: Other questions, then. You know, ever since that night, I've been wondering why, when you moved the paintings to the gallery, why'd you take all of them? I understand you were in a difficult situation, but it did seem pretty harsh. Why didn't you leave her just one?

WILLIE: *(Nervous now.)* Well, actually I didn't — I wanted to. But Lillian — she said she needed to see them all.

EUGENE: Really? Why?

LILLIAN: They're important work. They had to be catalogued. She doesn't have proper security in that apartment, not to mention the dust, the heat, the humidity, it's a disastrous environment for fine art. There were many reasons.

EUGENE: Objective reasons.

LILLIAN: What other kind of reasons would there be?

EUGENE: I'm just asking questions, Lillian. It's my nature. Actually, both of us, that may be the reason we first fell in love. We're both the kind of people who look for answers. We sit, we watch, we think. Somehow, we always know what the other is doing.

SYLVIA: *(Joking.)* Well, I don't know if *that's* such a good thing.

LILLIAN: It's neither bad nor good. It all depends on how one acts. Or doesn't.

EUGENE: On the basis of that knowledge.

LILLIAN: Yes.

SYLVIA: Well, now I don't understand what you two are talking about.

EUGENE: It's all right, mother, we understand each other. *(Standing.)* I've got to go.

SYLVIA: Oh Eugene, you can't! We haven't had the savory yet.

EUGENE: I'm full, Mother. Lillian, you and I — this clearly isn't working out.

LILLIAN: *(Cool as a cucumber.)* No, clearly not.

EUGENE: So that's it then.

LILLIAN: Yes.

(The others look around, surprised.)

LUCAS: What?

WILLIE: *(Sudden, to Eugene.)* Take the painting.

(Eugene stops; looks at him.)

WILLIE: *(Continuing.)* Take it.

(Eugene picks up the painting. The others react.)

SYLVIA: Eugene, what on — sit down. Sit — My Kidman! You can't!

EUGENE: It's not yours, Mother.

(He heads for the door.)

SYLVIA: Eugene, stop it! Stop it, thief! Thief!

(But before anyone can move, he goes. Blackout.)

Scene Twenty-one

Kidman's loft. Jenny and Charlie are watching television. Jenny fools with the rabbit ears.

JENNY: There . . . there . . .

(She backs up.)

CHARLIE: Oh.

JENNY: I hate that.

(She gets close again.)

CHARLIE: There it is!

JENNY: Yeah, but I can't stand here all night.

CHARLIE: Try a different thing with the antenna. Like, get it so the picture's not really right, and then when you back up, maybe it'll clear out.

JENNY: Does that work?

CHARLIE: Yeah, it works. Mac used to do it all the time. Here, let me.

(He goes to work on the rabbit ears. She goes back to the table.)

JENNY: I think we're gonna have to break down and buy another TV, Charlie.

CHARLIE: No, this is fine.

(Jenny picks up a pile of envelopes off the table.)

JENNY: No, we should just do it. Willie keeps sending these checks. I should just cash one of them, buy the both of us a nice dinner, and get a decent television set.

CHARLIE: Cable?

JENNY: Yeah, cable. Why not, cable.

CHARLIE: Whoa, whoa whoa, got it.

(He backs away from the set. The two of them watch, entranced.)

JENNY: That's beautiful.

CHARLIE: Okay. You want to cash one of those things, that's up to you. I'm just sayin', in terms of entertainment, our needs are taken care of. Ain't that right, Swee'pea.

(He turns to the bird and notices Eugene, standing in the door.)

EUGENE: The door was open.

JENNY: *(Startled.)* I know, I . . . Come in.

   (She turns the television off.)

EUGENE: I tried to call. Your phone is still unplugged.

JENNY: I know. I'm crazy.

EUGENE: No, it's totally understandable. I brought you this.

   (He brings forward the painting.)

JENNY: Oh.

EUGENE: I'm sorry I couldn't do more.

CHARLIE: *(Seeing the painting, stopping.)* Good lord, you found my duck.

JENNY: This is the duck?

CHARLIE: That's the duck!

JENNY: It's not a duck.

   (Happy, she takes it to a chair and sets it on it, so they can all look at it.)

CHARLIE: What do you mean, that's not a duck. That is a duck.

EUGENE: It's abstract, it can be anything.

CHARLIE: People say that, but I don't know.

JENNY: It's not a duck. It's me.

EUGENE: It is?

JENNY: Yes, of course it's me. Mac wasn't painting abstracts, all those years. He
   was painting me.

CHARLIE: Oh.

   (They look at it for a long moment.)

CHARLIE: *(Continuing.)* Well girl, you look like a damn duck.

JENNY: I do, don't I? I do.

   (They continue to look at the painting. Fade out.)

END OF PLAY

THE EXACT CENTER OF THE UNIVERSE
OF THE UNIVERSE
by Joan Vail Thorne

For the Tree House Gang

ORIGINAL PRODUCTION

The Exact Center of the Universe was produced by Elsa Daspin Haft, Martin Markinson, Judith Resnick, Sheilah Goldman, Jerome Rosenfeld and Allen M. Shore at the Century Center for the Performing Arts in New York City on September 8, 1999. It was directed by John Tillinger; the set design was by Michael Brown; the lighting design was by Brian MacDevitt; the sound design was by Laura Grace Brown; the costume design was by Carrie Robbins; the production manager was Joseph L. Robinson; and the production stage manager was Christine Catti. The cast was as follows:

VADA LOVE POWELL	Frances Sternhagen
APPLETON POWELL/MR. POWELL	Reed Birney
MARY LOU/MARY ANN	Tracy Thorne
ENID	Sloane Shelton
MARYBELL	Marge Redmond

The Exact Center of the Universe received its world premiere at Women's Project and Productions Julia Miles, Artistic Director; Patricia Taylor, Managing Director.) in New York City on April 7, 1999. It was directed by John Tillinger; the set design was by Michael Brown; the lighting design was by Philip Widmer; the sound design was by Laura Grace Brown; the costume design was by Carrie Robbins; the production manager was Pamela J. Traynor; and the production stage manager was Christine Catti. The cast was as follows:

VADA LOVE POWELL	Frances Sternhagen
APPLETON POWELL/MR. POWELL	Reed Birney
MARY LOU/MARY ANN	Tracy Thorne
ENID	Bethel Leslie
MARYBELL	Marge Redmond

BIOGRAPHY

Joan Vail Thorne has written for film and opera as well as theater. Screenplays are *High Cockalorum* and *The Living,* both commissioned by American Playhouse; and she both wrote and directed *Last Rites,* shown on PBS, and *Secrets,* shown on Cinemax. Opera libretti, written with composer Stephen Paulus, are *The Woman at Otowi Crossing,* produced by Opera Theater of St. Louis, and *Summer,* premiered at Berkshire Opera Company in 1999. Other plays include *Signs and Wonders* and *The Anatomy of a Female Pope.* She is also a director and has directed productions at The Alley Theatre, American Place Theatre, Arena Stage, Dallas Theatre Center, and The Women's Project, among others. Ms. Thorne is on the faculty of the Playwrights Horizons Theatre School and is a long-time member of the Women's Project.

CHARACTERS

APPLETON POWELL, JR.: Vada's beloved son, a definitely unusual, one might even say eccentric man, in his mid-thirties in Act One; in his mid-forties in Act Two.

VADA LOVE POWELL: A charming autocrat of a woman, who has never suffered from self-doubt and never will, in her late sixties in Act One; in her late seventies in Act Two.

MARY LOU MELE: A perfect match for Vada, even at age twenty in Act One; thirty in Act Two.

ENID SYMONDS: A retired second-grade schoolteacher, with starch and wit, over seventy in Act One; over eighty in Act Two.

MARYBELL BAXTER: The Southern belle par excellence because she really isn't one, almost seventy in Act One; eighty in Act Two.

MARY ANN MELE POWELL: Mary Lou's much more benign twin sister. Played by the same actor who plays Mary Lou.

MR. POWELL: Vada's husband as a young man. Played by the same actor who plays Appleton.

SETTING
Vada's sitting room and Enid's tree house in a small town in the deep South.

TIME
Act One takes place in the nineteen fifties. Act Two takes place in the nineteen sixties.

THE EXACT CENTER OF THE UNIVERSE

ACT ONE
Scene One

The sitting room of Vada Love Powell, an imposing, if not imperious, woman in her late sixties, somewhere in the deep South. The room is overstuffed and overdone, but not overwhelming. On the contrary, it is most inviting. "A surfeit of honey" describes the surroundings perfectly. A small table has been set for tea, and, as tea tables go, it looks sublime. There are photographs in ornate frames — of a male at all ages, from naked infant on satin throw to mature man in white linen suit — overrunning the room. They are all of Appleton Powell, Jr., Vada's only child — except for one formal portrait of Appleton Powell, Sr., wearing fine gentleman's attire of the twenties. The two men look very much alike.

The late fifties. A promise-of-spring afternoon in late February.

The stage is empty. When the lights come up, a warm sun fills the room. After several beats of silence, a definitely unusual, one might almost say eccentric but distinctive man in his mid-thirties enters. He wears steel rimmed spectacles and a white linen suit with a camellia in his lapel. He is Appleton Powell, Jr., and he speaks directly to the audience, with a not off-putting southern accent.

APPLE: My mother's sitting room! Used almost daily for some of the most remarkable social exchanges in the entire South — sometimes as an outpost, sometimes as a shrine, but more often as a battlefield. She has an army of friends! They march in an out in their armor — bosoms buttressed, waists corseted, to play bridge, plan bridal teas, conduct Church Guilds, steer Garden Clubs . . . or just "visit." That's what this room is meant for — *(He says the word with a pleasant buzzing sound.)* visiting. But today it's all set up to serve a more . . . predatory purpose. *(The doorbell chimes, and Vada enters one side of the stage and crosses off the other. As she crosses.)* There's the predator! My indomitable mother! Or is the visitor the predator? . . . You be the judge. *(The two women enter now, in a kind feminine flutter. Mary Ann is a vision of loveliness in a pushing-the-season pastel suit.)*

VADA: So you're Mary Ann . . . I'm Vada Love.

MARY LOU: I've heard so much about you, Miz Powell.

VADA: You young people! You mean to tell me you didn't wear a coat in this weather?

MARY LOU: But the sun's so kind.

VADA: It's still the middle of February.

MARY LOU: But it's up to sixty-eight degrees.

VADA: Mind you, I wouldn't want to cover up that pretty dress you're wearing. But I wouldn't want to take cold — not in the middle of the Mardi Gras season!

MARY LOU: I won't. I'm the warm-blooded one in the family.

VADA: Do you enjoy Mardi Gras as much as I do? I just dance right through it!

MARY LOU: You still go to the balls?

VADA: Oh, no, no, I only read about them in the paper — *every* adjective describing *every* debutante . . . Why don't you sit right here by me, so we don't have to shout at each other across the room.

MARY LOU: *(Looking around.)* What a lovely room!

VADA: My son says I should take half of what's in here out.

MARY LOU: Yes, he told me . . .

VADA: *(Quick as a cat.)* Told you what?

MARY LOU: About all the beautiful things you have.

VADA: Well, I don't know about beautiful, but every one of them has a history, and deep, deep sentimental value. It must all look a little *random* to a young person like you, no feeling for the past.

MARY LOU: Oh, I *love* the past! As a matter of fact, I intend to furnish my house with all antiques. I absolutely love antiques!

VADA: Your family's house doesn't look like it would have antiques.

MARY LOU: You know our house?

VADA: I know most every house in this town. Lived here long enough to watch it go . . . well, *down,* if you ask me. People don't take pride in their property any more.

MARY LOU: Not if they don't own it!

VADA: Now I don't mean you, dear. Your little house looks as neat as can be. I bet it's decorated very nicely. What kind of furniture do you have?

MARY LOU: Just furniture furniture. Sears, so to speak.

VADA: Then where do you intend to get all your antiques? I don't know if you've been to an antique store lately, but the prices are something criminal! *(Indicating the chair across from where they're sitting.)* I saw that very chair in a shop down in the French Quarter. Do you know what they wanted for it? Five hundred dollars! Highway robbery! Don't let that happen to you, dear!

MARY LOU: No ma'am.

VADA: Now! What would you like — tea or coffee? *(With a condescending sigh.)*

I have both. Some people insist on coffee — some of my own friends, mind you! But I think that just goes to show how everybody's losing all sense of the finer things, don't you?

MARY LOU: Yes ma'am.

VADA: Now, what would you like?

MARY LOU: *(After a beat.)* I'll have tea, please.

VADA: You have what ever you want, dear. Don't pay any attention to me. Apple says I'm old fashioned.

MARY LOU: No, I really like tea. I think it's elegant. My sister and I used to have tea parties for our dolls when we were little.

VADA: How sweet! I have an exquisite little Royal Doulton tea set packed away up in the attic. Never had any use for it. No little girls.

MARY LOU: You miss having a little girl?

VADA: I most certainly do not! Apple has given me all the joy a mother could possibly want . . . Now, Mary Ann . . . Beautiful name . . . *(Rolling it off her tongue.)* Mary Ann . . . Just give me a minute in the kitchen, and I'll return with the most exotic tea you've ever touched your pretty tongue to.

MARY LOU: Can I help?

VADA: I should hope not! You're the guest!

(Vada gets up and goes out to the kitchen. Mary Lou looks in the direction of her exit, then gets out of the chair, and begins to canvass the photographs of Apple that are crowding the crowded room. She smiles and shakes her head as she goes from one to another, and Apple again addresses the audience.)

APPLE: I'd have to give that round to Vada. That's my mother's name — Vada Love Powell — and she wears it like a tiara. Of course, she has the territorial advantage, but don't underestimate the invader. It's much too soon to tell.

VADA: *(Entering with an exquisite tea tray.)* I guess you're saying to yourself she's lost her famous touch. But you can't rush these things, you know . . . A good biscuit can't be coaxed. And I for one refuse to bake them beforehand. I wouldn't serve my worst enemy reheated biscuits in time of famine! *(She sets the tray down on the tea table, which is now replete with an exotic spread of homemade sweets, and begins to pour the tea.)* Help yourself to one of everything, my dear . . . And don't tell me you're on some kind of diet! I've never been on a diet in my life, and I've never been stout. Ample at times, but never stout! *(Offering her the biscuits.)* These are definitely *la specialité de la maison* — Vada's Bacon Biscuits! They're irresistible with my homemade fig preserves. *(Offering these.)* Here are my very own Not-So-Petit Petit-fours. And my luscious Lemon Squares. Bourbon Balls, and I do mean *bourbon!* I don't know why people are so stingy with the whiskey. And Vada's Pralines Parfaits! Help yourself, dear . . . Do you cook, Mary Ann?

MARY LOU: I'm a whiz with fudge.

VADA: Milk, lemon, sugar?

MARY LOU: Milk, please. My sister and I won first prize for our peanut butter fudge in the eighth grade.

VADA: I certainly hope you haven't resigned yourself to an eighth grade palate. I'm absolutely amazed at the number of otherwise intelligent people who remain children in two areas — their prayers and their palates! The very same people who never say anything but "Gimme" to God are the ones who put ketchup on their steak *au poivre!* You sure you have everything you want?

MARY LOU: And more! Everything's delicious!

VADA: Oh, I'm a good cook! I take no false pride in that! You should come for dinner!

MARY LOU: I'd love to.

VADA: I'm sure you would! Well, now that the food's on the table, let's put our cards there too, so to speak . . . Is it true you wish to marry my son, Apple?

MARY LOU: *(Without a moment's hesitation.)* I think it's true your son, Apple, wishes to marry.

VADA: Well, if you don't wish to marry him, what are we doing here?

MARY LOU: I believe you invited me to tea.

VADA: *(Deciding to take a more oblique approach.)* Yes, I did. I most certainly did. And you haven't told me a thing about yourself.

MARY LOU: What would you like to know?

VADA: Tell me about your family. You mentioned one sister. Are there any other siblings?

MARY LOU: No ma'am.

VADA: Do I know your mother? I know most everybody in this town, but I don't think we move in the same circles.

MARY LOU: I don't think you do. Mama works.

VADA: Out of necessity?

MARY LOU: Yes ma'am. She drives a school bus.

VADA: I saw a lady school bus driver! I couldn't believe my eyes! That was your mother?

MARY LOU: Yes ma'am.

VADA: Well, I can only admire people who dedicate themselves to the young.

MARY LOU: You should see her. She's terrific with the kids!

VADA: *Children,* dear. *Kids* are baby goats. . . How nice to hear a child speak well of her mother. I thought Apple was alone in that. And your father? . . . What does he do?

MARY LOU: *(Deftly avoiding the question.)* They both work very hard to send us to college.

VADA: What are you studying?

MARY LOU: Anthropology.

VADA: Whatever for?!

MARY LOU: I love people, and I love travel! I want to do my fieldwork on the tribes of New Guinea!

VADA: That's ridiculous! You can't go off with a bunch of savages if you plan to get married.

MARY LOU: That's what anthropologists do.

VADA: Not in my family! Anyway, you're much too young for Apple!

MARY LOU: He doesn't seem to think so.

VADA: My son is an incurable romantic. That's why he must have a realist for a wife.

MARY LOU: My twin sister is the realist in our family.

VADA: You didn't tell me you were twins. Identical twins?

MARY LOU: Yes, ma'am.

VADA: Oh, I'm so sorry . . . I've always thought there was something unnatural about identical twins. Nature never repeats herself, you know.

MARY LOU: It seems to me Nature does pretty much what she likes.

VADA: Well, Nature or no Nature, we must all put our trust in the Lord.

MARY LOU: *(With an edge.)* Which doesn't always work, does it?

VADA: Oh dear! Don't tell me you're an atheist! I have no patience with laziness!

MARY LOU: Laziness?

VADA: That's all it is! People who don't want to get up and go to church on Sunday mornings!

MARY LOU: What about Nietzsche? You've heard of Nietzsche?

VADA: Of course, I've heard of Nietzsche! He couldn't sleep a wink at night — God was already punishing him! Don't get me started on Nietzsche and his friend Hitler! I pray to God you're not an atheist.

MARY LOU: *(Not apologetic but expecting the worst.)* Oh, no ma'am, I'm a Catholic.

VADA: *(After a moment of silence, making the best of a bad thing.)* Well, one or two of my friends are Catholics . . . I'm an Episcopalian, thank God.

MARY LOU: *(Under her breath.)* Thank God. . . .

VADA: *(Not hearing.)* I'm sorry, what did you say? That's the only thing bothers me about my age. My hearing's not as sharp as it used to be. Mind you, I once had ears like a bird dog's. From the moment he had his first heart attack, I could hear Mr. Powell's breathing from any part of the house. A human heart monitor!

MARY LOU: Apple doesn't often mention his father. Except for his illness.

VADA: Well, all those years he was sick Apple was wonderful to him! And to me! Apple was . . . *(Deeply moved.)* well, I've already said it . . . everything I could ever hope for! Oh, dear Lord! Do you smell that? I just hope I haven't ruined them!

(Vada gets up abruptly and starts for the kitchen.)

MARY LOU: It's a miracle he survived!

(Mary Lou ponders as Apple continues.)

APPLE: No! No miracle! I was loved! You don't know what it's like to be loved like I was. It was hard — hard on both of us, but I didn't have to prove anything! To her or for her! I was the center of her universe. Therefore, given Vada, I was perfect! Oh, she had to hone me round the edges, point me toward the rainbow, but I was destined to touch it! . . . I know what people say about me . . . *(Mimicking the very people who make fun of him.)* "He's peculiar!" "That Apple's eccentric!" "Sissy!" — I got called that enough in my life! Why not?! A woman raised me! By herself! But that woman's one in a million! So . . . so am I!

(Vada returns with a silver salver with doily and macaroons.)

VADA: Macaroons! Apple's favorite! *(Presenting them.)* Have one. I think they cooled off on the way from the kitchen.

MARY LOU: These really are exquisite! My daddy loves them. I don't suppose you give away the recipe.

VADA: I most certainly do! I'll give anybody who asks me any one of my recipes. I consider them part of the public domain! . . . Now, we were just coming to something intriguing when I had to leave for the kitchen. What was it?

MARY LOU: Why I'm here.

VADA: Well, we both know that deep down, don't we?

MARY LOU: Actually, I've never been invited to tea before in all my life. I come from very simple people, Miz Powell. When we stop for a cup of something in the afternoon, it's instant coffee! — with a Twinkie! — to go! Or if my grandmother's visiting, we might have a Stella d'Oro cookie! She's Italian!

VADA: Italian?

MARY LOU: And if that's not bad enough for you, my mother's Irish!

VADA: I have to say that's the first thing I haven't liked about you, Mary Ann Mele. You're ashamed of your ancestors!

MARY LOU: I'm not ashamed of my ancestors. I just know they're not allowed in your circle.

VADA: They're not the ones trying to enter my circle.

MARY LOU: But I am?!

VADA: Are you? Do you wish to marry my son?

MARY LOU: *(Really attacking for the first time, but still in control.)* Are you proposing for him, Miz Powell?! . . . How many girls have you frightened off? Apple's thirty-five years old! He wants to get married and have a family. Are there any young ladies you would find eligible?

VADA: *(Fighting back.)* There are a great many young ladies I would find eligible!

MARY LOU: But do they find Apple eligible? That's the question! He's a most unusual man! Not your garden variety Gary Cooper! Some people think he's downright peculiar! Did you know that? Have you looked at him lately? Steel rimmed spectacles, rumpled white linen suit, crooked Panama hat! Have you looked at him?!

VADA: I look at him every day, Miss Mele, and I think he's perfectly beautiful. I'll never understand why women don't adore him. And I think he's one of the smartest men in the world!

MARY LOU: Forgive me, but for once in his life, what *you* think doesn't matter!

VADA: You know how to wound, don't you, young lady? I only want to protect Apple. I couldn't bear it if someone who didn't love him married him for the wrong reason.

MARY LOU: What would be the wrong reason? If it isn't his good looks or his great fortune, what else could it be? What do you fear so much that you'd invite an Irish-Italian Catholic girl, whose mother drives a school bus, to afternoon tea? You want to scare me off like the rest of them! You want Appleton Powell all to yourself.

VADA: I most certainly do not!!! Young woman, do you know the parable of the talents? About the man who buried his talent in the ground, he was so afraid he'd lose it. I think that man was the *stupidest* man in the world! . . . Apple is my talent! The Lord gave him to me to nurture and to cherish and then to let fly and bring his blessing upon his wife and his children and their children.

MARY LOU: Then what are you so afraid of?

VADA: I'm afraid no one will love him as I do.

MARY LOU: No one will! Apple's told me all about you. He's told me how you used to make him sit on the side of his poor daddy's bed when he was nine years old and read the paper to him. How you had him wear his necktie whenever there were ladies in the house, and made him work cheek by jowl with the yard boy, and stand up whenever the cook came into the room. I even know what you told him about the birds and the bees!

VADA: Why are you telling me all this?

MARY LOU: To prove to you that nobody will love him like that. And nobody needs to! Apple is already safe and sound because of what you've given him. It wouldn't matter if he didn't marry, but it'd be a pity. The talent ought not be buried! Not after all that!

VADA: I don't know what I told Apple about the birds and the bees.

MARY LOU: You couldn't get away with it nowadays.

VADA: Oh, I know. So much mystery and romance gone out of life. I feel sorry for you young people. You think love just happens. Well, let me tell you, you have to work long and hard to make it last. If you've got to stop to think, you've sure got to stop to love. *(The telephone rings.)* I can't believe it's let us alone this long. That telephone usually rings itself right off the hook this time of afternoon.

(Vada crosses to the telephone as Apple appears on the other side of the stage with a phone in his hand.)

Hello . . .

APPLE: *(Playing the game they always play.)* Hello, Mother, this is . . .

VADA: Don't tell me! Is it . . . the butcher?

APPLE: Nooo.

VADA: Is it the baker?

APPLE: Nooo.

VADA: Is it the Apple of my eye?!

APPLE: Yes ma'am.

VADA: You'll never guess who's sitting right here in the room with me.

APPLE: I might.

VADA: I bet you won't.

APPLE: I bet I will. How about Mary Lou Mele?

VADA: Mary Ann Mele.

APPLE: Mary Lou, Mother.

VADA: You mean you want to marry her, and you don't even know her name.

APPLE: *(Teasing.)* Who says I'm going to marry her?

VADA: I know the signs. You give me longer kisses on the cheek. You bring me blossoms from the yard. You hum — God help us! I know when you're in love.

APPLE: And you always manage to get me out of it.

VADA: And you always agree it was the right thing to do.

VADA:	APPLE:
And I did it for you . . .	Not this time . . . I beg your
What did you say?	pardon. What, Mother?

APPLE: You go first.

VADA: Of course, I go first!

APPLE: Mother, I'm calling long distance.

VADA: Long distance?! Where in the world are you?

APPLE: I'm at the airport.

VADA: The airport. How did you know Mary Ann Mele was here?

APPLE: It's Mary Lou. Ask her!

VADA: Is your name Mary Ann or Mary Lou?

MARY LOU: It's Mary Lou.

VADA: Why did you let me go on calling you Mary Ann?

APPLE: *(Raising his voice.)* Mother, will you listen to me?!

VADA: Appleton Powell, are you shouting at me?

APPLE: Yes, ma'am.

VADA: Well, you best have good reason.

APPLE: *(Very gently.)* Mother, I got married today . . .

    (He waits to see what's going to happen.)

VADA: Go on. You don't think I'm going to get hysterical, do you?

APPLE: I married Mary Ann Mele — Mary Lou's twin sister — at noon today
— in the rectory of the Catholic Church — with the Catholic and the
Episcopal priests both presiding. I thought it'd be better this way, Mother,
for you . . . and for us . . . Father Marshall's going to come by to see you
at five o'clock this afternoon . . . He'll explain.

VADA: *(Very taut.)* Explain?!

APPLE: Please, Mother! We're about to go off on our honeymoon. Father
Marshall's bringing our itinerary, so you'll know where to find me if you
need me. And he's standing by ready to help you if you need him.

VADA: Why should I need someone who betrayed me?

APPLE: He didn't betray you, Mother, I did. I begged him to do it this way. It
seemed easier for us all.

VADA: I wouldn't call this easy. Not easy for me! Not easy to see my only son
married . . . in the rectory of the Catholic Church! Oh, Apple!

APPLE: I really appreciate what you're doing for me, Mother.

VADA: What am I doing for you, Apple?

APPLE: Trying to forgive me. All those other girls were wrong for me. I knew that. I was glad you scared them off. But Mary Ann's different! You'll see. Mary Ann's very different! I have to go now. I love you, Mother. Wish me happiness.

VADA: I wish you all the happiness you've given me, and there isn't any more than that this side of Paradise.

APPLE: Goodbye, Mother. God bless you.

(Apple exits, and Vada slowly hangs up the phone. After a moment Mary Lou stands.)

MARY LOU: I'm sure you'd like me to leave.

VADA: No! I'd like you to stand right there and tell me how — I'm going to say it — the *hell* you had the gall to come here and deceive me. . . . You knew all along, didn't you?

MARY LOU: Yes, ma'am.

VADA: Were you at the rectory?

MARY LOU: *I* was, but my parents weren't.

VADA: I didn't for one minute think they were. I know my son!

MARY LOU: Do you?

VADA: *(Deliberately ignoring the question.)* Why did you lie to me?

MARY LOU: I didn't exactly lie to you.

VADA: You deceived me. Why?

MARY LOU: Twins are very close, Miz Powell. I love my sister as much as you love your son, and she loves Apple as much as I love her. And since neither one of us thinks anyone can love them like we do, I thought I'd make a good guinea pig for you to punish her, and you'd make a good guinea pig for me to punish him. And we'd get all that hurt over with. And you and she and Apple and I could start out without any scars. You said some things to me I wouldn't want you to say to Mary Ann. And I said some things to you, you wouldn't want me to say to Apple. And I don't think we'll ever have to say those things again, do you?

VADA: Are you quite finished, young woman?

MARY LOU: Yes ma'am. Are you finished with me?

VADA: No! There's one thing more. What does your father do for a living?

MARY LOU: Take a deep breath. . . . He's a cook.

VADA: A cook?

MARY LOU: At the hotel.

VADA: Well, it's the one place in town you can get a decent meal, except here, of course, and one or two of my friends.

MARY LOU: He runs the restaurant.

VADA: He runs it?

MARY LOU: Yes ma'am.

VADA: Then, for mercy's sake, tell him to call himself a chef. I see absolutely no reason to celebrate ignominity. From now on it must be clearly understood that the father of my daughter-in-law is a chef!

MARY LOU: Look, Miz Powell, about my folks . . . I'm sorry there wasn't any wedding, but they couldn't afford one — not the kind you'd want. It's not Apple's fault.

VADA: Oh, I bet Apple's glad.

MARY LOU: Why would he be glad?

VADA: He's proved to the world — for better or worse — he's not tied to his mother's apron strings.

(The doorbell chimes.)

MARY LOU: I guess that's your minister.

VADA: Father Marshall is a priest, dear. Priest — just like you have.

MARY LOU: I'll let him in when I go out.

VADA: No you won't! I want Father Marshall to see how well I'm getting on with my in-laws. And then I want *you* to watch *me* take on the entire Episcopal Church!

(The doorbell chimes again, and she starts off shouting.)

Coming!!! I didn't shoot myself if that's what you think!

(She exits as the lights go out on the scene.)

Scene Two

The same. But the room is now swallowed in shadows, which evoke a different reality — the internal workings of Vada's mind. Music underscores the scene to suggest that other reality. There is a glow on the photograph of Apple's father, Appleton Powell, Sr.

Twilight following the previous scene. The tea things are still on the table. Vada paces back and forth for a few moments in silence, taking in the photograph, and a dim light comes up on the figure of a man in deep shadow. He's dressed in a high stiff collar and twenties attire. He is Apple's father, Appleton Powell, Sr., at about the time he and Vada first met.

VADA: I don't understand it, Mr. Powell! I just don't understand it! What did I do?!

MR. POWELL: *(Quietly.)* Everything a mother could.

VADA: *(Not in the least startled by the voice but expecting it.)* And I did it alone, Mr. Powell!

MR. POWELL: I know. I was sick for so long. It was hard on you.

VADA: Hard on me and hard on Apple . . . but that doesn't excuse what he did to me this afternoon.

MR. POWELL: No, but it'll be all right, you'll see.

VADA: All right for you! You don't have to endure it! You never had to endure any of it! Walking up and down, talking to myself till his fever broke. Waiting up at night to hear his key in the door. *(After a beat.)* And now, if I've lost him, I don't have anybody to blame but myself!

MR. POWELL: I must say I'm surprised at you, dear. You're not one to feel sorry for yourself.

VADA: I just don't visit my feelings on anybody else.

MR. POWELL: No, you never did.

VADA: And tomorrow and the next day and the day after that, I have to go out of this house with my head held high and pretend to the world that my own son has not broken his mother's heart. That's what I have to do, Mr. Powell, and do it I will!

MR. POWELL: I admire you for it.

VADA: Thank you, sir.

MR. POWELL: You're most welcome, my dear . . . most welcome. . . .

(He retreats into the shadows, and she begins to clear the tea things as the lights go out on the scene.)

Scene Three

A tree house in Enid Symonds' backyard. It is little more than a platform with side rails and a ladder that reaches down to the ground; the tree branches form the roof. But there is ample room for a bridge table, four chairs, and a small serving table with a tray of lemonade and a beautiful homebaked strawberry cake. The sun streams through the leaves to produce a speckled light and suggest the movement of a gentle breeze.

The following day — so warm it could be April. Enid Symonds and Marybell Baxter sit on opposite sides of the table. They are counting, shuffling, and dealing cards impatiently. The lemonade pitcher is sweating, and there is an air of anxiety, even in this idyllic setting. A canasta game was scheduled for 2:00 P.M. It is 2:10, and Vada, one of the regulars in the Wednesday Canasta Club, has yet to arrive. The fourth member of the group is perma-

nently absent. Her name is Kitty Carter, but she died at the end of last summer, so one of her friends plays her hand. As the cards ripple and snap, Apple speaks again to the audience.

APPLE: I'm the one who dubbed them — "The Tree House Gang!" Of course, Mother doesn't approve. "Appleton," she says, "we're not a nest of criminals!" Then she looks at me, and she twitters, "A nest of rare birds maybe, fluttering their cards and flirting with God!" I wouldn't put it past that crew to flirt with God! Seventyish — every one of them — and they climb up to that tree house every Wednesday in nice weather to play canasta and consume sweets! Of course, canasta's way beneath their dignity! They're wicked bridge players! Canasta's just a good excuse for gossip! Today I'm bound to be the subject of discussion!

ENID: It's ten past two. You think she had car trouble?

MARYBELL: I do not.

ENID: Vada's never late, if God's in His heaven!

MARYBELL: Well, I'm sure God's not, far as she's concerned!

ENID: Marybell, why would you say a thing like that?!

MARYBELL: *(Chiding.)* I know that you know exactly what I know. So don't make such a big fuss about being *above* gossip!

ENID: If something's happened to Vada, it's not gossip. It's tragic!

MARYBELL: Depends on what happened.

ENID: Well, what did?!

MARYBELL: You mean to tell me you were home all morning long, and you haven't heard! I thought my phone would ring off the hook!

ENID: You know I go to the foot doctor on Wednesday mornings.

MARYBELL: Well, that explains it.

ENID: But I didn't go today.

MARYBELL: Why not?

ENID: I was too upset about what happened.

MARYBELL: Wait a minute! I thought you didn't know.

ENID: *(Devilishly.)* I'm holding out to see if you know more.

MARYBELL: Enid Symonds! You're acting like a nosy old lady!

ENID: Chicken clucking over the crow!

MARYBELL: Every time my phone rang, I said to myself, 'Now that's Enid! She wouldn't leave me in the dark any longer."

ENID: Your line was always busy! Just burning up the wires, weren't you, at our dear friend's expense!

MARYBELL: I resent that, Enid. I really do! I deeply resent the implication of what you just said. I would never do anything at Vada's expense. She's my right arm, and I'm hers! But I tell you right now, I really think she had this one coming.

ENID: So do I.

MARYBELL: Poor Vada's not used to being crossed.

ENID: Crossed?! I love Apple; he's my godson, but I'd say what he did to his mother yesterday wasn't crossed, it was downright cruel.

MARYBELL: First you say she had it coming, then you say it's cruel. Make up your mind, Enid!

ENID: *(Getting very upset.)* I'd appreciate it very much, Marybell, if you didn't order me around in my own tree house. Where's the rule I have to make up my mind?! I'll do what I please with my mind! I just hope I can hang on to it longer than my poor Bud did.

MARYBELL: I'm sorry, Enid, I really am. This business with Vada has gotten us both *so* upset. The whole town's in shock. . . . What exactly did you mean by cruel?

ENID: First off, that child's much too young for Apple. Second thing, she's not even an Episcopalian. And third, Marybell — you of all people should know — she's an Italian! What do you think that does to poor Vada?

MARYBELL: Why me of all people?

ENID: You nearly had a fit when Dr. Angelo put up that shrine with the blue Madonna in his front yard, right on your street.

MARYBELL: It had nothing to do with him being Italian!

ENID: Now, Marybell, be honest. I'm not blaming you. I know exactly how you feel.

MARYBELL: *(Suddenly lashing out.)* No, you don't! You don't have the least idea how I feel!

ENID: My goodness! Where in the world did that tongue of fire come from?

MARYBELL: You don't know, you just don't know . . .

(A car honks from the driveway below.)

Oooh . . . There she is! I'd recognize that honk anywhere! Oh, dear! What do we say to her?

ENID: Not a word till she does.

VADA: *(Off. Calling from below.)* Yoo-hoo!

MARYBELL: *(Feebly.)* Yoo-hoo!

VADA: *(Off)* You two up there already? I'm right on time.

ENID: You are not!!!

(Vada hoists herself up the last steps of the ladder and onto the platform of

the tree house. She seems totally together and is beautifully turned out. She's wearing white gloves and carrying her purse and a bottle of sherry.)

VADA: *(Without a moment's hesitation.)* You two know what today is?

ENID: My goodness! You're all dressed up.

MARYBELL: 'Course she is, Enid! It's only natural. When I feel *down*, I always dress *up*.

VADA: *(Triumphantly.)* It's Kitty's birthday! I dressed up for Kitty. I remembered her favorite sherry on the way out here, and I drove all the way back to the Piggly Wiggly to get it. I brought a little libation to toast her. And we'll sing "Happy Birthday."

MARYBELL: Isn't that kind of maudlin? You think Kitty would like that?

VADA: All right, we *won't* sing "Happy Birthday." We'll just sit here deaf as mutes!

ENID: *(Laughing along with Marybell.)* Deaf as mutes?!

VADA: Well then, let's just forget about Kitty. I guess she's beyond caring one way or another.

MARYBELL: Oh, I don't think so, Vada. Death isn't the end of life. It's the beginning of—

VADA: Please, Marybell, don't get started on your sermons! I'm not in the mood for —

MARYBELL: I can still see her in that hospital, thin as a toothpick. A fine stout woman like that! Shrunk to a string bean!

VADA: Oh, it's all right to be morbid about her, but it's not all right to give her a little birthday party.

ENID: I'm the hostess, and I say it's perfectly all right!

VADA: *(Sacrificing herself.)* No, no! Let's get on with our canasta! Who's going to be Kitty's partner today?!

ENID: Why don't you be?

VADA: I was last week.

MARYBELL: Not last week. I was last week.

ENID: Here we go again! If you all don't want to be Kitty's partner, why don't we get a replacement for her. It's not as if people weren't dying to play with us.

VADA: Which people?

ENID: Mildred Huey asked me —

VADA: You really want to play canasta once a week with Mildred Huey?! That whiney voice! I don't know how her husband stands it.

ENID: He's deaf as a post!

VADA: *(Sweeping all the dealt cards up into her hands.)* Time to play, ladies! Let's draw for the deal.

ENID: Vada, we already dealt!

VADA: You can't deal without drawing.

ENID: We had to do something while we were waiting.

VADA: You two are really trying to make it hard for me today.

MARYBELL: That's not true! Enid and I were just saying we'd like to be your right arm. That was one of Mama's favorite expressions. It meant being her strength in time of woe.

VADA: I know what it means, Marybell.

MARYBELL: *(Under her breath.)* You know just about everything, don't you, Vada?

VADA: You're mumbling again, Marybell. My hearing's sharp as a bird dog's, and I didn't hear a word you just said.

MARYBELL: I said my mama was from Mississippi.

VADA: You never told me that! Enid, did she ever tell you that? Where in Mississippi?

MARYBELL: Vicksburg.

VADA: *(Excited.)* My family's from Vicksburg — both sides. What's your folks' name?

MARYBELL: Oh, I doubt you'd know us, Vada.

VADA: We knew everybody!

MARYBELL: Where did you buy your shoes?

VADA: What does that have to do with . . .

MARYBELL: In Vicksburg — where did you buy your shoes?

VADA: You think I don't remember? I certainly do! The Imperial Shoe Store. Best in town!

MARYBELL: My daddy owned the Imperial Shoe Store.

VADA: I thought those people were Italians.

MARYBELL: They were!

VADA: Fardella, Farrara, something like that . . . *(Suddenly.)* What did you say?

MARYBELL: I said I'm Italian.

VADA: Enid, is this some kind of joke you two are playing, because I don't think it's funny.

ENID: It's all news to me, Vada.

MARYBELL: I just thought, in view of what's happened, this might be a good time to let the cat out of the bag. I, Marybell Baxter used to be Marybell Farrara! What do you think of that?!

ENID: *(Stopping her cold.)* All these years you never said a word!

MARYBELL: Not a word, or I wouldn't be here, would I? Wouldn't be allowed to contaminate your pure Anglo-Saxon blood.

ENID: I think that's disgusting.

MARYBELL: Answer me, Enid. If you'd known when I came here forty years ago that George Baxter had brought home an Italian bride, would you have invited me to your Christmas tea? And Vada, would you have taken me under your wing in the Guild, if George's mama hadn't called you up and lied! That's how important it was to the Baxters that nobody knew.

ENID: How in this world could you deceive us like that? All these years!

MARYBELL: I'd almost forgotten I did . . .

(Looking at Vada.) till all this came up. You live a lie long enough, you turn into it.

ENID: You're awful quiet, Vada. Cat got your tongue?

MARYBELL: You all want me to leave?

VADA: Oh, Marybell! It's ancient history, far as we're concerned. A lot of nice people are Italian.

MARYBELL: You're just going to forget about it?

ENID: We're not living in the Dark Ages!

MARYBELL: Some people are.

ENID: Not us! Right, Vada?

VADA: We're your best friends. What we don't know won't hurt us.

MARYBELL: *(Exasperated.)* But you do know. I just told you. I'm Italian!

ENID: So was Michelangelo! . . . Now, are we here to play canasta or not? It's almost two thirty!

VADA: Cut for the deal.

(They cut the cards for the deal; Vada cuts for Kitty. Nedding to Kitty's chair.) Happy Birthday, dear Kitty. *(The other two look at each other with raised eyebrows. They all show their cards, and the one Vada drew for Kitty is an ace.)* Oooh, Kitty has an ace! As her partner, I deal for her, of course. *(Vada begins to deal — eleven cards to each of the four places. She handles the cards exquisitely, like a cross between a river boat gambler and a concert pianist as Apple speaks to the audience again.)*

APPLE: You'd never know today was hard for her, would you? Under that corset: there's real grit! Lived all those years with an invalid. Not a word of complaint! After his heart attack I doubt they ever had sex! But she went right on living her life up to the hilt! Bringing him back news of the battle, puffing his pillows, brushing his hair. He called her his Florence Nightingale, she called him her wounded soldier. When Papa died, she went to work in the bank, and pretty soon she was "puffing their pillows." Wasn't long before the bank became the social center of the town!

(Vada has finished dealing. They all look at their cards and arrange them according to the rules of the game.)

ENID: No red treys, I suppose.

MARYBELL: If I had any red treys, Enid, I'd declare them.

VADA: *(Picking up Kitty's hand from across the table.)* Well, Kitty has one.

(She puts a red trey face up on the table and then draws from the stack.)

MARYBELL: My Lord! Do you realize we forgot to put up our money! How much will it be today?

VADA: A dollar a game!

MARYBELL: You must feel lucky!

VADA: In honor of Kitty's birthday.

ENID: You'll be mad as hog-*hell* if you don't win.

VADA: *(Sweet as molasses.)* Enid, you don't use that kind of coarse language. Something the matter?

ENID: *(Disgusted.)* I'd *like* to play cards, if you don't mind!!!

VADA: *(To Marybell.)* I don't know when I've seen her so testy. *(To Enid.)* Maybe you should go back on your Metamucil.

ENID: I'm regular as clockwork, thank you! Go on, Marybell!

MARYBELL: Go on what?

ENID: *It's your turn!!!*

MARYBELL: *(Throwing down her hand.)* I'm sorry. I can't continue with this charade! Here we are aggravating one another when Enid and I are worried sick about you, Vada. And you just go on pretending nothing's happened.

VADA: I'm not going to let a silly card game spoil my day.

ENID: We're not talking about cards! We're talking about Apple!

(There is a terrible silence.)

VADA: What about Apple?

ENID: It's all over town.

MARYBELL: *(To Enid.)* You sure you're doing the right thing? I thought we were going to let her bring it up.

VADA: *Her! Her!* Now ladies, you know I don't enjoy being talked about in the third person.

ENID: *(Angry and hurt.)* It may come as a shock to you, but you're not perfect, Vada. And neither is your son! You're keeping us out. We're your dearest friends, and you're not willing to trust us with a crumb of your feelings!

MARYBELL: Now, now, Enid, don't get yourself all worked up! Everybody has trouble with their children. Look at poor Kitty! What Little Kit did to that family was a scandal, and they all stood by her. And we stood by them.

VADA: I just want to say one thing, and that's all! There is absolutely nothing scandalous about what Apple did.

MARYBELL: I didn't say that. . . .

VADA: Oh, I'm sure it's on yours and everybody else in this town's slippery lips! People just love to talk about me and my son! We're some kind of freaks, because we have our standards, and we hold them high! There's a right way to do things, and that's the way *I* do them! Apple too!

ENID: Oh, not Apple, Vada! Apple does things his way. Always has. Didn't he go as far away to college as he could get? And then, when he graduated, didn't he move into those awful see-through apartments they put up, God knows why, right next to the cemetery. Even as a little boy, Apple used to ride his bike out here on a Saturday, to be with Bud and me, when you thought he'd gone on a hayride. Bud built this tree house for Apple!

VADA: *(Defensive.)* He missed having a daddy who could do things with him.

ENID: No. I think he felt sorry we didn't have any children of our own. So he came around once in a while to keep us company. That's why I love him like he was my own. But, Vada, I don't think what he did to you yesterday was decent one bit!

VADA: Now wait just a minute!

ENID: No! I wouldn't want a son who did that!!!

VADA: *(Hitting back — hard.)* Well, you don't have one, do you?!

MARYBELL: Now, Vada . . . Enid . . . Apple just knew deep down in his heart that his mother wouldn't approve, so he had to do it behind her back.

VADA: Apple never did anything behind my back!

ENID: *(Hostile.)* Did you go to the wedding?

VADA: There was no wedding!

ENID: All right! Did you go to the Catholic rectory for the nonwedding?!

MARYBELL: *(Trying to mollify.)* Doesn't matter, Vada dear. You never did like Catholics very much anyway.

VADA: You don't know what you're talking about! So will you please just shut up! *(After a terrible moment of shock.)* I apologize. I do.

ENID: No, I'm sorry, Vada. . . .

VADA: Well, that makes two of us . . . Enid, do you think we could have a piece of that perfectly beautiful strawberry cake? I always find a sweet settling to the stomach in times of stress.
(Enid begins to cut and serve four slices of cake, even one to Kitty's empty place. Then she pours the lemonade as Apple speaks.)

APPLE: You see, with Vada, you've got to present her with an inevitable and then she'll adjust. Anything less, and she'll just squash it. I think that's why she gets along so well with God! She's got a gift for dealing with the inevitable. He's got a gift for doling it out. Neither one of them's much good with give and take! In the hierarchy of command she'd rank somewhere between an empress dowager and a Marine Corps drill sergeant.

ENID: Aren't we ever going to talk about what we need to?

MARYBELL: You know, Vada, I know those Mele girls. They're junior candy stripers at the hospital on my day. So sweet and pretty! They're real nice girls, and so polite!

VADA: I've met them! One of them. She's very attractive. Blondish. The mother's Irish. I've never seen the father.

MARYBELL: *(Sarcastic.)* Oh, he's very Italian!

ENID: What does he do?

VADA: *(Very carefully.)* He's the chef at the hotel.

ENID: I didn't know that. He's a very good cook!

VADA: Italians usually are good cooks, Enid.

MARYBELL: I wish you two could hear yourselves.

ENID: What do you mean?

MARYBELL: You're such snobs! Both of you!

ENID: We're no different from anybody else in this town!

MARYBELL: Yes, you are! You're different from me.

ENID: After forty years of hiding from us, now you think you're better than us!

MARYBELL: I'm the same as I always was.

VADA: No, you're not! Now you're honest.

MARYBELL: Vada, I'm trying to teach you something. I'm ashamed of myself, and I don't want you to be.

VADA: Don't you worry about me, Marybell.

MARYBELL: *(Exasperated.)* Dammit, Vada! Now you listen to me! If an Italian wanted to join our church, would you let him?

VADA: An Italian wouldn't want to join the Episcopal church. They have their own church.

MARYBELL: Suppose your new daughter-in-law wanted to join our church.

VADA: She can join if Apple wants her to!

MARYBELL: Suppose Apple wants to join the Catholic church?

VADA: That's impossible! Apple's a lay reader in *our* church. He's not about to join another church.

ENID: Oh, dear God! Suppose he brings his children up Catholic.

VADA: Apple would never do that!

MARYBELL: Vada, when are you going to learn? Before yesterday you'd have said Apple wasn't about to marry Mary Ann Mele! But he did, didn't he?

ENID: Why are you being so hard on her, Marybell?

MARYBELL: I hate it when people think they're better than other people. Look what it made me do.

ENID: Nobody cares what you did right now, Marybell. *(Sweetly.)* Vada, you know what I've been thinking? Maybe it won't last.

VADA: *(Not believing her ears.)* What?!

ENID: You never know. Divorces are a dime a dozen these days.

VADA: Dear God!!!

ENID: What?

VADA: How can you say that?

ENID: Well, if you don't like it, you don't want it to last, do you?

VADA: Of course I want it to last!

ENID: Don't look at me like I'm some kind of criminal. I'm just saying what you're thinking.

VADA: You are not! I not only want it to last. I have every intention of making it last!

ENID: I thought you didn't like her.

VADA: I never said that. If Apple married her, she must be marvelous.

MARYBELL: Even if she's Italian?!

VADA: Marybell, you're beginning to get on my nerves.

ENID: My goodness! Such a fuss over a little secret. Everybody has her secrets!

VADA: Not I!!! There's not one skeleton in my closet, and I intend to keep it that way! Enid, it pains me to say it, but your strawberry cake begins to rival my own. *(Looking over to Kitty's place.)* Who ate Kitty's?

ENID: I served her one.

VADA: I know, and I was going to suggest we share it.

ENID: Too late now. Come on, own up. Who ate Kitty's cake?

MARYBELL: *(With guilt written all over her face.)* I didn't touch it.

(There's the sound of a car in the driveway, then a honk.)

ENID: Now, who's that? We'll never get to play canasta!

APPLE: *(Off. Calling from the bottom of the tree house.)* Mother! We're back!

VADA: Apple?

APPLE: *(Off.)* Our flight was cancelled. Some damn hurricane! And Mary Ann thought we ought to come back and check on you.

VADA: Well, you tell Mary Ann I don't need to be checked on! I'm doing just fine, thank you!

APPLE: *(Off.)* May we come up?

VADA: Why not? I'd like to meet the mother of my grandchildren.

ENID: *(Hating the thought of it.)* You want us to leave?

VADA: No indeed! We might need referees!

MARYBELL: Merciful heavens, Vada, what do you want us to do?

VADA: Watch me meet my Waterloo.

    (At this moment Apple's head appears above the tree-house floor.)

APPLE: Mother, I'd like you to meet my wife.

    (Now Mary Ann's head appears, and Apple helps her onto the platform. She's dressed in a lovely going-away suit and hat. There is a strained silence. The referees look sheepishly at each other, and Vada stares straight at Mary Ann.)

MARY ANN: I'm sorry it had to be. . . . *(She can't finish the sentence.)*

APPLE: What Mary Ann means. . . .

VADA: Let her finish, Apple! Had to be what?

MARY ANN: I'm sorry it had to be . . . this way.

APPLE: *(Finishing another gap in the conversation.)* Aunt Enid, Miss Marybell. . . .

MARYBELL: I know this pretty little girl, Apple. She's the best junior candy striper at the hospital. Hi, honey. I know what you're going through.

APPLE: . . . this is my wife.

ENID: Hello, dear.

MARY ANN: Hello . . . Miz Powell, I know how much you love your son.

VADA: No, you don't!!!

MARYBELL: Vada, the whole town knows that.

VADA: Keep out of it, Marybell.

ENID: You asked us to stay!

APPLE: Mother, maybe we should go home and continue this there.

VADA: Maybe you should have thought of that before you came barging in here.

APPLE: *(Angry.)* Come on, Mary Ann, I'm not going to subject you to —

VADA: *(Hitting back.)* No indeed! Don't subject *her!* Just your mother! Make her the laughing stock of the universe!

MARYBELL: There's not a soul laughing, Vada. We all feel terribly sorry for you.

ENID: You're not helping things, Marybell.

VADA: You present me with an earthquake and ask me to accept it. Well, I can't! I can endure it, but I can't accept it *or* condone it!

APPLE: But yesterday . . . on the telephone . . .

VADA: I've had twenty-four hours to think about what's been done to me!

MARY ANN: We shouldn't have come back so soon. It's my fault. But after sitting around that airport all night, I couldn't spend another minute not facing you.

VADA: *(Attacking.)* Aren't you a little late? Why weren't you willing to face me *before* the wedding?

APPLE: She was! Mary Ann always wanted to tell you about us.

VADA: Then why didn't she?

APPLE: I wouldn't let her. If we told you, you'd forbd it, and then we'd have to disobey you.

VADA: You wouldn't "subject" her to me, is that right?

APPLE: Mother, my wife's young —

VADA: *(Very sarcastic.)* Oh, I can see that! And *very* pretty!

APPLE: You're a powerful force. I might have lost her. I couldn't take that chance!

VADA: Enid, do I look like a tornado? Do I sweep you off your feet?

ENID: Vada, I think we should go.

VADA: No indeed! You're the hostess. This is your little nest . . . And Marybell? Do I strike you as a cannibal who gobbles up little girls?

MARYBELL: You better hold on to your tongue now, Vada. It'll run away with you if you're not careful.

VADA: Picture that! My silver tongue running down the road pulling me behind it . . . *(Hitting hard.)* And you, Mary Ann, do I really frighten you?

MARY ANN:. *(Respectfully.)* Yes, ma'am. But I think I frighten you much more.

VADA: And I'm sure you want to tell me why!!!

APPLE: Mother, please, don't be so hard!

ENID: She's hurting, Apple.

VADA: Your Aunt Enid's right as always. I am hurting, Apple. I'm ashamed to go out on the street. The earth has shifted under my feet.

MARY ANN: You're afraid.

VADA: Why? Because a girl from the wrong side of the tracks has stolen my treasure? Don't underestimate me, Mary Ann. Everybody's on the wrong side of somebody's tracks!

MARY ANN: I know that's not why I frighten you. That's just an excuse other people can understand.

VADA: *(Only slightly snide.)* Then do tell me why, dear!

MARY ANN: *(With absolute certainty.)* You're afraid of me because I love your son, and you think nobody in the world deserves to do that besides you!

VADA: How do you know anything about loving, at your age?

MARY ANN: I don't know anything about loving, Miz Powell. I just do it! I just *love* Apple!

VADA: Why should I believe you?

MARY ANN: You won't because you don't want to.

VADA: It may come as a shock to you, young woman, but I've never done just what I *want* to. Why don't you try me?

APPLE: Try her, Mary Ann.

MARY ANN: I didn't want to marry Apple. I know what people will say — "Gold digger! Social climber!" I have a good family — they don't deserve that. I didn't even want to get married right now. I'd just gotten my degree —

had lots of job choices. I gave up ever having the kind of wedding "a girl like me" always wanted. I gave up gaining your respect. I gave up my good name! I gave up all this to marry your son before you could frighten me away from him. And I'd do it again, and more, because I love him!

ENID: Out of the mouths of babes!

(Apple kisses Mary Ann impulsively in front of the ladies, and Vada takes it all in. Then she turns, in a different mood, on her friends.)

VADA: Well, have you two seen enough?

MARYBELL: Forgive me, but I just have to ask Apple what her parents think of him.

APPLE: They wish I was young and handsome . . . and rich!

MARYBELL: Well, I don't want to be a traitor to my friend here, but I just think you're the sweetest couple. . . . And, Vada, they're going to have the most gorgeous children.

VADA: *(To Mary Ann.)* What *about* children?

MARY ANN: I love children.

VADA: Apple's not getting any younger.

APPLE: Mother, please, do you mind?!

VADA: All you young women are so skinny, I can't tell a thing about your childbearing potential. No pelvis to speak of!

ENID: Everybody's so sure they'll have children any time they want. Such arrogance! As if God had nothing to do with it anymore.

MARY ANN: It *is* arrogant, isn't it, Miss Enid? My poor cousin's been trying so hard to have a baby for three years now.

MARYBELL: Is she Italian too, dear?

MARY ANN: Yes, ma'am.

MARYBELL: So am I.

VADA: Marybell, what does that have to do with anything?

MARYBELL: Just want the child to feel comfortable, Vada.

ENID: Well now, how about some strawberry cake? And there's lemonade. We even have sherry. We'll have a little wedding reception right up here in God's heaven.

MARYBELL: *(Always the peacemaker.)* And we'll ask his blessing on these young people. All right with you, Vada?

VADA: The question is, Marybell, is it all right with God?

APPLE: Mother, please forgive us. I do believe God does.

VADA: God's a lot quicker to forgive than I am. *(To Enid and Marybell.)* But I dare anybody in this town to say so! Mary Ann is my family!

MARY ANN: Thank you, Miz Powell.

ENID: You better not let her go on calling you Miz Powell, if you care anything about what this little ole town says.

MARYBELL: George Jr.'s wife calls me Mom.

VADA: That's so common.

MARYBELL: I resent that, Vada. I really do.

VADA: I meant "frequently used," Marybell.

ENID: Mildred Huey's daughter-in-law calls her Dearie, and she thinks it's sweet.

VADA: She would!

(By this time Enid has cut more slices of cake, and Apple has poured the sherry.)

ENID: *(Lifting her glass.)* God bless!

MARYBELL: *(Lifting hers.)* God bless!

VADA: *(After a beat, lifting hers.)* Well . . . that remains to be seen!

(The three of them drink to the bride and groom as the lights go out on the scene.)

END OF ACT ONE

ACT TWO
Scene One

Vada's sitting room, as described in Act One, with the following exceptions: a rather large and prominent picture of Mary Ann and several smaller ones of babies and children are crowded into one corner; and the table is set for coffee, not tea — a silver coffee pot, two cups, and a silver salver of beignets drowned in powdered sugar.

A decade after Act One; very early in the morning. Vada is sitting in her chair, quite still, and oblivious of all around her. She looks much older. Apple enters and addresses the audience. He looks older, too, and more distinguished.

APPLE: There's been a lot of tea poured in this room over the years. But not without purpose! My mother never does anything without purpose! . . . Well, never did . . . until a while ago . . . about a year ago . . . Sometimes now, if I come in and she doesn't hear me, I find her just sitting there. . . *still.* Can you imagine Vada *still?!* It's like this lapse in the Life Force . . . But it's only momentary, and then she's off again on her latest mission. *(The doorbell rings.)* My sister-in-law Mary Lou's home on a visit, and she's been summoned to stop by before she leaves town — for coffee, not tea! That's significant. It's amazing after what happened in this very room ten years ago, but those two are as thick as thieves. *(Vada and Mary Lou enter. Mary Lou has her car keys in her hand and her purse over her shoulder. She's dressed in jeans and a jacket.)*

VADA: We'll have a quick cup of coffee.

MARY LOU: Very quick! My plane leaves at eight twenty-five *(Not so sure.)* I think . . . *(Opening her purse to look at her ticket.)* I should check.

VADA: Wasn't that a nice goodbye party they gave you last night? All your family there — having so much fun —

MARY LOU: Loud! — as usual. Miss Vada, I want to thank you for being so sweet to my parents. They really appreciate it.

VADA: They're fine people! Wonderful grandparents. And your father's osso bucco is *bellisimo! (Suddenly remembering the tray of beignets.)* Have one of my little beignets. I know you love them.

MARY LOU: If I ate all that sugar this early in the morning, I could fly *myself* to the North Pole.

VADA: I was up at the crack of dawn to make these fresh for you this morning.

MARY LOU: Are you baiting a trap?

VADA: Oh, Mary Lou!

MARY LOU: *(Taking a beignet, eating, and loving it.)* Mmmm!

VADA: *(Pleased that she likes the beignet.)* When are you going to stop running around the world and stay home. . . .

MARY LOU: *(Teasing.)* . . . where I belong?

VADA: *(Teasing back.)* That wasn't what I was going to say.

MARY LOU: Oh no?

VADA: No! Stay home and . . .

MARY LOU: . . . settle down?

VADA: *(With feigned exasperation.)* No! Stay home and keep me abreast of the times. You're the only one does that.

MARY LOU: Picture that — Vada Love Powell "abreast of the times."

VADA: You just love to tease me, don't you?

MARY LOU: Yes ma'am. Now go on and tell me. What's up?

VADA: I need your help.

MARY LOU: Uh-oh!

VADA: I talked to Mary Ann at the party last night, about the pictures you took of those . . . I know you don't want me to call them savages.

MARY LOU: *(Enjoying her.)* No, I'd prefer indigenous peoples.

VADA: You can call them all the fancy names in the world, I still don't see how a nice girl like you ever gets used to living right alongside all those naked bodies . . . breasts swinging . . . privates dangling . . . If there's one thing in God's creation that always seemed to me a sad mistake, it's private parts! *(Mary Lou laughs out loud.)* It's not a laughing matter. In those pictures you sent home, everything's showing! Now, you're the godmother to my grandchildren, and it's my duty to tell you I've seen those innocent little girls *poring* over those pictures!

MARY LOU: *(Teasing again.)* Poring?!!!

VADA: Marybell Baxter says her grandson, Georgie, came home and told his mother the Powell girls were showing dirty pictures all around the school!

MARY LOU: Oooh, so that's what this is all about.

VADA: I tried to explain to Mary Ann that between those pictures and that poor excuse for sex education they get in school, those sweet things are so confused! I know because sometimes they ask me things they won't ask their mother.

MARY LOU: What do you tell them?

VADA: Oh, I'm very modern. Much as I hate it, I bought myself this little book about how babies are made. It's chock-full of all those distressing anatomy terms like . . . *(She finds it distasteful to say the word.)* vagina. *(Mary Lou bursts out laughing.)* Are you making fun of me?

MARY LOU: No ma'am, I'm not crazy about the word either.

VADA: If there's one word women ought to keep to themselves if they care anything about mystery and romance . . .

MARY LOU: *(Getting her back on track.)* And what did Mary Ann say?

VADA: I don't believe she realizes the consequences of all this. So, Mary Lou, if you could call her before you leave and just explain to her that *we* think . . .

MARY LOU: No, we don't!

VADA: What?

MARY LOU: Miss Vada, those people *exist,* that's the way they dress!

VADA: *Dress?!* That's an overstatement if I ever heard one.

MARY LOU: Do you really think it hurts our little girls to look at pictures of the human body?

VADA: If they look for the wrong reason, I do! . . . You may be an anthropologist, but those children are just normal! They don't have their doctorates in anything but curiosity. And we have to be careful they aren't curious about things they can't handle.

MARY LOU: What things?

VADA: Those people in your pictures, I felt ashamed for them.

MARY LOU: *They're* not ashamed. They're the purest people on earth. Looking at pictures of them couldn't hurt anybody.

VADA: Mary Lou, even Adam and Eve covered themselves up! Thank God, or we'd have to ban the Bible.

MARY LOU: Now, come on, Miss Vada, you love the museum. How do you deal with Greek sculpture?

VADA: I stand way back, and remind myself it's only marble . . . and I feel so sorry for them if their bits have been broken off.

MARY LOU: *(Teasing unmercifully.)* And what about those cute little Renaissance cupids?

VADA: I just thank the Lord they're not full grown! Furthermore, that's art, and art's beautiful. Those pictures of yours are real life!

MARY LOU: Which is *not* beautiful?!

VADA: There you go again!

MARY LOU: Look, Miss Vada, here's my suggestion. Why don't you sit down with Annie and Loulie and look at the pictures together. Talk about them.

VADA: We've already done that.

MARY LOU: Oh! And what did you say?

VADA: I reminded them of Adam and Eve in the Garden of Eden, and how God made their bodies the way they were, male and female, different . . . Then He gave them fig leaves to cover themselves up.

MARY LOU: No he didn't, and you know it!

VADA: Mary Lou, those little children aren't ready for the doctrine of original sin.

MARY LOU: Neither am I. Look, much as I love you, I can't help you with this. It's a different world out there, Miss Vada. Think how fast the earth's spinning right under our feet, it's no wonder we're all a little dizzy. I'm so sorry, I've got to go. Mama's home waiting to drive to the airport.

VADA: Aren't you ever going to settle down?

MARY LOU: I'm not finished sowing my wild oats!

VADA: Mary Lou, only men do that!

MARY LOU: Not these days.

VADA: Mary Lou! . . . Why don't you get yourself a nice beau like Apple?

MARY LOU: I have a beau . . . *(Hesitating.)* a . . . friend. We work together.

VADA: Is he going to ask you to marry him?

MARY LOU: I doubt it. He's a great scholar, and he's married to his work.

VADA: I don't care what he is, you can't give him your favors if he doesn't have the right intentions.

MARY LOU: *(Smiling.)* My "favors?"

VADA: Dear God, don't tell me you believe in free love!

MARY LOU: Is there any other kind? What do you believe in, Miss Vada? Duty love? I've got to go! *(She kisses Vada on the cheek and starts out with Vada following.)*

VADA: Why don't you bring your friend home with you next time. . . . Let me talk to him!

(Vada comes back into the room, and starts to clear the coffee and beignets. She suddenly feels weak and has to sit down. In her stillness, the lights dim, and the room is drowned in shadows, which again evoke a different reality — the internal workings of Vada's mind. And again music underscores the scene. After a moment Mr. Powell emerges from the shadows.)

MR. POWELL: Miss Love, may I be of some assistance?

VADA: Oh, no thank you, Mr. Powell, I'm just waiting.

MR. POWELL: For someone, Miss Love?

VADA: No sir, just waiting . . .

MR. POWELL: And that makes you anxious?

VADA: No. I just have time on my hands for . . . questions.

MR. POWELL: I don't remember you as someone who cared much for questions.

VADA: I didn't . . . not then. Now there're so much I want to know.

(The music changes to a twenties waltz.)

MR. POWELL: *(Offering his hand.)* May I have this dance, Miss Love?

VADA: *(Taking his hand and getting up.)* It would be my pleasure.

(They waltz together nicely, obviously enjoying one another.)

MR. POWELL: I declare, you're as light as air.

VADA: Thank you, sir.

MR. POWELL: You three Love sisters — the loveliest young ladies in Vicksburg. One prettier than the other! I was quite taken with your oldest sister, May, before you came of age.

VADA: Why didn't you marry May?

MR. POWELL: My heart was set on you, Miss Love.

VADA: Why didn't you tell me?

MR. POWELL: *(Avoiding her question.)* And you, my dear, what were your feelings for me?

VADA: Mama said a lady keeps her feelings to herself' A lady cultivates her very own kind of personal charm! And that's what I tried to do, Mr. Powell.

MR. POWELL: That's what you *did*, Miss Love! You were never one to want charm, or . . .

VADA: Or what?

MR. POWELL: Vitality! I was quite taken with your vitality. You just grabbed at life!

VADA: Mama taught us not to grab at anything.

(Vada suddenly stops dancing and has to sit down.) I'm sorry, you'll have to excuse me, Mr. Powell, I find myself a little indisposed. They told me at the Ochsner Clinic I had this little heart problem, but I'm not going to let it change my life.

MR. POWELL: Did you ever wonder what you could have done if you hadn't had to use up all that life on me?

VADA: I have no regrets about my life, if that's what you mean.

MR. POWELL: A life without regrets is a lie, Miss Love. Is there something you wanted to ask me?

VADA: I can't find the words.

MR. POWELL: Not you! At a loss for words?

VADA: Not yet . . . not now . . .

MR. POWELL: Well, don't wait too long.

VADA: No sir.

MR. POWELL: I'll be here when you need me.

VADA: Thank you.

(Mr. Powell starts to exit. For an instant Vada's lost in thought. Then she calls him back. Urgently.)

Mr. Powell!

MR. POWELL: What is it, dear?

VADA: May I ask you a favor?

MR. POWELL: Yes ma'am.

VADA: Would you say my name?

MR. POWELL: Vada . . . my darling Vada . . .

(Mr. Powell exits, the music fades, and Vada remains lost in her reveries. After a moment or two, she gets up and takes the coffee off to the kitchen. When she's gone Apple enters.)

APPLE: Mother!

VADA: *(Off.)* Yoohoo . . .

APPLE: Mother, why was Mary Lou over here so early? I saw her car in the driveway. If it's about those damn photographs —

VADA: *(Entering.)* Appleton Powell, are you spying on me? Just because you live next door . . .

APPLE: Mother, I need to talk to you.

VADA: Well, why don't we sit down? Or I could make you some pecan waffles.

APPLE: I don't want any pecan waffles.

VADA: Then, have one of these beignets Mary Lou barely touched.

APPLE: No thank you. Mother, it's about Mary Ann.

VADA: Oh, dear God! I was afraid of that. I've been waiting for something to happen between you and Mary Ann.

APPLE: Nothing's happened between me and Mary Ann.

VADA: Now, Apple, you know I'm always on your side. I don't blame you.

APPLE: No, Mother, I blame you!

VADA: *(Not at first taking in what he just said.)* But I do try to see both sides before I choose yours . . . What did you say?

APPLE: *(Clearly angry.)* I blame you!

VADA: Would you care to tell me what I'm accused of? According to Mary Ann!

APPLE: Mary Ann isn't the one who's accusing you. *I* am!

VADA: *(Dismissing it.)* You wouldn't accuse your own mother, and whatever it is, we know Mary Ann doesn't mean it. You're just putty in her hands.

APPLE: Goddamit, Mother! Will you please just shut up and listen to me?!

VADA: What did you say?

APPLE: I'm sorry.

VADA: You should be sorry! I've never in my life heard you use that kind of language, and I *always* listen to you.

APPLE: Well, you better listen to me now! I don't know what you said to her last night, but I've never seen her so upset.

VADA: I told her she was wrong to let our little girls take those . . . *suggestive* pictures to school.

APPLE: You had no right to do that!

VADA: She understood.

APPLE: No, she didn't! She just didn't want to cross you, with everybody there for Mary Lou's good-bye dinner. She's always deferring to you, Mother, and you never say anything kind or complimentary to her *ever!*

VADA: That's not . . . that's simply not true! Everybody knows how proud I am of my daughter-in-law.

APPLE: *She* doesn't!

VADA: I'm very fond of Mary Ann. She's a wonderful mother!

APPLE: Then why are you always telling her what do about the children? Mary Ann has a right to raise her children *her* way. And you have no right to interfere.

VADA: I never interfere, Apple, I intervene! I just want to save those sweet things from a lot of gossip and giggles. I only want what's best for them.

APPLE: How do you always know what's best, Mother, for everybody else?!

VADA: Well, I'm sorry, but right is right!

APPLE: No ma'am. Right is what *you* think it is — the rest of the world is wrong! . . . I want to warn you, Mother, if you so much as mention those photographs to the girls. . . .

VADA: *(For the first time blazing back at him.)* I would never, never hurt those precious children. They're mine too, you know.

APPLE: No, they're not! They're Mary Ann's children! They're *my* children!

VADA: I see . . . Well, I should tell you, Apple, I've already . . .

APPLE: No! Don't tell me anything else. I don't want to hear it. *(Starting out.)* I'm late at the courthouse.

VADA: But, Apple, I've . . .

APPLE: Not now, Mother! No more!!

(He goes, and the lights go out on the scene.)

Scene Two

The same. The table is now set for tea, but not quite as elaborately as in Act One. Afternoon of the same day. Enid and Marybell have arrived for tea. The tea has been poured, and Enid is reading a letter, while the other two remain remarkably silent and steal glances at one another. All three look a great deal older than they did, but it's Enid who's been hardest hit by the aging process: She has moments of obvious disorientation and distress. This condition is the sad cause of their meeting this afternoon. Apple enters, but they are, of course, oblivious of him.

APPLE: As Vada would say, "Be careful what you pray for, your prayers may be answered!" . . . I finally told my beloved mother off, but I didn't enjoy it one bit . . . Why did I wait till she got so old? *(After a beat.)* Even absolute monarchs age! Absolutely! The whole Tree-House Gang has grown *old.* There's something very sad and very grand about them, sitting there, trying to work out the large problems of their little lives. And, Vada, dear Vada, is still leading the pack. Of course, *she's* the one who called this "summit" about the . . . *unrest* in the Women's Guild of her beloved Episcopal Church.

(Enid finishes reading the letter, folds it carefully, and puts it on the table.)

ENID: Did we say our opening prayer?

MARYBELL: *(Very sweetly.)* Enid dear, remember now, we're not here for a meeting.

VADA: Yes dear, we had the meeting day before yesterday.

ENID: The meeting is now called to order!

(Vada and Marybell just look at one another.)

VADA: Well, let's get down to business. What about the letter?

ENID: Ignore it! They're obviously rabble-rousers. I think one of them's from New York.

MARYBELL: *(Sticky sweet with compassion.)* They mean well, Enid. They all have little children, some of them work. And poor things, they always look so *tired.*

VADA: *(Disgusted.)* Marybell, that's exactly the kind of talk that drags western civilization down! Are the Chinese tired? Do you hear about the Japanese being tired? But our young people, they're all *so tired.* It's become a national disease, and I for one refuse to catch it!

MARYBELL: All very well and good for you, Vada, but those young women are going to resign if we don't do something.

ENID: Where *is* everybody? Hattie never misses Guild. And Gladys . . .

VADA: Enid, will you listen to me for a minute? We're *not* having a meeting of the Guild this afternoon.

MARYBELL: You remember, we had one day before yesterday, and the young people walked out. *(She points to the letter.)*

VADA: Marybell, will you let me handle this . . .

ENID: Now don't you two start.

MARYBELL: Go ahead, handle it! Who's stopping you?

ENID: You know, girls, one of the reasons we're losing members is the way you two keep interrupting all the time. If I can't keep my two best friends in line. . . .

VADA: Everybody interrupted everybody, in the good old days.

MARYBELL: Well, things have changed, Vada! It's not the same anymore.

VADA: Thank you, Marybell Baxter, for those words of wisdom!

ENID: But we mustn't let the Guild go downhill, just because the rest of the world is! That's why I'm willing to remain on as President. What would have happened if St. Peter had given up? And look what he had to contend with. Every time I think about the twelve apostles, I can just smell the fish! . . . All those unwashed robes stinking of fish!

VADA: *There's* the problem! *Every* meeting — *all* that rambling!
(Enid stands and starts to leave the room.)
Enid, where are you going?
(It's obvious now that Enid's lost complete track of things.)

ENID: The meeting's adjourned.

VADA: No, it's not.

ENID: Well, I have to go . . .

VADA: To the bathroom?
(Enid is totally confused by the question. Marybell gets up and goes to her.)

MARYBELL: *(Whispering.)* You don't need to go potty, do you?

ENID: I don't think so.

MARYBELL: Well, why don't we sit back down?
(Marybell tries to help her back to her chair, but Enid shrugs her off and seems to come back to herself completely.)

VADA: Shall we have a sweet to settle the stomach? *(Passing the tray.)* Pennies from heaven? Mille-spice squares? I ground every single spice myself!

MARYBELL: You know, every time I eat sweets these days, I commence to feel dizzy. I guess it'll be diabetes next.

ENID: Oh, don't worry about diabetes. I've lived with mine for fifteen years. I take my little pill every morning, then I eat my sweets — in moderation, of course! Moderation is the seat of wisdom!

VADA: Says who?

ENID: The Greeks.

VADA: I thought they said wisdom came from suffering.

MARYBELL: Then I ought to be an oracle, after all I've been through.

VADA: Don't start, Marybell. We're not here to discuss your multitude of miseries. We all have our problems at this age. Some of us just don't choose to talk about them all the time.

MARYBELL: I'll forgive you for that, Vada, because *(Gloating over it.)* there'll come a day when you'll get good and sick like the rest of us, and then you'll see. *(Sweetly.)* Enid, have you noticed any changes in yourself recently?

ENID: Nothing but changes!

VADA: Maybe they're telling you something.

ENID: They're telling me you're jealous. Always have been. You'd just love to be President.

MARYBELL: *(Trying hard to get through to her.)* Enid, have you seen your doctor lately?

ENID: He's your doctor too.

MARYBELL: Well, he tells me you haven't.

ENID: That's none of his business. Bud spent enough money on doctors. That's what's so terrible! It costs too much to die.

MARYBELL: I know honey, I know . . . But haven't you noticed how forgetful you're getting? Remember how the firemen had to break down your door, and the key was right down your bosom the whole time.

VADA: I telephoned you last week, Enid, and you said you weren't in.

ENID: That's not so stupid.

MARYBELL: Dr. Delmar warned *me* to be on the lookout for things like that. There may not be enough oxygen getting to the brain.

VADA: And ever since Bud died, you don't eat right, we all know that.

ENID: You think I'm getting senile. That's what you think.

VADA: We don't think anything, except you're getting too forgetful to run the Guild anymore. Those young women are not going to come if a bunch of old ladies ramble on and forget to call the meeting to order.

ENID: I didn't forget to call any meeting to order!

MARYBELL: Yes, you did. We went right on sipping sherry for well over an hour before Father Marshall had to tell you to begin —

(The telephone rings, and Apple comes onto the side of the stage with a phone in his hand. Vada gets up and goes to answer her phone.)

VADA: Now, who's that? *(Talking to the phone as she crosses to it.)* All right . . . all right . . . *(Picking up the receiver.)* Hello.

APPLE: This is Apple.

VADA: I know who it is.

APPLE: Are Annie and Loulie at your house?

VADA: Of course not! They're at school.

APPLE: They're not at school, Mother.

VADA: Then where are they?

APPLE: If I knew, I wouldn't be calling you.

VADA: Did you call the police?

APPLE: Yes ma'am.

VADA: Oh, dear God!

APPLE: Now don't get yourself all upset. Mary Ann's looking for them.

VADA: What happened?

APPLE: I don't know. Mary Ann didn't have time to tell me.

VADA: Poor thing. She must be crazy with worry.

APPLE: Soon as I hear something, I'll call you.

VADA: We'll pray, Apple. Enid and Marybell are here — we'll put our prayers together . . .

APPLE: Then we know it'll be all right, don't we? Bye, Mother.

(Apple exits with his phone, but Vada doesn't hang hers up right away. There's a moment of hushed silence in the room.)

MARYBELL: What is it, Vada dear?

VADA: The twins have run away from school. That was Apple wanting to know if they were here.

MARYBELL: What happened?

VADA: He didn't know. . . . I told him we'd say a little prayer. Enid, as President of the Guild, would you lead us?

ENID: *(With great reverence.)* Let us bow our heads in prayer . . . *(And they do.)* Dear God, please hear us in this, our hour of need. We know Thou wast the One who said, "Suffer the little children to come unto me." But not so soon, dear Lord. Those little girls need to grow up to be workers in Thy vineyard. Wherefore, we pray Thee, send them back to us, Lord, and let us prepare them for Thy Kingdom. We ask this in Christ's name. Amen. *(The other two join in the* Amen.*)*

MARYBELL: That was beautiful, Enid. Thank you.

VADA: Yes, it was, Enid . . . *(Distraught.)* Please, dear God, keep them safe from harm.

ENID: Now, Vada, listen to me. In my second grade, not a year went by somebody didn't run off somewhere, and we never lost a one of them. You hold yourself together now, give everybody a little time, they'll turn up.

VADA: *(Very agitated.)* Who else should we call? Maybe I should go over there.
(Mary Ann enters.)

MARY ANN: *(Before anybody can ask.)* They're all right!

VADA: Thank God!

ENID: I told you.

MARY ANN: Up in their own room the whole time. Slipped right by Henrietta. . . .

VADA: Where were you?

MARY ANN: Grocery shopping. The phone rang just as I was coming in the door, and I panicked. I didn't even think to look for them in the house.

VADA: Does Apple know they're safe?

MARY ANN: Yes ma'am, he's with them now. I'm hoping he's going to drive them to dancing school.

VADA: Dancing school?! After what happened?

ENID: *(Warning.)* Vada!

MARYBELL: That's right! It's Wednesday! Little Marybell dances on Wednesdays. Margery and I went to watch a couple of weeks ago, and they looked like potatoes twirling around in toe shoes. All stomach!

MARY ANN: I wanted to come over and talk to you. . . .

VADA: Well, for heaven's sake, tell us what happened. Why did they take a notion to come home from school without telling anyone? I hope you're going to punish them.

MARY ANN: *(Sharply.)* No, ma'am. I'm not!

ENID: Don't keep us in suspense any longer.

MARY ANN: *(To Vada, indicating Enid and Marybell.)* I don't know if I should go into it right now.

MARYBELL: Enid, maybe we should be going.

VADA: Why in the world should you be going? It's just two little girls up to some of their shenanigans. Now, Mary Ann, don't be silly. Tell us what happened.

MARY ANN: I'm going to have to say some things. . . .

VADA: Well, go on and say them. These are my friends. They'll understand.

MARY ANN: I'm afraid it's your fault, Mother Powell.

ENID: Vada, if this is a personal matter. . . .

MARYBELL: Enid's right, Vada.

VADA: No, I'd like you to hear what I've done that's so terrible. Go on, Mary Ann, spit it out!

MARY ANN: All right! *(To Enid and Marybell.)* My sister took photographs of one of the tribes she's been studying, and the girls brought them to school . . .

MARYBELL: Oh, we know all about that, Mary Ann. Georgie came home and told his mother there were dirty pictures of naked people all over the place.

MARY ANN: Miss Marybell, they weren't dirty pictures —

VADA: *(Interrupting.)* Marybell, that's what I've been trying to explain. . . .

MARY ANN: Mother Powell, why didn't you —

ENID: *(Interrupting.)* I couldn't believe it when Marybell called and told me the people in the pictures were stark naked!

VADA: Now, Enid, that's the way those people dress. The point is little children shouldn't be looking at them.

ENID: Stark naked?! I should say not! They might as well go down to the bus station and buy one of those dirty magazines. Gladys told me they've got filthy pictures right in the middle, fold out like a map, made her sick to her stomach.

MARYBELL: How come Gladys got to see them?

ENID: Now, how would I know that, Marybell?

MARY ANN: Mother Powell, why didn't you tell me last night you talked to Annie and Loulie about the pictures?

VADA: I was too shocked to hear you didn't agree with me.

MARY ANN: And you said nothing to Apple this morning.

VADA: I tried to, but he walked out on me.

MARY ANN: Yesterday, when the teacher heard all the giggling out on the playground, she took the pictures away, but she planned to use them today in her section on Worlds and Peoples.

VADA: Dear God, she was going to show them in class?!

ENID: Who is their teacher, dear?

MARYBELL: Jane Bilderback.

ENID: Hilda Bilderback's child?

VADA: For God's sake, Enid, there's only one Bilderback family in this town!

ENID: Well, I've heard that young woman is a fine teacher.

MARY ANN: Even if she shows dirty pictures?!

ENID: Teachers make mistakes, Mary Ann. One little fellow in *my* second grade took out his dingle, right in the middle of the Pledge of Allegiance — I noticed because he didn't have his hand over his heart — and I just said, at the end of "liberty and justice for all," "Young man, that's a very nice thing you have there, but you better put it up, so nobody steals it." Of course, the word got back to the mother, and there was a big brouhaha, but it eventually blew over.

VADA: Are you quite finished, Enid? Go on, Mary Ann.

MARY ANN: The minute the teacher took out the photos, the giggling started up again, and before she could say a word about them, Annie and Loulie burst into tears. They said *you* told them the pictures were bad, and they should be ashamed to bring them to school. She couldn't get them to stop crying, so she sent them down to the nurse's office. But it seems they never got there — they ran home instead.

VADA: Mary Ann, you know I would never do anything to hurt our little girls.

MARY ANN: But you did hurt them, Mother Powell! They're still crying, and they don't want to go back to school tomorrow.

MARYBELL: Now, Mary Ann, you know how children make a big fuss over nothing, and then forget about it in a minute. Yesterday Little Marybell cried her eyes out when she spilled her cream of wheat, and two minutes later she was dancing the Sugar Plum Fairy all over my couch.

VADA: Marybell, this is not about cream of wheat, this is about right and wrong. . . . Mary Ann, I can't conceal my distress that you and I disagree. Disagreement's so bad for the children!

MARY ANN: Why? I think it's good for the children!

VADA: You mean those indecent photographs —

MARY ANN: *I* don't think they're indecent. The teacher doesn't think they're indecent. . . .

ENID: I don't know about that, dear, she may be trying to make the best —

MARY ANN: My sister doesn't think they're indecent — or she wouldn't have taken them!

VADA: *(To Enid and Marybell.)* But we think they're indecent, don't we?

MARYBELL: Well, I haven't seen them, but if the people are naked. . . .

ENID: And the children are titillated by them. . . .

MARY ANN: *(Very upset.)* I don't care! I don't want my children to be ashamed of the bodies God gave them! *(There is a silence.)* Look, Mother Powell, you're entitled to your opinion, but I'm entitled to mine. You got to raise Apple your way. I have to raise my children my way. Can't we disagree on some things, and go on trying to respect one another's opinion?

MARYBELL: Yes, Vada, this is a democracy after all.

VADA: Marybell, you are an oracle of platitudes!

MARYBELL: I resent that, Vada, I really do.

ENID: Now, don't you two start in again. We have enough strife in one room.

VADA: All that uncertainty, Mary Ann, it's not good for children. It breeds moral indifference! Everything relative — no absolutes! That's how it all began.

MARY ANN: What began?

VADA: The Decline of the West.

ENID: *(Almost under her breath.)* Talk about oracles.

VADA: I heard that, Enid.

MARY ANN: I don't care about the Decline of the West! I care about my children! I don't want them to be ashamed of their bodies! I don't want them to look down on people who're different from them! I don't want them to be afraid of what they don't know! I want them to be brave and loving!

VADA: *(After a beat.)* Mary Ann, I think this is the first time you've ever stood up to me.

MARY ANN: You did a terrible thing, Mother Powell. You told the girls their mother was wrong, and you told them behind my back.

VADA: I just didn't want to hurt your feelings.

MARY ANN: You hurt more than that. You hurt our little girls!

VADA: *(After a long beat and meaning it.)* I'm sorry. . . . I don't know what else to say except I'm sorry.

ENID: Vada Love Powell, I never thought I'd hear you say that.

MARYBELL: I just have to say, Mary Ann, much as I love you and Apple, we think Vada has a lot of right on her side.

ENID: Wait just a minute, Marybell! Personally, I don't know what to think now after hearing Mary Ann. It was beautiful what she said. I don't want our children to be ashamed of their own bodies either.

MARYBELL: Nor do we, Enid, nor do we. We just want people to keep their privates to themselves.

ENID: I don't know about that either. Maybe our whole generation needs to kind of. . . air out down there.

MARYBELL: Next thing we know, Enid, you'll be streaking down Main Street.

VADA: I don't know what to expect anymore. The world has changed so much!

MARYBELL: And not for the better, if you ask me!

VADA: Well, if it's not for the better, Marybell, what have we been doing here all these years?

ENID: *(Once again distracted.)* Is that Lij blowing for me?

VADA: What?

ENID: Lij — come to pick me up. I don't drive anymore, you know.

VADA: Nobody's blowing for you, Enid.

ENID: You don't hear that horn?

MARYBELL: Lij would never honk the horn. He always comes to the door.

VADA: He better not honk any horn at my house!

ENID: I have to go.

MARY ANN: Apple can drive you, Miss Enid.

MARYBELL: I drove you over here, honey. Certainly I can drive you home.

ENID: Where's Little Apple this afternoon?

MARY ANN: Right outside on his tricycle.

VADA: You mean to tell me you let that child play in the yard while you. . . .

MARY ANN: Henrietta's with him.

VADA: That good for nothing. Someone could whisk that child off before you could say Lindbergh.

ENID: You all just don't know how lucky you are. You have children.

VADA: Now, Enid, you have more children than all the rest of us put together. *(To Marybell and Mary Ann.)* You can't walk down the street with her without some burly truck driver yelling out from behind the wheel, "Hey, Miss Enid! Remember me, Cyrus Cranshaw, from second grade!"

ENID: Not any more . . . I have to go home.

VADA: Well, you go on and get a good night's rest. And tomorrow I'm going to start bringing you dinners that'll do you some good. We've got to get some nutrients in that system.

ENID: I couldn't let you do that, Vada.

VADA: You just try and stop me!

MARYBELL: Goodbye, Mary Ann. And Vada, thank you for a lovely tea. We can always count on you for at least a thousand calories. But we love it, right, Enid!

ENID: Yes, indeed.

(Marybell and Enid finally exit, and Vada and Mary Ann are left alone. There is a strained silence.)

MARY ANN: Do you have anything more you need to say?

(Vada just shakes her head.)

I'm really sorry, Mother Powell.

VADA: Well, as Apple says, they're *your* children . . . and I mustn't interfere.

MARY ANN: I wish Apple wouldn't speak for me.

VADA: Then you'll have to speak up for yourself, dear. We'll make our convictions known — even if they're wrong — and we won't make the children suffer for them.

MARY ANN: Mother Powell, can I ask you a favor?

VADA: *May*, dear. *May* I ask you a favor? *(Mary Ann just looks at Vada, and she realizes her mistake.)* I'm sorry.

MARY ANN: Please don't correct me in front of your friends.

VADA: When did I . . .

MARY ANN: Just now. About Little Apple playing outside.

VADA: Oh, well, that wasn't a correction. That was just a piece of good advice.

MARY ANN: *(Looking at her again.)* You see?

VADA: It's hard to teach an old dog new tricks.

MARY ANN: Yes ma'am . . . Can I help you clear the tea things?

VADA: No, you go on. I'm not helpless yet, thank God

(As Vada crosses the room to clear the tea things, she feels a sudden weakness, catches her side, and sinks down onto the sofa.)

MARY ANN: *(Rushing over to her.)* What's the matter?!

VADA: I lost my footing for a second.

MARY ANN: You look pale, Mother Powell.

VADA: It's just the light. We lose the sun so early this time of year. Now you go on and pick up the girls.

MARY ANN: Yes, ma'am.

VADA: And could you stop by for a minute on your way home? I'd like to talk to them . . . I'd like to . . . explain. . . .

MARY ANN: I'll drop them off.

VADA: No, I think it'd be better if we were all together this time.

MARY ANN: Yes ma'am. I'll bring the girls.

(Mary Ann pats Vada's hand and exits. Vada sits very still for a moment. The lights dim to shadow, and music suggests that other reality in Vada's mind as it continues to underscore the scene.)

VADA: *(Calling.)* Mr. Powell. . . . *(There is no answer, so she calls more urgently.)* Mr. Powell. . . .

MR. POWELL: Yes, my dear?

VADA: I was afraid you wouldn't come.

MR. POWELL: Why was that?

VADA: I'm so ashamed.

MR. POWELL: What are you ashamed of?

VADA: I was wrong.

MR. POWELL: You're ashamed of being wrong?

VADA: Yes sir.

MR. POWELL: It's only human, Vada dear.

VADA: What did you say?

MR. POWELL: It's only human.

VADA: But now I'm on the outside looking in.

MR. POWELL: That's where we always are, Miss Love.

VADA: No! It's not that way with them. I see them looking at each other when they don't know I'm watching . . . I must confess, Mr. Powell, I feel a little jealous.

MR. POWELL: Of Apple and his wife?

VADA: Sometimes they go to their bedroom in the middle of the day. They tell the children they're taking a nap, and the little girls giggle. I don't know why, but it makes me angry.

MR. POWELL: You find it disturbing.

VADA: I don't know. They argue and fight, and then they make up, and they seem so happy and loving. In the spring, they sit out on the patio talking way into the night. I lie there in my bed listening to them laughing and talking. And I think of us, Mr. Powell.

MR. POWELL: It was different in our day.

VADA: For a man? Or just for a woman?

MR. POWELL: I don't know . . .

VADA: Or just for me?

MR. POWELL: Oh, no, my dear, surely you weren't alone. It was different in our day.

VADA: We missed all that, didn't we?

(He begins backing out of the room.)

MR. POWELL: I'm sorry.

VADA: I missed all that.

MR. POWELL: I'm so sorry.

(Mr. Powell disappears, and Vada comments to herself.)

VADA: I should have asked a lot more questions.

(She gets up to clear the tea things, but has to sit back down. Closing her eyes, she sits motionless for a moment as the lights dim briefly. Then Apple enters, sees her "lifeless" in the chair and goes over to her with great concern.)

APPLE: Mother Mother! Are you all right?

(She opens her eyes.)

Mother, what's the matter?

VADA: Nothing! I must have dozed off after Mary Ann and the girls were here.

APPLE: Are you sure you're all right? You're very pale.

VADA: I'm perfectly all right. I had a nice little dream about your father.

APPLE: Mother, I want to apologize —

VADA: *(Interrupting him.)* No need. Mary Ann and the girls and I have it all worked out.

APPLE: Mary Ann and you?

VADA: And the girls. We had a little talk this afternoon. Even if we don't agree, we'll tell one another, and the children won't suffer for our mistakes.

APPLE: Well, good for you!

VADA: Apple, I'm sorry for what happened. . . .

APPLE: It's not the end of the world. We can all learn from our mistakes. The children love you, Mother, and they are so lucky to have you. I, of all people, know that.

VADA: How was your day?

APPLE: Good! Another big client from New Orleans.

VADA: That's better than good!

APPLE: Mother, Mary Ann called me. She said you didn't look good to her.

She's right! You *don't* look good. They warned you when you went through the clinic.

VADA: Shall we have our glass of sherry?

APPLE: *(Crossing to pour the sherry.)* What happened to you this afternoon?

VADA: I had one of my little spells.

APPLE: What kind of spells?

VADA: I just drop off for a minute or two.

APPLE: Just what?

VADA: Drop off, black out, the blood drains out of me.

APPLE: Oh, my God!

VADA: Apple, there's something I've been meaning to tell you, and this is a good day to do it . . . *(She takes a swallow of the sherry Apple has just handed her.)* I have an arrangement with Dr. Davis. I'm not ever having a by-pass! No pacemakers! And I won't take any of their high-powered pills! I want to die like my mother did, and my grandmother before her. God's way!

APPLE: Well, you can't stay here by yourself in this condition. We'll have to get someone to stay with you! Or you'll have to come stay with us!

VADA: Absolutely not! To both!

APPLE: Suppose some morning I walk in here and find you. . . .

VADA: Dead on the floor?

APPLE: I don't think this is a good time to talk about this.

VADA: No time is a good time! So everybody keeps silent. . . . Now, let me finish. I also have an arrangement with that new nursing home over in Covington. God forbid it's necessary, but I've put aside the money, just in case.

APPLE: You know how that makes me feel? Left out! Why didn't you tell me about this?

VADA: Same reason you didn't tell me when you got married. You wouldn't let me do it, would you?!

APPLE: No ma'am.

VADA: I can't live with your family. I'd destroy something wonderful.

APPLE: I still won't let you do it!

VADA: Well, Apple, you have to! Dying is the last thing I'm going to do with my life, and I want to do it well. You have to see that my wishes are carried out.

APPLE: What if you change your mind?

VADA: Appleton Powell, I ask you, do I *ever* change my mind?! Furthermore, this is not about my mind, it's about my soul! I *believe* in heaven, Apple, and I don't want to be all worn out when I get there.

APPLE: *(After a beat.)* Mother, about this morning, I feel bad, but Mary Ann —

VADA: *(Interrupting him.)* I understand. . . . "Therefore shall a man leave his father and mother, and shall cleave unto his wife . . ."

APPLE: Yes, but whither I go, you'll go with me, Mother, you and all your strength sealed in the marrow of my bones.

(There is a moment of silence.)

VADA: I'm glad! . . . Oh, and Apple, there's one more thing. I want you to plan my funeral! There's something so satisfying about a nice funeral. . . . I'd like a blanket of pink camellias on a steel gray casket — which will be *closed,* no matter how good I look. *(She begins again to clear the tea things.)* I don't want any overwrought eulogies, no charming anecdotes. Just any Scripture readings *you* choose *(After just an instant of thought.)* "through a glass darkly" or "unless ye be born again." . . .

APPLE: *(Amused, helping her clear.)* That doesn't leave very much for me to do.

VADA: Well, you be on the look-out for a good epitaph . . . something from Shakespeare maybe . . . or The Lives of the Saints. . . .

APPLE: *(Much amused.)* Oh, Mother. . . .

VADA: *(Pressing right on.)* Now that's all settled, I can get on with my life! I picked enough figs this morning to put up my preserves. And I promised Little Apple an angel food cake.

APPLE: Mother, I'm afraid I have a confession to make.

VADA: Oh, dear!

APPLE: I'm not wild about fig preserves.

VADA: Don't be silly, Apple! You *love* fig preserves!

(She exits with the tea things, and Apple follows her — with a knowing glance to the audience — as the lights go out on the scene.)

END OF PLAY

A SMALL DELEGATION
by Janet Neipris

For Donald,
and my daughters Cynthia, Carolyn, and Ellen

ORIGINAL PRODUCTION

A Small Delegation was written with a Rockefeller Fellowship to Bellagio, an NEA grant, and first produced under a W. Alton Jones grant. The play opened at the Harold Prince Theater, Annenberg Center, Philadelphia, in June 1992 and was produced by The Philadelphia Festival Theater for New Plays. The cast and creative contributors were:

REMY	Joyce Lynn O'Conner
SUN	Freda Foh Shen
PHILIP	Terry Layman
ELIZABETH	Anne Newhall
MEI YEN	Tina Chen
COMRADE WU	Mel Duane Gionson
SHERWOOD/PASSPORT OFFICER	Shi-Zheng Chen
LILI	Bai Ling

DIRECTOR	Susan H Schulman
DESIGNER	Ming Cho Lee
ASSISTANT DESIGNER	Karen Teneyck
COSTUMES	Vickie Esposito
LIGHTING	Curt Senie
ORIGINAL MUSIC COMPOSITION	Tan Dun
MUSICAL DIRECTION / CHOREOGRAPHY	Shi-Zheng Chen

A revised script of *A Small Delegation* was produced in Beijing in April 1995, produced by the China Youth Arts Theater under the direction of Shi-Zheng Chen. The cast were:

REMY	Wang Li Yun
(SUN) LIU XIN	Yang Qing
PHILIP	Shi Wei Jian
ELIZABETH	Zhang Xiao Li
MEI YEN	Zhang Ying
OLD WU	Chen Qiang
SHERWOOD/PASSPORT OFFICER	Wang Nan
LILI	Wang Qing Mei

The Beijing production was made possible with the help of the following: The Asia Society, Asian Cultural Council, The China Institute, Geraldine and John Kunstadter Foundation, New York University and the Starr Foundation.

BIOGRAPHY

Janet Neipris, playwright and screenwriter, received a B.A. from Tufts University and an MFA in playwriting from Brandeis University. Her plays have been produced at major theaters in the U.S. and internationally, including the Manhattan Theatre Club in New York; the Women's Project; the Arena Stage, Washington D.C.; Studio Theatre, Washington, D.C.; Center Stage, Baltimore; Milwaukee Rep, and the Annenberg Center in Philadelphia. Her play, *A Small Delegation*, was produced in Beijing at the China Youth Arts Theatre. She is the author of *The Agreement, Statues, Exhibition, The Bridge at Belharbour, Separations, Out of Order, 703 Walk Hill, Almost in Vegas, Notes on a Life, Southernmost Tip, Natives,* and the award-winning play, *A Small Delegation.*

She has also written extensively for film and television, as well as National Public Radio and BBC.

A recipient of grants including an N.E.A. in playwriting in 1981 and 1997, a Rockefeller Grant to Bellagio, a U.S.I.A. Grant, and a Schubert Fellowship.

A member of the Dramatists Guild Council, Tony Committee, Writers Guild of America, East, Pen, and Chair of the Dramatic Writing Department, Tisch School of the Arts, New York University, 1983–1999. She has taught in China, Indonesia, Australia, London, Florence, and Prague.

A collection of plays *Plays by Janet Neipris,* was published by Broadway Play Publishing, 1999.

She is represented by Patricia McLaughlin, Beacon Artists, New York.

INTRODUCTION

A Small Delegation was based on an incident in Beijing two summers before Tiananmen Square. As a group of four American screenwriters, including Richard Walter, head of UCLA Screenwriting, I was invited to China to teach the next generation of Chinese screenwriters. It also was an attempt, following the Cultural Revolution, to better relations between the U.S. and China. It was Richard who aptly named our foursome "the small delegation." Our students, incidentally, would go on to become the talented "fifth generation" of Chinese screenwriters, including Chen Kaige and Zhang Yimou.

The play grew out of a politically incorrect gift I gave my translator. Because so many books had been destroyed or "misplaced" during the Cultural Revolution, I decided to give my new friend in Beijing, a western-educated woman, a valuable book. We had been advised by the State Department to bring gifts, as the Chinese, by custom, would greet us with many presents. Protocol, which was never directly stated, was that all members of the institute where we were teaching should receive gifts of equal value. The translator subsequently got into trouble for accepting the special book. If she hadn't accepted it, however, she would have insulted the visiting Americans. Catch-22 in Beijing.

At first glance, post-Cultural Revolution China seemed free, but the longer we stayed, I had the feeling things were not as free as they appeared. The differences between East and West were more complex than could be found from reading history books. Meanwhile, the idea for a play was growing.

A Small Delegation is the story of a group of Americans who come to teach in China the summer of 1988. It's the story of two women, the American professor, Remy, and her translator, Sun, and the eventual impossibility of their friendship. Remy, in meaning to do good, but failing to understand the cultural differences between East and West, ends up ruining the life of her Chinese friend. If the play is about good intentions gone wrong, it's also about the impossibility of any two cultures or people wholly understanding each other. Of all the areas on the stage, the hardest to locate and the most important to reveal is the dangerous space where two lives touch.

A Small Delegation, after productions in the U.S., went to Beijing where it was directed by my friend and colleague, Chen Shi-Zheng. It was closed down after the first presentation due to "cultural differences" but not before we met with a group of prominent Chinese critics after the performance, as is customary in China. The translator for this epic meeting was none other than my original translator, the one who had sparked the idea of the play eight years before. So, there in Beijing, I had come full circle and home.

CHARACTERS

REMY: an American professor, a woman in her early thirties.

SUN: a Chinese translator, a woman in her early thirties.

PHILIP: an American professor, about forty.

ELIZABETH: Philip's wife, a doctor.

MEI YEN: Chinese government official, in charge of Summer Institute.

COMRADE WU: Chinese government tour guide; he is in his mid-forties.

SHERWOOD: Chinese graduate student and engineer.

LILI: a young Chinese actress.

PASSPORT OFFICER: a young man.

MUSICIANS (optional)

Casting note: Passport Officer may be played by same actor as Sherwood. The Musicians may be played by Lili and Sherwood or Passport Officer.

SCENES
ACT ONE

On The Great Wall, Summer 1988

Scene One. *Temple of the Sleeping Buddha, near Beijing, courtyard, early morning, June 1988.*

Scene Two. *Classroom, immediately following.*

Scene Three. *Hotel room, Beijing, early that same evening.*

Scene Four. *Great Wall Sheraton Hotel, Beijing, banquet hall, later that evening.*

Scene Five. *Mei Yen's office, a week later.*

Scene Six. *The Friendship Store, Beijing, a few weeks later.*

Scene Seven. *Beihai Park, Beijing, mid-June.*

Scene Eight. *Tiananmen Square, Beijing, later that week.*

Scene Nine. *Temple of the Sleeping Buddha, the next morning.*

Scene Ten. *Classroom, immediately following.*

Scene Eleven. *Hotel room, Beijing, three days later.*

Scene Twelve. *Hotel lobby, Beijing, immediately following.*

Scene Thirteen. *A street in Beijing, the same night.*

On The Great Wall.

ACT TWO

Scene One. *Courtyard, Beihai Park, sunrise, the next morning.*

Scene Two. *Forbidden City, later the same day, noon.*

On The Great Wall.

Scene Three. *PRC passport office, Beijing, the next day, early morning.*

Scene Four. *Temple of the Sleeping Buddha, classroom, the same morning, the fourth of July.*

Scene Five. *Tiananmen Square, the next afternoon.*

Scene Six. *A tearoom, Beijing, several days later.*

Scene Seven. *Hotel room, Shanghai, three days later.*

Scene Eight. *Classroom, Beijing, three days later.*

Scene Nine. *Ming tombs, Xian, one week later, late July.*

Scene Ten. *P R C passport office, Beijing, two hours later, the same day.*

Scene Eleven. *Public Security Bureau, detention room, Beijing, several hours later.*

Scene Twelve. *Hotel room, Beijing, a few days later, late at night, the first of August.*

On The Great Wall.

They knew themselves as residents of the Celestial Empire; their ruler they called the Son of Heaven. Surrounded by peoples less culturally advanced, they felt they were a kind of chosen people, chosen not by God but by virtue of their superior attainments. Foreigners were known as barbarians. And the land of China was called Zhongguo, or Central Kingdom. It was a luminous domain, the global seat of civilization and of ethical conduct; it was quite simply — the center of the earth.

— Richard Bernstein, *From The Center Of The Earth,*
The Search For the Truth About China

A SMALL DELEGATION

ACT ONE

The action of the play takes place on The Great Wall of China in the summer of 1988, and in Beijing, Xi'an, and Shanghai during that same summer. The central image of the play is a large simple circle, representing a circular section of The Great Wall.

The continuous action of the play is the climb on the wall, intercut with a series of scenes during that summer, played out on points on the inside of the circle.

Little scenery is needed. Just a suggestion of reality. Only the scenes on The Great Wall are out of sequence in time and meant to be as in a dream. Scenes on The Great Wall should be lit differently, as if the clock had been stopped.

Lights fade up. In the background is heard, as if in a distance, a flute. Remy, an American professor, about thirty, and Sun, a Chinese translator, thirty, are at downstage center, six o'clock on the circle. Remy wears large sunglasses and Sun wears a traditional cone-shaped bamboo hat.

On The Great Wall

(Remy and Sun downstage center on the Great Wall.)

REMY: *(Wiping herself with a handkerchief.)* It must be a hundred degrees out today.

SUN: Only ninety-eight.

REMY: I should have brought a hat. American women, you know, have been warned to stay out of the sun because of cancer.

SUN: You mean the government doesn't allow it?

REMY: *(Out of breath, stopping, and Sun stops along with her.)* No. You can do whatever you want. It just may be bad for you.

SUN: In China, we're governed more by rules. For example, you are not a hero until you've climbed the Great Wall.

REMY: In the U.S. we go to the top of the Empire State Building or ride down the Colorado River on a raft.

SUN: Is it true that in New York you can order pizza on the telephone and it's brought to your house?

REMY: Chinese too. You call, and ten minutes later, Boom! Pork dumplings and lo mein. They deliver on bicycles, and promptly.

SUN: Oh sure. We're an obedient culture. Congenial too. For instance, notice my quick smile. Sun, like the sun. *(Taking off her hat, offering it to Remy.)* Here, take my hat. Let's begin the climb.

(Remy takes the bamboo hat and the two start to walk, silently at first, Sun leading the way. Note that they should begin downstage center, six o'clock on the circle, so that by the end of the play, they have completed a full circle.)

REMY: How many steps until we get to the top?

SUN: Fourteen hundred. But when we're there, it's extraordinary — many springs, large evergreen trees, wildflowers.

REMY: This trip is the farthest I've ever been from home.

SUN: On this wall is the only place high enough, and far enough away, so one feels at home . . . so I can breathe without asking permission.
(Beat.)

REMY: Is it a mistake to think we could be friends this summer?

SUN: No. But I think for good face, we should stick to the group. It's protocol and also politic.
(Lights down on them.)

Scene One

Time: June 1988, early morning.
Place: The courtyard of the temple of the Sleeping Buddha, in the hills, outside Beijing. The open flagstone courtyard, with a single banyan tree, is surrounded by several small buildings used for conferences and a temple that houses a figure of a sleeping Buddha. Sun, dressed in a simple skirt and flowered blouse, stands in the courtyard waiting. The sound of a car driving up.

SUN: They're here! There they are!
(Mei Yen, a woman in her late forties, with long dark hair, pulled back in a pony tail, and dressed in a cotton summer suit, comes walking quickly into the courtyard, looking toward the front gate.)

MEI YEN: *(To Sun.)* Ask them if they want to pee, then offer them some orange soda. *(Beat.)* I like the tall *(Please adapt for specific production.)* one's earrings. *(Remy, in high heels, sheer stockings, a silk dress, and dangling earrings enters with a book bag, followed by Comrade Wu, dressed efficiently but impeccably, together with a much-wilted Philip and Elizabeth Milton. Mei Yen comes forward.)*

REMY: You must be Mei Yen. *(Shaking Mei Yen's hand.)* I'm Professor Remy

Martin, American Literature. *(Turning to others.)* This is Professor Milton
. . . his wife, Elizabeth. Philip's in the History Department at N.Y.U.

PHILIP: European.

ELIZABETH: Medieval, actually, between the Greeks and the Italian Renaissance.

MEI YEN: *(Exchanging handshakes.)* Welcome to the Summer Institute. Welcome
to the Temple of the Sleeping Buddha. How was your flight?

REMY: They stopped us in Shanghai at bloody three in the morning; and when
we were coming through customs in Beijing, they went through our books.

PHILIP: They confiscated one of my magazines.

COMRADE WU: There was a question it was perhaps pornographic.

ELIZABETH: It was the *New York Review of Books.*

COMRADE WU: We'll get it back later.

PHILIP: How?

MEI YEN: Later. *(Then introducing Sun.)* This will be your translator while you're
here.

SUN: *(Coming forward, extending her hand.)* Sun, like the sun.

REMY: *(Shaking it.)* Remy, like the cognac. My parents were in Paris when I
was conceived and thought it was adorable to name me for an after dinner drink.

PHILIP: I speak Chinese, so I won't be needing a translator.

ELIZABETH: Philip is fluent in six languages, not counting English.

MEI YEN: Very good.

REMY: What a ride here from the Jing Jang Hotel! And I thought New York
taxicabs were scary.

MEI YEN: There's a lot to contend with on the streets of Beijing. It's the question of the equestrian versus the pedestrian.

REMY: Yes. Mr. Wu, in fact —

MEI YEN: *(Correcting her.)* Comrade Wu.

REMY: Comrade Wu, yes, told the driver to slow down. We came to some sheep
in the road, and he just kept plowing through, giving them the horn, and
the people and animals, carts with cabbages, grandma on a bicycle, carrying a chicken on one handlebar and a grandchild on the other, just got
out of the way, parted like the Red Sea to let us through.

MEI YEN: They could see you were foreign visitors.

SUN: The people manage to escape, but sometimes there's an accident.

COMRADE WU: Like when Nixon was here.

SUN: *(Squealing.)* Oh yes, the pigs! What a sight! Right on Janhuachi Road.
Pigs everywhere!

REMY: I thought I'd lose my insides.

ELIZABETH: I kept my eyes closed all the way.

PHILIP: I kept my legs crossed. I've had to urinate ever since we left the hotel.

SUN: Then you should use the toilet first. The students are in the classrooms waiting.

MEI YEN: Remy will be teaching in the Flower Pagoda. Philip will be in the Great Hall. *(Beat.)* Very good. And Professor Milton has been appointed Head of your delegation. He sits to the left of the Guest of Honor at banquets and makes the first toast.

SUN: By tradition the Leader is always a male scholar.

PHILIP: I told Mei Yen, I'm honored.

REMY: *(To Philip.)* You didn't tell *me*.

MEI YEN: We asked Philip to be secret; things can change.

COMRADE WU: Kuai. Bing-bang.

REMY: God, yes, bing-bang.

ELIZABETH: Philip's been reviewing his lectures all the way over, from Dante to Disraeli.

MEI YEN: "The East is a career," Mr. Disraeli said. Before the Cultural Revolution, of course, that was read.

SUN: Which is why we're excited about your visit. Some of our books were misplaced during the C.R.

COMRADE WU: Temporarily taken by the Red Guard.

MEI YEN: In the Cultural Revolution. But then they were certainly returned.

COMRADE WU: Most were returned.

SUN: But some were lost. So this generation knows little, for example, by William Wordsworth or Walt Whitman.

REMY: *(Excited.)* Walt Whitman! That's my first lesson! *(Taking a leather volume out.)* Look at this! Walt Whitman. That's a coincidence. I think that's fate. Isn't that fate?

MEI YEN: A question for the gods; but Whitman, of course, is admired here, now in 1988, for his views on democracy.

REMY: *(Taking a breath, becoming more formal but exhilarated.)* We hope our small delegation can share with our Chinese colleagues our American spirit, the pioneering spirit. That's what we bring across the ocean, from west to east, building a bridge of new friendship. . . .

PHILIP: Ditto.

MEI YEN: Our expectations are simpler. We want you to teach us whatever we can learn. *(Pointing to Remy's book.)* And that's a handsome book. Is it an original edition?

REMY: It was my father's. He was an eminent Whitman scholar.

SUN: (*Breaking in.*) We should go. It's important to start on time.

REMY: How long should the lecture be?

MEI YEN: Not over four hours.

PHILIP: Not over four hours.

COMRADE WU: In the afternoon we've planned a trip to the cloisonné factory.

MEI YEN: We've made special arrangements. Last year, Professor Nick Hunter, from UCLA bought two large vases there — so big, he had to buy an extra suitcase to cart them home.

COMRADE WU: And we have permission to see Chairman Mao.

SUN: He's in a see-through box.

REMY: If it's okay, I'd rather see The Forbidden City.

COMRADE WU: The Forbidden City is *next* week. This afternoon we visit the cloisonné factory. Any questions about coming or going, ask me. Tonight we'll go to the Great Wall Sheraton where there'll be a Texas-style barbecue in your honor.

MEI YEN: The cloisonné factory is famous; all the work is done by hand. (*To Remy.*) And, by the way, those are earrings to be admired.

REMY: They're street jewelry. They sell them in the streets in New York.

MEI YEN: We sell food on our streets.

REMY: So do we.

PHILIP: Hot dogs.

COMRADE WU: And this isn't always true that we eat dogs. It's a quite vicious rumor.

ELIZABETH: (*To Comrade Wu.*) I'm sure. In the morning I like to run. Is there a park where I can run?

COMRADE WU: No. I don't think so. But there's sunrise discoing in a nearby park where you can go for aerobic exercise. They do the tango there. It's the newest rage. (*Pointing to the right.*) And the washrooms are that way.

MEI YEN: On Sunday we'll climb the Great Wall.

SUN: Unless it rains.

MEI YEN: Then we'll take umbrellas.

Scene Two

Time: Immediately following.
Place: Classroom, Temple of the Sleeping Buddha. Remy and Sun sit side by side at a desk. On the desk is a thermos of water. Remy gets up, moves down-

stage, faces audience as though we were the class. As she speaks, Sun translates into Chinese, waiting for Remy to pause. The speeches can overlap.

REMY: *The American Spirit,* as found in the poetry of Walt Whitman.
   (Pause.)

SUN: *Wa er te Hui te de shizhong suo zheo de "Mei Li Fan Jing shen."*

REMY: When I first read Walt Whitman, it was summer and I was in Italy.

SUN: *(Holding up her hand, signaling Remy to stop so she can translate.) (Wo di yi ci du Wa Er Te Hui Te Man shi wo zai Yi Da Li de xia tian.)*

REMY: And because I was twenty-two — *(Holding up two fingers twice.)*—and in a foreign country, afraid to be alone, it was the only connection with my own country — the language.

SUN: *Yin wé wo zai waíguo, hái pá gu dú, yu yán shi wo he Wo de Zuquó baochi lianxi de weí yí tújíng.*
   (Imitating Remy, holding up two fingers.)

SUN: *(Pause, scanning the class, sighting a raised hand.)* A student would like to know, what was Whitman's approach to the Civil War?

REMY: He saw Lincoln as the savior of the slaves, which he was.

SUN: *(Ta ba Lin Ken shi wei nei nu de Jiu xing, Ta que shi ruci. Pause, scanning class.)* Someone has asked if it was true that your President, Thomas Jefferson, kept slaves although he professed to be against slavery.

REMY: *(Obviously rattled.)* Yes. It's true. Well it's complex.

SUN: *(To the class.) Shi de, zhe shi zhen de, dan shi, zhe li henfu za. (Then to Remy.)* Here in China, we're accustomed to doing what we say. This way, the action matches the word.

REMY: *(To Sun.)* You're never hypocritical then.

SUN: Only in our hearts. We've perfected the art of biaotai — giving a performance.

REMY: Tell them Jefferson had slaves, but in his heart, he was against it. Then say:
   (Quoting Whitman, and as she does, Sun translates simultaneously, as she knows the poem.)
   "I celebrate myself, and sing myself
   And what I assume you shall assume"

SUN: *Wo zanmei wo ziji, gechang wo ziji/Wo chengdan zi ye jiang chengdan*

REMY: The individual means everything to Whitman . . . privacy. . . .

SUN: *(To Remy.)* I can't translate that.

REMY: Why not?

SUN: There's no word for privacy in Chinese. Just go on quickly. Cover up.

REMY: *(To class.)* So, Whitman, spent most of his time alone in a room.

SUN: It's better not to say that either. No one has a room of their own in Beijing, except for punishment.

(Lights down.)

(Lights up. A few hours later, a weary Remy; Sun fans herself.)

REMY: And so, as Confucius said, "I transmit, but I do not originate."

SUN: *Zheng ru kong zi shuo de: "Shu er bu zuo." (Beat.)* They liked that, that you quoted from us, sixth century B.C.

REMY: The thing about China is it's so damn authentically ancient.

(Turning to Sun.) Am I done yet?

SUN: Good. Four hours, ten minutes. Overachiever.

REMY: *(Much relieved, to class.)* At our next class we'll discuss the works of Henry Wadsworth Longfellow.

SUN: *(Chinese translation.)* — Longfellow *(Applause.)* They're pleased. They admire Longfellow because he rhymes. Now stand up. The lecture is over. The students won't leave until you do. Respect for authority.

REMY: For the teacher.

SUN: The *American* teacher.

(They stand, turning downstage, as Comrade Wu and Elizabeth enter with teacups, chatting, at far end of courtyard.)

REMY: *(Softly, to Sun.)* Elizabeth came to assist Philip with his slides.

SUN: I thought you had Women's Liberation in your country.

REMY: We do. Elizabeth's a public health doctor. She works in an AIDS clinic. But this is her vacation, so it's a relief just to be a wife.

SUN: She looks unsure.

REMY: She's made of steel. She lives with Philip.

SUN: The fine art of performance again.

REMY: Women are experts; *which means* I have no idea what *I'm* saying to the class is what *you're* saying to the class.

SUN: Unless we plan to trust each other. *(Beat.)* I sometimes think about going to a brave city like New York. There are more books at Columbia University, I hear, than in the entire world.

REMY: If you come, our apartment has a pull-out couch. And you can see Central Park out the window.

SUN: Don't tempt me . . . But, like everyone, I enjoy a good daydream.

(Remy begins packing up her books and lecture notes. Sun, watching each book disappear into Remy's bag.)

SUN: We owned a copy of *Leaves Of Grass* that was my mother's, but it was misplaced in the Cultural Revolution. But that's the past.

REMY: *(Pause, then frantically searching in the depths of her enormous bag for the Whitman book, finding it, holding it out.)* Why don't you take the book. Here. Take it. Take the Whitman. It would make me happy.

SUN: I think absolutely not. This is a very valuable book.

REMY: *(Insisting.)* No. It's a gift. I know where to get another one. *(Pushing it on her.)* Look, at home I wanted all this stuff. Now my house is full of stuff. You have to take it.

(Sun stands frozen. Then Remy quickly pushes the book into Sun's hand as Mei Yen and Philip join Elizabeth and Comrade Wu in the courtyard.)

SUN: *(To Remy.)* Books are still scarce, since the Gang of Four. We think they ate them for dinner, since they all had big bellies. We intellectuals are hungry for books. Others dream of Sony TVs. *(Pause.)* Those are nice too.

(Sun quickly stuffs the book into her bag. They both stand, moving down stage, toward courtyard.)

SUN: *(Whispering, as they walk.)* See Mei Yen? She's a single woman. She lives permanently without her husband and independent. *(Beat.)* Are you married?"

REMY: To a historian. He teaches with Philip. *(Beat.)* We're on a trial separation. I'm here, he's there.

MEI YEN: *(Walking up to them.)* So how did it go? Philip was a great success, especially with the ladies.

REMY: The students wrote down every word. I mean, not everything's a pearl.

(Sun is silent. Perhaps Mei Yen has seen the book.)

ELIZABETH: Comrade Wu took me to see the discoing in the park. There were dozens of people doing the tango.

COMRADE WU: The old ones still do T'ai Chi.

SUN: Out of habit.

MEI YEN: Out of tradition.

COMRADE WU: I taught Elizabeth "White Crane Spreads Wings."

(Elizabeth assumes the above position, Comrade Wu joins her.)

MEI YEN: One of our most direct moves, because it takes concentration, is "Step Forward And Punch." It's a warning position — Don't cross this line, or you may find my fist in your mouth. *(Assuming the position.)* It's why we built a wall. Like your Robert Frost says, "Good fences make good neighbors."

Scene Three

Time: Early that evening.
Place: Remy's hotel room, Beijing. An open suitcase is on a bed. Remy, in a bathrobe, a towel around her just-washed hair, goes through her suitcase, frantically looking for something. Philip, already dressed for the evening, smokes a cigarette and paces. Elizabeth is writing in her journal.

REMY: How was I to know we're expected to bring everyone a present? No one told me.

PHILIP: They told me.

REMY: The History Department is just more efficient.

PHILIP: Or maybe I'm a better listener.

REMY: How would you like my fist in your mouth?

PHILIP: We brought these Statue of Liberty thingamajigs. *(Getting out of his bag a bunch of souvenir Statue of Liberty statuettes.)*

ELIZABETH: Are those tacky or *what?*

REMY: *(Now really rattled, plowing through her suitcase.)* Maybe I can give Comrade Wu my watch. *(Holding up her watch.)*

ELIZABETH: *(Continuing to write in her journal.)* Too extravagant.

REMY: My belt then! *(Pulling out a belt.)* Genuine American. I got it in Montana. It has a buffalo on the buckle.

PHILIP: I heard these welcoming banquets are very formal.

REMY: *(Still looking through suitcase, pulling out.)* . . . A scarf. Jesus, Ted bought this for me in Venice. *(Holding up the scarf.)* What the hell! For Mei Yen. *(Wrapping scarf in tissue.)* What about Bic ball point pens for the drivers?

ELIZABETH: Too cheap.

REMY: *(Grabbing her wallet.)* Perfect then! Plain old dollar bills. The drivers will love it. *(Waving bills.)* And think of the symbolism. *(Beat.)* I gave Sun my Whitman book.

PHILIP: Why did you do *that?* It's a first edition.

REMY: Look at all this stuff we came with. *(Pulling clothes out.)* Sweaters, skirts, jackets, silk underwear! Did you see how simply they dress? I'm not wearing any of my jewelry. I feel like a conspicuous consumptive.

PHILIP: Let me assure you, you're just a run of the mill capitalist like the rest of us.

REMY: What are you going to say for your toast tonight at our Great Wall Barbecue?

PHILIP: You're pissed. It was either you or I to head our delegation.

ELIZABETH: Even though Remy's senior faculty.

PHILIP: You heard their tradition — the male scholar

ELIZABETH: Please don't be an academic prick. Or do the two go together?

PHILIP: *(To Elizabeth.)* I hope they serve bear's paws tonight, and you can't refuse, because if you do, it's an insult, and they never give you anything again.

ELIZABETH: We should leave for the barbecue. You know they're there waiting for us early so they won't be late.

REMY: And I may give Sun some of my jewelry.

ELIZABETH: That's like saying "Here we are, us rich Americans." I plan to talk Comrade Wu into letting me visit a hospital. What interests me is how they're treating infectious disease. I'll bet more aggressively than we are. How do you say *please* in Chinese?

PHILIP: *Ching.*

ELIZABETH: *(Exits, repeating.) Ching.*

PHILIP: Did you know Elizabeth has refused to sleep with me? She says I've become uncreative.

REMY: You should try a sex therapist or a book. *(Beat.)* What are you going to say for your toast?

PHILIP: I don't know.

REMY: Then say *gan bei (Lifting her glass.)* Bottoms up!

Scene Four

Time: Later that evening.
Place: The Great Wall Sheraton Hotel. There is a Texas-style barbecue banquet as a welcome for the Americans. Gathered, drinks in hand, are Mei Yen, Comrade Wu, Sun, Remy, Philip, and Elizabeth. If possible, two musicians, a man and a woman, (Lili) play traditional Chinese instruments. Strains of "Oh Susannah" are heard. Mei Yen wears the scarf Remy has given her.

MEI YEN: *(Holding her glass.)* Dear delegation, hello. *Ni hao.* Welcome to the Great Wall Sheraton. We've prepared a Texas-style barbecue to say how happy we are you're here. And entertainment by the quite famous Zhou Minh and Miss Lili Chan. *(Clinking her glass against Philip's.)* Cheers. *(All drink, then referring to the liquor.)* First, I should caution you about our maotai. It's known to be lethal for foreigners.

PHILIP: *(Holding up his glass.) Gan bei.*

(He clinks glasses with Mei Yen, then all clink with each other, and so on.)

MEI YEN: *(Clinking again, drinking.)* Gan bei! Before we attack our Kentucky Fried Chicken — our newest store in the PRC *(People's Republic of China.)*, we should tell the saying, "Eat the fish before the fish eats you." The Chinese have a saying for everything.

COMRADE WU: Later, we're planning a more traditional banquet.

SUN: Two thousand-year-old eggs and drunken chicken.

REMY: *(Holding up her glass, trying to think of something very Chinese.)* "To spring, to the bloom of a hundred flowers."

(Clinking glasses with all. There is silence, then slowly the Chinese drink. Remy has obviously said something wrong.)

COMRADE WU: *(Raising his glass to the Americans in a toast. There's a great relief as the silence is broken. This next section should all go fairly rapidly.)* "Remember the Red River Valley"!

(They all clink and drink.)

ELIZABETH: *(Raising her glass.)* "Remember the Alamo!"

(All clink and drink. Comrade Wu refills glasses.)

SUN: *(Raising her glass.)* Sunshine on my shoulders makes me happy. . . . John Denver, "Rocky Mountain High."

(Clink and drink.)

PHILIP: *(Raising glass.)* To the wisdom of the east. . . .

MEI YEN: *(Raising glass.)* To the riches of the west .. . . . *(Putting glass down.)* Let's eat. Dig in. *(Handing Philip a newspaper.)* Oh, and Philip, the *New York Review of Books* was declared noncontroversial. *(Comrade Wu and Philip exit followed by Mei Yen and Elizabeth. They move upstage on the circle to a table set with fried chicken. Lights fade as they serve themselves; and up on Sun and Remy who remain behind.)*

REMY: What did I say wrong?

SUN: Nothing. *(Then, without missing a beat.)* I think Mei Yen saw you give me the book. Did you give her a book?

REMY: A scarf. The one she's wearing. It's a very good scarf.

SUN: Not good enough. It's not a book.

REMY: Then I'll give her a book.

SUN: But it won't be the *same* book. It's tricky. China is a plate of sand. *(Beat.)* Remy's wrong-saying . . . "Let a hundred flowers grow." The government said the same thing once, "Let flowers grow, speak any words you want." So we put up posters on a Democracy wall. *Then* the government said "We don't like these ideas," and the soldiers came and tore them down, and you couldn't do the ideas anymore. It reminds us not to be foolish. *(Beat.)* But, *xie xie.*

REMY: What does that mean?

SUN: Thank you for my Whitman.

REMY: *Xie xie.*

SUN: *Bu xie.* You're welcome. And I think it's stupid how they made a barbecue. I could be punished for saying that. It was Mei Yen's idea. She enjoys being an original thinker.

REMY: Is this an original thought, Sun? You'd like to leave someday?

SUN: I want to *stay;* I want to *leave.* My unruly ancestors are sometimes demons. But we're missing the Kentucky chicken.

REMY: What if we choose instead to go to the restaurant here in the hotel?

SUN: *Choose.* This is a new foreign concept. And have American drinks? Bloody Mary?

REMY: You bet! I invite you! You're my guest.

SUN: You bet! And after we could ride up and down in the glass elevators. *(Pause.)* Then everyone would see us alone. *(A hesitation, then.)* I invite you instead to my house for dinner. Sunday. *(Writing on a piece of paper, handing it to Remy secretly.)* My address. Later I'll draw you a map. *(Excitedly.)* You'll meet my husband and son and I'll cook *haizhe pi,* jellyfish. Close your eyes and it tastes like scallops. And you won't be surprised by my son. He's one of the new rascals. He watches television and dreams of riding a motorcycle.

REMY: *Xie xie, xie xie, xie xie.*

SUN: We better teach you a new word.

Scene Five

Time: A week later.
Place: Mei Yen's office. Mei Yen is seated behind a desk. Sun sits in a chair.

MEI YEN: What did you say when you were given the book?

SUN: I said "Thank you." I said, "This is a very valuable book."

MEI YEN: Of course. You had to be polite.

SUN: Of course, I had to be polite.

MEI YEN: But you didn't report the book. It wasn't listed in the register.

SUN: Because I had mistaken information.

MEI YEN: That can happen.

SUN: It happened to me that Professor Remy said the book *was* valuable. But

I was told it *wasn't*. So she was misinformed. Otherwise, I would have reported such a valuable gift.

MEI YEN: Of course. *(She takes the Whitman book from her lap and opens it on the table.)* Only this book of Walt Whitman *is* valuable. It's a first edition. *(Beat.)* Who told you the book wasn't valuable?

SUN: A bookseller near Fu Xinmen Street. I don't remember exactly where. I neglected to get his name. But it's very clear to me he was a stupid man and didn't give me the right details. But now I know. I was right in the first place and should have reported this important gift, a first edition of *Leaves of Grass* by Walt Whitman.

MEI YEN: Don't get too involved. It's only a summer romance. Be honey-tongued but correct. You wouldn't want to be branded a spy mistakenly.

SUN: Appearances.

MEI YEN: Just caution. You're up for a promotion at the university. Comrade Wu is a true party guy. You have a short memory.

SUN: For God's sakes, it's 1988! Things have turned around! Our doors are open.

MEI YEN: Don't be stupid. Don't be an ostrich.

SUN: I already died once. What could I fear?

(Beat.)

MEI YEN: I heard you were reconciled with your father.

SUN: It's true.

MEI YEN: He must have been angry or sad.

SUN: He understood. I simply was misinformed by the Red Guards, like most of us. They said "Your father is bad," and I believed them. *(Beat.)* In America, you know, since Gloria Steinem, women have loyal and giggling friendships.

MEI YEN: That's not a luxury we can afford.

SUN: Why not?

(Beat.)

MEI YEN: *(Considers it.)* We have higher pursuits.

SUN: Like what?

MEI YEN: Sun, one could be exasperated by you! *(Beat.)* Here are four books to translate. *(Handing Sun four large volumes.)* You have a month, but earlier would be better. That should keep you busy while the Americans are here. *(Beat.)* They come in, Sun, like a breeze in the middle of the night, blowing hot and cold, getting us stirred up, and then they'll sweep out of here and we'll be left. They'll send Christmas cards once a year and we'll be left. You need that job at the university. I need my job. I don't count on kindness of strangers.

(Sun stands, moves to get the book from on top of the desk. Mei Yen picks up the book.)

MEI YEN: I'll hold onto the Whitman.

Scene Six

Time: A few weeks later.
Place: Friendship Store, filled with Chinese goods, only for foreigners. Elizabeth and Mei Yen are at the counter.

MEI YEN: Most Americans like to buy the silk pajamas at the Friendship Store. But wait for Shanghai for the leather jackets.

ELIZABETH: We're not silk pajama people. We're not leather jacket people either. We're quite sensible.

MEI YEN: Then maybe you should be frivolous. What a poor fate to be like a monk with an umbrella — no hair, no sky.

ELIZABETH: Mei Yen, not to be blunt — I'll be blunt. I didn't ask to come here. I was told "Be outside your hotel at two o'clock."

MEI YEN: You could have refused. They just do the plan to be polite. Everyone wants to go to the Friendship Store.

ELIZABETH: Okay, then, I'll buy something. *(To an unseen clerk.)* That sweater. The peach-colored one. How much is it?

MEI YEN: *(Whispering.)* It's cashmere.

ELIZABETH: I'll take it. Charge. Do you take American Express?

MEI YEN: Don't you want to try it on?

ELIZABETH: No.

MEI YEN: Chinese sizes are smaller.

ELIZABETH: If it doesn't fit, I'll give it away.

MEI YEN: The thought's occurring that you're buying it to please *me*.

ELIZABETH: What if I am?

MEI YEN: Then you are acting in a typically correct manner for a Chinese person.

ELIZABETH: Then it may be the first time I'm doing anything right since I got here. *(Beat.)* I'm not a Goody Two Shoes like Remy, or a lecturer in six languages like my husband. *(Beat.)* What is it like to be alone? Sun said you live alone.

MEI YEN: Sun should mind her business.

ELIZABETH: No. I asked her.

MEI YEN: Sun has a loose mouth. The walls in China have ears. There are baby spies in every crack.

ELIZABETH: *What is it like?*

MEI YEN: What do you think?

ELIZABETH: Frightening.

MEI YEN: *(Shaking her head.)* Powerful.

ELIZABETH: In America, for a time, everyone left their husbands.

MEI YEN: Here no one divorces. Only sometimes they get busy with work and disappear. And Sun's one to gossip! Her husband was in the U.K. for two years, and now he's leaving again. He came home to do his laundry.

ELIZABETH: I *believe* in practical arrangements. *(Beat.)* Where were you in the Cultural Revolution?

MEI YEN: You're *very* forward.

ELIZABETH: I'm a doctor. I'm trained to ask questions.

MEI YEN: And I'm trained to evade them.

ELIZABETH: I studied ballet but didn't have talent; so I went to medical school instead. And I'd like a favor. Could you persuade Comrade Wu to take me on a tour of your hospital?

MEI YEN: *(The two pick through the clothes, like any two women shopping.)* Possibly Tuking Union.

ELIZABETH: Tuking Union's all American doctors. I want to observe the Chinese.

MEI YEN: There's no AIDS here. Just a few cases.

ELIZABETH: *(Skeptical.)* So Comrade Wu explained.

MEI YEN: If you take no for an answer, that's appreciated. Professor Remy could learn from you. *(Beat.)* Sun's mother, you know, was a dancer with the ballet in Beijing. In the Great Proletarian Revolution, they made her dance for hours with a corpse in the schoolyard and made us watch. So, Sun for sure was one who denounced her own mother. She applauded after the dance.

ELIZABETH: They must have threatened her.

MEI YEN: Hey, the Gang of Four bullied everyone; but no one put strings on people's hands to make one clap against the other. Remy should be told to be cautious in her friendships.

ELIZABETH: No one tells Remy anything. Sun's even invited her home for dinner Sunday.

MEI YEN: But Wu takes us to the circus Sunday to see the famous tigers who jump through hoops. The seats were a last minute gift from your Ambassador,

Mr. Lord. You warn Professor Remy to stop stirring up winds. And Sun, of course, is unpredictable, a little *fangele* — crazy.

ELIZABETH: Is Sun's mother still alive?

MEI YEN: My God, no. She died while she was dancing with the dead person. Thirty-one hours. That's when Sun applauded. You call it a dance marathon. Is that correct? *(Silence.)* After, her father was in shock and they put him in a mental ward. When the GPR was over, he wanted to stay there. It was one of the only places where there still were flowers. He was a botanist. No more questions, except, what is "Goody Two Shoes"?

ELIZABETH: It means to be an excellent tap dancer.

MEI YEN: Like Fred Astaire.

ELIZABETH: Like Fred Astaire.

Scene Seven

Time: Mid-June, a Sunday afternoon.
Place: Beihai Park, Beijing. Sun and Remy are in the park.

SUN: This is how you play "fish." We both lie down on the grass like this. *(Sun lies down flat on her stomach. Remy follows.)*

SUN: Then, we face each other, lying flat likes fishes, face to face.
(Sun and Remy arrange themselves, lying flat on their stomachs, face to face.)

SUN: Then we look at each other eye to eye. Then we tell what's in our heart. Fish never lie. We used to play this game . . . my girlfriends and I. We'd come to Beihai Park, like this, in front of the Bridge of Perfect Wisdom, in this spot near the lake, and so our ancestors couldn't hear us, we'd whisper.

REMY: *(Turning face up to the sun, then back again into the fish position.)* Finally, a day off. They've been working us like dogs.

SUN: Tell me about it. Mei Yen gave me four American books to translate into Chinese, including *Bonfire of the Vanities*.

REMY: *Bonfire of the Vanities* is very long.

SUN: Yes, I know.

REMY: You should complain.

SUN: That's considered a bad attitude.

REMY: When do you have to finish?

SUN: In one month.

REMY: That's impossible.

SUN: *(Whispering.)* No. Mei Yen wants to keep me busy while you're here. I think she's jealous. She's an independent woman, so she has no friends. *(Beat.)* We may have to cancel when you're coming to my house. There could be no time.

REMY: Then we'll steal time. But we have to change the day. I'm expected at the circus Sunday. They got front row seats. I said I was invited to your house for dinner, but Mei Yen said "no."

SUN: Oh boy.

REMY: So another night.

SUN: Probably not; but you must see the amazing circus. The tigers are terrifying fun in the first row. One prays they don't mistake the audience for the hoop.

REMY: I thought you wanted to be friends.

SUN: Tell me a secret.

REMY: About what?

SUN: Anything no one else knows is a secret.

REMY: My brother taught me how to eat animal crackers. You eat the feet first, so you save the best part for last. He also taught me never to walk on yellow snow.

SUN: *(Considering it.)* Never walk on yellow snow. *(Beat.)* Now you say *fish.*

REMY: Fish.

SUN: In Geneva, Switzerland I saw a young girl with golden hair sipping a lemonade the color of the sun. *(Beat.)* Fish.

REMY: Once I stole perfume from a store. Fish.

SUN: I shit in my pants when my mother died. *(Beat.)* Who was the first boy to touch you? Fish.

REMY: Brian. He had blond hair and he put his hand on my blouse and squeezed my nipple hard. *(Beat.)* Fish.

SUN: My cousin Chen Wei was home from the University, and in the cool cellar, he put his fingers inside my shorts and touched my furry fuzzy. How could something that feels so good be so bad, so bourgeois? *(Beat.)* Fish.

REMY: I'm not as strong as I look. *(Beat.)* Fish.

SUN: A bicycle repairman makes more than a teacher. I want Ray Ban sunglasses like the boys who sell T-shirts, and a tape machine and the lamps the tourists buy. I like beautiful jewelry. I have red-eye disease. I don't want to stay up all night to read the American's books so I can return them in the morning, smile politely. "Thank you." Xie xie. "Would you care for a cup of tea?" *(Sun bows head.)* I want a job at the United Nations with an apartment and a window to look out and see the sky, like it was your own. *(Beat.)* There are things I could kill for. *(Beat.)* Fish. *(Silence.)* Why do you eat the feet first on the crackers?

(Remy hesitates, then —)

REMY: So the animals won't run away.

Scene Eight

Time: A few days later. In the afternoon.
Place: Tiananmen Square, Beijing. Philip and Elizabeth are in a line to see Mao's glass-cased tomb. Elizabeth has on a red blouse. Philip, in sneakers, holds an official letter.

ELIZABETH: I don't want to stand in this line. I don't want to see a dead person in a glass case.

PHILIP: Mao looks as good as new.

ELIZABETH: I want to go home.

PHILIP: The tickets can't be changed. There's a penalty.

ELIZABETH: I don't care.

PHILIP: Keep moving or someone will break into the line.

ELIZABETH: I'm not looking at the dead man.

PHILIP: We're in enough trouble. If you leave early, you'll disgrace us.

ELIZABETH: Wrong. They'll never let on. They'll be terribly polite and say they're so sorry my mother's sick.

PHILIP: How can your mother be sick? She's dead. . . . God, Elizabeth, hang in there. It's only another four weeks.

ELIZABETH: *(Pointing to the sign.)* Look at the sign — "Welcome" and "Keep Off Our Grass." *(Reading.)* "Chinese admitted Mondays, Foreigners admitted Fridays. Decorous attire is encouraged — no shorts, sneakers, or bright colors." Outsiders are still the barbarians. I'm wearing red, so we can't go in.

PHILIP: So I'm wearing sneakers. We've been in the damn line for an hour. We've got our permission letter. I'm staying.

ELIZABETH: Well I'm *not*. Ever since we got here, I keep ending up in places I don't want to be, like the Forbidden fucking City, or in this line to view the corpus delicti. I can't even get in to see a real hospital. *(Beat.)* I called work and they're short-handed at the clinic.

PHILIP: Always.

ELIZABETH: That's not my fault! *(Beat.)* I'll leave it to you and Remy to *xie*

xie. Only keep an eye on yours with a smile, Sun. I understand from Mei Yen she's slightly *fangele. (Circling her finger.)*

PHILIP: Mei Yen hates Sun.

ELIZABETH: Mei Yen doesn't like to be crossed. But hey, this is just the country where they kill the calligrapher if one letter of a word is wrong. That's too much pressure for me. I'll see you back at the hotel.

PHILIP: What am I supposed to tell Wu when he comes to pick us up?

ELIZABETH: That I went to the Friendship Store and I'll take a taxi home. I feel like buying a pair of pajamas. *(Starting to leave.)* And my best to Chairman Mao. Tell him my favorite saying of his is "Enough of your farting." He forbid the people to fart. Some even died from holding it in.

Scene Nine

Time: The next morning.
Place: Temple of the Sleeping Buddha, courtyard. Comrade Wu and Philip are talking.

COMRADE WU: It's not allowed for the delegation to go anywhere alone. It's for protection.

PHILIP: It was Sunday. My wife was looking for a church.

COMRADE WU: There are no churches in China.

PHILIP: *(Taking in a deep breath.)* Elizabeth may have to leave. She has an emergency at home. A relative is sick. Her mother is ill. Very ill.

COMRADE WU: Oh, I'm sorry. Was she ill before you left?

PHILIP: Probably. Yes. We aren't sure. She lives in Florida. *(Beat.)* It's a place for old people. They like to go there because the sun shines, and they do fun things. *(Beat.)* Shit. She just wants to go home, Wu. She feels like an outsider here. She's outside the delegation and the delegation is on the outside of the inside. She wants to tour your PLA Hospital, but you won't take her.

COMRADE WU: I know.

PHILIP: How come you asked us here in the first place if you already know everything? I didn't hold back. I gave distinguished lectures. That's my job.

COMRADE WU: And this is mine.

PHILIP: You're a tour guide.

COMRADE WU: Exactly. In fact, I never would have toured Mongolia if it wasn't for my "re-education." I was married also. Now I'm a confirmed bachelor man. *(Pause.)* But I don't want to get sentimenta_ on you, Philip, about "the good old days." You know what they say about the good old days? They're mostly a product of bad memory. *(Pause.)* I'll make arrangements for Elizabeth's perhaps sudden departure, and I know I speak for Mei Yen and the Government in sending our regrets for your mother-in-law's poor health. May she have an unusually speedy recovery. *(Pause.)* We'll have the Embassy ensure your wife's safe arrival, but there's red tape, so be patient.

PHILIP: Can't you pull strings to get Elizabeth into the Army Hospital? I don't want her to leave. Being away alone can bring out the worst in people.

COMRADE WU: Or the sad bottom.

PHILIP: . . . When the crusaders left for the Holy Land they had no idea where they were going and how they'd get there. It was a land like no other they'd seen, with sun and fruits on the trees, and it smelled of figs and honey and seemed like Paradise; and who could have imagined they would be, months later, one morning standing knee deep in their own blood. They were as distant from home, they might as well have been on the moon.

Scene Ten

Time: Immediately following.
Place: Classroom, Temple of the Sleeping Buddha. Remy and Sun at table facing downstage, the class.

REMY: By the shore of Gitche Gumee
By the shining Big-Sea Water . . .

SUN: *(Interrupting.)* One of the students would like to know . . . where *is* Gitche Gumee?

REMY: Longfellow tells us it's somewhere in the Northland.

SUN: *(Acknowledging a question.)* Another student asks what your take is on the American Indian problem regarding the sale of Manhattan.

REMY: I believe the American Government is paying the Indians reparations. End of class. The class is over. The next class will cover Birds' Eye View, Modern American poetry.

(They exit, walking toward courtyard.)

REMY: The students seem more interested in the politics of America than the poetry.

SUN: You put a Kentucky Fried Chicken into the middle of Beijing, you're bound to make people curious.

(Pause.)

REMY: I have a present for you.

SUN: You already gave me a present. The book.

REMY: No. This is the *official* present.

SUN: There's no need.

REMY: Yes there is. I *need* to give it.

(Thrusting a wrapped package into Sun's hands. Sun hesitates.)

SUN: The hope is that you didn't have so many "needs."

REMY: Open it! Come on, open it!

(Sun opens the package reluctantly, painstakingly. She takes out a small box, opens it slowly, as though it were either a bomb or Pandora's box. She stares into the box. At first we don't know what's in there. She takes out the contents, holding up a long pearl necklace.)

SUN: Well, they're pearls.

REMY: Cultured pearls *(Beat.)* It means . . . *(Thinking of something, anything.)* . . . you conquered the Cultural Revolution.

(Silence.)

SUN: It's difficult to accept these.

REMY: No. I want you to have them. It's okay.

SUN: Hold it! You don't know what's okay, Remy, so please don't tell me! *(Beat.)* It would be easier not to take this gift. *(Sun hands back the pearls.)*

REMY: I came here with too much. Please let me give you the pearls. It's our secret. My God, your country gave us two panda bears. They're right in the Washington Zoo.

(Remy takes pearls and puts them on Sun.)

SUN: These are too important.

REMY: They're faux pearls. They're not valuable. *(Silence.)* Well, do you like them? *(Silence.)* I asked do you like them?

SUN: They're not valuable.

REMY: No, they're faux . . . fake.

SUN: I understand the translation. *(Beat.)* It's not ingratitude. There *are* things I would want. If I get an advanced degree, I have a better chance for my promotion, so instead of a hundred twenty yuan a month—thirty-nine dollars and fifty cents American, I get a raise to a hundred eighty yuan. *(Beat.)* I'm considered an intellectual, but I can't eat culture. And yes I like the pearls. I never had any. And it's the Japanese, of course, who are famous for their pearls.

REMY: Then I know what I could do.

SUN: Why do you have to *do* something? Why don't you volunteer in an orphanage?

REMY: Please don't patronize me. I want to recommend you to our department. You could come as a guest lecturer and get paid good money. I could find you a place to stay, or you can stay with us. I'm sending a letter.

SUN: If you write a letter, it could be found out and considered that I asked you for a favor, taking away your important time from teaching our students. For the same reason, I'm apprehensive about you coming to my house. *Don't. (Taking off the pearls.)* And please, no offense, but take back the not-valuable pearls.

(Sun holds the pearls out, but Remy refuses to take them.)

REMY: I'm not taking them back and you are not asking me to write the letter; it's my idea. *(Beat.)* Want to play fish, Sun? Tell me a secret.

SUN: *(Hesitating.)* I really like the pearls. Each one is different, cultured . . . And, Remy, a young actress in my unit, plans to come to the States. Lili's twenty-two, and with the Youth Theater. She doesn't speak English, but she's learning rapidly. She wants to be rich and famous. She's asked me, would you meet with her and tell her about New York? The only thing I know, I told her, the Bronx is up and the Battery is down.

Scene Eleven

Time: Three days later.
Place: Remy's hotel room, Beijing, Two chairs, a table, and a lamp.

PHILIP: Mei Yen told Elizabeth. Sun ratted on her mother, stood in the middle of People's Square and accused her mother of being a counterrevolutionary. Then they made the mother dance until she dropped dead and Sun laughed and clapped like a crazy person.

REMY: A lie I'm sure, or they beat her up.

PHILIP: Everyone was beat up. How do you think Mei Yen ended up in solitary for eight years? You better watch it with Sun. Once a rat, you don't turn into a pussy cat. She led the Red Guards on a guided tour through her house, straight to all the valuables. That's why she got an easy job out of town.

REMY: Mei Yen is just jealous Sun and I are friends.

PHILIP: No. Mei Yen is angry because Sun spent the Revolution cutting grass in the sun, and Mei Yen spent it in a stinking hole in the ground.

REMY: The Chinese were taught to obey authority.

PHILIP: So were the Germans.

REMY: And I wrote to the university inviting Professor Sun. She needs an advanced degree.

PHILIP: Are you crazy? Sun's some kind of a desperate nut. And we're being cut back on budget. How can you promise to add a foreigner?

REMY: I didn't promise.

PHILIP: She made you feel guilty.

REMY: She did not. She wants to come. I can tell. I sent them her résumé. She's published. She's a well-known scholar!

PHILIP: *(Interrupting.)* Has it ever occurred to you to want something and not go after it?

REMY: I wanted to do something for her.

PHILIP: Why?

REMY: I like to help.

PHILIP: Why?

REMY: It makes me feel good.

PHILIP: *(Grabbing Remy's arm.)* It's not as free here as you think. You listen to me. I'm the Head. You're going to get us all murdered, chopped into chow mein.

REMY: *(Breaking free.)* I understand this place, you know. I studied all year before we came. I read every history book about China. Everyone who ever took a ride down the Yellow River has written a journal and I've read it. Test me. Go ahead. *(Going on rapidly.)* The Opium War, 1839–1842, the Taiping Rebellion, 1850–1864, the Sino-Japanese War 1894–95, 1908, the Empress Dowager dies, 1912, the child Emperor, Pu Yi, as seen in the movie *The Last Emperor* . . . .

PHILIP: Enough!

REMY: *(The wind out of her sails.)* If you don't mind, I'm expecting a guest, an actress friend of Sun's I've agreed to meet in my room. And yes, I have permission from the ministry. *(Pause.)* And you don't know a damn thing about friendships. They have nothing to do with position.

PHILIP: They have everything to do with position. See you this afternoon at the Temple of Heaven. And take a hat to protect your head. It's supposed to be a scorcher. *(Beat.)* This is not our country. We're just here for a shot. You're not Joan of Arc and I'm not Marco Polo. *(He exits.)*

REMY: *(Picking up phone.)* Room 5. I'm expecting a Miss Lili Chan and a Miss Sun.

Scene Twelve

Time: Immediately following.
Place: Hotel lobby. Lili sits in a chair, on edge. Sherwood sits in the chair beside her, reading a Chinese newspaper. Note that the two same chairs can be used as in the previous scene. Remy enters.

REMY: Is there a Lili Chan here? I'm Remy. (*Going over to Lili, speaking slowly.*) Are you Lili Chan?

LILI: (*Very excited.*) Remy? Remy?

REMY: Lili?

(*The two embrace excitedly.*)

REMY: I was waiting for you in the room, but you didn't come up, so I didn't know what to do, so I came down. I don't know where Sun is.

LILI: (*Cutting into Remy's speech above, becoming simultaneous.*) *Wo bu zhidáo Sun zái na li. Wo yi jing déng le yí gé zhang tóu le.* (*I don't know where Sun is. I've been waiting for one hour. She's reliable. I don't understand.*)

(*During the above, Sherwood continues reading his paper.*)

REMY: Well what are we going to do? I don't speak Chinese, you don't speak English. (*Beat, slowly.*) Do you speak English?

(*Lili looks at Remy perplexed. Sherwood puts down his paper.*)

SHERWOOD: (*To Lili.*) *Ni shuo Yingwen ma?* (*Do you speak English?*)

LILI: *Wo hui shuo yidian.*

SHERWOOD: (*To Remy.*) She speaks a little.

LILI: (*To Remy.*) Good morning.

REMY: *Ni hao.*

(*The two woman nod approvingly, as though they've had a momentous communication.*)

SHERWOOD: Excuse me. My name is Sherwood. I'm an engineer and I'm here waiting for a group of Americans to arrive. I'm the translator for my company. (*Handing Remy and Lili each his business card.*) I have a half hour before they come. I'd be happy to help you out. I'm a technical translator, you understand.

REMY: No, no, it's fine! Thank you! *Xie xie!* It's a miracle. I'm an American Professor. I don't know where Professor Sun is. She's our translator. She's very punctual. This isn't like her. She's the one who asked me to have this meeting. This is Lili Chan. She's an actress.

SHERWOOD: (*Bowing.*) Lili Chan! Oh my God! Miss Chan. I didn't recognize you. Usually in the films you play a peasant, or the one where you were in the army and had fallen on hard times. What an honor. I saw you in *The Old Well. (To Remy.)* She won the Golden Rooster Award. It's like your Academy Awards. *(Excitedly.)* This is one of the greatest days of my life! Lili Chan! *(To Lili.) Wo hen rongxing. (Then, to Remy, translating.)* I'm honored.

REMY: *(To Lili.)* I understand you want to come to New York.

LILI: Hollywood.

REMY: This isn't easy.

LILI: Hollywood, exactly. Paul Newman, Robert Redford, Meryl Streep.

REMY: They're megastars, you know.

LILI: I know *that*. You know them?

REMY: No. *(Turning to Sherwood.)* I think we should call Sun to see if she's okay. Could you ask Miss Chan if she has Sun's phone number. . . . I have her address.

(Sherwood whispers to Lili, Lili whispers back to him in Chinese.)

SHERWOOD: She doesn't have that information.

REMY: This is the address.

(Remy takes out a piece of paper and hands it to Sherwood.)

SHERWOOD: *(Shaking his head.)* This is just an address. It's complicated. Many people live in that block.

REMY: But this is where she lives.

SHERWOOD: Yes. In that block, somewhere. *(Shrugs.)* Who knows? But if you want to speak with Miss Chan, you'd better hurry. I don't have a lot of time. So we'll begin. Miss Chan has many questions to ask you. . . . *(Bending over, whispering with Lili in Chinese, then to Remy.)* . . . like what books or videos you brought . . . *(To Lili.) Ni jinwan you kong ma, Xiaojie Chan? Xianzai qing kaishi.*

REMY: What did you say to her?

SHERWOOD: "Now please begin" . . . and . . . *(Hesitating.)* . . . "Are you possibly free this evening, Miss Chan?"

(Lights down.)

Scene Thirteen

Time: That same evening.
Place: A street in Beijing. Remy, paper and map in hand is wandering the street trying to find Sun's apartment house. It's raining.

REMY: *(Reading from the piece of paper.)* Excuse me. Can you tell me where 25 Dongbin He Road is? Compound of the Ministry of Culture, Building 67, Entrance 5, Unit 2D? I'm looking for Sun Hong Tian. *(Silence.)* Does anyone speak English? *(Looking in her Chinese dictionary.)* Duibuqi, ni hui shuo Yingwen ma? *(Silence.)* My translator is lost. *(Silence.)* Oh, shit.

(A man enters from the shadows. He holds an umbrella. We can not see his face.)

REMY: Excuse me . . . *Laojia* . . . Excuse me . . . *Laojia* . . . Hong Tian . . . Sun Hong Tian . . . I'm an American. I can't speak Chinese . . . *(Looking in her dictionary.)* Wo bu hui shuo Zhongguohua . . . I'm sorry . . . *baoquian* . . .

COMRADE WU: *(Only his voice, his face still hidden.)* The people are afraid of *"baoquian."*

REMY: *(Surprised.)* Wu!

COMRADE WU: When the people saw they had misinformation about the government, the offenders naturally wrote self-criticisms, *baoquians* and then they were re-educated, *"aojiao,* which means excuse me. So, your words remind them of bitter times. But how could you know?

REMY: What are you doing here?

COMRADE WU: I could ask you the same question.

REMY: I'm looking for Sun. I have a letter for her. She didn't show up for a meeting.

COMRADE WU: Between you and the actress Lili Chan? You should have told me about that meeting. You said you were staying in to wash your hair.

REMY: I did wash my hair.

COMRADE WU: The others enjoyed the trip to the Temple of Heaven. They bought dozens of postcards. *(Silence.)* It was explained if you wanted anything to ask me. Professor Sun, of course, is working for us, and you are our guest.

REMY: I can meet with somebody privately if I want to. The actress wanted some information on Los Angeles.

COMRADE WU: But that's not what you're here for.

REMY: What *am* I here for?

COMRADE WU: You tell *me.*

REMY: To get to know the Chinese better.

COMRADE WU: You won't.

REMY: For the Chinese to know us better.

COMRADE WU: They won't. That's not what they're after.

REMY: And what's that?

COMRADE WU: To take what's useful and spit the rest out. *(Beat.)* Why did you come to our country?

REMY: You know why. To exchange cultures.

COMRADE WU: We invented culture.

REMY: It seems the Chinese invented everything.

COMRADE WU: You shouldn't have given Sun the pearls. It got her in trouble and makes you suspect *and* your small delegation.

REMY: *(Now frightened.)* They weren't valuable, Comrade Wu.

COMRADE WU: Like the Whitman book? Sun, of course, reported the gift immediately.

REMY: If she reported it, what's the problem?

COMRADE WU: She shouldn't have accepted it. Questionable corruption.

REMY: Sun didn't want to take them. I insisted.

COMRADE WU: *(Angrily.)* Well, that's not *our* problem. We're not a poor hungry pig-cow! Sun, of course, couldn't refuse. It would have been an insult to you. No Chinese would have refused. They'd rather die than humiliate.

REMY: Then it's not Sun's fault.

COMRADE WU: Look Miss Martin, you're a guest in China. Don't bite the hand of the Emperor. Sun will be at your next lecture.

REMY: I thought things were changed here.

COMRADE WU: They are. But you go back to New York; we get to stay.

REMY: I demand to know what's happened to her.

COMRADE WU: Home translating. There is a sudden demand now for all of William Faulkner's books . . . *The Sound And The Fury, Light in August.* *(Beat.)* Did Sun share stories with you about the hard times in China?

REMY: She wasn't complaining.

COMRADE WU: Just passing information about current injustices to the outside world. That's a serious crime here. It loses face. *(Beat.)* And it would be impossible to find Sun's apartment. Even I don't know where it is. If one wanted, one could go to the Public Security Bureau, but it takes weeks to get an appointment, and then, their files are *nan* — difficult. They will say something like *Zhongguo hen da* — China is a very big place. *(Beat.)* Go home and leave Sun alone.

REMY: I do have some kind of conscience.

COMRADE WU: I don't care *what* you have. You can't tease her fantasies. It will give Sun a twisted heart. There are few opportunities for us. You don't need to teach us the "pioneering spirit." *(Beat.)* Teach and go home. Don't break your heart. Don't break ours. We're the ones who play Weiqi where you win by surrounding your opponent while he's trying to surround you. This is a Chinese game and not for Americans.

On The Great Wall

Remy and Sun advance clockwise on the wall to twelve o'clock, up stage center and top of the circle. They ascend very weary from the long climb.

SUN: The Middle Kingdom is the center of the earth, and China is the center of that center. Everything there is in harmony and order. The rest is chaos. *(Pause.)* We're almost to the top.
(They stand looking over the edge.)

REMY: Hyacinths and lilies and the wall goes on forever across the mountains. There's a river and lotuses. Sun, look at this!
(They start to walk clockwise.)

SUN: Sometimes I think maybe Marco Polo never was to China because there's no mention of the Great Wall in his writing, and it was here when he was here. And he was a student of architecture. If *he* wasn't here, maybe *it* wasn't here. All of the West trying to come to Dongfang, the Orient, and all the time, we're not even here, so you can't get to China.

REMY: At the beach, in the summer, I'd dig a hole, deep as I could, sure any minute a dragon would leap from the sand, and I'd know I was there.

SUN: This year is The Year of the Dragon. It means a year of strength and fire.

REMY: To The Year of the Dragon.

SUN: To the dragon, to the days of China's glory. *(Beat.)* The Year of the Dragon, it's believed, is unlucky for travelers, so maybe I'll remain here until next year. *(Beat.)*

REMY: A letter came. It came this morning.

SUN: What did it say?

REMY: They want you. The University wants you. They want you to come.
(Remy and Sun start to walk clockwise down the wall, toward the place where they began. The lights fade.)

END OF ACT ONE

ACT TWO
Scene One

Time: The next morning, sunrise.
Place: Courtyard, Beihai Park. Early morning aerobics. Tango music is heard.
The lights fade up slowly and we see three couples doing the tango — Sherwood
and Lili, Philip and Remy, Comrade Wu and Mei Yen. Their movements are
precise and perfect; they move swiftly, as if in a dream. The figures are lit so
that they appear as silhouettes. After the beginning beats have been established,
Comrade Wu, without missing a beat, changes partners, dancing with Philip,
leaving Remy and Mei Yen. The two women, also without missing a beat,
take on each other as partners, continuing to dance the tango. The music esca-
lates in tempo. The lighting becomes brighter, as the sun rises higher. After a
few minutes, Philip changes partners, taking Mei Yen. Remy is left to dance
with Comrade Wu. There should be a good deal of tension, as each changes,
and the abandoned partner dances with the only choice, as in Mei Yen with
Remy and Remy, finally, with Comrade Wu. Only Sherwood and Lili stay
together for the entire scene, dancing closer and closer.
The music finishes. Lights slowly down. The dancers stop and the scene
is in frieze.

Scene Two

Time: Later the same day, close to noon. It is very hot.
Place: The Forbidden City, the courtyard in front of the Imperial Palace, Gate
of Supreme Harmony. Comrade Wu stands encircled by Mei Yen, Remy, Philip
and Elizabeth. Mei Yen holds up a white umbrella, leading the group, as there
are many tour groups in the vast courtyard of the Forbidden City.

COMRADE WU: The Imperial Palace, also known as the Forbidden City, is located in the heart of Beijing, covers two hundred fifty acres, and is surrounded by a wall thirty-five feet high. The complex contains over nine thousand rooms, which may soon be converted into hotel space for tourists.

MEI YEN: This courtyard could hold ninety thousand people during ceremonies.

ELIZABETH: I think we should move out of the direct sun.

COMRADE WU: *(Moving ahead.)* We'll proceed now to the Hall of Supreme Harmony.

REMY: Where's Sun this morning?

MEI YEN: She has work.

COMRADE WU: It seems there's a Faulkner emergency.

REMY: *(Politely.)* Begging your pardon, may I request a meeting with Sun? I haven't seen her and we have the next lecture to review. *(Silence.)* If I can't meet with her, I'm unable to do my next class.

MEI YEN: Such arrogance. This could shock our students. Some of them have saved for over a year to come to the Summer Institute.

REMY: *(Under her breath.)* I don't give a flying shit.

PHILIP: Cool it, Remy!

REMY: You cool it! Go eat a hotpot, Philip!

COMRADE WU: Sun has the flu.

MEI YEN: Sun hasn't the time for sight seeing.

REMY: *(To Mei Yen.)* Because you're doing something with her.

MEI YEN: Sure. Chinese water torture.

REMY: I thought everything was so free here — 1988, the new democracy. You throw up a Sheraton, but you tell a woman she can't have an American friend. And I don't want to see the Forbidden City. Probably a million people's bones are buried under here. I'm going back to the hotel. I have the flu too. *(She starts to exit.)*

COMRADE WU: You can't go to the hotel yourself. How will you get there?

REMY: By paying someone for the use of their bicycle. I plan to report Sun's disappearance to your police.

COMRADE WU: We have no police in China.

REMY: Who are the ones in the uniforms then?

COMRADE WU: In uniform? Hmm . . . traffic cops. Of course we have a Public Security Bureau, the PSB.

REMY: Then I'll tell the PSB, unless you want to tell me where she is.

MEI YEN: At her home.

REMY: It would be easier to find the Middle Kingdom than to find Sun's home.

COMRADE WU: The Middle Kingdom isn't a real place.

REMY: *That's* what I mean. It's impossible to locate. *(Turning to Mei Yen.)* You're jealous because I gave Sun a book, because I gave her dumb jewelry!

MEI YEN: The pearls.

REMY: The pearls.

MEI YEN: Not jealous. Jealousy is wanting what someone else has. *(Beat.)* Envy is wanting what someone else has and you don't want them to have it. I have envy. Maybe I want to play fish.

REMY: How do you know about fish?

MEI YEN: I also know how to be clear-headed. Be alone in a dungeon for one thousand days. I never let my guard down.

(Remy exits.)

MEI YEN: *(Pulling herself together, putting forward the public "face.")* There's no concern. The PSB will assure Remy, Sun is safe and busy.

PHILIP: I apologize for my comrade's spirit. And I apologize for my wife. She's not feeling well.

ELIZABETH: Dead wrong. I *am* feeling. I am absolutely feeling!

MEI YEN: *(Quickly, to cut off any more emotional outburst.)* In fact, Professor Sun tells me she is so taken with *The Sound And The Fury,* she doesn't sleep or eat and has even lost a stone of weight.

COMRADE WU: And now, this way to the Temple of One Hundred Buddhas, each in a different position. Though some call it No Buddha Temple since so many of the statues were misplaced during our Cultural Revolution.

(Comrade Wu and Philip exit, Mei Yen and Elizabeth linger behind in the courtyard.)

ELIZABETH: *(To Mei Yen.)* This morning I took a walk by Yuyuan Lake, and everyone stared to see a westerner. *(Beat.)* I'm changing my ticket and going back early. It has nothing to do with my mother. I have my work at home.

MEI YEN: How long have you been married?

ELIZABETH: Fifteen years.

MEI YEN: Do you love him?

ELIZABETH: Now *you're* being forward. Philip does the cooking, I do the bills, and we sleep together in the night. For Remy, it's different. She goes for passion.

MEI YEN: She's already separated.

ELIZABETH: *Quite* separated. *Left.* Adorable Remy wakes up one morning last month to find the cock has flown, so to speak, with her best friend. And not a whisper of a warning. She gave all his Armani suits away to Goodwill before she came to Beijing. *(Beat.)* Remy loves China. There's so much missionary work here.

On The Great Wall

Remy and Sun walk very slowly now. The light is dimmer than before, as in late afternoon in summer. They walk toward six o'clock, now closer to where they began on the wall, downstage center.

REMY: So the Universe is China.

SUN: No. The *center* of the universe is China. Everything else is away from the center.

REMY: Don't you consider that self-centered?

SUN: I never considered it.

REMY: And if you leave?

SUN: Only you can't, because it's in the center of you.

REMY: Then how will you come with me?

SUN: I would want to, and maybe have no choice.

REMY: But I made plans, wrote letters.

SUN: But I have a son here and a room, and every morning it's still uncertain which way the wind blows. We watch the sky like sailors.

REMY: If you don't come *now,* it may not happen. The University can change it's mind, bing-bang. You'll see. You'll love it — Radio City, Rockefeller Center. *(Adding.)* I have a guest room. You could stay longer. *(Beat.)* My husband is actually gone, gonzo, *fei,* flying, fly away *(Making the motion of a bird.)* Like a bird.

SUN: *(Hearing, not hearing, Now circling downstage on the circle.)* Look, they're signaling! It's Philip! He's bought a T-shirt. It says I CLIMB THE GREAT WALL. And Elizabeth's waving *her* purchase, a statue of a Chinese warrior. Wave back to Philip and Elizabeth. They're waving to us. *(Waving back.)* Yoo hoo! We're coming!

REMY: *Ni hao ma!* Hello! *Ni hao ma!* Wait for us!

SUN: We're coming together. *(Beat.)* It's strange that in other countries they study the Orient, but here in the Orient, we see no need to study ourselves; instead, our scholars go to Harvard and study with American Orientalists, and then come home and teach us ourselves reflected. *(Beat.)* You know we invented gunpowder, but then the British came a thousand years later with cannons, and everyone forgot we were the place where it began. . . . How can we be a third world country if we were the first?

Scene Three

Time: The next day, early morning.
Place: PRC passport office, Beijing. Sun is with the Passport Officer.

PASSPORT OFFICER: Sun Hong Tian, you're applying for a passport?

SUN: To the U.S. for advanced study, so I can be a greater teacher, sponsored by Professor Remy Martin, New York University.

PASSPORT OFFICER: Will you be selling or trading anything in America?

SUN: No, no, I want a J-1 Passport for professional work.

PASSPORT OFFICER: What unit?

SUN: Beijing Institute of Foreign Languages, Literature Department.

PASSPORT OFFICER: *(Shaking his head.)* I'm looking at my list here. No. I don't see you under the list from your unit.

SUN: That's impossible. I'm with the Beijing unit.

PASSPORT OFFICER: It's *quite* possible. Let me see your papers.

(Sun hands over her papers. The Passport Officer looks them over, then returns them.)

PASSPORT OFFICER: You don't have enough papers. Please return in two weeks with more papers and an application for B-2.

SUN: B-2! That's ridiculous! That's only for one month. That's for a tradesman, not a teacher! What can I do in one month?

PASSPORT OFFICER: The passport is delayed.

SUN: I assure you I am a loyal member, sponsored by my unit, approved to go abroad for advanced degree, and opposed to bourgeois liberalization.

PASSPORT OFFICER: *(Stamping her application.)* Delayed. More research. More papers. B-2.

Scene Four

Time: Later that same morning, the Fourth of July.
Place: Temple of the Sleeping Buddha, classroom. Mei Yen stands in front of the class rather stiffly, clears her throat, and begins.

MEI YEN: This is a puzzling situation. We have no idea where your professor is. She wasn't in her room this morning. As for your translator, Professor Sun has a reputation for being speedy on her *zixing che*, a daredevil on two wheels, so perhaps she has run into a road accident. And under our new free China, I worry about hooligans on the highway. Comrade Wu has gone to look for her. *(Beat.)* Today is the Fourth of July, which is a holiday of independence in the U.S. Perhaps Professor Remy is celebrating early. . . . *(Beat.)* Class dismissed. We'll meet tomorrow at Tiananmen Square for the kite-flying competition.

(Comrade Wu comes running in followed by a much disheveled Sun on a bicycle.)

SUN: *Wo hen baogian!* I was riding along, and a woman with a cart full of chickens came colliding into me with her bicycle, and then she was screaming at me and screaming at the running chickens. And then a truck came along and ran into the chickens, and they were then running around truly like chickens without their heads on, crashing into the man on the bicycle with cabbages. Smell me! Full of cabbage! *(Holding up the sleeve of her dress to Mei Yen. Beat.)* Where is Remy? *(Smoothing down her hair.)* I am ready for my class.

MEI YEN: *(To the class.)* Class will be over, please.

(Beat. Mei Yen waits for them to leave, then turns to Sun.)

MEI YEN: You don't talk in front of the class like a wild monkey! And your professor has taken off and refused to teach. What a humiliation, and all because of your damned complaints, and how you failed to show up at our trip to the Forbidden City.

SUN: Begging your pardon, Mei Yen, but I had the translations to finish.

COMRADE WU: Your absence yesterday was disruptive. Unfortunately, it was not a successful outing.

SUN: Am I expected to do the work or tour the Forbidden City?

MEI YEN: Both. We're expected to show our faces.

SUN: Which face of our two faces?

COMRADE WU: I would be cautious with your rudeness, Sun.

SUN: Why? Is there a rat in this room?

MEI YEN: The superior man hesitates before condemning his neighbor's roof to be rotten.

SUN: Speak plain, Mei Yen.

MEI YEN: No one forgets what you did.

COMRADE WU: To your own parents.

SUN: *(To Comrade Wu.)* So what your children did to you. It's all the same. We were made to be like refrigerators in that time. Open the door, close the door. Did you forgive your children, Wu? Then forgive me.

COMRADE WU: I don't even know their names anymore. Even my dreams are without their names.

SUN: I saw your son, Wu Yiding. He's well and has two children. He lives in Canton.

COMRADE WU: My ears aren't listening. *(Beat.)* And what do you know about my not public only-ness?

SUN: Oh Wu, come on. You lick up the party line like a true shit!

COMRADE WU: My wife was a god-beautiful painter. *(Then angrily.)* Okay! So, I was sleeping in my house, one morning, and she called me. "You hear the shouting? 'Down with Wu Xinguo, down with rightist Wu Xinguo.' " Then they brought me to the school where I was teaching, and there were some student leaders, and my son with them, haranguing my crimes. My son joined the Red Guard and took on the name Li, Li the Faithful.

SUN: See. You do know his name.

MEI YEN: *(To Sun.)* Don't invoke sentiment!

COMRADE WU: Excuse me, but I have an appointment at the Bureau to re-register for the Party. With my apologies, please go fly a kite in Tiananmen Square for Wu.

(Comrade Wu exits.)

MEI YEN: *(Making certain Comrade Wu is gone.)* Your American friend went to the Bureau to report you missing. Of course, I called them to correct the misinformation. We have to grease Wu's palms. We don't know where he stands. That's why I act like I do.

SUN: You gave me the work for spite.

MEI YEN: I gave you the work to keep you away from the Americans. You drool too much over them.

SUN: But I love the life of the scholar. I dream of the University, of going to Geneva as a translator, or maybe New York City.

MEI YEN: Remy is no ticket to a passport. She'll go home and you'll be forgotten, snow in a field of rice. Have some discipline! *(Calming herself, reciting, with accompanying Tai Chi movements.)* Hsu — Patience and confidence will bring prosperity.

SUN: *(Frightened, but chiming in. This is a catechismlike recitation known to most educated Chinese, often recited during the CR.)* Hsu is a combination of water and heaven.

MEI YEN: *(Still reciting, Sun joins in.)* Without them everything would die. The sun is yang and the rain is yin. The earth needs light and water and we need help from those around us.

SUN: But Mao was crazy.

MEI YEN: You could be punished for that.

SUN: You still think I'm a traitor because I acted with the rest of the young Red Guards.

MEI YEN: You have no idea *what* I'm thinking.

SUN: *Baotai.*

MEI YEN: No! No *Baotai. (Banging her hand against her forehead.)* Kong! Kong! Kong! Empty! *(Softly.)* I can't remember how to have an original thought.

(Beat.) You turned on your mother. You could do the same to me. You might even clap.

SUN: *(Angrily.)* I clapped so she could hear me while she danced! *(Beat.)* I want to go to New York, but I need more papers — a permission letter from you. Please. My heart is leaping to get my advanced degree. And not selfish, but to soak it in, then bring it back here so we aren't dumb Asians. Professor Remy has absolute permission in a letter. How can I humiliate the American offer? I have been popular, obedient, and even dreamed once of being in love with Mao and knitting him a sweater, which proves my loyalty. My son will stay with strict relatives, and then I'll come home, Mei Yen. I was just crazed before. Afterwards, when the clapping was over, I even twisted the head of a rooster. Since then, everything has been in a straight line.

MEI YEN: Perhaps you were crazed in those years.

SUN: I was crazed. Let me go. I promise I'll come home. *(Beat.)* I was crazed. *(Lights down.)*

Scene Five

Time: The next afternoon.
Place: Tiananmen Square. Sherwood, Lili, Philip, Elizabeth, Mei Yen, Remy, and Sun are scattered in the Square, flying colorful kites, some in the shapes of animals, some with musical instruments on them that whistle in the wind.

REMY: *(Moving closer to Sun, in a whisper.)* I thought you'd been murdered.

SUN: *(With no emotion.)* My position requires many hours of work. I'm happy to do what's asked of me. Our goal is to educate the students in official policy.

REMY: *(Whispering.)* I even went to the Security Bureau to report you missing. *(Silence, as Sun takes this in.)*

REMY: But they were closed for lunch, open again at three. So I went back at three, but there were lines around the block. When I went back at four, they said it was closed for a special meeting, "No more appointments." And then it was just closed.

SUN: The Security officials are hard workers and vigilant defenders of our government and thought reform. Their paperwork is heavy. *(Whispering.)* You didn't say my name?

REMY: *(Whispering.)* I didn't get that far.

SUN: *(Whispering.)* Never do that again. It could put me on the "hit list."

REMY: *(Softly.)* I have more information. The visiting fellowship is for one year. They said "Yes! Good! We encourage multi-cultural!" You'll teach, even get faculty housing, and can take all the classes you want *free*.

(The others come closer.)

SUN: The sky is Ming blue today.

MEI YEN: *(Moving closer to them.)* The wind is brisk northwest, a good sign for kite flying.

SHERWOOD: If it were raining, that's the best luck.

SUN: The kites are an offering to Heaven, telling the gods we're here and to have pity.

MEI YEN: The prize is, the one whose kite stays up the longest gets to live the longest.

ELIZABETH: *(Having trouble keeping her kite aloft.)* A questionable trophy.

MEI YEN: Long life is good fate. That's why such a crowd is out today, hoping.

SHERWOOD: I can't tell you the last time I took a summer day off just for pleasure. I have Lili to thank. She is such an opportunist.

LILI: Sherwood is like all scientists — work, work, work.

SHERWOOD: What about last weekend? Lili is such a party butterfly. We went to the Jingjiang Club in Shanghai, and sat in the first row.

LILI: And were lucky the topless dancers didn't jump into our laps. Sherwood thought it was funny. *(Playfully nudging Sherwood.)* Didn't you, Xuehua. *(His Chinese name, meaning "snowy birch tree.")*

(Accidentally, Lili knocks his kite down.)

SHERWOOD: Oh, no. Lili! Look what you did! You knocked down my kite!

LILI: It was a mistake.

MEI YEN: Sherwood is *out*.

LILI: *(To Sherwood.)* I'm sorry. I was only being a playful kitten.

SHERWOOD: I have to go back to work anyway. *(To Lili.)* Next time, be more careful. How will you be such a great actress if you make other people fall off the stage? *(Sherwood exits.)*

ELIZABETH: This is the perfect outing for my last day here. A lovely diversion before it's back to the wars.

(Moving closer to Remy, away from the others.)

REMY: *(Sarcastically.)* Thanks for running home.

ELIZABETH: *(Sticking close to Remy, whispering.)* The heat's oppressive, the government's oppressive, the bathroom's like a rice paddy, and the food is nothing like Chinese food. Why should I stay? I have nothing to prove.

REMY: And I do?

ELIZABETH: That you can fix everything. That's supposed to be my job.
  (Struggling harder with the kite to keep it from falling.)

REMY: You don't think I'm playing with fire?

ELIZABETH: *(Moving toward the rest of the group.)* Oh, I do.
  (Elizabeth's kite finally falls.)

ELIZABETH: Maybe if I stayed another few weeks, I might really understand China.

PHILIP: *(Now struggling to keep his kite up.)* Come on! Stay up there! I'm not letting go!

LILI: That Sherwood is such a foolish boy. He has too much pride.

ELIZABETH: He's in love with you.

LILI: *(Letting go of her kite.)* How do you know?

ELIZABETH: *(As she exits.)* I watched him watching you.
  (Lili exits.)

MEI YEN: The wind's changed to the south. We should move to the foot of the Peace Gate, near Mao's portrait. If the breeze dies down, it's more favorable in that spot.
  (Mei Yen exits, followed by Philip. Sun and Remy remain, their kites still up and just the music of their two kites.)

REMY: *(Whispering.)* Are you okay?

SUN: *(Beat, whispering to Remy.)* When would the job begin?

REMY: As soon as you get your passport.

Scene Six

Time: Afternoon, several days later.
Place: Tea room, Beijing. Remy and Sun have tea.

REMY: Fish.

SUN: No fishing today.

REMY: What about the passport?

SUN: Still delayed.

REMY: Why?

SUN: Complex. I brought them the more papers and permission from Mei Yen. I go back in one week.

REMY: In a week *(Flying motion, like a bird.)* free as a bird.

SUN: If you were my sister, I would come and be roommates. Do you have grass in Central Park or just murderers?

REMY: This is a quite vicious rumor that we have only murderers.

SUN: We kids were all asked to join the Red Guard and Sun was shipped off to Binyang in the South to cut grass. Our quota was three hundred catties of grass a day. I spit at grass.

REMY: When your mother danced and died . . .

SUN: Correct . . .

REMY: And you clapped . . .

SUN: Correct . . .

REMY: So . . .

SUN: So . . .

REMY: What kind of person does that make you?

SUN: What kind? . . . Somebody says one day blue is dangerous and lists the reasons, which seem logical. So you throw out all the blue. The next year, they say blue is good, and the arguments for that are just as logical. So then you reconsider. Maybe the blue wasn't so bad. *(Beat.)* I clapped so she could hear me. *(Starting to clap — clap, clap, clap.)* I'm sorry. *(Clap, clap, clap.)* I love you. *(Clapping faster and faster — Clap, clap, clap.)* I'm sorry. *(Clap, clap, clap.)* I love you. *(Clap, clap, clap.)* I'm sorry. *(Clap, clap, clap.)* I love you.

(Sun, then seeing Lili and Mei Yen enter the tea room, changes the subject rapidly.)

SUN: *(To Remy.)* . . . So, a B-2! That's for a noodle salesman, I told him.

MEI YEN: *(Now in the tea room, to Sun.)* Maybe the Passport Officer was given a "small report." *(Explaining to Remy.)* We call this a "little report." There are watchdogs around with soft ears who hear gossip and report it. It could be your best friend. *(Passing plate of cookies.)* Almond cookies make you happy. Everyone take one, please. This is a real girl party.

REMY: Comrade Wu. Maybe he's a watchdog. He followed me when I was looking for Sun.

SUN: When?

REMY: When you didn't show up at my hotel. *(Beat.)* You didn't come to the tour of the Forbidden City either.

MEI YEN: Perhaps now I think Sun saw plenty of the Forbidden City when the Red Guard was stationed there.

LILI: She brought the best sweet rice pudding every Sunday to her husband and the rest of us. We gobbled it like turkeys. Her husband was a great supporter of the arts. He encouraged my acting career.

SUN: He encouraged *numerous* actresses.

LILI: He put me in charge of the "free workers" theatricals. Now, when I go to the U.S., I plan to dedicate my first performance to Comrade Sun.

MEI YEN: To the U.S.? But what about Sherwood? What are you, Lili? A western woman, about to choose a career over love?

LILI: Oh, Sherwood is applying to UCLA for graduate work. He's smart and one hot guy. We plan to live in Los Angeles. Oranges grow on trees there. First we have to get our passports. There are quotas, and one has to move quickly to the front of the line.

SUN: They're in a violent mood at the Passport Office. Questions, more questions, new rules, blah, blah, blah. You should be prepared.

LILI: No problem. I have comrades in that office. *(Turning to Sun.)* And if you come to the U.S. next year, Sun, maybe we'll meet in the Central Park.

MEI YEN: Am I to be the last Chinese left in Beijing? Lili is love-struck, and Sun can't wait to leave, like a frog about to swallow the moon.

REMY: My university has invited Sun.

SUN: If I get the passport.

REMY: They can't refuse, or we'll get the students to write and say what a great teacher she is, what an honor to China she is.

LILI: This is not the sixties. You have a wrong attitude. The government doesn't listen to students.

REMY: *(Frustrated.)* What do they listen to?

MEI YEN: Flattery.

LILI: *(Shaking her head "no.")* Bribery. I know those officials. Some of them were in my old unit. As for myself, of course, I'm not concerned because my history is clear.

SUN: Is that supposed to mean mine is cloudy? To this day I could recite a self-criticism with such conviction, you would swear it was true. I could flatter the face of a mongoose without blinking an eye. Isn't that proof Sun Hong Tian is re-educated, therefore suitable for passport? Only once was I put under house arrest, because I complained for a hat in the summer. I was told I was insolent.

MEI YEN: You sometimes are.

SUN: True. I then expressed deep sorrow to the Guards for my "erroneous views," to show my Party spirit. What a splendid liar I became. *(Beat.)* There are things I could kill for.

REMY: You were brave, Sun.

SUN: No. All the brave ones are dead.

Scene Seven and Scene Eight

Time: Three days later.
Scene Seven Place: Hotel room, Shanghai. Sherwood and Lili in bed.
Scene Eight Place: Classroom, Temple of the Sleeping Buddha. Remy is fin-
ishing her lecture downstage. Sun translates.
Note: Scenes Seven and Eight are performed intercut, as indicated on stage
right and stage left.

(Scene Seven.)

SHERWOOD: Did your meeting go well?

LILI: *(Tracing her finger around the moons of Sherwood's finger nails, one by one.)*
It always goes well in Shanghai. They served French champagne at lunch
and escargot. But then it was a little spoiled by some rotten apples who
shouted rude slogans outside on Nanjing Road. These dissidents, they
ruin it for the rest of us and are to blame for all China's troubles. It puts
me in bad humor. Tell me a story. . . .

(Scene Eight.)

REMY: Robert Penn Warren is known for his poetry and novel *All The King's*
Men, taken from the Mother Goose rhyme, *Humpty Dumpty*.

(Scene Seven.)

LILI: . . . a bedtime story. I'll close my eyes. *(She does.)*

(Scene Eight.)

REMY/SUN: *(Simultaneous translation.)*
Humpty Dumpty sat on a wall,
Humpty Dumpty had a great fall,
All the king's horses and all the king's men
Couldn't put Humpty Dumpty together again.
Han pu di, dang pu di, zai giang shang zuo
Han pu di, dang pu di, zai le ge,
Suo you guo wang, de ma he suo you guo wang di ren
Duo bu len be Han pu di dang pu di chong zu he.

REMY: And the final poem, by that curmudgeon, Robert Frost.

SUN: *Zui hou yi shou shi, zuo zhe lin se gui Luo bo te Fu luo si te.*

(Scene Seven.)

SHERWOOD: My parents named me *Xuehua*. *Xue* is snow, and *hua* is birch tree, and Sherwood is like forest.

(Scene Eight.)
REMY/SUN: *(Simultaneous translation.)*
"The Oven Bird"
There is a singer everyone has heard,
Loud, a mid-summer and mid-wood bird,

(Scene Seven.)
SHERWOOD: When I was born, at the beginning of the Cultural Revolution, my parents were sent to the Russian border, near Lake Xingkai.

(Scene Eight.)
REMY/SUN: *(Simultaneous translation.)*
The bird would cease and be as other birds
But that he knows in singing, not to sing.

(Scene Seven.)
SHERWOOD: There was only snow and birch trees covering the earth there.

(Scene Eight.)
REMY/SUN: *(Simultaneous translation.)*
The question that he frames in all but words
Is what to make of a diminished thing.

(Scene Seven.)
SHERWOOD: They wanted the name Xuehua for me, to remember I was born in the difficult times. *(Beat.)* Are you asleep?

(Scene Eight.)
REMY: Some say Frost was speaking of sex; others, that he was predicting the fall of America.

(Scene Seven.)
LILI: No, no. I'm listening, but the sound of your voice makes me sleepy — nice.
SHERWOOD: Are you going to fall asleep before we make love?
LILI: No. Just after.

(Scene Eight.)

SUN: Our farewell banquet will be at the Sick Duck Restaurant, a week from today. At that time we'll say *zai jian* — goodbye.
(Lights fade.)
(End of Scene Eight.)

(Scene Seven.)

SHERWOOD: Out of politeness, I'm asking if this is the first time.

LILI: In Shanghai, it is the first time, brother.

SHERWOOD: Then do you prefer the lights out?

LILI: No — *on*. I like to see. I like to compare.

SHERWOOD: *(Embracing her.)* Naughty girl. Compare to whom?

LILI: I have practice saying bad things like this because of my experience in the theater.

SHERWOOD: Then how will I know who is you and who is the character you're playing?

LILI: Come inside and find out. . . . But first, woo me.

SHERWOOD: *(He begins.)* Once upon a time . . . Tang Qi was a poet and my friend. . . .

LILI: Tang Qi was a famous dissident.

SHERWOOD: *(Correcting her.)* Lili, he was a famous hero. *(Then reciting.)* "Dawn and our train will soon arrive *(He kisses her.)* Blue light *(Kissing her again.)* Pure white snow *(And again.)* Countless hearts, a long chain *(Kissing her once more.)* Marches into the forest . . . " *(Again. Beat.)* You're asleep.

LILI: No, dreaming. Dreaming of you, and how in the morning, I'll wake up first, and you'll be lying on the white sheets, still dreaming of me, and how it was to be on the inside of me.
(End of Scene Seven.)

Scene Nine

Time: Later that week, late July.
Place: The Ming tombs, Xian. Comrade Wu, Lili, and Philip (camera slung over his shoulder) stand inside a large dimly lit tomb, viewing the 80,000 life-size terra-cotta warriors buried with the First Emperor.

COMRADE WU: The eighty thousand life-size terra-cotta warriors in this underground tomb, were discovered in Xian when a group of peasants were digging a well. It's estimated that forty thousand more clay warriors and horses are still buried here. The Emperor didn't want to be lonely in heaven.

(Philip snaps a photo of the terra-cotta warriors.)

LILI: *(Grabbing Philip's camera from him.)* NO CAMERAS, PLEASE!

COMRADE WU: *(Grabbing the camera from Lili, putting it into his knapsack quickly.)* Do you want to get us arrested? Didn't you see the "obey" sign, Philip? NO CAMERAS.

LILI: *(To Comrade Wu.) Mao zou le.*

PHILIP: *(To Comrade Wu.)* What did she say?

COMRADE WU: "The cat is gone out of the bag." You've made trouble. They see us. The guards are discussing it.

PHILIP: I wanted to take a photo to show Remy.

LILI: Yes, it's a shame she was sick and couldn't come. This is our major tourist sight. We're honored to be in the presence of such important history. My patriotic feelings here make me close to tears.

(Mei Yen enters.)

MEI YEN: The good news is our entrance fee is waived. One of the guards has seen Lili on television and also knew her from the Youth League. The bad news is that they want Philip's camera.

(Comrade Wu takes camera out of his bag and quickly hands it over to Mei Yen.)

COMRADE WU: *(Frightened, to Mei Yen.)* Did they see me put the camera in my bag?

MEI YEN: It's okay. They said they know Lili.

PHILIP: *(Grabbing the camera back.)* It's not okay. They can't have my camera.

LILI: They give it back.

PHILIP: Sure, two weeks from now, like the *New York Review of Books,* when I'm in an airplane over the Atlantic.

MEI YEN: *(Taking the camera back.)* Let me have the camera, Philip. I'll wait outside. I'll call the hotel and see how Remy is, poor girl, lying in her room with the Beijing flu.

LILI: And how Sun is making out at the passport office. Sherwood had no trouble this week when he showed the "yes" letter from UCLA. And I meant to say earlier, Philip, how sorry I was that Elizabeth had to depart so speedily because of her sick mother. How *is* her mother?

PHILIP: Better.

LILI: American women seem so sensitive. At least that's the impression I get from reading *Vogue* magazine. *(Beat.)* Mei Yen and I will wait outside. The breath of too many people in here at one time can destroy the art.

(Lili and Mei Yen exit.)

COMRADE WU: *(To Philip.)* Is your wife's mother truly ill?

PHILIP: Of course not.

COMRADE WU: I didn't think so.

PHILIP: My wife and I aren't in love anymore, and we don't know why.

COMRADE WU: My wife was an artist. But now I'm night-lonely.

PHILIP: I know. I think about women. That Lili is one hot pistol.

COMRADE WU: Keep away from Lili. She's taken.

PHILIP: Oh Sherwood's just a kid.

COMRADE WU: *(Looking around to make sure no one is watching them.)* No. Not Sherwood. Someone high up in the party, with *guan-xi* with connections.

PHILIP: If she wants to be an actress, she'll need plenty of *guan-xi*.

COMRADE WU: *(In a whisper.)* Lili's not always an actress. She just acts like an actress. *(Shrugs.)* China is a plate of sand. I'm sorry. A saying for everything.

PHILIP: But aren't you high up in the party? One night you followed Remy in the street.

COMRADE WU: Small cabbages. I used to be something, but I'm nothing now. I act like a cadre, but my only morality is survival. *(Beat.)* I think about women also, Phillip. I have a part of a book. An old pal had three chapters he hid away and they never found it in his home when they looted it . . . *Lady Chatterly's Lover . . . Whew!*

PHILIP: When I get home, I'll send you the rest of the chapters. I have them in my house.

COMRADE WU: It's okay, Philip. I like the first three chapters very much.

Scene Ten

Time: The same day.
Place: Passport Office, Beijing. Sun sits silently, stiffly, clearly terrified. The Passport Officer enters with stack of papers. Sun stands.

PASSPORT OFFICER: *(Dismissing Sun with a wave, sitting down, taking his time going through the papers. Sun waits, then finally he begins.)* We would like to say Yes, approved, no problem, *wenti, but* Sun Hong Tian . . .

SUN: But . . .

PASSPORT OFFICER: You are so special and valuable, so needed here. How can we let you leave? Your translating skills are too important. In fact, there's a possibility you'll be transferred . . . let me see here. . . . *(Looking through his papers.)* Yes, here it is . . . *(Studying the piece of paper.)* A position in the First High School in Gansu Province.

SUN: Gansu! That's practically in Tibet. I'm a university professor, not a high school teacher. I've done nothing wrong.

PASSPORT OFFICER: *(Accusingly.)* It isn't good enough for you here! It's good enough for the rest of us! You have a swollen head, Sun Hong Tian. *(Remy enters. Sun doesn't see her at first. Passport Officer to Remy.)*

PASSPORT OFFICER: Excuse me. Yes?

SUN: *(Turning around, panicked.)* Remy! What are you doing here?

REMY: I have the list. The students just finished signing their names saying how valuable a teacher you are.

PASSPORT OFFICER: What list? Let me see this list. *(To Sun.)* Who is this person?

SUN: *(To Passport Officer.)* She's an American professor and my visiting friend. I'm her official translator.

PASSPORT OFFICER: *(To Remy.)* You have no business here. *(Pointing to Sun.)* Even she has no business here.

REMY: But I have an official letter of invitation from my university. *(Handing him the envelope.)* Here. Look.

PASSPORT OFFICER: *(Opening the envelope, scrutinizing the letter and the list of students as he speaks.)* The students on this list are also questionable, well known as dissidents. And if our Sun is so valuable, how can we let her go? *(Closing his file, standing, as though the meeting is over.)*

REMY: But I have a very good job for her in the United States.

SUN: *(Turning to the Passport Officer.)* I'm telling you, I have nothing but my country in my heart.

PASSPORT OFFICER: You have yourself in your heart.

SUN: *(Very angry now, to the Passport Officer.)* What do you know? You know nothing! You're just a machine doing paperwork, stupid work. You know nothing about me!

PASSPORT OFFICER: Shut up foolish woman! I know plenty! *(Waving the papers.)* Conspiring with foreigners, stirring up the students, trying to bribe an official —

SUN: That's not true! I did everything right! I did just what you asked! I filled out all the forms, I learned every song *(Singing, with increasing intensity and loudness.)* Dongiay hóng tái yang sheng Zhóng gúo chule yige Mao Tse Tung Chule. (The East is Red, The Sun Rises . . . ./China has a Mao Tse-Tung/ He finds happiness for the people/He's the Great Savior of the people . . .) *(Continuing at a fevered pitch.)* I joined the Thought Reform Move-ment.

I even clapped for my mother while she danced to her death, I named every villager, I gave directions to their houses!

PASSPORT OFFICER: Everyone knows how you incriminated your mother and father, confessed lies rather than be shot. Who would be stupid enough to trust you now?

REMY: You told her, her parents were bad, in the Cultural Revolution.

PASSPORT OFFICER: The American professor recites *our* history to us. *(Beat.)* This is my table, my office. *(To Remy.)* Your passport.

REMY: I don't have it with me.

PASSPORT OFFICER: Always carry your papers, ID.

SUN: They're at her hotel.

PASSPORT OFFICER: *(Paying no attention to Sun, directly to Remy.)* Your papers please, delivered here today.

SUN: Yes, sir, delivered promptly. We both respect your good judgment and approval for exit.

REMY: *(To Passport Officer, realizing they both are in trouble.)* Give me my letter back, please.

(The Passport Officer remains motionless.)

REMY: Maybe she could come next year, if Sun is needed here that badly.

SUN: That's a lie!

PASSPORT OFFICER: Shut up your Chinese face. The purpose of the teacher is to reverse the thinking of the students.

SUN: *(Furiously to the Passport Officer.)* Wo cao ni ma! *(Bastard!)*

PASSPORT OFFICER: For that obscenity I spit in your face.

(He spits at Sun. She just stands there. He slaps Sun's face. She doesn't move. This is not the first time she's been slapped.)

REMY: *(Frightened.)* There's no job! It's a mistake! Someone else applied first. Give me my letter. No job. Sun stays here. No room in my apartment anyway. Filled with cockroaches. I only have one bedroom. I want to live alone. I need my privacy.

SUN: *(To Remy.)* Traitor. Two-faced visiting friend. Why did you start up with me? I'm happy here. I have a fine life, everything a girl could want

PASSPORT OFFICER: *(To Sun.)* Quiet, you. *(To Remy.)* You leave. *Zou!* ID papers here today.

REMY: *Xie xie.* (She exits.)

PASSPORT OFFICER: *(Pulls the pearls out of his pocket, the same ones Remy had given Sun.)* And what are these?

SUN: Those are my pearls.

PASSPORT OFFICER: Then how did I get them? *(To Sun.)* Who is Mei Yen?

SUN: My superior.

PASSPORT OFFICER: Tell your superior she's dumb. It would take more than pearls. *(Beat.)* This meeting is over. *(Standing.)* You should start packing your bags for Gansu, Sun Hong Tian, and don't forget your boots. There's much rain there. *(Then, holding out the pearls.)* Here, take them. Go ahead. Take them back.

(No one moves, then.)

SUN: *(Grabbing the pearls from the Passport Officer.)* The pearls are *not even valuable!*

(As Sun grabs the pearls from him and starts to hit him with the pearls.)

PASSPORT OFFICER: You'll be punished for this Sun Hong Tien!

(Blackout.)

Scene Eleven

Time: Several hours later.
Place: Public Security Bureau, detention room, Beijing. Sun and Remy are separated by a screen. They talk through the screen.

SUN: They hold me here for a day. Questions, more questions.

REMY: The guard said *kuai wu*. He shouted.

SUN: This is Beijing Detention House, not Central Park. Five minutes quickly and don't come again.

REMY: The Passport Officer sent me here. He said it was okay.

SUN: Ha! Lili said it was okay to give pearls for a bribe. I trust no one.

REMY: I brought you rolls.

SUN: Thank you, I've been fed. *(Beat.)* Do you know where Gansu is?

(Remy shakes her head no on the other side of the screen, not answering.)

SUN: The end of the world. The Yellow River crosses the Great Wall there, and the winds from the Gobi desert blow cold in your face. Why did you lead me on? Pursue Sun like a pet to bring home in your sleeve? *(Not waiting.)* I asked you for nothing! *(Recalling Remy's earlier speech.)* "We hope our small delegation can share our American spirit, our pioneering spirit." What does that mean, *pioneer*? I looked it up — "To colonize, ride in and take over land, annex it, make it yours." I had the good life before you came.

REMY: That's a lie. *(Starts to eat the rolls, slowly at first, then frantically.)*

SUN: If it is, then it's the lie I choose.

REMY: Sun, we're friends, like sisters . . . Fish . . .

SUN: You must have been mistaken. You exaggerate some friendship between us. We are acres apart. I invite you to my house, but I'm just being polite to a visitor. You know us Chinese. *(Beat.)* And the Whitman. *Xie xie.* I'm finished. *(Taking the Whitman book out of her bag and pushing it under the screen out to Remy.)* As I'll be traveling, it's important to lighten the load. *(Remy accepts the book, holding it, as though it weighed a hundred pounds.)* *(Lights fade.)*

Scene Twelve

Time: A few days later. The first of August. It is late at night.
Place: Hotel room in Beijing. Remy sits very still, in a large overstuffed chair.
White crocheted doilies are on each arm of the chair. The only illumination
is from a small lamp. After a minute, she gets up, puts on a small tape recorder.
American music. The sound of a knock at the door.

REMY: Who is it?

MEI YEN: *(Off stage. In a whisper.)* Mei Yen.
(Lights up more fully as Mei Yen enters the room.)

MEI YEN: Is it too late?

REMY: *(Staring straight ahead.)* What time is it?

MEI YEN: Past eleven.

REMY: It's okay.

MEI YEN: There's all this paper work, closing the Summer Institute. *(Silence.)* The students were sad. This is the first year we didn't have a farewell banquet. Last year the Americans sang *Yankee Doodle Dandy*, and also, *I'd Like to Get You on a Small Boat to China*, and everyone danced. *(Silence.)* I saw Philip downstairs in the bar.

REMY: Philip likes to drink.

MEI YEN: I'm sorry about the pearls. I did it with good intentions for Sun. Lili insisted it would be an excellent bribe. She even offered to bring the pearls personally to the Officer. It was, now it seems, careless.

REMY: Lili — the actress who isn't really an actress.

MEI YEN: Also, as it seems, she was lying.

REMY: Oh, Christ, Mei Yen! Lili is an actress, but not, and Comrade Wu is loyal, but isn't, and Philip is together, but he's not, and you honor your mother, but spit at other women because you have red envy, and Sun spits at her mother's grave because she's loyal to the Government, but then the government screws *her*, or Lili screws her, or I screw her, or she screws herself.

MEI YEN: The meaning of *screw*, please.

REMY: We sometimes use it to mean making love. Also, it's like being a rat; doing someone in. *(Beat.)* I was stupid. I got Sun wanting.

MEI YEN: Sun was already wanting. We never know here what one thing it is which makes the government irritated. It could be Sun only ate noodle in the wrong shop.

REMY: I wish I hadn't come.

MEI YEN: Except you did. When Marco Polo came to China, our land extended from the Yellow Sea to the Mediterranean, from Siberia to India. China was the jewel in the Empire. Marco Polo passed through cities of such greatness, even he was astonished. *(Beat.)* Sun is a lucky one. She still knows her own heart. Mao warned that people are not like leeks. If you cut off their heads, they don't grow back.

REMY: It's possible she planned to kill herself if they didn't give her the passport.

MEI YEN: Perhaps. Comrade Wu tells me she's now in Prison No. 1 and that's all we know. She may have a trial. Maybe not.

REMY: I should see her. I should apologize. *(Knowing what a mess she's made of it.)* I should tell her in High School I was voted "The Girl with the Most School Spirit." *(Silence.)* I should do nothing for once.

MEI YEN: Sun knows you're her friend. *(Beat.)* So, she is perhaps in solitary. . . . Yes, she's in solitary, Wu said. So she is alone but possibly dreaming. We're used to *Hsu*, patience, and just consuming time. Time is the only thing we have plenty of. That's why, perhaps, we're no longer the jewel of the Empire. *(Beat.)* Want to play fish with me?

REMY: Eat the fish before it eats you? Sure.

(Remy and Mei Yen face each other.)

REMY: Fish.

MEI YEN: Next year, my husband may come back from New Haven with an advanced degree. Yale. There's a new democracy movement, perhaps, and he'll be part of it. *(Beat.)* Fish.

REMY: When we were climbing the Wall, I had a feeling so high, higher even than making love. *(Beat.)* Fish.

MEI YEN: The Emperor had seventy concubines, and still he built the Wall. What do you think? *(Beat.)* Fish.

REMY: I'm leaving Sun in Beijing, like a monk without an umbrella. *(Beat.)* Fish.

MEI YEN: Just a monk. *(Beat.)* She didn't need the umbrella after all. She never got to Gansu. *(Beat.)* Fish.

REMY: Fish.
MEI YEN: Fish.
  (Lights fade.)

On The Great Wall

It is almost dark. Remy and Sun walk, as in a dream, completing the circle, ending up where they began, six o'clock, downstage center.

REMY: Easier going down the Wall than up. There's everyone! We're at the end.
SUN: And the beginning.
REMY: If we wanted to climb again. Yes.
SUN: It's almost dark. Another day. I worry about being up here at night with mountain lions and thousand-year-old rats hidden in the cracks.
REMY: Maybe next year I'll come back. Next summer.
SUN: Next summer will be the Year of the Snake. People born in the Year of the Snake are known for their wisdom and determination. The snake is known for its cleverness. The Year of the Snake is supposed to be more peaceful.
REMY: To the Year of the Snake, then.
SUN: To next year then, the Year of the Snake.
  (Lights fade out.)

END OF PLAY

Playwright's note: The next year, June 1989, the Tiananmen Square massacre occurred.

LOBSTER ALICE
by Kira Obolensky

ORIGINAL PRODUCTIONS

Jungle Theatre production

ALICE HOROWITZ . . . . .Julie Briskman

JOHN FINCH . . . . .Bob Davis

SALVADOR DALI . . . . .Charles Schuminski

THORTON/THE CATERPILLAR . . . . .Jamison Haase

DIRECTOR . . . . .Bain Boehlke

SETS . . . . .Bain Boehlke

LIGHTING . . . . .Barry Browning

COSTUMES . . . . .Amelia Busse Breuer

SOUND . . . . .C. Andrew Mayer

COMPOSER . . . . Roberta Carlson

VOCALS . . . . .Bradley Greenwald

SOPRANO SAXOPHONE . . . . .Sarah MacDonald

WIG DESIGN . . . . .Ivy Loughborough

CHARGE PAINTER & PALETTE DESIGN . . . . . . .John Clark Donahue

STAGE MANAGEMENT . . . . .John Novak

DRAMATURG . . . . .Buffy Sedlachek

Playwrights Horizon production

ALICE HOROWITZ . . . . .Jessica Hecht

JOHN FINCH . . . . .Reg Rogers

SALVADOR DALI . . . . .David Patrick Kelly

THORTON . . . . .Derek Richardson

DIRECTOR . . . . .Maria Mileaf

SETS . . . . .Neil Patel

COSTUMES . . . . .Ann Hould-Ward

LIGHTING . . . . .Frances Aronson

ORIGINAL MUSIC/SOUND . . . . .David Van Tieghem

PROJECTIONS . . . . .Jan Hartley

CASTING . . . . .James Calleri

DIRECTOR OF DEVELOPMENT . . . . .Jill Garland

PRODUCTION MANAGER . . . . .Christopher Boll

PRODUCTION STAGE MANAGER . . . . .William Joseph Barnes

FACT: In 1946, the Surrealist Salvador Dali went to Hollywood. He spent six weeks at a large studio where he had been commissioned to create a short animated surrealist ballet based on the popular song, *Destino* or *You Tempt Me*. He spent most of his time with a young animator who was working on the color styling and design of *Alice in Wonderland*. This play is a fictional speculation on the course of those six weeks.

CHARACTERS

JOHN FINCH: an animator.

ALICE HOROWITZ: Finch's assistant.

SALVADOR DALI: a Surrealist.

THORTON/THE CATERPILLAR: a beautiful boy, nineteen or so.

SETTING

The play takes place in John Finch's studio in Burbank, California. There is a window, through which the landscape of Burbank can be seen. There is a desk, for Alice. Finch's studio is the space of a creative, organized person. There's a large drawing board. Various drawings are pinned up. A few photographs around. A storyboard. Finch is working on *Alice in Wonderland*.

LOBSTER ALICE

Scene One

Finch's office. A Monday morning. Alice enters. She turns on the lights. She opens the blinds. She puts down her purse. She looks at the office, as she always does, for things to throw in the garbage. There's a cup on Finch's drawing table. It has DRINK ME written on one side.

So she drinks. And then she puts it down. She sits at her desk. She puts her lunch in the drawer. She sees a list on her desk from her boss. She picks up the phone, and requests an inhouse extension.

ALICE: 123, please. This is Alice Horowitz on Lot B Hi Shirley, I've got an order. Are you ready? Three rolls of vellum, fifty-two charcoal sticks, Prismacolor set, deluxe. Gouache, tempera, standard issue. We're going to need another drawing table. And then there's this list of things. Here goes. Three white doves in a cage.

A clock.

A chunk of ice. *Ice.* Big chunk, that would be my guess.

A silver bell.

A jug. I don't know. It says a jug.

A bucket of worms.

A box of grasshoppers.

I'm not kidding.

A cotton tail.

A cow hide. Black and white.

The remnants of a 1964 Chevrolet. Yes, you heard right. It says 1964. Yes, I realize it's 1946. But it says 1964. No. . . maybe it is 1946.

Remnants. That's what it says.

A tortoise shell.

Boy, this just gets curiouser and curiouser.

Mustache wax. From England.

A gold fingernail file. That's what it says. Gold.

Ten pounds of black tea.

Silence. No, Shirley, not you, it's on the list. Silence. Uh huh. See what you can do.

A wooden boat.

And a dozen lobsters. Real, I suppose.

And that's it.

Thanks so much. Here's the billing number: IRP, 304432PQ.

It says by tomorrow.

You can only do your best.

Oh it was nice. My younger sister. She was radiant. He was handsome. Got some rice in my eyes. No it's fine, Shirley. Just a little rice.

Same old questions. When are you going to get married. What's a pretty girl like you doing without a husband. What's a pretty girl like you doing without a family. What's a pretty girl like you doing with a job. Folks just can't get used to the idea of a girl with a job.

Oh no, Shirley, I didn't. Well, he's dead. The war. Oh a long time ago since we were sweethearts. A really long time.

Anyway, I was glad to be back. First thing I did, lit a cigarette.

I brought my lunch today. But tomorrow? Tomorrow would be good—
(Finch enters the office. He hangs his hat. Takes an orange out of his pocket.)

ALICE: Listen, Shirley. I got to run. See you later.

(She hangs up.)

ALICE: Good morning, Mr. Finch.

(Finch approaches his desk. He takes off his coat. He hangs it up. He opens his briefcase. He removes a file. He hangs up his hat. He sharpens a pencil, as he speaks.)

FINCH: Good morning, Alice. Did you have a nice vacation?

ALICE: I was at a wedding.

FINCH: I worked all weekend. On the Drink Me sequence. You know. Drink Me. Well. It's good to get away. I could use a break myself. If I could I'd go to New York City.

ALICE: You would?

FINCH: Absolutely. Always wanted to live there.

ALICE: So have I.

FINCH: But Burbank is nice. There's no place else for someone like me. I've got an orange tree in the backyard. I have a nice life.

ALICE: I imagine you do.

FINCH: Well here we are. Monday. Did you have a nice weekend?

(A beat.)

ALICE: I was at my sister's wedding.

FINCH: You were away? Of course you were. I'm sorry. I'm a little distracted.

ALICE: Can I get you a cup of couch this morning?

FINCH: *(A beat.)* No, no. Did you say . . . cup of couch?

ALICE: Cup of *coffee*.

(She busies herself.)

FINCH: Oh no. Thank you. Not just yet.

ALICE: Did anything happen while I was gone?

FINCH: No. Well nothing really. I met with, uh, him. And he didn't like it. Not Alice. Not the Caterpillar. The Cheshire Cat was too friendly. The Duchess was, what did he say? Too much like a society matron. He said the work was "vanilla pudding," and I said "exactly." I love vanilla pudding.

ALICE: I prefer tapioca. Something with a bit of texture. Something to roll around on my tongue.

FINCH: *(A little scared.)* Tapioca?

ALICE: The way it feels in my mouth.

FINCH: Vanilla pudding is soft, it's silky. It's a superior texture, Alice.

ALICE: It's bland. Not interesting.

FINCH: Well then. Doesn't seem like I can convince you.

(Pause.)

ALICE: This list — are we getting another project?

(Finch laughs.)

FINCH: Come here.

(Alice approaches his desk. He opens a file. He shows it to her.)

FINCH: Look at this. What do you see.

ALICE: My goodness.

FINCH: Tell me what you see.

ALICE: A murky landscape, with a skull and a tower.

FINCH: Now move three steps to the left.

ALICE: Oh, how interesting. Something different altogether. A naked man and a woman.

FINCH: To the right. Go on, three steps —

ALICE: And now a cornucopia with a boat and a grasshopper.

(She takes the file, flips through it.)

ALICE: Is that Shirley Temple?, with the hairy red body of a, I don't know, monster.

FINCH: *(As if to stop the discussion.)* Thank you, Alice —

(But she flips through the file.)

ALICE: — an enormous, my it's enormous . . . a woman painted like a piano. A woman wearing a lobster. My.

FINCH: Thank you, Alice.

(He holds out his hand for the file. She gives it to him.)

ALICE: Thank you, Mr. Finch.

(And Alice returns to her seat. She shuffles through her papers.)

FINCH: I've spent the past week staring at all of these pictures. From every possible direction. To see what else they say — how they infiltrate the brain. What is really there, that's the question. I mean beyond the offensive naughty stuff.

ALICE: You think it's naughty.

FINCH: Yes. It is offensive and naughty.

ALICE: I thought I saw the bust of Voltaire.

FINCH: You didn't!

(Looks again.)

I see what you mean. Is that Voltaire?

ALICE: Sure looks like him to me.

FINCH: What else will reveal itself. Under your eyelids. Maybe you look at it and then three days later, the horrible message occurs to you. Or maybe it reveals itself as the paint fades. Every decade an ugly truth emerges until we can no longer face the world with any hope.

ALICE: What has gotten in to you?

FINCH: I'm upset, Alice.

ALICE: I can see that.

FINCH: I'm profoundly upset.

ALICE: You seem paranoid.

FINCH: I wish I had fortified myself earlier. Gone to church on a regular basis. I wish I had said something to you, sooner, earlier.

ALICE: Said what.

FINCH: Something. I've always had this feeling I wanted to say something to you, but I don't know what it is. I look at you and I feel an urgency. And then, I don't know. It goes away.

ALICE: About the couch?

FINCH: The couch —

ALICE: My couch, the night we —

FINCH: No. That's not it.

ALICE: You can say whatever you like, John. Mr. Finch. It's not as if we are strangers.

FINCH: Of course not.

Did you, uh, what did you think of those pictures I showed you?

ALICE: I liked them.

FINCH: You liked them.

ALICE: I thought they were interesting.

FINCH: Many things in this horrible world are . . . interesting.

ALICE: You should not be condescending toward me, Mr. Finch.

FINCH: I'm sorry, Alice. I didn't mean to be condescending. I feel I have to warn me. Warn you.

ALICE: Whyever would you need to do that. I am perfectly capable of taking care of myself.

(Finch approaches her. He is so earnest he is almost hysterical.)

FINCH: Alice, you have to promise me. Pledge to me your allegiance.

ALICE: Pledge the allegiance?

FINCH: No. Pledge your allegiance.

ALICE: I'm not quite sure what that means.

FINCH: To me, Alice!

ALICE: It's not like I'm a spy, Mr. Finch.

FINCH: It is critical that I understand that you trust and respect me.

ALICE: Of course I trust and respect you.

FINCH: Do you? Do you think of me, outside of work, with respect.

ALICE: You're a decent boss, Mr. Finch.

FINCH: Do you think of me?

ALICE: Sometimes I think of you. With affection.

FINCH: That's nice, Alice. Thank you.

But you would never repeat what goes on in this room to other people in the studio?

ALICE: Why would I do that?

FINCH: Gossip!

ALICE: Frankly, Mr. Finch, there isn't anything really interesting enough to talk about.

FINCH: But if there were?

ALICE: Then I couldn't help myself. I am a slave to the interesting. That is why I left my home in Oklahoma. I relish the world only when it is interesting. I live my life to be interesting. Why else do I study Chinese, Mr. Finch? Why else do I read medieval texts?

FINCH: You've always been a fantastic resource. I know I consider you my right-hand man.

ALICE: Uh huh.

FINCH: I always give you credit when credit is due.

ALICE: That's right. There's nothing I enjoy more than seeing my name fly by on the screen at the end of the credits. Special thanks to Alice Horowitz. If you blink you miss it.

FINCH: Do you talk about . . . interesting things . . . with your friends?

ALICE: Oh I do.

FINCH: If something interesting were to happen in this office, then could I count on you to keep your mouth shut.

ALICE: No.

FINCH: Could I pay you to keep your mouth shut?

ALICE: Mr. Finch!

FINCH: We are about to embark on six weeks of . . . I fear the word interesting is too pale. There is no word. For what is about to happen. I can only warn you and ask you, Alice, to be my friend.

(The phone rings. Alice picks it up.)

ALICE: Mr. Finch's office. I'll tell him. How *interesting.*

(She hangs up.)

There's a gentleman to see you, Mr. Finch.

(And Dali appears like a devil or a magician. He is a dapper, slender reed of a man. He has a mustache. He carries a bouquet of oversize forks. He presents them to Finch.)

DALI: For you. A bouquet of appetite.

FINCH: *(Takes them.)* Thank you. Alice, will you get a . . . vase?

(Who hands them to Alice, who says.)

ALICE: I'll just go get a vase.

DALI: I am here. Dali is here.

FINCH: Welcome.

(Dali takes off a red scarf. He throws it on the floor. He steps to the window.)

DALI: *(Referring to the view.)* Magnificent. I would blow it up with dynamite and build a castle. A monument to Dali.

(He turns to Finch, casually.) The money is not sufficient. I asked for a certain amount — I asked for a phenomenal sum and I expect more than pigeon droppings.

(Alice might exit here.)

FINCH: I'm not personally in charge of the money.

DALI: Then what are you?

FINCH: The man I work for is, of course, well known to you. I am one of his employees. I am your *liaison* while you are here. For six weeks. In charge of your efforts, as they say.

DALI: My efforts.

FINCH: Your commission. Yes.

DALI: I do not understand. Something is expected of me?

FINCH: As you most likely know he saw your . . . thing at the World's Fair. The, uh, Dream of Venus. He wants something similar. On film.

DALI: It was not a thing. It was a phantasmagorical mirage, an impossible taste of desire.

FINCH: I am not unfamiliar with your work, Mr. Dali. It's implications do not escape me.

DALI: You know my work.

FINCH: I have made some efforts to understand it. You've had a lot of press in this country, as I am certain you are aware. Here are a few memorable headlines: "Salvador, the MadCap Artist." "Making Sense of No Sense." "Putting the F Back in Art."

DALI: *(Pleased.)* I love your country. Will you bring me a cup of tea.

FINCH: I'm afraid that is impossible.

DALI: Why?

FINCH: Because Alice is gone.

DALI: Alice brings the tea.

FINCH: She does.

DALI: I thought you were to be my servant.

FINCH: No, your *liaison.* Your facilitator. The direct connection between the song and the film.

DALI: The song?

FINCH: "You Tempt Me."

DALI: Do I?

FINCH: The song. "Destino." Also known as "You Tempt Me."

(Finch goes to a record player. He puts an LP on, the scratchy sounds of "Destino, You Tempt Me." You tempt me with your two lips of scarlet and your two eyes so starlit — you stand there so enticing in your splendor And I behold a vision sweet and tender So it would be complete surrender, if I fell 'neath your spell. You tempt me —)

(Alice enters with a vase. Actually it's a bucket. She hears the song — and Finch removes the needle from the record.)

FINCH: The song. You are to animate it.

DALI: What does it mean —

FINCH: To bring it to life.

DALI: I want the sudden materialization of the suggested image! For you, it is to animate. For me, something different altogether. The imagination, my friend — that is the place where we are to bring it.

FINCH: My imagination, I should make perfectly clear, suits me very well. It is a clean, pin-striped, smut-free thing. And I plan to keep it that way.

DALI: Do you.

FINCH: Yes, I do.

DALI: My imagination is reality and delirium. I make no distinction.

(Dali takes off another scarf and throws it on the floor. Alice approaches the two scarves and is about to pick them up —)

DALI: STOP!

(Alice freezes.)

DALI: No one touches my scarves.

(Alice straightens. Dali suddenly charming.)

DALI: I am Salvador Dali.

ALICE: Alice Horowitz. I'm Mr. Finch's assistant.

DALI: You have firm turds, Miss Alice. I can see this from looking into your eyes. A regular constitution.

FINCH: Miss Horowitz's . . . intestinal fortitude . . . is of no consequence to either of us.

DALI: Oh but it is. We are three people together in a room. We must know everything.

FINCH: Mr. Dali, my only hope is that we will maintain a professional distance, marked of course by respect.

(Dali takes takes a framed photograph from Finch's desk.)

DALI: What is professional distance?

(Finch takes the photograph away from Dali.)

FINCH: There. A professional distance.

DALI: Who is the cow?

FINCH: My sister.

DALI: Who is the giant mouse?

FINCH: That's me, Mr. Dali. Halloween some time ago —

DALI: I have received not enough money.

FINCH: We will relay your concerns —

DALI: And my hotel is unacceptable.

ALICE: Where are you staying, Mr Dali?

FINCH/DALI: In the Belaire.

ALICE: That's a nice hotel.

DALI: Carpeting, everywhere.

(Dali takes off another scarf and throws it on the ground.)

DALI: My accommodations are infected. Carpet is a breeding ground. Carpet is the source of all sinus infections. I ripped up the carpet. And we will be okay.

FINCH: You ripped up the carpet. What did you do with it.

DALI: I put it in the hallway and called for room service.

FINCH: Of course.

(Dali picks up another picture.)

DALI: Look at all these smiling people. Happy people. Incredible. In Europe, there are no smiles. Not one to be found. And yet look at this. Nowhere in my life have I seen so many people who look like white bread.

ALICE: How long will you be here with us, Mr. Dali?

DALI: Six weeks.

FINCH: Mr. Dali is here to work on a project. We are to assist in whatever way we can. There will be weekly meetings — every Monday morning shall we say? — in which he presents his ideas.

DALI: We are going to have a marvelous time.

(Finch takes the photo from Dali's hands. Dali sits elegantly in a chair.)

FINCH: We'll have to begin right away. I imagine we should start with a meeting to hash out the story.

DALI: Who are those people in that photograph?

FINCH: My family.

DALI: Ahh. Are you a good child?

FINCH: I'm an adult.

DALI: Are you a good child?

FINCH: I'm a good son, I suppose. Yes.

DALI: When I was a child, I liked nothing more than to torment my parents. My favorite activity — to defecate in some strange hidden place in our house. Announce the fact. And watch the adults tiptoe around, carefully opening drawers, sitting on chairs with great fear. . . .

(Finch checks his chair, Alice laughs at him.)

DALI: Oh, Mistress Alice. You I would like to get to know.

ALICE: Mr. Dali, I'm flattered —

FINCH: Alice is really very busy now. We've also got *Alice* in the works.

ALICE: *Alice in Wonderland.*

DALI: I know this story. I know it very well. Perhaps this is why I am here.

FINCH: It is my project.

DALI: One cannot own a dream.

FINCH: Yes one can. In America one can. And for now, for the next few weeks, I own *Alice.*

(Dali takes off another scarf. Throws it on the floor.)

ALICE: Are you warm, Mr. Dali?

DALI: I am on fire!

(And Dali exits. A beat. Alice moves to the scarves and then stops herself, returns to her desk.)

FINCH: You're not going to pick those up?

ALICE: I'm not.

FINCH: I don't blame you.

ALICE: Well. That was interesting.

FINCH: Yes it was. I apologize for his rude questions —

ALICE: Oh I don't mind. He reminds me of my father. My father always talked about blood and bowels. I'm not squeamish at all.

FINCH: You're a good kid.

ALICE: I'm not a kid.

FINCH: You're a good gal.

ALICE: Yes, I am.

FINCH: That wasn't so bad. I expected worse.

ALICE: Salvador Dali, here. Incredible.

FINCH: You've heard of him?

ALICE: I read *Life* magazine.

FINCH: I mean, it was a bit touchy, at points. I had to insist on my position.

ALICE: I don't think he cares about your position.

FINCH: All in all, it went well. Maybe it will be interesting. To see what he comes up with.

(Alice retrieves a brown paper sack from her desk.)

ALICE: I didn't know she was your sister.

FINCH: Oh — Susan? Did I say sister?

ALICE: You told me she was your fiancée.

FINCH: Did I?

ALICE: We went on a date. We sat on my couch. The next Monday she appeared on your desk. I asked, you said, *Fiancée*.

FINCH: That's right.

ALICE: That's right?

FINCH: I was protecting her.

ALICE: You were protecting *her*.

FINCH: I was protecting someone.

ALICE: Uh huh. I can see that.

(She's on her way out, with her bag lunch. Finch's phone rings. He picks up.)

FINCH: Oh, put her through. Thank you —

ALICE: The caterpillar, Mr. Finch.

FINCH: My what?

ALICE: The caterpillar. It needs something.

FINCH: It does?

ALICE: I think it would be better served if you looked at the American furry klondike.

(And Alice exits.)

FINCH: Hello, Mother. Do I? No. Everything's just fine. Everything's pretty much the same as it was yesterday. Pretty much.

Oh I'm working on Alice. Can't get it out of my mind. No, *Alice in Wonderland*. No, no. Yes I see how that might have led you to think I was —

Uh huh. Uh huh. You've got plenty of time left.

Say, we've got an artist visiting. Salvador Dali. Uh huh. That's him. That's right. Uh huh. Uh huh. Uh huh. You sound like a fan. I didn't realize — Oh, I'm in charge of his efforts. Oh, he's helping out. That's all. I hope it will be. Interesting.

Oh it's sunny, here. Always sunny.

(As the lights fade.)

Scene Two

The next Monday. The office in morning light. The scarves have turned into lobsters.

Finch enters, as he does every morning, with this ritual: He takes off a trenchcoat, he hangs it on the wall. He removes from a pocket of the trenchcoat an orange, which he puts on his table. He takes from his front shirt pocket an eyeglass case. He puts his glasses on. Then he removes them, wiping them clean. He approaches his desk — flexes his fingers, snapping and cracking the muscles. He loosens his neck in the same way. While engaged in these exercises, he notices the lobsters. He stops. He looks. He takes off his glasses. He approaches, carefully — bends down, as if to touch. Alice enters.

ALICE: Good morning, Mr. Finch.

(Finch straightens.)

FINCH: Good morning, Alice.

Well. Here we are. Monday.

ALICE: Did you have a nice weekend?

FINCH: Very nice. Thank you for asking.

(Alice is going through her ritual, her coat, her lunch. Her chair. She takes pencils from a drawer and sharpens them Finch is waiting for her to notice the lobsters. But she doesn't. In her trajectory across the room, she merely steps over them.)

FINCH: And how was your weekend?

ALICE: Well, I cried starting Friday night until Sunday afternoon. Cried, Mr. Finch. Sobbed. Like a monster faucet had been turned on by a monster God who made me mourn for everything I've lost and every single broken dream. But my heart is not broken. My sense of humor is intact. My life seems by all accounts to be sailing along. But these tears, Mr. Finch. Could have filled four buckets.

FINCH: Crying? And you say you're not upset? Did something happen.

ALICE: Nothing happened.

Did you want a cup of coffee this morning?

FINCH: I'm so sorry. That you cried. Gosh.

ALICE: Do you want a cup of coffee?

FINCH: Yes, Alice. That would be nice.

Wait. I'll get it. And let me bring you a cup of coffee.

ALICE: Don't be ridiculous. I drink tea, Mr. Finch. Tea.

(And Alice exits for coffee. Finch sits at his drawing table. He begins to draw. The Cheshire Cat appears. A grinning feline face from above.)

CAT: You like to color in the borders, don't you.

FINCH: I draw the borders.

CAT: Your Alice is . . . what's the word? She's pale. Tentative. She needs something.

FINCH: Would you stop smiling.

CAT: Impossible.

FINCH: God, that smile. Gives me the creeps.

CAT: Who's going to get her?

FINCH: No one gets her.

CAT: Oh but they do.

FINCH: This is a children's story.

CAT: Oh but it's not.

(The Cat springs onto the table. Alice enters with the coffee.)

ALICE: Hello, Mr. Dali. We didn't expect you so early this morning.

(Dali leaps from the table and bows before Alice.)

ALICE: Just don't ask me about my weekend.

DALI: What exactly is a weekend.

ALICE: Saturday and Sunday.

DALI: I had a most satisfying weekend in my hotel room.

FINCH: Shall we get him a chair?

ALICE: I'll get him a chair.

(Alice exits for chair.)

DALI: The pursuit of pleasure is very interesting in this country. The way young women and men meet and share alcoholic beverages. The alcohol gives them a freedom, I see the women begin to want to take off their clothes. And vice versa for the men. Drink me, the alcohol says and I will show you the way to freedom. But to the Surrealist, the world is a door, and one only needs a dream to achieve the reckless feeling of pleasure.

FINCH: This meeting is not about pleasure.

DALI: Every meeting should be about pleasure. Miss Alice. Is her heart broken?

FINCH: I have no idea. I don't know her heart. That's not to say that I don't care. It's just that I hope we can maintain our working relationship.

DALI: How do you expect to know her if you don't love her?

FINCH: I'm not required to know her, or to love her.

DALI: Yet you work on her.

FINCH: No, I work on something else. It is only coincidence that Alice and the heroine of my project share the same name.

DALI: Is it?

FINCH: It is.

DALI: What do you do when you are awake?

FINCH: I focus. I Concentrate. I pay attention.

DALI: With your desires.

FINCH: I really ask you, please, to respect the fact that whatever desires I have, and I do have them, they remain my desires and not a topic of conversation.

DALI: While I am awake, I incessantly increase my desires. I develop my desire — because it is connected to imaginative possibilities.

(Alice enters with a chair.)

FINCH: Thank you, Alice.

DALI: We were just talking about desire.

ALICE: Desire on a Monday. Fantastic.

(And she sits expectantly.)

DALI: Do you have anything you wish to say about desire?

ALICE: I might. Let me think . . . I am ruled by it. I have felt it since I was a baby. Need. A gaping chasm in my soul. I am *haunted* by desire.

DALI: I would like to eat you —

FINCH: Mr. Dali!? —

DALI: Because beauty is edible, or there is no such thing as beauty.

ALICE: I'm flattered. Thank you.

DALI: And you, Mr. Finch, what do you desire?

(Finch looks surreptitiously at Alice.)

FINCH: I would like to ask that I be given some time to think about my relationship to desire. And in the meantime, that we turn our attention to our weekly meeting.

DALI: Permission is granted.

FINCH: I am not asking for your permission.

ALICE: It sounded like you were.

FINCH: I am leading this meeting.

ALICE: Very well.

FINCH: Alice, will you take record of it.

(Alice pushes herself out on her chair. She holds a stenographer's pad, expectantly.)

DALI: My thoughts. *Destino.* A red cape. A tortoise. A bell tolls.

ALICE: When you say a tortoise, do you mean —

DALI: Large, ancient. Perhaps a wall of tortoises.

ALICE: Yes, I see.

FINCH: I think that the idea, the general gist of the project, was to use the song as a starting point for something sweet. About love.

ALICE: Love?

FINCH: Yes, love. Sweet love, the sort we all understand from our childhoods.

ALICE: Because the song seems to me to be about temptation.

DALI: Seduction.

"Ay! vida, ay! que negro destino, qu difficil camino y lo tento quendar."

ALICE: "You tempt me, 'Til I lose self command, dear; And my heart's out of hand, dear As soon as I've been kissed."

FINCH: I hear love.

DALI: I see — red cape. Ruins. The ancient dilemma of desire. A wasp, perhaps.

ALICE: How interesting.

FINCH: I wonder if we drive down a dangerous road in this interpretation —

DALI: Oh, I hope so. All roads should be dangerous, don't you think, Alice.

ALICE: Some roads. Not all roads.

DALI: My story has to have people in it. A woman, a beautiful man. Two innocents who grow old and besotted.

FINCH: Besotted?

ALICE:. My.

DALI: After a great amount of time has passed.

FINCH: We're looking at a minute, minute and a half maximum. I only mention that because it seems difficult to consider a love story with a great deal of time passing —

DALI: We will make the man the God of Time. That way he will have the powers you think impossible.

ALICE: The God of Time. I would like to meet him.

DALI: Would you?

FINCH: Alice, perhaps Mr. Dali would like a cup of coffee.

DALI: I don't want a cup of coffee.

FINCH: Because I would like a cup of coffee.

ALICE: Then you can get it yourself. I'm busy now.

FINCH: All right then. I'll get it myself.

> *(He stands and heads for the door. A moment while he considers the possibilities. He exits, cautiously. Dali smiles at Alice, like the Cheshire Cat. An awkward moment.)*

ALICE: Are you enjoying Burbank, Mr. Dali?

DALI: Yes.

ALICE: I trust you find the facilities here comprehensive . . .

DALI: I do.

ALICE: Your work on film, well, it's quite interesting to consider.
Where it will go, I mean.

DALI: Go?

ALICE: The directions it could take —

DALI: The question is where Alice would like to go.

> *(Finch enters.)*

FINCH: I'm back! Coffee. *(He sips.)* What's the question?

DALI: Where she wants to go.

FINCH: Alice? Wants to go?

ALICE: We were speaking hypothetically.

FINCH: Mr. Dali, while I was filling my cup, I had a few thoughts.
Number one. We are quite concerned that you have not provided us with preliminary sketches. Quite concerned. Number two. This is an animation studio. We do not, we cannot, afford to behave like artists here. We work, Mr. Dali. And while I do appreciate your situation, we don't have the time to wait until the spirit moves us.

DALI: I should like to begin with the solution. Alice will become my assistant.

FINCH: That simply is impossible.

DALI: The problem is that I am lonely.

FINCH: If you think that I'm going to allow — Alice is my secretary.

ALICE: Alice is Alice.

FINCH: I will not be able to fulfill my responsibilities; besides, it is not up to you to decide who works where.

DALI: Dali does not believe in anything other than the hierarchy of art.

FINCH: This is the hierarchy of art! Alice is paid to be my secretary.

DALI: We have put Alice in a difficult position to which I have the solution. Alice will remain your secretary. And she will work for me in the evenings. That is when I need the most stimulation.

FINCH: Alice? No!

DALI: I shall pay you, Alice.

ALICE: Do you want me to leave with you now?

DALI: Tomorrow in the evening, perhaps we take in a Western film. Or discuss the wonders of the universe.

ALICE: I look forward to that, Mr. Dali.

FINCH: *(To Dali.)* Have you forgotten who you are working for?

DALI: I work only for me. And that is the difference between us. That is why my ballet will become famous in all of time, and your efforts, reductive and simplistic, will fade from the American memory.
    (Dali exits.)

FINCH: You are not going to work with him. Please don't tell me, you're going to work with him.

ALICE: Okay.

FINCH: Okay, what?

ALICE: I won't tell you.

FINCH: You have to tell me!

ALICE: Your mother called, late on Friday. After you left. I spoke with her. I introduced myself. I asked her about Susan. Susan is your sister!

FINCH: Exactly, that's exactly what I told you!

ALICE: You did not. You said she was your fiancée!

FINCH: I told someone she was my sister.

ALICE: You told me she was your fiancée.

FINCH: I told the truth eventually.

ALICE: Uh huh. Why did you say she was your fiancée.

FINCH: To protect myself.

ALICE: From what.

FINCH: From . . . him.

ALICE: He doesn't want to hurt you.

FINCH: Oh but he does.

ALICE: I think he wants to save you.

FINCH: Save me? From what.
    (Alice approaches him, about to tell him. And then leaves in frustration.)

FINCH: *(Calls after her.)* You are an enigma, Alice Horowitz!
    (And Finch sits at his desk.)
    (Alice returns. She's got lobster claws for arms.)

ALICE: I forgot my purse.

(She retrieves her purse and flings it over her lobster arms.)

(She exits.)

Scene Three

The next Monday morning. Finch at his drawing table. The record is playing:

"You stand there so enticing in your splendor

And I behold a vision sweet and ten-dor

So it would be complete surrender

If I fell 'neath your spell.

You tempt me —"

Alice enters, pushing a white couch. He removes the needle, quickly. A loud scratch.

ALICE: Good morning, Mr. Finch.

FINCH: Good morning, Alice. What's, uh, this.

ALICE: It's my couch.

FINCH: Your couch. The couch where we, well, you know.

ALICE: This is the couch.

FINCH: Why is it here.

ALICE: Because I brought it to work.

FINCH: Ah.

ALICE: I thought it might be useful.

FINCH: Useful?

ALICE: Yes, useful.

FINCH: Well, that's nice Alice. Um. Thank you. Here we are Monday. Did you, uh, have a nice weekend?

ALICE: Oh very nice. Thank you.

(She starts looking for something.)

FINCH: What did you do?

ALICE: I went to a party. To two parties. Fantastic parties. Filled with interesting people. Charming people. And I assisted Mr. Dali with his project.

FINCH: I don't want to hear another word.

(She's looking for something.)

ALICE: Can I get you a cup of . . .

(Looking, looking.)

FINCH: Have you lost something?

ALICE: Yes.

FINCH: What.

ALICE: It's round.

FINCH: Lots of things are round. Marbles. Balls.

ALICE: Not those.

It's furry.

FINCH: Furry? With fur?

ALICE: Round and furry. I had it just a minute ago. And now I've misplaced it.

FINCH: It'll turn up. What is it? I mean, do you know what it is?

ALICE: It's a cotton tail.

FINCH: A cotton tail? What were you doing with a — Never mind.

ALICE: Oh well. It will turn up.

(She sits at her desk and begins to type. An interlude of dialogue with typing in the background —)

FINCH: We need to collect the storyboards at some point today.

And I expect Mr. Dali will be here shortly to report on his progress.

ALICE: Oh, yesterday he mentioned to me that he would not be coming in this morning.

FINCH: Did he? Oh? Good. We can get some work done.

(He goes to his desk. He keeps looking back at the couch; she's typing again. He is quite flummoxed by the couch.)

FINCH: Alice?

ALICE: Yes?

FINCH: What are you working on?

ALICE: I'm typing up the desire line. For Alice. From Friday.

FINCH: That's terrific. Thank you.

ALICE: You're welcome.

FINCH: What was it exactly that we decided on —

ALICE: It starts on the riverbank. It ends on the riverbank. The riverbank — dry, a few green moments, a leaf, a bug. A caterpillar.

FINCH: Yes, well. The caterpillar.

(She types again.)

FINCH: You know, it's awfully hard for me to concentrate —

ALICE: Do you want me to type softer?

FINCH: No, no. I mean with that couch.

(She stops typing.)

FINCH: I was horrified by my actions. On that couch. I was like an animal.

ALICE: You were like a mouse.

FINCH: A mouse is an animal.

(She starts to type.)

FINCH: I know I fell asleep on that couch.

(She stops typing.)

ALICE: And told me you were engaged to be married to your sister.

FINCH: And yet you brought the couch to work.

ALICE: Sometimes I wonder if . . . what might have happened if we had —

FINCH: Do you? Because, this is exactly what's been going through my head, day after day. Thinking, if only I could do it over. If only I could do it over. Sometimes I wonder if that's what life is. Missed chances that amplify in your brain, tormenting you like a drumbeat. If only I had kissed Alice on that fateful day. If only. If only.

Oh. I . . . should sit down.

ALICE: Please.

(Finch sits and lets out a nervous giggle.)

FINCH: You are really something. This is really something.

ALICE: What is.

FINCH: That you went to all of this effort to recreate the scene of the crime.

ALICE: *I'm* not recreating the scene of the crime.

(She returns to her desk.)

FINCH: Will you let *me* recreate the scene of the crime.

ALICE: Sure.

(She joins him.)

FINCH: *(Thinks.)* So. I had taken you out for a banana malt. At a diner you thought was boring. And you didn't like the banana malt. Then we went to your place. I tripped over the stoop, ripped my pants, tried to kiss you. Fell asleep. . . . So, instead I take you out for Cuban food. In West Hollywood, a little place with a banana tree in front. Oh, sorry. Bananas again.

ALICE: Yes, but different. More interesting.

FINCH: You know the place?

ALICE: I do.

FINCH: So we go there and we eat — what do we eat?

ALICE: Plantains, black beans, and squid.

FINCH: My.

ALICE: According to the recipe books I've eaten — I've *read*.

FINCH: We eat. Maybe you have a drink.

ALICE: A Mojita.

FINCH: That's right.

ALICE: Rum and mint. Sugar and water.

FINCH: And then we get to your place. I ask to come in.

ALICE: I ask you to come in. For a beverage.
And you do not check your watch.
(Finch checks his pocket watch.)

FINCH: My watch is gone. What time is it?
(He looks at the clock on the wall. It melts.)

FINCH: Do you know what time it is?

ALICE: No.

FINCH: *(Looking at the clock.)* What are we going to do.

ALICE: You don't know? Remember, you're standing on my stoop.

FINCH: Oh yes. I wipe my feet.

ALICE: Why?

FINCH: For mud.

ALICE: I have never seen mud in West Hollywood.

FINCH: I suppose it's a reflex from the past.

ALICE: Shit on the past.

FINCH: What did you say?

ALICE: You heard me. The past is dead. The past is excrement.

FINCH: It's that man. He is not a good influence.

ALICE: He is a *fantastic* influence. I can't live in the past, anymore. I can't. I have to break free. We all do —

FINCH: I don't want to argue with you, Alice.

ALICE: Good.

FINCH: I want to sit on the couch.

ALICE: Sit.
(He sits.)

ALICE: I'll sit down here next to you.
(Finch thinks for a moment.)

FINCH: We could talk about our childhood.
(Alice yawns.)

FINCH: No really. It will be interesting.

ALICE: Go on. Tell me.

FINCH: I wanted to fly. An airplane.

ALICE: Don't most boys?

FINCH: Maybe.

ALICE: Well why did you want to?

FINCH: To see things from above. I always liked patterns. The earth makes sense when it's so far away.

ALICE: Did you learn how to fly?

FINCH: Thankfully, no.

ALICE: Yes. Of course. The war.

FINCH: Lucky.

ALICE: Well. That's all?

FINCH: I guess so.

> *(A moment of awkward silence.)*

FINCH: What did you want when you were a girl?

ALICE: Dig a hole to China.

FINCH: Really?

ALICE: I started with a small spade and a beach bucket. I was very diligent.

FINCH: You still are. Diligent Alice.

ALICE: I only got as far as what looked like an open grave. And then my sister buried me alive. Now that was terrifying. I don't think she intended to, but I crawled into the hole. She put a handful of dirt in, I squeezed my eyes shut so the dirt wouldn't fall in. And soon I was completely covered.

FINCH: This is incredible.

ALICE: Only child's play.

FINCH: Did it scare you.

ALICE: To this day, I am terribly frightened of being buried alive.

FINCH: I imagine so.

> *(Awkward silence.)*

ALICE: The small talk is over.

FINCH: Yes it is.

ALICE: And so I offer you an alcoholic beverage.

FINCH: I don't drink.

ALICE: *(Disappointed.)* You don't.

FINCH: My mother is a drunk.

ALICE: *(More interested.)* She is?

FINCH: Oh yes. Never touch the stuff myself.

ALICE: Makes sense. I spoke with her on the phone. She didn't seem drunk.

FINCH: Gin. It makes you tight. Did she sound tight?

ALICE: She did a little.

FINCH: I put my arm around your shoulder.

> *(He does.)*

ALICE: Nice. Very nice.

FINCH: Scootch in a little.

ALICE: *(Bolts up.)* Should I put a record on.

FINCH: You could.

ALICE: Jazz?

FINCH: Oh no. Please not jazz. It makes me jittery.

ALICE: *(Disbelief.)* It makes you jittery?

FINCH: All jangled up.

ALICE: It's supposed to.

FINCH: I never thought of it that way before. I could use some jangling. Let's hear jazz.

("You Tempt Me" on a scratchy LP from off.)

(Alice sits again. Stands again.)

ALICE: I forgot the beverage.

FINCH: No you didn't.

ALICE: That's right. You don't drink.

(She sits again.)

FINCH: Are you nervous?

ALICE: A little.

FINCH: You don't need to be nervous.

ALICE: I'm expecting somebody else to show up.

FINCH: *You are?*

What a cad.

ALICE: We don't know Mr. Dali yet. A boy I knew a while ago. My sweetheart. A long time ago. He was a soldier. He's dead now.

FINCH: And he's going to show up.

ALICE: He might. He really might.

FINCH: In the meantime, I'll just. There, arm is back in position.

ALICE: Snuggle in. You're warm.

FINCH: Am I perspiring? I hope I'm not perspiring on your shoulder?

ALICE: Shhhhh.

(A moment of silence. Alice closes her eyes and leans in. He gently kisses her on the hair.)

ALICE: Do that again.

FINCH: Like this?

(He kisses her again.)

ALICE: Again.

Again.

Again.

(Getting faster.)

Again. Again. Again. Again.

Now.

On my lips.

(And Finch hesitates.)

FINCH: Wait.

(He sits up and starts to take off his shoes. As he is taking them off, Thorton appears from the couch. Thorton is holding a red rose.)

ALICE: Thorton, what a beautiful rose.

THORTON: Because I think you're beautiful.

ALICE: I want . . . Thorton . . . I want to kiss you!

THORTON: Alice. I want you to wait for me.

ALICE: I'm tired of waiting behind the barn. Why can't we go into town and share a banana malt?

THORTON: No, not behind the barn. Wait for me.

ALICE: Are you going somewhere?

THORTON: I'm going to make my way in the world. And when I come back, I'll be a hero, and if not that, then at least a man. And we'll get married.

ALICE: We'll get married?

THORTON: And we'll go dancing on Fridays.

And eventually my parents will like you.

ALICE: Your parents don't like me?

THORTON: They want me to date American girls.

ALICE: American girls? I am American!

THORTON: I know. Shhh. Someone's coming. Let's kiss.

(Alice and Thorton kiss.)

ALICE: You make me melt. Oh, Thorton.

FINCH: Did you call me Thorton?

ALICE: Again —

(They both are kissing her.)

ALICE: Again —

THORTON: Promise me you'll keep being my little Alice.

ALICE: Little Alice?

THORTON: You'll wait for me, exactly like you are. Will you say yes?

ALICE: I don't know what else to say.

THORTON: Shhhhh. Shhhh.

(Thorton exits.)

ALICE: I am so tired of waiting!

(Finch grabs her and kisses her. When he is finished, there is a pause. As if this gesture will solve everything.)

ALICE: John. What would our life be like together?

FINCH: It would be nice. I'd like a wife.

ALICE: A wife.

FINCH: Someone who acts like a wife. Yes.

ALICE: I don't cook.

FINCH: Then I'll cook.

ALICE: I don't clean.

FINCH: Then I'll clean.

ALICE: And what else.

FINCH: We could stroll in the park together.

ALICE: There isn't a park.

FINCH: We'll move to a place with a park.

ALICE: New York City has a park.

FINCH: You're right.

ALICE: Go on.

FINCH: That's all I know.

ALICE: A walk in the park?

FINCH: A fine place to start a relationship.

ALICE: Maybe so.

FINCH: And there will be more. If we're blessed. Two little children. And church on Sunday, And pot roast on Sunday. And piano lessons.

ALICE: Piano lessons?

FINCH: For the children.

ALICE: Isn't there more?

(A beat. Finch doesn't know what to say.)

ALICE: *Isn't there more?*

FINCH: This is a nice couch.

ALICE: Yes . . . it . . . was.

FINCH: Is.

ALICE: I'm selling it.

FINCH: You are?

ALICE: Big sale. Starts tomorrow.

FINCH: Why?

ALICE: There's got to be something different, John.

FINCH: Is there?

ALICE: Would you like to hear about the party I went to this weekend?

FINCH: Not necessary.

ALICE: I went swimming in the nude. Perhaps I had a bit too much to drink. Champagne. Mr. Dali was there. Wearing a snakeskin suit. Resplendent man. There were lots of people there. From the studio, waiters in the hotel. We met in his room. He really did rip up the carpet. And put the mattress on the floor. The champagne did something to me. It made me fascinating. Suddenly, the information I've been accumulating all these years, all these articles I've read in so many magazines. there was a place for it. A place for small talk. I was probably the best person there at small talk. I met a man from Egypt. He thought I should star in my own movie. What did he call it . . . *Alice in Wonderland,* which I though was incredibly amusing. And there was a lady, with some kind of title, maybe she was a duchess, who trains snakes and another lady, very rich. Covered with jewels. Salvador says gold and jewels are the same as excrement. But her emeralds, so many emeralds. She looked positively green with emeralds. Did you know the reason emeralds are green is that the air is really green if you examine it on a molecular level? Emeralds are frozen air. That's why they are so beautiful. It was a wonderful party.

FINCH: I'm glad.

ALICE: Did I mention I went swimming in the nude?

FINCH: You did.

ALICE: It shocks me, a little. But once I took off all my clothes. It all made sense. Suddenly, this existence of mine, my white couch, our date, the boy I loved, all of it, so very far away.

FINCH: Alice —

ALICE: I have a feeling that my life is going to change in a magnificent way.

Scene Four

The next Monday.

Finch is visibly tired. He's at his desk. There's something on his chair. It's clear on his face. He is horrified. For he thinks, for one terrifying moment that . . . He stands and examines it. It's a furry white cotton tail. He puts it on his desk. With relief. And then with some regret, jealousy. Irritation. He takes out a pair of scissors. Enormous scissors. It seems as if he may plunge the scissors into his heart. But instead, he plunges them into the wall behind him.

As if recent events have made a hole between this world and another. And voices —

ALICE: *Shall I never get any older than I am now? That'll be a comfort — never to be an old woman — but then — always to have lessons to learn!*

DUCHESS: *Off with her head!*

ALICE: *I'm falling, falling. Soon I may very well be near the earth's core — Good-bye feet!*

A jumble of Alice in Wonderland *noise.*

Alice enters. The noise stops.

ALICE: Good morning, Mr. Finch.

FINCH: Good morning, Alice. Here we are. Monday. How was your, uh . . . weekend?

ALICE: *(Yawns.)* Exhausting.

(A beat.)

ALICE: I see you found the cotton tail.

FINCH: Yes.

ALICE: Where was it.

FINCH: On my chair.

ALICE: I'm not crazy then. I knew I left it in the office.

FINCH: Why would you have a cotton tail, Alice?

(Alice laughs, remembering something naughty.)

FINCH: You are driving me mad. Punishing me with your goddam vitality. Sexuality. Whatever. Punishing me.

ALICE: Am I?

FINCH: Because I'm too . . . what was the word, pedestrian? Smug? Settled? Content?

ALICE: Scared. Did you want a cup of coffee this morning?

(Alice starts to exit.)

FINCH: Sit down, Alice. Please.

ALICE: All right.

(She sits at her desk. Finch exits and returns with a pot of tea. He takes a tray of baked goods from his desk. He sets the work table with tea paraphernalia.)

ALICE: What are you doing?

FINCH: We're having tea.

ALICE: But you drink coffee.

FINCH: And you drink tea. My attempt, however feeble, to remind us that we are civilized creatures, not fiends who run around with rabbit tails.

ALICE: *(Correcting him.)* Cotton tails. Rabbits don't have tails, per se.

FINCH: We live in a civilized world, Alice.

ALICE: No, we don't.

FINCH: I don't care that everything is suddenly upside down. I will prevail.

ALICE: Goodness gracious, you are dramatic. For a dormouse.

(And Dali enters.)

DALI: *(Opens eyes wide.)* Why are fifty small goblets filled with lukewarm milk hung on a rocking chair exactly the same as the plump thighs of Napoleon?

ALICE: I think I know.

DALI: You know or you think you know?

ALICE: That's right.

DALI: Not the same at all. I think I know is very different from I know what I think. You might just as well say that I like what I get is the same thing as I get what I like!

FINCH: *(Looking at Alice.)* Or that I see what I want is the same thing as I want what I see!

ALICE: Yes. Both.

DALI: I see what you mean. And she's described it perfectly. Why fifty small goblets filled with lukewarm milk hung on a rocking chair are exactly the same as the plump thighs of Napoleon.

ALICE: That's a relief. Please, gentlemen sit.

(They sit.)

ALICE: And now there's no place for Alice. I'll get a chair.

(She retrieves a chair.)

ALICE: Isn't this nice? Like being in another country.

FINCH: I haven't had tea, like this, since, goodness. I can't remember when.

DALI: I find that a tea party in the afternoon can add an element of civilization to any setting. Even Burbank.

FINCH: *(To Alice.)* Crumpet?

ALICE: No thank you. I'm reducing.

DALI: *(Takes a sweet.)* Now if we had met for tea at the beginning of my stay, I imagine it would have been quite civilized —

FINCH: This is *my* tea party!

DALI: Of course.

FINCH: And I have invited you both in the spirit of true artistic camaraderie.

(A beat of expectation.)

FINCH: Not to discuss Mr. Dali's work, which we all agree is important and invaluable. But my own. Which has been recently, for unknown reasons, difficult. Wonderland. I would like to discuss Wonderland. There, I've said it. Wonderland.

ALICE: What an interesting question.

DALI: Yes it is.

FINCH: What does Wonderland look like.

ALICE: I don't think that matters.

FINCH: Actually —

ALICE: What it looks like . . . it's what it's like. Goodness. I feel as if I know it, instinctively.

DALI: It looks like this studio!

FINCH: *(Dubious.)* It could. . . .

DALI: There. Dali has solved it.

ALICE: It should be beautiful. An escape from this ugly world.

DALI: Nonsense. There is nothing more beautiful than something that is profoundly ugly.

ALICE: *(Absentmindedly.)* There is nothing more ugly than something that is profoundly beautiful.

DALI: Bravo!

ALICE: There is nothing more real than that which is surreal. There is nothing more surreal than that which is real.

DALI: You are an excellent student, Miss Alice.

ALICE: I know.

FINCH: Wonderland. Are there trees in Wonderland?

ALICE: Upside down.

DALI: Right side up.

FINCH: What color is the sky?

DALI: Brown.

ALICE: Blue.

FINCH: And the animals.

DALI: They smile all the time.

FINCH: Certainly the cat does.

(Dali smiles at Finch.)

DALI: The cat and the finch.

ALICE: It should be filled with surprises.

DALI: Of course.

ALICE: And danger.

DALI: Shit.

FINCH: No. Not that.

(Dali shrugs.)

DALI: It's everywhere. Even Wonderland.

ALICE: Wonderland is a land filled with wonder. The quality of wondering. . . . A land filled with I wonder if . . . I wonder if. . . .

DALI: You can "wonder if" anywhere, Alice.

ALICE: Yes I know.

DALI: And "wondering if" doesn't get you anywhere.

FINCH: But there are certain questions that don't even deserve the wondering.

DALI: No there aren't.

ALICE: Oh maybe it's something far less obvious. Just a series of doors that open.

And when they do, you walk through. And as you walk through the rules, the silly rules that govern us, break down and as they disappear —

FINCH: Chaos reigns.

ALICE: Yes, chaos reigns.

DALI: *(Claps his hands.)* Magnificent!

FINCH: Mr. Dali, I think you preach chaos, but I think you live a very disciplined, structured life.

DALI: Do you?

ALICE: My sense of Mr. Dali is that he has a way of thinking that isn't logical. It's more like elastic. Everything . . . stretches. There are no rules in his world —

FINCH: Oh yes there are.

ALICE: No, I don't think so.

FINCH: He has rules about rules! And don't you forget it!

ALICE: Don't raise your voice —

FINCH: I'm not, Alice. I'm really not. Because that would imply that I was engaged in some sort of struggle for your heart. Which I'm not.

DALI: Excuse me, but what time is it?

(Finch takes a pocket watch from his pocket, checks it.)

FINCH: It's 1946.

ALICE: No, he asked for the TIME.

FINCH: And I said it's 1946.

ALICE: Mr. Finch. The time.

FINCH: 1946.

ALICE: *(Takes the watch.)* It says 1964, John.

FINCH: 1946.

ALICE: 1964.

(Dali takes the watch and puts it in his teacup.)

DALI: There. That settles that.

(Finch is stunned.)

FINCH: That pocket watch belonged to my grandfather.

DALI: Who cares.

FINCH: I care, very much. You've muddled the works now. A watch is not supposed to get WET.

DALI: You need to relax.

FINCH: Don't tell me to relax! I am relaxed!

ALICE: You're not.

FINCH: You can carry on the two of you together. Anarchists — that's what you are. Both of you. Watch yourself, Alice.

ALICE: Watch myself!

FINCH: Yes!

(And Finch exits.)

DALI: Do you have the answer to the riddle yet?

ALICE: What riddle?

DALI: How does Alice grow a mustache?

ALICE: No, I don't know the answer. How Alice grows a mustache.

(Dali presents her with a key.)

ALICE: Is this the answer?

DALI: I'm having a small party on Saturday night. I hope you can attend.

ALICE: A party?

DALI: A small party.

ALICE: Well thank you. I happen to be free on Saturday night. I'd love to attend.

DALI: I am delighted.

(He bows and exits, leaving Alice holding a key.)

Scene Five

The next Monday.

> *The office has transformed into a Surrealist landscape. The office is filled with the detritus of Dali — the objects from Alice's list drape the room.*

> *Finch enters. He miraculously finds his desk. He bravely attempts his hat, his coat, his orange. He calls out —*

FINCH: Alice?

(The door opens. It's Dali.)

DALI: I am precisely on time.

FINCH: I am sure you are.

DALI: Monday morning. Week number five! Dali has been here for more than one month.

FINCH: *(Distracted.)* Yes. I am aware.

DALI: Where is she?

FINCH: I don't know. She's late.

DALI: Most likely. And understandably.

FINCH: Why is that understandable?

(Dali is about to answer.)

FINCH: Never mind. She's late because she has the sniffles.

DALI: How was your weekend?

FINCH: Very fine. Thank you. Worked most of it. Deadline approaching.

DALI: Ah yes. The dead line.

(Dali draws on the wall.)

DALI: You see. Dead.

Dead line approaching.

FINCH: Why is it dead?

DALI: It doesn't have any life. The straight line. It is completely dead in art.

FINCH: Well, of course. That's obvious.

DALI: Dali never resists opportunity to teach about his life and thoughts.

FINCH: I've noticed.

DALI: Aren't you going to ask me about my weekend?

FINCH: No.

DALI: I rode on his model train. I sat upon it as if it were my mother's lap. He clapped his hands in glee!

FINCH: The secret of his success — he hasn't forgotten what it's like to feel the wonder of a child.

(Dali lies on the couch.)

DALI: Forgive me for noticing, but this office has taken on a certain familiar charm. What a comfortable davenport.

(Dali luxuriates horizontally.)

FINCH: Mr. Dali, we have a meeting scheduled.

DALI: I can meet on my back. It's my finest position.

FINCH: Very well. As you have mentioned, it is the fifth week of your stay here, and we are all quite curious as to the status of your project.

DALI: It is finished.

FINCH: Is it?

DALI: From beginning to end. With a very seductive middle I might add.

FINCH: Well that's fantastic. When do we get to see it?

DALI: When I put it on paper.

FINCH: I see.

DALI: There is nothing to see.

FINCH: Then we have a sort of situation.

DALI: Do we?

FINCH: According to your contract, there is need for a finished product.

DALI: Of course.

FINCH: But there is no finished product.

DALI: It is finished in my head. Now all that is required is for the minions to put it to paper.

FINCH: The *minions*.

DALI: I will tell you Dali's story.

It is a myth. It is a tragedy. It is a love story. As every story should be.

We begin at the edge of the world. Luminescent, phosphorescent, fluorescent, tumescent! The edge of the world looks like the cliffs of Dover. A watch running out of time. A drain sucking a sinkful of water.

The edge of the world. Stand on it and you will find yourself near the edge of death. Or life.

A young girl about to be an old woman. We are, each of us, the culmination of every instant, every part of our life, from the past to the future.

And, I might add, it's a moment I personally adore. When beauty flares for one brief fling before settling into something ordinary. My heroine. We first see her in a field, picking strange daisies as big as trees. She is oblivious to the eyes that gaze upon her. Eyes as large as the world. Eyes in the daisies. Eyes in her own eyes.

Chronos, the God of Time. Time looks like a blank watch, a portrait of a dead person, ice, a beautiful boy. He will be her lover.

What would you do if you stared Time in the eyes? What will she do when she stares into his eyes, which are like pearls and chocolate.

She sees him first in the flowers, and then in the sky. And perhaps someplace more ordinary. A swimming pool.

(Blue light of a swimming pool. A splash.)

First there is an introduction.

And then there is a seduction.

Seduction is a red cape.

You Tempt Me.

Seduction is a crevasse, wet with sweat.

Seduction is easy when Chronos is in the bed.

('You Tempt Me' from off. And laughter.)

The second movement is very seductive. I see a plethora of creatures, each more fantastic than the last. I want floozies and flotsam, daggers spitting out of the mouth of a tiger. Nipples like mountains, climbed by a kiss. A woman sodomized by her own chastity. A puddle of lust. A puddle of pride. A puddle from Paris. A puddle of puddles, each filled with desire.

The heroine of my story, I'd call her Alice only that would upset you. The heroine of my story and Chronos unite.

They make monsters together.

The monster of shame. Shame is a woman with a mustache and a cake on her head.

The monster of lust, a wet seal.

The monster of youth, which looks like a watch. Water rushing down a drain. A beautiful boy.

(The sound of ripping paper.)

The lust, shame and youth leak into the world, in a chaos of umbrellas shaking themselves of excrement.

And there is rain.

The sound of ripping paper.

You Tempt Me

And You Tempt Me.

And You Tempt Me.

There is blood. Perhaps.

There are tears

Which wash the earth clean.

And dissolve the story.

Leaving traces on the screen and in the memory. Of all that we search for. All that we love.

The sad sounds of violins.

(Dali, spent, throws himself again on the couch.)

DALI: Magnificent. That was magnificent.

FINCH: *(After a beat.)* Yes. It's, well, it's quite beautiful, I think, to look at.

DALI: Of course.

FINCH: Animation has never been used in such a way.

DALI: I know.

FINCH: A revolution of sorts.

DALI: Yes.

FINCH: It's like *Fantasia,* only it will be successful.

DALI: *Fantasia* is not successful.

FINCH: The critics hate it.

DALI: Not so with Dali. America loves me.

FINCH: What do you imagine the palette to be.

DALI: The colors of the body.

FINCH: Yes.

DALI: Many shades of various flesh. And ochre. And blue for the sky.

FINCH: The challenge will be how to make it something He will like.

DALI: Something I will like.

FINCH: Wonderful ideas, but they need some taming, don't you think? Goodness, I see it all. From start to finish.

DALI: I can imagine what you see.

FINCH: We have two weeks, Salvador. The deadline.

DALI: I do not worry about dead lines.

FINCH: Yes, but I do.

DALI: If it isn't finished, then I will ask for more money and stay for even longer.

FINCH: Do you know the time?

DALI: No.

FINCH: Because Alice is really late. I wonder if I should call her house?

DALI: How is the progress of Alice?

FINCH: There is no progress with Alice.

DALI: So much for your dead line.

FINCH: Alice — I want her. She doesn't want me.

DALI: Is she your shadow?

FINCH: No.

DALI: Then it is no good.

FINCH: She is my muse.

DALI: Ahh. Yes. But then she is your shadow, just as my Gala is. My Gala, the great true love of my life.

FINCH: Who is Gala?

DALI: My wife!

FINCH: Your wife. You love your wife?

DALI: I adore my wife. She is my 9th Symphony.

FINCH: That relieves me. I wondered if perhaps you and Alice —

DALI: No, no. Although.

FINCH: Although what.

(Dali is silent.)

FINCH: She mentioned to me that she went swimming. In the nude.

DALI: Yes.

FINCH: Tell me. Is there more?

DALI: Now you want me to tell you.

FINCH: Yes!

DALI: Oh, I have been amusing myself. That is all.

FINCH: With Alice?

DALI: Alice has been amusing herself and I have been amusing myself.

FINCH: Did you see her this weekend?

DALI: Yes. She was at my soirée.

FINCH: What the hell is a soirée?

DALI: I arrange for meetings to happen between my friends. That is all.

FINCH: She had a meeting? Like we had a meeting?

DALI: Similar in spirit, yes.

FINCH: Who did she have a meeting with?

DALI: A beautiful young man who works at the hotel.

FINCH: Is his name Thorton?

DALI: His name is Juan. Like your name, only wahhhn.

FINCH: Where was this meeting?

DALI: On my bed.

FINCH: Alice and a young man on your bed. What were they doing on your bed?

DALI: What one does on a bed.

FINCH: And you watched?

DALI: It is impossible for me to create without the stimulation of desire. And I told to you the results of such stimulation. You said yourself that it was the work of a genius.

FINCH: The work of a madman.

DALI: The only difference between a madman and myself is that I am not mad.

FINCH: Alice? My Alice? Not some other Alice?

DALI: It is imprinted on my imagination.

FINCH: Your imagination?

DALI: Yes, from start to finish. And now it is in your imagination.

FINCH: Yes it is.

DALI: Now what do you see?

FINCH: Impossible. Alice, well it's simply impossible.

DALI: Do you feel an octopus of gold sparkling with a thousand precious stones of anguish?

FINCH: (Surprised.) Yes.

DALI: Do you feel—

FINCH: It's none of your business what I feel!

DALI: Just think, if I had not told you my story, Alice would appear to you the way she always has. She would be a silver bell and now suddenly — she is what you always suspected — a ripe lobster.

FINCH: A lobster? Alice?

DALI: Exactly. This is Dali's method. To put two things together in the imagination in such a way as to change both forever.

FINCH: In the imagination?

DALI: Yes.

FINCH: So everything you've said is about your imagination?

DALI: Always. This is always the case.

FINCH: Everything you've told me is all just something to get to me, to shake me up. To affect me in some way so that the work starts to get interesting. Am I right?

DALI: Does it shake you up?

FINCH: Like an earthquake.

DALI: It is healthy to have the world crumble. Every once in a while.

FINCH: Alice is late, because . . . Alice is late. My god. You had me going . . . Mr. Dali your method. . . is understood.

DALI: Then we are ready to begin. I will provide you with master shapes and color configurations by Wednesday.

FINCH: I'll see who I can assemble. We'll draw and draw and draw and draw and see what we can do in the next week. I can't promise completion, but I think we can find at least fourteen seconds.

DALI: Miniscule!

FINCH: Enormous. Fourteen seconds is hundreds of drawings.

DALI: I want fourteen minutes.

FINCH: Impossible.

DALI: Everything is possible.

FINCH: Within limits.

(The men exit.)

Scene Six

The couch. An eerie blue light. A Caterpillar slithers out from between the pillows as if it's being born. Slither, slither. (The Caterpillar looks like the essence of a caterpillar, not like any cartoon version.) And then Alice emerges, feet first.

ALICE: Up! — Oh.

CATERPILLAR: *(Languid.)* Who are you?

ALICE: I'm Alice.

(And she sits.)

(A beat. She looks at the Caterpillar.)

ALICE: Are you a caterpillar?

CATERPILLAR: Very.

(And he slithers on top of her.)

ALICE: My. How very . . .interesting.

(The Caterpillar wraps himself around her.)

ALICE: Because if you are a caterpillar, I really shouldn't be doing this. In the office. In my office.

(He kisses her. She kisses him back, with some amount of desire. Caterpillar pins her to the couch, legs and arms akimbo.)

ALICE: Oh.

CATERPILLAR: Will you marry me?

ALICE: Marry you? Well, I don't think so. I can't, you see. It's impossible.

CATERPILLAR: *(Warning her.)* Don't tarry, dear.

(And he sits up and lights his hookah. The stage fills with smoke.)

ALICE: Dear John.

CATERPILLAR: Dear Juan.

ALICE: *(Insistent.)* Dear John. Shh. Shh.

CATERPILLAR: Shh, shh.

(And the Caterpillar disappears into the couch, taking Alice with him.)

Scene Seven

The next Monday.

Dawn. Finch is in the office. He appears as if he's been in the office, every day for the last week. He is half asleep — half awake. He clutches a piece of yellow paper.

Alice in Wonderland, *through the hole in the wall.*

ALICE: It was much pleasanter at home, when I wasn't always getting bigger and smaller and being ordered around by mice and rabbits! I almost wish I hadn't gone down that rabbit hole — and yet — it's rather curious, you know this sort of life! I do wonder about what has happened to me!

FINCH: Alice.

ALICE: What.

FINCH: Will you sit on my lap?

ALICE: I most certainly will not.

FINCH: Why?

ALICE: Because I don't want to.

FINCH: Will you climb out of the wall, then? So I can see you.

ALICE: I'm stuck. I'm real big now. And there's not much more room to get any bigger.

FINCH: Will you accept my apology?

ALICE: Will you stop saying I'm sorry.

FINCH: All right. Sorry.

(Alice screams with frustration.)

ALICE: Ohhh — you make me so —

FINCH: Shhh. Please don't scream. It's too early and I haven't had my coffee.

ALICE: Would you like me to get you a cup?

FINCH: Oh that would be nice.

(Dubious.) But can you?

(The door bursts open.)

DALI: Finch! Where are you GODDAM IT!

(Alice is gone.)

FINCH: I'm here. Where I've been for the past 144 hours.

DALI: I had a thought.

FINCH: A thought?

DALI: About the second movement.

(Music from off, from the second movement.)

FINCH: Is that you, Salvador?

DALI: Of course it is.

FINCH: Salvador Dali. In my office.

DALI: Yes. It is amazing. I agree.

FINCH: I wonder what it would be like if you never came.

DALI: Impossible to consider.

FINCH: Is it?

DALI: It's all wrong.

FINCH: What do you mean.

DALI: You seem tired.

FINCH: I am tired!

DALI: You need a shower.

FINCH: Of course I need a shower! I told you, I've been here for six days and seven nights.

(Finch approaches Dali like he's going to throttle him. Instead, he catches a whiff —)

FINCH: (Continuing.) You smell. Like . . . roses. Is that worrisome? Is that supposed to mean something awful, like I'm on the verge of death, the scent of roses?

DALI: It's orange blossom water. From Seville. I douse myself with it after my ablutions.

FINCH: I'm sorry?

DALI: My morning wash.

FINCH: When did you have time for a morning wash.

DALI: This morning. Earlier.

FINCH: Where did this morning wash occur?

DALI: At the hotel, of course. Along with my customary hot tea and chocolate croissant.

(*A beat.*)

FINCH: *(Snarling.)* Did you sleep well?

DALI: I never sleep well.

FINCH: Good!

DALI: Especially not last night. I was positively dizzy about the second movement —

FINCH: I don't want to hear what you're going to say.

DALI: It has to be changed.

FINCH: Impossible.

DALI: The red is wrong. The balance of the entire section is off.

FINCH: Off? It moves like the wind.

DALI: Precisely.

FINCH: Is it a pacing thing?

DALI: It is an everything thing.

FINCH: We can correct the color.

DALI: I am thinking first about the bell man. The manner is incorrect. He's a bell. He should ring.

FINCH: He does ring.

DALI: In a very melancholy way.

FINCH: You said it should be melancholy.

DALI: I was wrong. It should be bright. Ding ding ding ding ding ding —

FINCH: You said melancholy. Ding ding ding.

DALI: Faster.

FINCH: *(Helpful.)* We can make it faster.

DALI: And then the jellyfish.

FINCH: I'm pleased with the jellyfish.

DALI: How does a jellyfish move.

FINCH: I'm not sure what you're getting at —

DALI: Does a jellyfish climb trees?

FINCH: Is this a test?

DALI: Does it move like a squirrel?

FINCH: Are you getting at something here?

DALI: The jellyfish should move like a jellyfish. Not like a squirrel.

FINCH: *(Slowly.)* It should move like it's a jellyfish instead of squirrel?

DALI: Yes!

FINCH: Did not you say specifically that it should — scurry — I think was the word you used? Scurry? Does a jellyfish scurry?

DALI: If it's in a hurry.

(A beat.)

FINCH: No.

DALI: And the entire character of the floozie is wrong. Wrong. It's a floozie —

FINCH: That's why it's red!

DALI: Where is the languor?

FINCH: We're saving it for the sloth.

DALI: What is the primary quality of a sloth?

FINCH: Slothfulness.

DALI: This is my point exactly. And I want to make certain that the sloth doesn't look like a sloth!

FINCH: Nothing looks like it's supposed to —

DALI: Except for the floozie, which blurts out *floozie!!*

FINCH: That's what I thought you wanted. You said languor, you said floozie!

DALI: And you delivered a red squirrel!

FINCH: Are you sure you're not confusing this with the squirre?

DALI: *(Incredulous.)* There's a squirrel!?

FINCH: Maybe I'm not remembering correctly.

DALI: THERE'S A SQUIRREL AND A FLOOZIE BEHAVING LIKE A SQUIRREL!!!

FINCH: Apparently.

DALI: Let me explain to you my feelings. I am MISERABLE. Not only is the second movement ENTIRELY WRONG, there has been an invasion of squirrels.

FINCH: The squirrel refers to a shape that actually looks far more like a spoon.

DALI: *(Wailing.)* A SPOON!!

FINCH: *(Soft.)* A spoon.

DALI: Never in my life have I even uttered such an odious word. Spoon!! My brilliant ballet is going to be called the dancing nature show, with table setting! A SPOON!!!

FINCH: Yes. A SPOON!

DALI: I have never been in more incompetent hands.

FINCH: I'm sorry, did you say incompetent?

DALI: I did.

FINCH: Because myself, myself and my team has generated close to 700 drawings in the past week. And you think that's incompetent?

DALI: Yes. Anybody can generate drawings.

FINCH: (*With righteous dignity.*) No, Salvador. *Anyone* can't. The team of artists attached to your project may be composed of nameless, pimpled young men wearing thick spectacles, but let me assure you, they are among the finest artists this country has to offer. Crackerjack artists. Boys dripping with imagination and references to Greek myth and animal behavior. Boys that know information on the tango, the papaya, the mating habits of skunks, Wittgenstein, and pickles. There is no better artistic think tank in this country. You are working with the absolute TOP of the HEAP. You are lucky to be in our presence, you and your snakeskin soul. We are taking the scribbles you take out of your pockets, smudged with GOD KNOWS WHAT, and we are transforming them into reality. Into more than reality. Into art.

DALI: Where's Alice? Has she left you?

(*Finch clutching a piece of paper, which he waves in front of Dali.*)

FINCH: She's VISITING HER MOTHER!! IN OKLAHOMA!

(*Finch grabs Dali, shakes him, and throws him out the window. This is what you might call a "cartoon moment," and should be played as such. And then, Dali enters through the door, as if the previous never happened. He assumes the same position as before and asks —*)

DALI: Where's Alice?

FINCH: She is visiting her mother. In Oklahoma.

(*Finch shows Dali the door.*)

DALI: (*As he exits.*) It is better, my friend, to die of love than to love without regret.

(*And Dali slams the door and then Finch unfolds the letter. Which is from Alice.*)

FINCH: (*Tenderly.*) Dear John —

(*We hear Alice from off — the two of them sing a duet/notes are indicated.*)

ALICE: Dear John. (C-A)

FINCH: Dear dear John. My dear John.

(C-C-A. C-C-A)

ALICE: I'm sorry, but I will be out —

(F-G-A-F-A-A-G-F)

FINCH: Dear John. She thinks I'm dear —

(C-A. A-A-A-A)

ALICE: for the following week —

(F-G-A-A-A-F)

FINCH: I will be far, but my heart is near.

(A-A-A-A-F-G-A-G-F)

214 Kira Obolensky

ALICE: My mother is sick —
    (C-A-F-F-G)
FINCH: Her mother is sick —
    (C-A-F-F-G)
ALICE: With a bad case of gout —
    (C-C-C-C-C-C)
FINCH: Poor Alice, her mother is ill; her mother has gout!
    (C-A-F-F-F-F-F-F-F-F-F-F-F-F)
ALICE: Love, Alice.
    (C-A-F)
FINCH: Love, Alice.
    (C-A-F)
    LOVE, Alice. I love Alice.
    (C-A-F. F-C-A-F)

Scene Eight

The last Monday.
    The office is a mess. But the lobsters are gone. Finch is a mess. He sits, forlorn, at Alice's desk.
    And then Alice enters. She is wearing a light blue suit.

ALICE: Good morning, John. Sorry I'm late.
FINCH: Good morning, Alice.
    (Finch is stunned. They stare at each other. Alice approaches her desk. Finch returns to his desk.)
FINCH: Well. Here we are. Mon . . . . day.
    Did you? . . . Did you . . . did you . . . did you . . . have a nice week away?
ALICE: Fine. Actually, I was at the hospital.
FINCH: You were ?
ALICE: My mother. Appendicitis.
FINCH: Oh. That's right. I thought you said gout.
ALICE: Did I? No. Appendicitis.
FINCH: I'm sorry. Gosh. Is she okay?
ALICE: They took it out. It was the size of an apple. The doctor actually showed
    it to me. In a metal tray.
FINCH: He actually showed it to you? What is the world coming to?

ALICE: Oh it didn't alarm me. It was satisfying. And mother couldn't get over it. She'll be describing it for the rest of her life.

FINCH: I imagine so. The size of an apple!

ALICE: Bigger.

FINCH: Gosh. And you came back? You returned.

ALICE: Of course I did. I'm certainly not going to stay in Oklahoma.

FINCH: Why should you? A woman like you. That is a very attractive color you are wearing.

ALICE: Is it?

FINCH: Oh yes. What do you call that color?

ALICE: Blue. Light blue.

FINCH: Very becoming. I missed you, Alice.

ALICE: Thank you, Mr. Finch.

(The "Mr. Finch" is a slight wound. Finch becomes businesslike.)

FINCH: Your skills, I missed them last week. You've never witnessed such a week. Like a tornado.

ALICE: The office looks like a dump. I'm not going to clean it up.

FINCH: No. I sort of like it this way. All out of whack.

(Alice is silent.)

FINCH: His project. All fourteen seconds of it. All fourteen brilliant seconds. Supreme. Positively a light shining in what has been the dark closet of my mind. The lyric quality. The humor. The strange juxtapositions of umbrellas and pigs feet. There on the drawing table. The strange combinations of things. That's how he thinks. How can I put two things together in such a way as to change both forever.

ALICE: Pig sties and umbrella feet?

FINCH: Exactly! Oh, he is a son of a bitch. Forgive me for swearing, but this last week was . . . I've never experienced anything like it. And he broke me down before we even started. He told me all sorts of odd stories . . . some of them quite horrible. About people I care about. He broke me down so I would do his work. I did it, and I have come out the other side unscathed. And you, Alice?

ALICE: No questions. Asked or answered.

FINCH: I can respect that.

ALICE: You will.

FINCH: Even though it would be very interesting to discuss various things. Interesting. Just the way you like it.

(Alice's eyes well up with tears. She takes a hanky out and dabs at them.)

FINCH: Are you okay? I'm sorry. That's not a question —

ALICE: I am extremely sensitive to mildew. Has there been moisture in this office?

FINCH: On Thursday we flooded the office so we could swim. And record the movement.

ALICE: I thought so. I have a very sensitive nose.

FINCH: I know! I used it as the model for the rabbit.

ALICE: For the rabbit?

FINCH: The way it . . . twitches. Yes.

ALICE: No woman likes to be told she's a rabbit. Just as no man likes to be told he's a mouse.

FINCH: Water under the bridge, Alice. I have totally recovered from that reference. I'm certain you didn't mean it. I understand the sort of stress you've been under lately —

ALICE: Understand the sort of stress? What is that supposed to mean?

FINCH: Nothing. Really.

ALICE: Because I don't think you can understand the sort of stress a woman like me feels at this particular point in her life when she discovers that the high point of her life is skinnydipping in a hotel swimming pool with a bunch of drunks!

FINCH: I liked it better the way you described it before.

ALICE: I went to the hotel this morning. And that whole place, the splendid magical beautiful place had melted. The swimming pool was dirty. The lobby was smoky. The people were all checking out. And no one recognized me. As if I were very small. So small I was invisible.

FINCH: I'm going to make her dress blue. That blue. The one you're wearing.

ALICE: Whose dress?

FINCH: Alice's.

ALICE: You are?

FINCH: We'll be the only two who know. That's how Alice's dress came to be that particular shade of blue.

ALICE: Well that's nice. That is nice. But it doesn't make up for the rest of it. For me.

FINCH: Oh come on.

ALICE: No really, John. It's shocking the way I've been always wanting life to be different. And now everything is . . . different. And there's no place for Alice.

FINCH: Well. I'm not sure what that means.

(Alice doesn't respond.)

FINCH: I've been thinking about us, Alice. You're right. It's silly the way I am.

Falling asleep when I should be awake. I didn't sleep the entire week you were gone.

ALICE: Sounds like you've been thinking about you.

FINCH: I have been thinking about you.

(Silence from Alice.)

Did you think about me, Alice? Even for a minute?

(But she doesn't say anything.)

FINCH: You know, everything absolutely everything worked better when we maintained a professional distance.

ALICE: Yes it did.

FINCH: Without professional distance, nothing can be accomplished.

ALICE: I agree.

FINCH: And nothing has been right since we . . . since I fell in love with you. Nothing.

ALICE: I agree.

FINCH: I feel like a fool most of the time —

Am I a fool, Alice? Is that all I am to you?

(A beat.)

ALICE: (Simply.) No.

FINCH: Well. That's good. I'm glad. Anyway, I've been thinking about Alice, Alice. Alice in Wonderland. It *was* too vanilla pudding. There are some changes I'd like to make, fundamental changes in how the story is told.

ALICE: Sure.

FINCH: Sure?

ALICE: Sure.

FINCH: I was thinking about that whole tea party scene. It might be fun to introduce all sorts of things, like melting clocks.

ALICE: Did you want me to get you a cup of coffee?

FINCH: No.

ALICE: All right.

(Alice sits again. She checks the clock. And takes out her lunch bag.)

ALICE: It's lunch time.

FINCH: Look at that. Are you going out?

ALICE: No, I brought a bag. Thought I'd eat at my desk. Try and get organized.

FINCH: I brought mine today, too. I'll do the same thing.

(Both Finch and Alice take sandwiches out of their bags. They clear space from their desks and begin to unwrap.

FINCH: *(Examining his sandwich.)* Peanut butter and grape jelly. What do you have?

ALICE: Lobster salad.

FINCH: Lobster salad?

(And Finch notices the lobsters are gone.)

ALICE: It's my special recipe. Mayonnaise. Celery. And grapes. Something to surprise the tastebuds.

FINCH: Well that certainly sounds fancy.

ALICE: It is fancy.

FINCH: I'm trying to remember the lobster thing, from Alice. How does it go? *It's the voice of the lobster, I heard him declare, blah blah too brown, I must blah blah my hair —*

ALICE: That's not it.

FINCH: How does it go, then? *It's the voice of the lobster, I heard him declare —*

ALICE: *You have baked me too brown, I must sugar my hair.*

(And Alice takes out a Life *magazine. She sits back and opens it. She brings the magazine up, so that it covers her face. We see the word* Life, *clutched by two hands. Finch, munching on his sandwich, looking at Alice, as the play ends.)*

END OF PLAY

FALL
by Bridget Carpenter

You're walking. And you don't always realize it,
but you're always falling.
With each step, you fall forward slightly.
And then you catch yourself from falling.
Over and over, you're falling.

— Laurie Anderson
Walking & Falling

ORIGINAL PRODUCTION

Fall was originally presented in developmental readings as part of the 1999 US West Theatrefest produced by the Denver Center Theatre Company, New Works Now! at the New York Shakespeare Festival/Public Theater, and the 1999 New Work Festival at the Center Theatre Group/Mark Taper Forum.

The world premiere of *Fall* was at the Trinity Repertory Company, Oskar Eustis artistic director, Neal Baron, director; Eugene Lee, set designer; Yael Lubetzky, lighting designer; Sharon Jenkins, choreographer; Marilyn Salvatore, costume designer; David Van Tieghem, music and sound designer; FOY flying, design; Rosetta E. R. Lee, stage manager; and Ruth E. Sternberg, production stage manager. The cast was as follows:

LEAD and FOLLOW	Jones and Boyce
JILL	Anne Scurria*
DOG	Dan Welch*
LYDIA	Ari Graynor*
GOPAL	Ronobir Lahiri*
MR. GONZALES	Mauro Hantman*

* *denotes members of Actors' Equity Association*

BIOGRAPHY

Bridget Carpenter is a member of New Dramatists. Her latest play *Fall* is the recipient of the Susan Smith Blackburn Prize and had its world premiere Spring 2001 at Trinity Repertory Company in Providence, Rhode Island. Recently the NEA/TCG Playwright in Residence at the Guthrie Theater, she is also the recipient of a 1997 Princess Grace Playwriting Award. Other prizes include two Jerome Fellowships, a Minnesota State Arts Board Artist Grant, a McKnight Advancement Grant, a Ford Foundation Grant, and an NEA Arts Corps Fellowship.

Her work has been produced and developed at Arena Stage, Berkeley Repertory Company, Center Stage, the Getty Center, Shakespeare & Company, Joseph Papp's Public Theater New Works Now!, the Mark Taper Forum's New Works Festival & Taper, too, ASK Theatre Projects, and the Denver Center Theatre Company, among other venues. Recent plays include *The Death of the Father of Psychoanalysis (& Anna), Mr. Xmas, Typhoid Mary, West,* and *Tiny.* With composer Libby Larsen, she has recently completed *Barnum's Bird,* a commissioned opera liberetto to be produced in 2001 in Minneapolis and Washington DC.

As a director Bridget has directed new plays in Los Angeles at The Actors' Gang, as well as theaters in Austin, Providence, and Minneapolis. She holds an M.F.A. in Creative Writing from Brown University and has taught playwriting in grammer school, high school, college, and prison.

Bridget, born in New York, is based in Los Angeles. Currently she is completing a new play commission for the Atlantic Theater Company and *Fall* will be seen this season at Berkeley Repertory Company and Center Stage with Lisa Peterson directing.

CHARACTERS

LYDIA: Fourteen.
JILL: Thirty-four.
DOG: Forty-four.
GOPAL: Twenty-four.
MR. GONZALES: Twenty-four.
LEAD
FOLLOW

TIME

Late summer. The present.

PLACE

Southern California

SETTING

Outside, inside, around, and about an enormous 1920 ballroom that overlooks the sea.

There is a wide-open camp feel.

DANCE NOTES

Swing is a general term — an umbrella designation for many specific dances: Lindy Hop, East Coast Swing, West Coast Swing, Shag, Balboa, the Big Apple, to name a few.

"Lindy Hop" is a *specific* dance. There are times I have used *lindy* as a verb ("Lead and Follow lindy through the room"), and where this occurs, I envision the dancers to be Lindy hopping, rather than six-count swinging, or some other variation.

The characters in this play do *not* have to be professional dancers (that's why Lead and Follow are there). But actors should understand the rudiments of moving in rhythm.

Please, please: If you are producing this play, learn about the Lindy Hop. Watch videos of Frankie Manning, father of the Lindy Hop and originator of the aerial. Learn the steps to the Shim Sham. Hire wonderful Lindy Hoppers who are savvy swing dancers and can demonstrate style to the actors. And above all, be brave: Go out swing dancing; observe — and partner with — as many dancers as possible to get a sense of the wide range of dance styles.

CHARACTER NOTES

Lead and Follow are nonspeaking roles. They are *superb* swing dancers, to be used in transitions and the background of many scenes.

Jill is sexy and wears cute clothes.

Gopal's parents are from India. Everyone is from California. People speak with a standard American accent, whatever that means.

MUSIC NOTES

Scene titles are often songs which I was listening to when I wrote the scene, thus, something from the song may have found its way onto the page. It is *not* essential (indeed, it's inadvisable) to use the particular song to underscore the scene in production.

Exquisite, exuberant, joyous period swing music and dance is essential to this world. At times movement and music may take over. Actors might keep in mind that swing should be easy like breath.

AUTHOR NOTE

Fall was written during a Princess Grace Fellowship in residence at New Dramatists in New York City.

Innumerable thanks go to Daniel Alexander Jones and Maria Mileaf, my first, priceless readers. To Cindy Geiger, swing instructor extraordinaire, and Lindy Bruce Moreira, erstwhile partner in the midwest. To Julie-Anne Robinson, who hosted me in London while I completed *Fall* and who put together a reading the day after I finished it. To Mimi Kilgore and the generous patrons of the Susan Smith Blackburn Prize. And to the fine actors who read *Fall* and gave feedback during its development.

Most important, thanks to all my dance partners from Tapestry, Mario's, Jitterbugs, the 100 Club, Irving Plaza, Swing 46, and many, many more; I was listening, every moment, every breath. Thank you.

FALL

Scene One: Honeysuckle Rose

Ella Fitzgerald's version of "Honeysuckle Rose" *plays.*

Jill stands in a suburban bedroom, packing clothes in a suitcase. She's wearing a "do-rag." She seems not to hear the music, but once the horns kick in she does a break that shows she's been listening all along. Now her movements are in perfect time. She adds a little footwork, nice and easy. She hears a noise, looks up: It's Dog, he's thrown his jacket aside and is holding out his arms. Like a musical.

One jump and they're together in perfect time. They do a respectable six-count swing, the occasional fancy move thrown in — maybe Jill's a little better than Dog. They look good together. They dance a while.

Lights come up on Lydia, separate.

LYDIA: *(Calling.)* Jill! *Jill!*

(Throughout the following conversation, Jill and Dog dance.)

JILL: Are you all packed, honey?

(To Dog.) You know why she's calling me by my first name now? Because she knows I hate it.

LYDIA: I'm not going!

DOG: We talked about this Lydia, you are too going.

LYDIA: I have scuba lessons! I can't miss them!

JILL: *(Calling.)* They have scuba instruction there, I checked.

(To Dog.) She's mad at me.

DOG: At you? Her mother? No.

LYDIA: This camp will make me miss the first TWO DAYS of fall term of my *freshman year,* Jill! That's socially handicaping me for life.

JILL: I'll write you a note.

LYDIA: Explaining that I'm not in school because I had to *swing.* With my *parents.* That'll get me in with Kool and the Gang. Let's just tattoo "winner!" on my forehead.

DOG: *(Dancing.)* It's family camp, Lids. We're a family.

LYDIA: We're not the *Partridge* family! I don't want to learn your stupid dance so we can take an act on the road!

DOG: *(To Jill.)* Now there's a thought. She could play a tambourine. Lids, come on in here! Dance with your old man!

LYDIA: No way, Dad.

JILL: She calls you Dad. I don't get it.

DOG: I'll teach you a step . . .

LYDIA: I. DON'T. WANT. TO. GO. TO. SWING. CAMP!
God! Three weeks of SWING. It's like you *want* me to be an outcast.

JILL: Three weeks on a family vacation, and you'll miss two days of school. It happens all the time.

LYDIA: Why aren't you two into the Grateful Dead like normal people your age?

JILL: *(Gritting teeth.)* It's going to be fun, Lydia!

DOG: *(Calling.)* That's right, sweetie! You're going to have fun with your mother and me if we have to beat it into you with a stick!

LYDIA: When did you lose your connection to your own people?

JILL: Mr. and Mrs. Gonzales are going to be there.

LYDIA: Those are *your* friends!

JILL: The Gonzales' have a little girl, remember?. You like Nina.

LYDIA: Jill. She's five. I'm fourteen. Are you smoking crack again?

JILL: Don't ask if I'm smoking crack!
(She stops dancing to talk to Lydia.)

DOG: (Oh, here it comes.)
(Lydia sees her mother and starts to laugh.)

JILL: What is with you?

LYDIA: Nothing, Aunt Jemima. Can I have some pancakes?

JILL: Okay! That talk is unacceptable!

LYDIA: What talk? I'm making an observation.

JILL: A racist observation!

LYDIA: It's not racist, it's astute.

JILL: You are being disparaging and disrespectful.

LYDIA: *(Giggling.)* What do you want me to call you, Rosie the Riveter?

JILL: I want you to call me Mom. Why are you always behaving this way to me?

LYDIA: Why are you always doing things for yourself, and pretending it's for me, when it's not?

JILL: This camp is for *all* of us.

LYDIA: Sorry I'm not the flawless dancing daughter you want.

JILL: I want my flawless daughter to *pack*.

LYDIA: I'm not going!
(The final straw.)

JILL: You are going to swing camp with your father and me. This is our *family time*. Don't fuck with family time. Is that clear?

LYDIA: You. Are ruining. My life.

(Lights out on Lydia. Dog checks his watch.)
DOG: Refresh my memory. She's fourteen?
JILL: Last I checked.
DOG: So we're right on time.
(The bedroom scatters; the ballroom becomes apparent.)

Scene Two: The Bends

LYDIA: There was this scuba documentary. And this diver got the bends. His
tank was empty — he panicked — he had to release his weights. Too fast.
Too fast. He fell *up* — through schools of silver fish — he fell toward the
sky.

There are two parts to the bends. There are the rushes, which means
nitrogen bubbles have gotten in your blood. Rushes are not fatal, but you
feel prickly, like ants are crawling on your skin. My scuba teacher said it's
sort of horrible and exciting at the same time.

But. Full-on bends. Are different. Nitrogen is no longer just in your
blood — it's now in your joints and in your muscle tissues, and it's like
you've shaken up a can of coke and pricked it with a pin and the whole
thing explodes.

That is what happens to your body. It is fucked up.

Know why they call it the bends? Cause when it happens to you, you
bend.
(She clutches her stomach and bends over to demonstrate. Straightens up.)

The only sex I've ever had, and it wasn't really even sex, is the night
my grandmother died, I went over to Julie-Anne Mariano's house, and
we were all sitting there in the dark watching *Saturday Night Live* and pretending to drink Coors Light, and Sleazy Joe Rotella put his arm around
me and sort of tried to make out, but I didn't want to. So he took my
hand, and kissed my palm. And then for about a half hour he sort of sucked
on my fingers.

It was interesting.

Because I didn't like Sleazy Joe at all, I still don't, but I felt sad because
of my grandmother, and at the same time my stomach was jumpy and
excited.

Julie-Anne has had sex with four people since seventh grade. She says
it's no big deal, but if it's no big deal then why does she talk about it every

day of our whole lives? Every day. Blah-blah-blah-I-slept-with-four-guys. I'm all, I *know.* Jesus.

Julie-Anne says she had sex with those four guys because each time she fell in love.

I cannot believe I have to go to swing camp.

Scene Three: Walk Right In (Walk Right Out)

Gopal sits at a registration desk outside the ballroom, shuffling papers. Jill, Dog, and Lydia stand with bags. Music plays over a creaky PA system.

DOG: *(To Jill.)* . . . I had wings, and you didn't know who I was.

JILL: *(To Gopal.)* It's Joss . . . J-O-S-S

DOG: I said, "Jill, Jill — you can't resist me — let's dance" and you said, "I don't dance with strangers." And then I was at my desk, and the wings were gone, and so were all my papers.

JILL: Your dream ends up in the office.

GOPAL: Here's a map to the campsite.

DOG: . . . You were there, too.

LYDIA: Is this music playing *all the time?*

JILL: Zip it, Lydia.

LYDIA: Like the *Twilight Zone.*

DOG: *(Listening.)* I love this song.

LYDIA: You would.

DOG: You know, this is a famous ballroom. Movie stars used to come to this island.

LYDIA: *(Looking around.)* Children of the Corn. Children of the Swing.

GOPAL: You don't like to dance?

JILL: She's never tried.   LYDIA: You got it.

GOPAL: What's your name?

LYDIA: I don't remember. My mom hits me a lot, so I forget things.

JILL: *Lydia.*

(Gopal looks on his clipboard.)

GOPAL: Lydia. So you are Jill and . . . Dog. — Oh I'm sorry, this must be a typo —

LYDIA: No, my dad was switched at birth with a German shepherd.

JILL: Please excuse Lydia's bad manners. I'm Jill — you have it right — this is my husband Dog.

LYDIA: His name is Doug, but nobody calls him that. Because that would be too normal.

GOPAL: I'm Gopal.

LYDIA: *Gopal.* What's *that* mean?

GOPAL: Loosely translated, it means cowboy.

LYDIA: How about tightly translated.

GOPAL: Herder of cows.

(Dog laughs.)

LYDIA: You expect me to fall for that?

GOPAL: Everybody falls for something.

(Mr. Gonzales has arrived.)

DOG: Heyyy — it's the young Jack Gonzales.

MR. GONZALES: Hi, Dog. Jill.

JILL: Jack. Lydia, say hello to Mr. Gonzales.

LYDIA: Hello to Mr. Gonzales.

MR. GONZALES: Hi, Lydia.

(Tousles her hair. She moves away.)

JILL: She's in a rotten mood, don't pay any attention.

LYDIA: Isn't it weird, we only pay attention to the *good* moods? It seems unfair to leave all the other moods out. That must be why they're so pissy.

JILL: *(To Jack, pretending not to hear Lydia.)* Isn't this beautiful?

DOG: Hey, Jack, where's everybody else??

MR. GONZALES: Michelle and Nina are home. They — decided not to come.

DOG: Oh.

JILL: Oh.

LYDIA: What's up with *that.*

JILL: Lydia!

MR. GONZALES: I thought — you know — why waste the reservations —

DOG: Sure! You can take home a new move!

JACK: *(To Gopal.)* So it's just me.

GOPAL: Gonzales . . . here you go . . . and cross off. . . .

JACK: Michelle. And Nina. Right.

GOPAL: O-kay.

And swing passports for everybody!

(Gopal gives Jill, Dog, Mr. Gonzales, and Lydia tags which they cheerfully place around their necks. Lydia holds her neck tag out, staring at it in disbelief.)

LYDIA: Swing passports. I was wrong. This camp *is* cool.

(Jill pretends deafness.)

GOPAL: You guys are all set. The next session isn't 'til 3:30.

JILL: Lydia, why don't you register for your classes with Gopal, and Dog and I will go and explore camp.

LYDIA: *(Withering.)* Neat.

DOG: See you, kiddo!

(To Jack.) Why don't you follow us —

MR. GONZALES: . . . Okay.

(They exit. Lydia looks steadily at Gopal.)

LYDIA: So you're a swing kid?

GOPAL: Mm. I guess so.

(Lydia sighs heavily.)

LYDIA: You live here on this island: you are surrounded by the best diving ever: you *swing*. God. Have you ever gone scuba diving?

GOPAL: I teach scuba.

(Little pause.)

LYDIA: No way.

GOPAL: Sure.

LYDIA: You teach scuba here.

GOPAL: Well, I'm teaching dance this month, but usually, yeah.

LYDIA: You're *certified.*

GOPAL: Yeah.

LYDIA: Oh. . . . Why would you teach swing instead of scuba?

GOPAL: You can't be underwater all the time.

LYDIA: I wish. . . . My parents practice swing all the time. All the time. Every day.

GOPAL: I guess they want to be good.

LYDIA: I guess they want to be freaks.

(Gopal looks over some papers.)

LYDIA: Have you heard of spontaneous combustion?

GOPAL: I think so.

LYDIA: My friend Julie-Anne told me about this girl who got out of the pool and burst into flame. In thirty seconds she was a pile of ashes.

GOPAL: Right out of the pool, huh.

LYDIA: I read about it. Spontaneous combustion. It happens. Do you even know what it's like, being stranded here with your *parents?*

GOPAL: Yeah. I do. My family runs this place.

LYDIA: *Chh.* So how does it make you feel?

GOPAL: Useful.

LYDIA: Well it makes me feel invisible. Transparent. Like water.

GOPAL: But you're not.

(Little pause.)

LYDIA: So what dance classes should I take.

GOPAL: What do you want to take?

LYDIA: I *want* to take scuba, but that's only once a week.

GOPAL: How about beginning Lindy Hop?

(Lydia covers her face with her hands for a moment, horrified.)

LYDIA: This embarrasses me just to talk about. It is *so severely lame.*

(At this moment the Lead and Follow dance through. Clearly, they have been practicing for a long time. They glide through the registration area, doing the Lindy Hop gorgeously together. Lydia and Gopal watch them — the Lead and Follow are oblivious to everything but their own steps. After a wonderful, showstopping episode of dance, they dance out.)

LYDIA: Was that Lindy Hop?

GOPAL: Yeah.

LYDIA: Fine. Sign me up for that.

GOPAL: *(Smiling.)* Okay.

LYDIA: Just cause I have no idea what else to put down.

GOPAL: Right.

LYDIA: I still think it's lame.

GOPAL: Oh, I know.

(Music comes from the PA system, and a voice.)

PA VOICE: Those who have registered, come to the ballroom for an intermediate workshop in the Balboa!

(Lydia puts her head in her hands again.)

Scene Four

Lydia and Dog sit together. After a lesson.

DOG: That was good, huh? You did great, Lids.

LYDIA: You're such a bad liar, Dad.

DOG: Well. You *will* do great. It was just the first one. There's a lot more to come.

LYDIA: Goody gumdrops from the gumdrop tree.

Look, there's that guy Attilla. He was my partner today.

HEY ATTILLA!

(She waves.)

DOG: *(Hopefully.)* Good partner?

LYDIA: He writes science fiction as a *hobby*. Why not just say the words, "I'm an asocial weenie" and be done with it?

DOG: You might tone down the sarcasm, Lids, just for variety's sake.

LYDIA: I dance for an hour with a guy named Attilla and I can't say anything? Get real.

DOG: *(Sigh.)*

LYDIA: Are you and Jill going to break up?

DOG: Lydia WHY do you keep asking that? Your mother and I love each other very much. We love you very much. We're all here together, and we are going to stay here together. WHAT have we done to make you think we're breaking up?

LYDIA: Nothing. Just if it happens, I don't want to be surprised. *(Rest.)* Everything is about sex.

DOG: Ah, I don't think I caught that segue, honey.

LYDIA: It is. Sex, sex, sex, sex, sex, sex, sex, sex, sex, sex, sex, sex, sex, sex, sex, sex, sex, sex, sex, sex, sex. It's everywhere. It's disturbing.

(Dog is fairly uncomfortable.)

DOG: Lydia. honey. is there something you want to talk about? Because —

LYDIA: It's everywhere, you know, SEX — I just think it's *twisted* and I'm sick of it. All my friends — especially Julie-Anne — have this never-ending assessment of guys, this *debate* about whacking off, and whether it's just boys who do that, or whether *everybody* does it, or if we all just *think* about it, sex, sex, sex, sex —

DOG: I get it.

(Rest.)

LYDIA: I have my period. That's why I'm so moody.

(Dog gets more uncomfortable but tries to deal with it.)

DOG: Oh. Well. We can tell your mother and —

LYDIA: I've had my period for the last four years. Has Jill told you that?

DOG: *(Momentarily shocked.)* What?

LYDIA: I've been bleeding for four years. I mean bleeding *every single day*. "It'll stop soon," Jill told me. *Four years* without a break! Then I read that constant bleeding over several years often leads to spontaneous combustion —

(Okay, now he's pissed.)

DOG: *(Angry.)* That is enough, young lady.

LYDIA: I'm going to turn into a pile of ashes!

DOG: You want to be a moody teenager: fine. That's what I see. You want me to quit being understanding? Cause I can just be Dad — you know, the dad you *want*, the dummy who doesn't get anything.

(Lydia and Dog look at one another. Lydia looks repentant and sad. She leans forward, as though to impart a secret. Dog leans forward too.)

LYDIA: Have you ever wished you had a vagina?

DOG: *(Long exhalation of breath. He gets up and exits.)*

LYDIA: You think you see me, but you don't. You don't.

Scene Five: An Unheard Question

Dance class.
Gopal stands in front of the audience.

GOPAL: What you want is a state of *light resistance.*
Face your partner.
Hold your hands up.
Now, the *leads* should *push* with one hand.

All right it's resistance not rigor mortis.
Mrs. Clyde, you need to allow your husband to lead you.
— I'm sure that's unfamiliar.
Try again.
(Gopal watches. They're not good.)
Mr. Chin, *light* resistance.
Light tension, Ethyl.

Tension plus resistance equals momentum.
(The Lead and Follow come on. They dance slowly — Lead pushes, Follow spins. Follow pushes, Lead spins. They spin faster and faster until they are whirling in an arc, and it is impossible to tell who is pushing who.)

Scene Six: The Devil and the Deep Blue Sea

Underwater. Blue/green ocean light.
Lydia appears in snorkeling gear. She moves slowly, with wonder, reaching up to touch a fish. Lydia swims very slowly, blissful in the ocean. She reaches down to pick up a conch shell and places it to her ear.
There is the sound of swing music underwater.
Lydia hears this music. She tries desperately to swim away from the music, but cannot. She swims faster, faster; the music follows her as she goes.

Scene Seven

Lydia sits, legs dangling over the side of the wall. She wears snorkeling mask and has a tube in her mouth.

Mr. Gonzales approaches. He might be carrying a book, reading.

LYDIA: *(Something unintelligible with her mouthpiece in.)*
(No response.)

LYDIA: *(Something unintelligible with her mouthpiece in. LOUDER.)*

MR. GONZALES: So. Lydia. Hello.
(Lydia salutes.)

MR. GONZALES: Are you practicing your scuba?
(Lydia looks at him in utter disbelief. How can any adult be so stupid. She removes the snorkel from her mouth.)

LYDIA: *(Slowly, as though to a child.)* Well. First of all, this is snorkeling gear. Scuba requires a tank. Second, I'm not *in* the water. The ocean looks like it's, I don't know, five stories below. So no, I'm not practicing my *scuba*.

MR. GONZALES: I guess not.

LYDIA: How do you know my dad again? You're certainly not his *age*.

MR. GONZALES: I know your mom.

LYDIA: Uh huh.

MR. GONZALES: We work together. Teaching.

LYDIA: Uh huh. You guys, like, hang out in the faculty room. Drinking coffee.

MR. GONZALES: We're at the same school.

LYDIA: Uh huh. That is incredibly illuminating.
(Long pause.)

LYDIA: Thinking some big thoughts, huh.

MR. GONZALES: Oh I don't know.
(Long pause.)

LYDIA: Query. Do you have anyone to talk to? Like, do you actually *say* things. That are revealing.

MR. GONZALES: *(Shrug.)*
(Lydia waits.)

LYDIA: Well nice talking with you, Mr. Gonzales.
(Lydia replaces the snorkel mouthpiece and stares out to sea.)

Scene Eight

LYDIA: First scuba class today. First week. First ocean dive.

(Lydia beams with pleasure.)

I fall toward the ocean floor, slow.

Quiet underwater. Just the sound of my heart.

Thick. Heavy.

There are hundreds of tiny fish around me, thousands.

I touch a spiny cucumber that feels like moss.

My teacher looks at me, and makes the sign "okay" like "are you okay" and I make the sign back. Because I am. Okay.

I'm underwater. Jill's somewhere on the shore. No one sees me but the fish. I'm Okay.

Scene Nine: I'm Beginning to See the Light

Music. Gopal gives a private lesson to Jill and Dog. He's demonstrating the opening stance of an aerial.

GOPAL: To begin with, Dog, your center of balance should be low.

JILL: Ooh, Dog, you're vibrating.

(Wait a minute.)

JILL: You're *vibrating*.

DOG: Excuse me! I'm swinging.

JILL: I don't believe you.

DOG: What! Oh, I completely forgot that was there.

(Jill has answered his cell phone.)

JILL: Hello. Yeah, well he can't talk right now, he's dancing. Hi, Karl.

DOG: Oh, geez —

JILL: Have you pitched a *tent* in the office?

DOG: Honey!

JILL: I bet that's neat.

DOG: You see, she thinks this is funny.

JILL: No I don't. *(Back to phone.)* It must be fabulous there. At work. I mean why else would you call on *someone's vacation?*

(Dog grabs phone.)

DOG: Karl? Yeah, no, I'm sorry, what's up.

Well you need to tell them that's unacceptable.

(He looks at Jill.)

DOG: Karl, I've told you a thousand times, don't call me! I'm *dancing*, and *dancing comes first*. Talk to you in an hour.

(He hangs up theatrically.)

JILL: *(To Gopal.)* Does this happen to you often? Do other people bring their *phones* to class?

DOG: Hello? I hung up!

JILL: You did, didn't you. I'm going to give you a cookie.

DOG: Well, good.

GOPAL: So Dog, you need to lead this combination from a strong base.

DOG: I'm not so sure about this aerial moves stuff. . . .

JILL: You should try everything once.

DOG: *(Muttering.)* " . . . try everything once, except aerials and incest."

(Jill rolls her eyes.)

GOPAL: I think the saying is, "You should try everything once, except for *incest* and *folk dancing.*"

(Jill and Gopal think this is funny.)

DOG: Didn't I read somewhere about a guy killing his dance partner when he tried to flip her? Broke her neck.

JILL: Dog, don't be asinine.

DOG: I *read* something. . . .

GOPAL: That was years ago.

JILL: *What?*

GOPAL: *Kidding,* I'm kidding. You two are going to be fine.

DOG: I don't think we're advanced enough for this, hon.

JILL: Come *on,* I want to learn aerials! That's what we came here for! Aerials!

DOG: What *you* came here for.

(The following Dog/Jill lines occur simultaneously, ending with Dog's "I am here.")

JILL: *(Overlapping.)* It's supposed to be a vacation, a VACATION, and you insist on being half here, half somewhere else, I mean really!

DOG: *(Overlapping.)* Just because I feel nervous about picking you up and tossing you around does not mean I'm not on vacation — I *am* here!

(Gopal is starting to get uncomfortable.)

GOPAL: Now, to do aerials well, you have to trust your partner. . . .

DOG: Maybe you want to find another partner. Mr. Leo maybe, you can trust him.

JILL: You are being such a *baby!* I want *you* to be my partner.

DOG: It's *advanced.* It says so in the brochure. Advanced.

JILL: We're advancing!

GOPAL: These particular dance moves are about balance and momentum, not force.

DOG: Tell *her!*

JILL: (Jesus.)

GOPAL: You'll be going at your own pace . . .

JILL: *(To Dog.)* You have to attempt to *move* before you can pick a pace!

DOG: Hey. You know what, Jill? *You* pick a pace. I'm out of here.
    (He stomps out.)

JILL: *(Calling off.)* Where are you going!

DOG: *(From off.)* Tap!
    (Gopal and Jill are left in an awkward quiet.)

GOPAL: Um. That's a good class, tap.
    (Rest.)

GOPAL: We can still work on some support basics.
    (Rest.)

JILL: You know why I wanted to learn aerials?

    I want to be thrown *straight up.*

    Some people dream about having wings, or about being lost, or about running away to the circus.

    I dream about being swung out — swung up, and over, and letting go. Because when you're in the air like that, you're not somebody's teacher, or somebody's wife, or somebody's mother. You're just — whsssssshhhhh.
    (She closes her eyes.)

Scene Ten

The ballroom. Dance lighting. Lydia sits alone in a folding chair. Music.

PA VOICE: . . . so find a partner, and welcome to swing camp's dance-o-rama!!
    (Jill and Dog dance by, immersed in the music. They don't see Lydia. Mr. Gonzales approaches, stands by her, in his own world.)

LYDIA: Hi, Mr. Gonzales.

MR. GONZALES: Lydia.

LYDIA: *(Holds up her hand.)*

MR. GONZALES: Is anyone sitting in this chair?
    (Lydia gives a withering glance. Mr. Gonzales sits.)

MR. GONZALES: You're not wearing your snorkeling gear.

LYDIA: (Jesus.)

(They don't talk for a moment. They watch people dance. One song ends [clapping, cheers from off] and another begins.)

LYDIA: Mr. Gonzales. How come you're here alone?

MR. GONZALES: Well, Lydia. Good question.

LYDIA: But no answer.

MR. GONZALES: *(Shrugs.)*

LYDIA: There you go again. Chatty.

(He looks at her. She looks away.)

MR. GONZALES: Some concept, isn't it?

LYDIA: What.

MR. GONZALES: Whole room full of men and women, all of them getting along.

LYDIA: Huh.

MR. GONZALES: I imagine your parents didn't consult you before they planned your summer vacation.

(A steady gaze from Lydia.)

LYDIA: Are you trying to bond with me? Did my mother tell you to sit here?

MR. GONZALES: No.

LYDIA: You're gonna go dance, huh?

MR. GONZALES: Eventually.

LYDIA: How come you're not out there now?

(Mr. Gonzales doesn't know.)

MR. GONZALES: . . . I'd rather talk. To you.

LYDIA: Oh.

MR. GONZALES: What did your friends say about swing camp?

LYDIA: You think I *told* people? Think again.

MR. GONZALES: No one's going to be a bit curious over your missing the first couple days of school?

LYDIA: I told everyone I was getting a nose job.

MR. GONZALES: But you have a beautiful nose.

LYDIA: *Chh.* I'm not *really* getting a nose job. That's just what I'm telling people.

(She is secretly quite pleased at his statement.)

LYDIA: Lots of people get nose jobs at my school.

MR. GONZALES: Maybe lots of people at your school need nose jobs, but you're not one of them.

(She successfully hides her smile.)

LYDIA: Even if I did need one I wouldn't get it. Would you ever get one?

MR. GONZALES: Do you think I need one?

LYDIA: No.

MR. GONZALES: Whew. Good.

LYDIA: Don't make fun of me.

MR. GONZALES: I wasn't.

LYDIA: Okay.

MR. GONZALES: Okay.

(They watch the dancers.)

LYDIA: Do you ever think that swing dancing is like the revenge of the lames? Look at these people. Mr. Leo. Check out Mr. Leo.

(They watch Mr. Leo.)

MR. GONZALES: (Contemplative.) Mr. Leo can *swing.*

LYDIA: That's what I'm saying.

You see that guy over there? The eighty-four year old. Four feet tall.

MR. GONZALES: Dancing with the bald woman.

LYDIA: Right. That's Ethyl and Bob. They're from Lancaster: one vacation a year: Camp. This is a room filled with the most boring people alive.

MR. GONZALES: You dance with any of them?

LYDIA: No.

MR. GONZALES: Your mother can really —

LYDIA: Yeah I *know.*

MR. GONZALES: Hard to believe you're not up on your feet, too.

LYDIA: Nobody *asked.* (Beat.) Every person here dances better than me. I am so bad. Look at them. They . . . I don't get, get how just — they're *themselves* and so awkward and so —

MR. GONZALES: Pure.

LYDIA: Yeah. They are.

You'd never know how boring they are. It changes. When they start. The men just open their arms and the women fall. It's —

MR. GONZALES: Like a fairy tale.

LYDIA: Like that story about the twelve dancing princesses.

MR. GONZALES: Feet barely touching the ground.

(Both Lydia and Mr. Gonzales lean forward, transfixed. Then the spell is broken.)

LYDIA: It is so unfair. That I have to come here and watch them. Like it's not enough at home. They dance; I watch. Same old.

MR. GONZALES: It is unfair. I know exactly what you mean.

LYDIA: I'm invisible here. It fucking sucks.

(Dog and Jill dance by again. Dog waves merrily at Lydia.)

DOG: HI LIDS! (Blows her a kiss.)

BYE LIDS!

LYDIA: He is so disturbing. Do you know how embarrassing it is to have a father who *swings?*

MR. GONZALES: Can't say that I do.

> When I was fourteen, my father had me drink with him, man to man. And after a few beers, my father turned to me and said, I like your mother better than you. That's all. And I, uh, didn't say anything.
>
> *(They watch the dancers.)*

LYDIA: You know why I wouldn't ever get a nose job? Because I think it's important to like somebody *because* of their flaws. Not to *wait* until they're perfect. Not everything can be fixed. Not everybody learns how to dance.

MR. GONZALES: Not everybody tries.

LYDIA: *(A challenge.)* I think my parents are going to break up.

> *(Mr. Gonzales is taken aback but hides it.)*

MR. GONZALES: What makes you think that?

LYDIA: I don't know. I just do.

> *(She goes back to watching the dancers, sneaking a glance at Mr. Gonzales, who is watching Jill.)*

LYDIA: *(Pointedly.)* You know if you're gonna ask my *mother* to dance, you should find her before the next break. She's a woman in *demand*.

MR. GONZALES: Maybe later.

> *(Lydia looks away, shy.)*

LYDIA: Have you ever gone scuba diving?

MR. GONZALES: No.

LYDIA: You'd like it.

> *(Dance music changes. Clapping from off.)*

MR. GONZALES: You gonna take me?

LYDIA: "Maybe later."

> *(They sit companionably. Mr. Gonzales stands up.)*

MR. GONZALES: Well. Why don't we give it a try.

> *(He touches her nose, holds out his arms.)*

LYDIA: *(Internal freakout.)* Um, no. Thank you.

Scene Eleven

Jill and Lydia sit in arts and crafts. They are concentrating hard on making candles in milk cartons.

PA VOICE: Calling all swing kids: Wear your vintage finery to this week's dance and win a prize! And dancers, remember to give your feet a rest. If your dogs have been barking, take a break! You can weave a basket, throw a pot, and much more when you visit the Craft Hut!

JILL: Right now the kids have finished their spelling tests . . . and they're lining up for recess . . . and there's a teacher counting heads . . . and it's *not me.* Isn't this great?

LYDIA: We swing . . . we make sand candles. This is the best vacation of my whole life.

JILL: Lydia, don't use so much sand.

LYDIA: *(Disbelieving.)* You're an expert *candle maker,* too?

(Lydia begins to mutter to herself as Jill busies herself with her own candle.)

LYDIA: I'm sorry that I missed the issue of Martha Stewart Living that had the Big Candlemaking Exposé. Jesus. It's a sand candle, a five year old could do it, I mean, what's next, a seminar on *macrame?* Or maybe if I'm lucky I'll win a prize for a *pot* holder!

(Triumphant music swells over her words. Lydia stares. Over a crackled and strange PA system we hear:)

PA VOICE: And the Grand Jury First Prize for . . . Lydia, are you listening?

LYDIA: *(Unnerved.)* What?

PA VOICE: *(Overlap)* The Grand Jury First Prize for Amazing Candlemaking goes to . . . JILL!

LYDIA: *(Overlap)* No. No!

We are now deep inside Lydia's fantasy. Sounds of applause, whistles, trumpets. Gopal marches carrying a shiny, enormous, glittering candlemaking trophy that reads: JILL! Jill's hands fly to her face like the Miss America Pageant winners who are like "I don't believe it!" Music swells even louder. Jill accepts the trophy from Gopal.

JILL: *(Mouthing soundlessly.)* Thank you! Thank you so much. . . .

Dog is behind Gopal, carrying a garish banner that reads: #1 CANDLE MAKER. He waves it over Jill's head.

Jill clutches the trophy to her chest with emotion. Gopal and Dog are applauding. He holds out his arms; Jill puts down the trophy, takes Mr. Gonzales's hands and the two begin spinning in slow motion, like lovers in a meadow. Lydia watches, aghast.

Music shifts from triumphant to romantic.

Gopal keeps applauding, Dog keeps waving the banner; Jill and Mr. Gonzales keep whirling around and around wearing sappy expressions.

Music shifts, gets a bit static perhaps . . . a voice can be heard under the music . . .

P.A. VOICE: And there is once again a Grand Jury Prize for best vintage costume, so start planning now. We want to see you hepcats dressed to the nines!

Things have returned to normal. Gopal, Dog, Mr. Gonzales, and the Candlemaking Trophy are all gone. Jill is intent on her candle.

JILL: . . . I just think you want to have a wax-to-sand ratio that's higher on the wax . . . Lydia? Something the matter?

LYDIA: . . . it's just . . . those PA announcements are really annoying. They're freaky.
(Gopal enters.)

GOPAL: Hey, Lydia. Jill. Hm. If it's candles, it must be Tuesday.

JILL: Hi, Gopal.

LYDIA: It's Cowboy.
(He sits and begins knotting small pieces of plastic.)

JILL: You're not teaching right now?

GOPAL: My mom likes it when I help her out in arts and crafts.

JILL: See, some people help their mothers.

LYDIA: Yeah, Gopal is perfect. What are you making?

GOPAL: A lanyard.

LYDIA: And what is that?

GOPAL: . . . .I don't know.
(He takes a key chain out of his pocket. There are perhaps twenty other lanyards on it. He adds his new one.)

JILL: God, the air is different here. You probably don't notice — you're here all summer. So it doesn't feel *different* to you. This is your normal. Lucky.

LYDIA: Chh. How long have you worked here?

GOPAL: Probably since I was your age.

LYDIA: Is there swing in India?

JILL: Lydia.

GOPAL: Don't know. Never been.

LYDIA: But your *parents* were born there.

GOPAL: Right.

LYDIA: And they came here to . . . swing? What is that about?

JILL: Lydia don't be rude.

LYDIA: I'm interested! I'm not being rude!

GOPAL: My folks came to California when they were still teenagers. My dad had this accounting job, really an amazing opportunity for an immigrant, but he was really lonely, homesick, ready to leave. One night they were out for a walk, and he was telling my mother that he couldn't take it, he was going to quit his job so they could go home. And they stopped inside this club to talk. And onstage . . . Ella Fitzgerald was singing, just sitting in with the band. My father says that when he heard her sing, he forgot his brothers and sisters. Forgot his parents and school friends. Forgot everything. He stopped talking, he took my mother's hand, and they watched everyone dance, listening to Ella. He says her music was why they stayed.

LYDIA: That's cool. Jill and Dog are breaking up.

JILL: We are not! Lydia, stop it!

LYDIA: I was just kidding.

JILL: It's not funny.

LYDIA: *(Concentrating.)* My candle is going to kick butt. . . .

JILL: Lydia, honey, I do think you're using too much sand. . . .

LYDIA: Jill, you make your candle, I'll make mine.

JILL: O-kay.

PA VOICE: Come one, come all — advanced east coast swing is taking place in five minutes at studio four!

JILL: Oops — that's where I'm meeting Dog — Lydia, want to finish my candle?

LYDIA: Okay.

JILL: Bye, baby!

LYDIA: Happy swinging.

(Jill exits.)

GOPAL: These look ready to try — you want to go first?

LYDIA: Sure.

GOPAL: Let's see yours.

(Lydia pulls her candle out of the milk carton by the wick. The wick is attached to nothing. She turns over the carton to dump out her candle, which is in fact a miniature pile of rubble.)

LYDIA: Well that sucked.

(Gopal takes Jill's candle out of the milk carton by the wick. It is perfect. Stellar. A beautiful candle. Lydia and Gopal stare at the wondrous candle.)

Scene Twelve

Lydia by herself, awkwardly practicing a dance step. Sometime during her practicing, Mr. Gonzales enters, holding a book.

LYDIA: Step step triple-step, step step triple-step.
Step step triple-step, step step triple-step.
One two three-and-four, five six seven-and-eight.
One two three-and-
— OH MY GOD.
(Lydia stops dancing immediately.)

LYDIA: Hi.

MR. GONZALES: Hi.

LYDIA: Were you just watching me?
(Mr. Gonzales is settling in with his book.)

MR. GONZALES: No.

LYDIA: Oh.
(Mr. Gonzales reads. Little moment.)

MR. GONZALES: Falling right into the rhythm I see.

LYDIA: Hardly — you just said you weren't watching.

MR. GONZALES: I saw — this much.
(He holds up his fingers in a pinch.)

LYDIA: Oh.
(Mr. Gonzales returns to his book.)

LYDIA: Were you in class this morning?

MR. GONZALES: Yes.

LYDIA: I didn't go. Was it hard?

MR. GONZALES: I suppose it was pretty basic.

LYDIA: I didn't go because I can't stand being the worst one there. It's exhausting.

MR. GONZALES: You want me to show you what we did?

LYDIA: No.

MR. GONZALES: Okay.
(Rest.)

LYDIA: You don't seem to care about swing very much.

MR. GONZALES: Neither do you.

LYDIA: That's because I stink.

MR. GONZALES: I see.
(He reads. Lydia slumps in despair.)

LYDIA: It's a special kind of hell to be crappy at something while everyone around you is wonderful.

MR. GONZALES: That's how I feel about parties.

LYDIA: What do you mean?

MR. GONZALES: Everyone likes to go to parties. I always feel uncomfortable.
(He reads.)

LYDIA: Well do you bring your *book* to parties?

MR. GONZALES: Do you think it would help?

LYDIA: No. Ha, ha.
(Rest.)

MR. GONZALES: You're sure you don't want me to teach you what I learned this morning?

LYDIA: Pass.

MR. GONZALES: If I don't practice right away, it's like it never happened.

LYDIA: Um. Okay.

MR. GONZALES: It was something like —
Here —
Tuck, turn and back —
(They try.)

MR. GONZALES: Almost. Again. Tuck, turn and back —
(Jill has entered and is watching.)
(Lydia missteps.)

LYDIA: Sorry.

MR. GONZALES: No, it's me. See, I forgot the lead already.
(Lydia giggles. Jill steps in.)

JILL: *(To Lydia.)* — Look at you! Come here, you, I missed you in there. Let's cut a rug.
(She holds out her arms to her daughter. Lydia is appalled; maybe she recoils.)

LYDIA: *Please. (As in, "Bitch, please.")*
(Rest.)

JILL: I think Lydia's going to be really good.

LYDIA: What could possibly lead you to draw that conclusion.

MR. GONZALES: I was showing Lydia what we learned in class this morning.

JILL: Oh, sweetie, you would have had fun. It's flashy.
(Opening her arms to Mr. Gonzales.) Here, show her the pinwheel —
(Mr. Gonzales glances at Lydia.)

MR. GONZALES: You know: I think I just got a little foot cramp. I'm gonna stop for right now.

JILL: *(Nonplussed, maybe.)* Okay. — Lydia, want to come to a Smooth Lindy workshop after lunch with your father and me?

LYDIA: Maybe. But I should go and round up my "swing homeys" for practice.

MR. GONZALES: Sure, a bunch of us thick-headed ones are going to put in some time, really nail that footwork.

(He winks. Lydia hides a smile.)

JILL: Well whatever you want. I'd love it if you came to the workshop. See you later.

(Jill exits. Mr. Gonzales picks up his book.)

MR. GONZALES: I think I'm going to go find a party, somewhere to read. Thanks for helping me practice.

(He exits. Lydia watches him go.)

Scene Thirteen: Petootie Pie

Jill and Dog sit in silences, holding cards. Jill discards, draws. Dog looks at his hand. Jill clears her throat. Dog looks up, discards, draws. Both look at their hands. They play throughout their conversation, punctuating their words with the slap of cards.

JILL: Did you talk to what's his name about the thing?

DOG: Mm hm. Worked out for now.

JILL: Good.

We should visit that couple.

DOG: They are nice.

JILL: When we get back.

DOG: Sure. We can go to that place, remember the time, after the long thing.

JILL: That's a good idea.

DOG: Ran into Jack this morning when you were at Lindy stretch. Quiet guy.

JILL: I guess.

DOG: You think he feels odd here? Without his wife?

JILL: He hasn't talked about it. I don't think he ever talked about her a lot, though. Even before.

DOG: That's a bad sign.

JILL: Why?

DOG: Because when you love someone, they come up.

(Jill and Dog look at each other.)

(Lydia enters.)

LYDIA: It's the parents.

JILL: Gin.

DOG: I'm going to call, I gotta check in.

JILL: Yes you do.

DOG: Yes I do.

(*Dog kisses Jill on the forehead; she's shuffling cards and doesn't look up.*)

DOG: Bye, Lids.

LYDIA: Bye, Dog.

DOG: *Backwards,* Lid . . .

LYDIA: Bye, God.

(*Dog exits.*)

JILL: You want to play?

LYDIA: I guess.

(*Jill: Surprise.*)

JILL: *Great!* All right . . . here we go. . . .

(*Jill shuffles and deals.*)

JILL: Did you have your scuba class with Gopal yet?

LYDIA: It's this lady instructor. Not Gopal.

JILL: Oh.

LYDIA: It's tomorrow.

JILL: Oh.

LYDIA: Gopal knows someone who spontaneously combusted. He said it started in her heart and spread like a forest fire. Instant ashes.

JILL: Well I'm sure it will be very nice. — Okay!

LYDIA: Jill.

JILL: Mm. Hm.

LYDIA: How did you meet Dad?

(*Jill looks at Lydia. This is new.*)

JILL: In college.

LYDIA: . . . You guys were not in college at the *same time.* What was he, your babysitter?

JILL: Ha, ha. He was an instructor.

LYDIA: (*Horrified and fascinated.*) He was your teacher?!

JILL: *No,* Lydia. A *visiting instructor* in the business school.

LYDIA: Did he give you an "A"?

JILL: I didn't take his class. I was in education, and I had a friend in econ, and he introduced me to your father. We were friends.

LYDIA: *How* old were you?

JILL: Sophomore.

LYDIA: And how old was he?

JILL: He was twenty-nine, thirty.

LYDIA: And you guys were friends. And then you stopped. Being friends.

JILL: He wanted to be more than friends.

LYDIA: And did you?

JILL: . . . I wanted to be around your father all the time.

LYDIA: Why?

JILL: Because he was . . . so . . . happy. He was the happiest person I'd ever met. That's why everyone called him Dog.

LYDIA: *(Amazed.)* You got married while you were *still* in *school.*

JILL: We did. I was just nineteen. It seems crazy now but it made sense then. And then we had you, which was the best thing that ever happened to either of us.

LYDIA: Did grandma and grandpa freak out?

JILL: They were a little worried about the age difference at first. But then they met him. And saw what a . . . decent human being he was. Is. Everything worked out. Things work out when you fall in love.

LYDIA: So after you stopped being friends. . . .

JILL: We didn't *stop* being friends.

LYDIA: Oh. You got married.

JILL: And we're *friends.*

LYDIA: Whatever. So you say.

JILL: Yes, I say. And Lydia — you don't judge your father and me.

LYDIA: I'm not judging! I'm just asking!

JILL: Okay. Your discard.

(They play.)

LYDIA: So are you and Dad monogamous?

JILL: What kind of a question is that?

LYDIA: Julie-Anne's parents have an open marriage.

JILL: You're kidding.

LYDIA: That's what her mom said.

JILL: Really.

LYDIA: Because Julie-Anne's father has a girlfriend. It's no big deal.

JILL: Ah, yes it is.

LYDIA: So does Dad have a girlfriend?

JILL: No.

LYDIA: If he did would you guys break up?

JILL: No, we wouldn't.

LYDIA: So it's no big deal.

JILL: We wouldn't break up, but it doesn't mean it's not a big deal. You make choices in a relationship. Nobody is perfect. People make mistakes. And when that happens, you make a decision to forgive them, and you move forward.

LYDIA: Has Dad made mistakes?

JILL: No.

LYDIA: Have you?

JILL: . . . Yes.

LYDIA: Whoa.

(Lydia decides not to pursue this.)

JILL: Your father is my other half. I don't know who I'd be without him. Or you. I wouldn't be myself. And…that's all I'm going to say.

(They play.)

LYDIA: So did you "know" right away that he was the one? When you met Dad?

JILL: Not right away. But there was a moment. And then I knew.

LYDIA: Tss. But *how* did you know? How do you know it wasn't just *random,* like he could have been talking to anybody and it didn't mean anything and it just *happened* to be you. An accident.

JILL: Oh, honey. You just—you know, people talk. Men and women. And someone will be talking. And suddenly you'll know that they're really talking to you. Saying something to you they couldn't say to anyone else. And it's very special — that connection. That's how you know.

(They play.)

LYDIA: Cards are stupid. I'm going to go make a lanyard.

(She exits.)

Scene Fourteen: An Unheard Question

GOPAL: When you hold your partner, You don't grip. You don't clench. You don't wring the life out of the hands.

It's a shared endeavor.

So you hold one another appropriately.

It means *appropriately,* Mr. Peterson.

Well, passion is not something that fuels swing.

If you want passion, go to Tango Camp.

In October.

Scene Fifteen

Mr. Gonzales sits, legs over the side of the wall, lost in thought.

LYDIA: Hi, Mr. Gonzales. . . . Hi, Mr. Gonzales.

MR. GONZALES: Lydia. You can call me Jack.

LYDIA: Okay. Jack. What are you doing.

MR. GONZALES: Just thinking.

LYDIA: What are you thinking about.

MR. GONZALES: This beach reminds me of — someplace else.

LYDIA: What kind of name is Jack Gonzales.

MR. GONZALES: An American name.

LYDIA: But are you from Mexico?

MR. GONZALES: No.

LYDIA: Do you speak Spanish?

MR. GONZALES: No.

LYDIA: How come?

MR. GONZALES: My father didn't want me to.

LYDIA: Oh.

MR. GONZALES: "Speak English, be American." So I did. I spoke English. I
    spoke English, I went to Yale, I majored in education, I had a daughter,
    I married a girl from Connecticut. Not the right order, but . . . just like
    my father wanted.

LYDIA: What about your mother?

MR. GONZALES: She's dead.

LYDIA: Sorry.

MR. GONZALES: Don't be. You didn't kill her.

    (Silence.)

LYDIA: Was it recent?

MR. GONZALES: No, no. When I was little. Five.

LYDIA: Do you remember her?

MR. GONZALES: A bit.

LYDIA: Do you miss her?

MR. GONZALES: Questions. Questions.

LYDIA: *(Hurt.)* Sor-ry. Forgive me for thinking you might want to talk. To me.
    My mistake.

    (Silence.)

MR. GONZALES: When I was five, my mother, my father and I came here to
    the seaside. A picnic. My mother had made little cakes, and I had brought

a kite which didn't fly. There was a balloon. The kind you ride in. Dollar a ride. My mother wanted to go. Not my Dad. And I was too little. So she got in the basket — and he stayed on the ground, holding my hand.

The sky was no color at all. We watched my mother go up, up, up. The balloon grew smaller and smaller as the wind pushed it above the low clouds. She was just a tiny . . . thing . . . in the basket. And I let go of my father's hand, I jumped up and down. I held my arms high in a V to her. I waved and waved. I wanted her to see me. And she waved back! She imitated me exactly, both arms high. And then . . . she was in the air. Arms still waving. I watched her fall. She was dark against the pale sky, a doll.

When I looked up at my father, his hair had turned white. And instead of running in the direction where she fell, he turned his back.

He never spoke my mother's name aloud again. He could not forgive her for leaning out too far. He could not forgive me for —.

And — why should he. Why should he.

(Silence.)

LYDIA: Your mother, I bet she always wanted something. Something she couldn't name.

In the air — she saw her little boy. She looked down, and there you were. It must have felt so perfect. She had to raise her arms. Because she was happy. She wasn't holding you, but she *wanted* to. That's why she leaned into the sky. She couldn't contain her joy. Did you ever think of that?

Scene Sixteen

LYDIA: Second scuba class. Second week. Second ocean dive.

Today, we go deeper.

The surface of the sea is far above.

I could stay and stay down here in the perfect clear blue.

Just me and the fish.

When we're back up on the deck of the boat, sitting in the warm air peeling off our wet suits, I can feel it happening to me.

Rushes. Rushes. Lightheaded, this feeling of buoyancy, dizzy in my stomach. Cold sweat. Fast heartbeat. Falling.

Rushes. I have to lie down, I can't talk.

At night alone in my cot, I close my eyes and I can still feel it, I can still feel everything.

I taste ashes on my tongue.

Scene Seventeen: Is You Is, Or Is You Ain't (Ma' Baby)

Dog is dancing with Jill. Gopal watches. They're having a ball. On a break.

DOG: Switch!

Gopal swoops, taking the lead from Dog. Now he and Jill dance while Dog watches. The leads go back and forth this way, switching again and again on the appropriate beat, Jill deftly following one lead, then another. It's an impressive demonstration.

DOG: *(Clapping.)* That's my wife, baby!
    (On a break, Dog jumps in again.)
DOG: Did you miss me, darling?
JILL: I always miss you.
    (Lydia enters and watches her parents. As the song ends, Dog dips Jill low.)
DOG: And they lived happily . . . ever . . . after.
    (He kisses Jill, still in the dip.)
DOG: *(Seeing Lydia.)* Oh, *my* bad! No Parental PDA!
JILL: Lydia! Sweetie! Were you there the whole time? I didn't see you!
LYDIA: You guys look pretty good.
    (Rest.)
    (Jill and Dog look at one another.)
DOG: She thinks we look good.
LYDIA: Yeah.
JILL: Well thanks, honey. So Gopal. Can you quickly go over the footwork on that first break? The bob bada THREE —
    (Gopal goes over the footwork with Jill.)
DOG: How's it going, cutie?
LYDIA: Fine.
DOG: You okay? You look a little flushed.
    (He feels Lydia's forehead.)
LYDIA: I'm fine. I'm excellent. I'm okay.
JILL: Okay, great, so take me through one more time from the beginning. . . .

LYDIA: Actually I wondered if I could steal the dance instructor and have a lesson right now.

(They all look at Lydia.)

JILL: *Really.*

DOG: Honey, why don't we go to the jazz intensive.

JILL: Sure. Of course. Have a wonderful class, plum. See you tomorrow, Gopal.

GOPAL: See you.

(Jill and Dog exit. Lydia and Gopal look at one another.)

LYDIA: So. You want to teach me something?

GOPAL: You been practicing?

LYDIA: Sort of. — No. Not at all.

(She's beaming.)

GOPAL: It's sort of unusual for a student to be so happy about that. Well, hold out your arms, and let's begin. We'll just start with some six count, okay?

(He leads a turn. Lydia is somewhere else.)

GOPAL: Okay . . .

(He leads another turn less successfully.)

GOPAL: . . . You're resisting my lead.

LYDIA: What?

GOPAL: You're resisting my lead. A little resistance, good. Too much resistance, you don't get invited to dance again.

(He leads a turn. She doesn't get it.)

GOPAL: Resisting.

(He leads yet another turn less successfully.)

GOPAL: Resisting.

LYDIA: You know Gopal I'm a feminist. Maybe that's why I'm bad at this.

GOPAL: Take my word for it: feminism and swing are compatible. But *I* lead, and *you* follow.

LYDIA: Yeah, "separate but equal."

(They dance.)

GOPAL: Now you're anticipating.

LYDIA: *Jesus!*

GOPAL: I didn't *lead* that turn. You decided to go.

LYDIA: You know, when Mr. Gonzales dances with me, he's not always telling me how lame I am.

GOPAL: Mr. Gonzales isn't your teacher. Plus, he is not a particularly strong lead.

LYDIA: He is too. He is to me.

(They dance.)

GOPAL: There! That's it!

LYDIA: What.

GOPAL: *That's* a follow.

LYDIA: Fine.

GOPAL: See? We're dancing. I'm not trying to make you fall for a trick.

 (They dance.)

GOPAL: You feel the difference? You're following. — She's following!

LYDIA: I am?

GOPAL: Yeah. Good!

 (They dance.)

LYDIA: Gopal.

GOPAL: Mm hm.

LYDIA: If I learn to follow like a dream will other people find me irresistible?

GOPAL: Just listen to the music. Follow.

 (They dance. Lydia smiles, just a little.)

Scene Eighteen: The Shim Sham

PA VOICE: Hey, cats and kittens, it's time for the *Shim Sham!*

Everyone is out on the floor for a group lesson, a swing line dance that is cooler than country line dancing. Everyone does the Shim Sham. Initially Lydia and Mr. Gonzales are laughing together, trying to do the steps in time.

LYDIA: *(To Mr. Gonzales, over the music.)* I am the shim shammer, my friend. . . .

Then Jill bumps Mr. Gonzales, both laugh, and they partner up and swing together, apart from the rest of the line. Gopal, Dog, Lead, Follow and Lydia continue the line dance — no partners.

 Lydia stops dancing, watching her mother and Mr. Gonzales together. She stands alone and watches them dancing. They are very happy. No one notices her. Gopal and Dog and Lead and Follow continue to do the Shim Sham.

 Jill and Mr. Gonzales dance in a light separate from Lydia's. Lydia's face changes.

LYDIA: Mr. Gonzales and my mother.

 Mr. Gonzales and Jill are . . .

They . . .

Mr. Gonzales And my Mother are having an affair.

Everything makes sense. No wife. Jill wanting to go to swing camp at the same time. Bringing Dad is the perfect cover.

And me.

Look at them.

Mr. Gonzales and Jill, who have been dancing in a nonintimate way, stop and stare at each other.

Music changes from 'Shim Sham' to 'Romantic.'

Mr. Gonzales and Jill begin to neck passionately, theatrically, like in the movies: Lydia's fantasy. Lights fade on them in a clinch. Everyone continues the Shim Sham.

Scene Nineteen

Lydia sits outside on the steps. Head on knees. Gopal sitting next to her.

GOPAL: Hey. Lydia . . . It's your lesson. Lindy Hop time.

LYDIA: Who the fuck cares. Why don't you go Lindy with Jill. Everyone does.

GOPAL: What are you talking about?

LYDIA: This is the most fucking depressing place I have ever been in my whole entire life. Everyone has a partner. *Some* people have two!

GOPAL: What's the *matter?*

LYDIA: You know, my mom told me that before she married my dad, she went on a diet and ate only eggs and grapefruit for an entire year. So when she married my dad she was a *perfect size four.* I could NEVER eat eggs and grapefruit for a whole year!

GOPAL: So.

LYDIA: So. She's the prettiest. She's the best dancer. She's been everywhere first. And now *I* have to be *here,* at *Swing Camp* and watch her be first. Again.

GOPAL: You're a good dancer. And beautiful in a way that's all your own.

LYDIA: Why don't you say I have a charming *personality.* Jesus *God* Gopal you are depressing.

GOPAL: You've got a lot going for you Lydia. But I wouldn't put a charming personality at the top of the list.

LYDIA: Do you like my mother?

GOPAL: What? Sure.

LYDIA: I mean, do you *like* her.

GOPAL: Do I like her?

LYDIA: Yeah. Like, are you trying to get in her pants.

GOPAL: Christ.

LYDIA: Are you?

GOPAL: No. That's ludicrous. I would never. Do you believe me? Lydia. *(Simply.)* No. Just no.

LYDIA: Okay.

GOPAL: Okay?

LYDIA: *Okay.*

GOPAL: So we're friends.

LYDIA: Chh. You want to be my friend.

GOPAL: Call me crazy. I do.

(Lydia considers.)

LYDIA: Okay. Friend. When was the first time you had sex?

GOPAL: This is totally inappropriate.

LYDIA: Gopal, come ON. Talk to me. Almost nobody *talks* to me!! I'm just asking how *old* you were. I'm not talking about a pubic hair on my coke. *(Rest.)*

GOPAL: I was fourteen.

LYDIA: God. *Everybody* did it before me.

GOPAL: Boys are idiots. Believe me.

LYDIA: So you regret it?

GOPAL: Not — It's not age that matters. Look. You're too smart to —

LYDIA: Everything is about sex.

GOPAL: Not always. But —

LYDIA: *(Interrupting.)* Shh.

(Dog and Mr. Gonzales walk above. Lydia pulls Gopal so that they are unseen by Dog and Mr. Gonzales.)

LYDIA: *(Whispering.)* My mother and Mr. Gonzales are having an affair.

GOPAL: What?

LYDIA: Jill and Mr. Gonzales are having an affair. I can tell.

GOPAL: I don't think so.

LYDIA: My mother and my dad are breaking up and my mother and Mr. Gonzales are having an affair.

GOPAL: Your parents don't act like people breaking up.

LYDIA: Shh.

(Dog and Mr. Gonzales are chatting.)

DOG: Remember the back-and-forth Charleston?

MR. GONZALES: Yeah, I think so.

DOG: What's the lead there, how do you get into it, is it on the three-four?

MR. GONZALES: *(Counting to himself.)* one-two-three-and-four . . . I dunno how to — let me show you.

LYDIA: *(Whispering.)* See. He's being extra nice to my dad. Cause he feels guilty.
(Mr. Gonzales and Dog begin to practice dance together.)

LYDIA: Oh. My. God. I was wrong.

GOPAL: Well I'm glad you realize it.

LYDIA: It's not my MOTHER and Mr. Gonzales. It's my DAD and Mr. Gonzales.

(Mr. Gonzales and Dog, who have been dancing in a nonintimate way, stop and stare at each other. Mr. Gonzales and Dog begin to neck passionately, theatrically, like in the movies. Lydia's fantasy.)

LYDIA: Do you see that?

GOPAL: *(Looking.)* They're getting good.

LYDIA: They're *together!* They're going out! I have a *gay dad!* Don't you see it?

GOPAL: *(Looking.)* No.

(Lights fade on them in a clinch. Lydia watches.)

LYDIA: This camp is *fucked up.*

END OF ACT ONE

ACT TWO

Scene Twenty: Somewhere (The Bends)

Blue/green light. Ocean shimmer. Underwater.

Three figures move slowly across the sandbar. Their scuba gear obscures their features.

The only sound is the dull thud of a faraway beating heart. Bubbles rise from the mouths of the figures.

A school of silver fish streaks through the water; the figures are transfixed, watching.

Very faintly . . . a great distance away . . . we hear the tinny sound of Big Band music, as if being played up at the surface of the water from a transistor radio.

The underwater figures look up then at each other. The heartbeat speeds up.

One figure releases weights and flies up, bubbles in its wake. The other figures watch it, necks craned.

The two remaining figures look at each other. One holds out its arms. They begin to dance to the distant music, but slowly, underwater.

One figure suddenly flies upwards, leaving the last figure alone. The last figure looks up, craning its neck.

Music continues. Lights fade.

Scene Twenty-one: Now or Never

Lydia perches somewhat precariously high atop a ledge of a wall outside the ballroom.

LYDIA: Mr. Gonzales: gay. Mr. Gonzales — with my dad, not Jill. Maybe.
  (*Dog exits the ballroom below her, practicing.*)
DOG: One two, three-and-four, five six, seven-and-eight. One two, three-and-four, five six, seven-and-eight.
LYDIA: Dad!
DOG: Oh hey, honey. What are you doing way up there?
LYDIA: Reading.
DOG: Oh. Hey, I just came from a styling workshop. Check it out.
  (*He does a move.*)
LYDIA: (*Bored.*) Right on.

Hey, I have to show you something.

(She pulls out a men's skin mag and throws it down to him.)

DOG: *Jesus,* Lydia! Where did you get this?!

LYDIA: Paid Oliver in the kitchen to buy it for me when he went into town.

DOG: For Christ's sake! You should not be reading this!

LYDIA: Does it turn you on?

DOG: *What?!*

LYDIA: Dad, if you're a man who loves men, it's okay.

DOG: I'm not a man who loves men!

LYDIA: Don't get homophobic about it.

DOG: I'm not — Lydia get your ass down from there!

LYDIA: Why!

DOG: Because — *(He doesn't know why.)*

Never mind! — I'm taking this!

LYDIA: You can have it.

DOG: *I don't want it.* Jesus Christ on the cross!

(He stalks off. Throws the magazine violently aside.)

LYDIA: Huh.

(Mr. Gonzales strolls on. Lydia stands up on the ledge when she sees him. He doesn't see her at first. She is far above him.)

LYDIA: Mr. Gon — Jack. Jack.

MR. GONZALES: Well, hello there.

(Mr. Gonzales looks at her. She just smiles a little goofily.)

MR. GONZALES: And — see you.

LYDIA: I'm going to ask you a question, okay?

MR. GONZALES: *(Bemused.)* Ask me a question.

LYDIA: Are you gay?

MR. GONZALES: Am I . . . ? No.

LYDIA: You're sure.

MR. GONZALES: Fairly sure. Why do you ask?

LYDIA: Because.

(To us.) Right now, I'm looking at Mr. Gonzales, and I *see* him.

And he's looking back at me, right into my eyes, and he sees me.

And I understand that everything that's happened in my life up to now has been about preparing me for this moment, this instant of recognition. I know, I *know* that I am meant for him. That's all. And when you *know* something that big, you have to *do* something big. So I do. I raise my arms high, I lean forward, and I fall.

I fall from an impossible height, I fall with my back flat, I fall through the air and even as I'm falling, I know that I'd be really hurt, maybe killed, if I wasn't caught.

But, see, I know, I know he's going to catch me.

And he does.

(Lydia is in Mr. Gonzales's arms.)

LYDIA: I love you.

MR. GONZALES: Jesus! Jesus Fucking Christ!

(He drops her or puts her down roughly.)

LYDIA: I do. That's why I'm here.

MR. GONZALES: Lydia, what you just did was *crazy!* Do you understand that? *Insane!* What if I hadn't caught you!

LYDIA: But you did.

MR. GONZALES: But what if I *hadn't?*

LYDIA: But you did.

MR. GONZALES: *Jesus!*

LYDIA: I love you.

MR. GONZALES: I'm going to pretend for your sake that you didn't say that.

LYDIA: But I did.

MR. GONZALES: *Stop it!*

LYDIA: You danced with me. You listened to me. You told me things. You talked to me, really talked to me. You caught me. I want — I want. . . .

MR. GONZALES: I have nothing to say. No. Don't talk. You should not have done that.

(He stalks off.)

LYDIA: But I did.

Scene Twenty-two

Dance class. Gopal stands with Lead and Follow.

GOPAL: Falling into a dip. This movement is *led* by the man. But how *far* the dip goes is up to the woman.

(Gopal listens to a question from the class. The audience does not hear the question.)

Because usually the lead *is* a man.

(Another unheard comment from the class.)

Not in your case, that's true Sharon.

(Another unheard comment.)

For the purpose of this class, let's assume that the follows are *women* and the leads are *men*.

(Another unheard comment from the class.)

Except for Sharon. And Emily.

My point is, the *follow* decides how fast and how far to fall.

(Gopal demonstrates. Lead dips Follow, holding her parallel to the ground, and then steps away. Follow stays in the exact same position.)

You trust your partner to give you the appropriate lead.

(Lead and Follow dance, demonstrating a low, low dip. Follow is an inch from the floor.)

Scene Twenty-three

Jill is drinking tea. Mr. Gonzales comes in.

MR. GONZALES: Jill. There you are.

JILL: Hi there.

MR. GONZALES: Hey. Where's Dog?

JILL: Phone call.

MR. GONZALES: Have you seen Lydia lately?

JILL: Not since this morning. By now she's probably found a place to go get a tattoo.

MR. GONZALES: I wanted to check with you, see how she was doing . . .

JILL: Oh, God, has she unleashed something at y — because she has a talent for saying exactly the most inappropriate thing, and you need to know, it's not personal, it's just — Lydia.

MR. GONZALES: Our last conversation. Took kind of a turn.

JILL: I'm sorry if she's been abrasive. Obviously you're dealing with major family issues of your own, you don't need that kind of — God. That just came out — insanely, wrong. Jesus. Sorry.

MR. GONZALES: No. It must be obvious. I know.

JILL: Are you and Michelle talking.

MR. GONZALES: No. You don't — think it's weird that I came here without them.

JILL: No. I don't know. Maybe. Yes.

MR. GONZALES: I just — it got bad, uh unexpectedly, and I didn't know really what to do, or. Well. So. We're just taking some space.

JILL: Sure. No, I understand. I mean, I don't — know, but. Sorry. I feel like an asshole.

MR. GONZALES: Then stop.

JILL: All right.

MR. GONZALES: Things seem to happen for a reason.

(Jill nods.)

MR. GONZALES: But I just wanted to check on Lydia, with you. . . .

JILL: She's at that age. You know.

(Little rest.)

MR. GONZALES: I remember.

JILL: Do you.

MR. GONZALES: Yes.

JILL: Well you're younger than me. There are days when I look at her, and I barely recognize . . . this *tall* person . . . who used to be my *baby.* It's amazing. She's not a baby any more.

MR. GONZALES: No. She's a remarkable young woman.

JILL: With a remarkable mouth.

MR. GONZALES: Well, she thinks something, and she says it. . . . I probably don't do that often enough.

JILL: She's fearless.

MR. GONZALES: She is. It's a wonderful trait to be around. Rare.

JILL: Listen, I'll talk to her — she can't go around just being rude anytime she feels like it.

MR. GONZALES: Oh — she's not rude.

JILL: Well she needs to be reminded to respect other people. Not to just say anything she wants to you because she thinks it's funny.

MR. GONZALES: I'd feel badly if, because of me, you said something. I mean, she hasn't done anything wrong. Don't mention anything.

JILL: All right. And I am sorry about — Everything.

MR. GONZALES: You're saying that a lot.

JILL: True. Sorry. . . . It's so much easier, isn't it?

MR. GONZALES: Hm.

JILL: Dancing.

MR. GONZALES: Than what.

JILL: Talking.

(Lead and Follow dance into the scene. Jill and Mr. Gonzales watch.)

MR. GONZALES: Maybe.

JILL: Or, just a better conversation.

(Mr. Gonzales is left alone.)

Scene Twenty-four: Too Close For Comfort

Music. Gopal has taken Dog's phone away. They dance together.

GOPAL: Don't be afraid to simply hold a moment.

DOG: How do you mean.

GOPAL: You don't always have to be moving right into the next combination. It's good to break. Listen.

DOG: And what's your partner doing?

GOPAL: She's with you. She's waiting with you.

DOG: What if she doesn't want to wait?

GOPAL: Well. You're dancing together. And you're the lead.

DOG: Right. Right.

GOPAL: So you give her space to do her thing. While you hold. You give her space, she doesn't take space.

DOG: Right. Right.

GOPAL: Listen. Here the music takes you high — then you can go low, then back. That's the break.

DOG: Right.

GOPAL: Here. Feel this. *(Gopal leads Dog in some breaks.)*

DOG: Your partner knows this is going to happen?

GOPAL: My partner's waiting for my lead. We're working together, listening. To the music. To each other.
(Concentration.)

DOG: That's the trick of it, isn't it? Listening to both.

GOPAL: It is.

DOG: Huh.

GOPAL: You don't want to throw every step you know into a single dance. It's simply about your partner, and you.
(An attempt at a move.)

DOG: It's hard to stay with a partner.

GOPAL: Sometimes. You seem to have done all right.

DOG: Yeah. You know, I came here to make Jill happy. Be the best lead she'd ever have in her life. I love dancing with my wife. But if she *didn't* want to dance, that would be okay with me too.

GOPAL: You're a good dancer. A good lead.
(Dog sees Gopal's father dancing.)

DOG: Your dad knows what he's doing.

GOPAL: These days, he mostly does the books: columns and columns of numbers. Until he hears that music. Then he straightens up, his eyes glow, and he looks around to find my mom.

(Dog thinks about it.)

DOG: — You know you're right, I don't break enough. In the songs. I should just stop, listen to the music. Think about what comes next.

(They dance again.)

GOPAL: Listen for the break.

(He hums the music to highlight the break. Dog listens to Gopal humming. They break — and hold — for eight beats, then start up on the same beat. Dog has been a little off the break.)

DOG: I'll keep working at it.

Scene Twenty-five: Paper Moon

Dance lighting. Lydia sits alone outside the ballroom.

PA VOICE: . . . And remember, tonight's After Hours Dance will take place at Pier Six, starting at midnight through the wee hours!

(Clapping, music from far away. Gopal approaches Lydia.)

GOPAL: Lydia. You left the dance, now I have no one to lindy with.

LYDIA: Quit being retarded, Gopal, you can dance with anybody.

GOPAL: You skipped your lesson this afternoon. I missed you.

LYDIA: You know, did you ever consider that I might be here for a reason other than dancing?

GOPAL: Sure. Scuba.

LYDIA: Other than scuba.

(Gopal clutches his heart.)

GOPAL: *Other than scuba!*

LYDIA: Forget it.

GOPAL: Come on. I'd like to dance with you.

LYDIA: Gopal, do you think it's possible for one person to be totally certain of something, and the other person not to get it at all?

GOPAL: Yes. For example, I'm certain that you should follow me into the ballroom and be my partner for the next dance, and you don't get it at all.

LYDIA: What's the point. It doesn't matter anyway. I'm never going to be good. I suck.

(Gopal is taking off his tie.)

LYDIA: What, you're going to *strangle* me because I ditched the fucking swing shindig?

GOPAL: We're trying something.

LYDIA: I'm *not* going inside to dance.

GOPAL: You don't have to.

(He puts his tie around her eyes like a blindfold.)

LYDIA: Whoa. Okay, this is officially weird.

GOPAL: This is going to help you follow.

LYDIA: "Marco!" "Polo!" *(Giggling.)* Gimme a bat, where's the pinata!?

GOPAL: Just listen to the music, smarty pants.

LYDIA: Ooh, smarty pants. Trash mouth.

(Gopal takes the blindfolded Lydia in his arms and dances a complicated Lindy with her. She follows.)

LYDIA: So, should we — Oh my God.

(She dances. It takes all her concentration since it's fast. Gopal is leading advanced moves.)

LYDIA: Jeez. *Jeez. (Missing a step)* — Sorry.

GOPAL: No "sorry," Lydia, it's a *dance*.

LYDIA: Okay. Okay.

They dance beautifully, better than she's ever danced before. The blindfold has created a momentary magic. Lydia has become a brilliant dancer: confident, graceful, joyous. Mr. Gonzales has entered and is watching from afar. The music ends, and Lydia is laughing, spinning, thrilled. She doesn't take off the blindfold.

LYDIA: Wow. Wow. Wow. This is so excellent. I feel like Luke Skywalker. You're the Obi-Wan of swing, Gopal.

Gopal becomes aware of Mr. Gonzales, who puts a finger to his lips "Shush" — and motions for Gopal to "leave, it's okay." Gopal looks at Mr. Gonzales, at Lydia, and steps away from Lydia reluctantly. Lydia holds out her arms. She takes a step forward, arms outstretched, still laughing. Mr. Gonzales shoos Gopal again, who begins to walk back toward the ballroom.

LYDIA: I'm like that blind ice skater they made that movie about.

(Mr. Gonzales steps up to Lydia and takes her in his arms in a lead.)

LYDIA: You know, the one in the seventies with Robbie Benson —

She stops talking when she feels the dance lead. Mr. Gonzales holds her for a moment, and then they dance. Lydia keeps the blindfold on. The dance ends with Mr. Gonzales holding Lydia in a low dip. They hold this position, trembling. She takes the blindfold off. Mr. Gonzales stands up and steps away from Lydia. She takes one step toward him, another, leans forward, and kisses him. She stands back, looking him in the eyes.

LYDIA: Okay.
MR. GONZALES: Okay. Okay.
　　(Gopal sees from far away.)

Scene Twenty-six: Zip Gun Bop

Dog is putting shirts in a bag. Jill keeps taking them out again.

DOG: Okay, okay, ha ha ha.
JILL: It's not funny. Stop packing.
DOG: You just *ripped* one!
JILL: That was ripped before.
DOG: No it wasn't!
DOG: Baby, come on. It's not such a big deal.
JILL: It is to me.
DOG: It's a few days. I have to take care of this.
JILL: You promised.
DOG: Jill, you're being very silly.
JILL: No *you* are.
DOG: *This is important.* Everything could fall apart if I'm not there.
JILL: I could say the same thing about here.
DOG: No you couldn't, sweetie. — okay, cut it out with the shirts.
JILL: No.
DOG: That's pathetic.
JILL: *You're* pathetic! Can't keep a promise!
DOG: What, are you gonna call me an Indian giver next?
JILL: *(Withering.)* You didn't give me anything.
DOG: I just want to get this deal over with, I want to keep my business from falling and collapsing into itself, I want to make a decent living and I want to be reasonably happy.

JILL: Why reasonably? Why not *un*reasonably? Why can't we be unreasonably happy? That's such a stupid thing to say.

DOG: *Will you stop taking my shirts out of the bag!*

JILL: No!

DOG: Fine. I'll go with no shirts. Because I am going.

JILL: I don't want you to.

DOG: That's abundantly clear.

JILL: You are always paying attention to your business and not to what matters.

DOG: Sorry it doesn't matter to you. Happens to feed our family, but other than that.

JILL: We said we were going to have time away together.

DOG: We have. We *are*. *I'm just going to be gone a few days.*

JILL: The most amazing capacity for shortsightedness, you.

DOG: Not going to respond to that.

JILL: Of course not.

DOG: I'll miss you.

JILL: Easy. Easy to say.

DOG: Easy to say because it's true.

JILL: Well don't go and you won't miss me.

DOG: I like to miss you.

JILL: Big fucking deal.

　　(A moment.)

DOG: Right. Fine. Can I please have a shirt.

JILL: No.

DOG: Fine. Tell Lydia good-bye, and I'll *see* her in a *few days.*

JILL: No.

DOG: God. Fine.

　　(Dog starts to go.)

DOG: I had been thinking up to now that dancing with you was bringing us closer. You in my arms every day. But it's not, is it?

JILL: I don't know.

DOG: Right. Me too.

　　(Dog leaves without a bag. Jill looks at the beautifully folded shirts, shakes one out, puts it on. she unfolds another, ties it around her waist. She unfolds a third shirt, tosses it over her shoulders. She sits wrapped in dog's shirts, biting a nail, lost in thought.)

Scene Twenty-seven: The Frim Fram Sauce

Slow music. Gopal and Lydia dance simply. Too simply. Lydia's bored.

LYDIA: This is kind of slow, Gopal.

 (Gopal doesn't answer.)

LYDIA: Don't you want to teach me something new?

 (Gopal doesn't answer.)

LYDIA: Hey, Cowboy. Hellooo.

GOPAL: I can't dance with you right now.

 (He stops.)

LYDIA: Are you mad at me?

GOPAL: Don't act dumb.

LYDIA: I'm not dumb.

GOPAL: I know. Don't act it. You are how old?

LYDIA: You know how old I am.

GOPAL: I want to hear you say it.

LYDIA: Age doesn't matter.

GOPAL: Just say it. If you asked, say, a policeman, it would matter.

LYDIA: Fourteen. I'm fourteen. I'm going to be fifteen in three months. You said you were fourteen when *you* —

GOPAL: *(Cutting her off.)* All *right*.

LYDIA: I'm happy. I've never been happier in my whole life.

GOPAL: It's wrong. What that man is doing is wrong. Wrong, illegal, immoral, and I wish to God I had never seen it.

 (Lydia can't really contain her joy.)

LYDIA: I love him. I've fallen in love. And he has too. He says, he tells me, "You. Are everything. I want."

GOPAL: Yeah, he wants you, and he wants a sandwich too, because he's hungry.

LYDIA: What's that supposed to mean?

GOPAL: Life is not only about *wanting* and *having*. His behavior, forget it, it's shameful. You're a minor.

LYDIA: Gopal, it's not him. It was me: I did everything. Me. I started it. And he, he saw me.

GOPAL: I saw you. I see you. But I don't have to piss all over you to make sure you belong to no one but me.

LYDIA: I want to belong to him. That's the difference. It's going to be okay. Things work out when you fall in love. I'm okay. I am. Okay.

GOPAL: Aside from being illegal, the man is married. He has a family.

LYDIA: Most of the time, I'm all — I'm not even here, I'm invisible, I'm underwater and then when he touches me, I never . . . I. . . . He, he and then — I'm in my body. Julie-Anne never described it right.

GOPAL: I have to tell your parents. Or you do.

LYDIA: You're shitting me.

GOPAL: I'm serious.

(Lydia is trembling with rage.)

LYDIA: No you're not.

GOPAL: I am.

LYDIA: FUCK YOU. You don't understand.

GOPAL: Goddamn it. I do understand. I went out with a woman who was married.

(Lydia looks at Gopal.)

LYDIA: My mother?

GOPAL: *Not your mother!*

LYDIA: Okay. Jeez.

GOPAL: Two years ago. I just, I couldn't help myself. — No. I decided: I *allowed* myself to. To do this one thing. And I got hurt. Everyone gets hurt.

LYDIA: So you know. You fell in love.

GOPAL: Lydia, are you *listening??* Whether I fell or not isn't the point. The whole thing was a mistake! A mistake! She was married. She had a family. She had a life. And *those* are the things that endure. Not the lapse in judgment.

LYDIA: So I'm just a lapse. A fuckup. A mistake. No one could possibly fall in love with me.

GOPAL: No. No, that's —

(She is upset. He hugs her, awkward, guilty. holding her. Lydia looks up, tries to kiss him. He pulls away. Lydia runs off.)

Scene Twenty-eight

Dog and Jill are playing dominoes. Lydia enters. Jill looks up absently.

DOG: Hi sweetie. You just come from the Lindy intensive?

LYDIA: No. Dad. Jill. I have to tell you something.

JILL: What is it honey?

LYDIA: I'm having — I'm going out with Jack.

DOG: Jack who.

LYDIA: Gonzales. Jack. I've been going out with Jack.

(Rest.)

DOG: Okay is this some kind of joke?!

LYDIA: No.

DOG: I'm going to get very upset in a minute. I'm taking this in.

LYDIA: Dad. We're in love. I'm not kidding. I know he loves me. And his marriage is not working out. They got married too young.

DOG: Too Young! I am not hearing this!

LYDIA: *(Overlap.)* He's twenty-four, and I'm fourteen —
it's just like you guys — and we talked
about it, and I don't want to . . .
lie to you and neither does he, because
it. . . is real.

JILL:
WAIT A MINUTE,
WAIT A MINUTE . . . !

(Mr. Gonzales appears.)

MR. GONZALES: I should probably say something about now.

DOG: Oh JESUS!

JILL: *What* is going on!

MR. GONZALES: What she said.

DOG: The only reason I'm not upset yet? I'm in shock. I DON'T BELIEVE THIS — I WANT A RATIONAL EXPLANATION —

JILL: What are you talking about! What about Michelle?

MR. GONZALES: She's left. Michelle and I are still friends. We're in therapy; we'll co-parent. But the marriage is over.

LYDIA: Mom, Dad: we're in love! Things work out when you fall in love.

JILL: *(Overlap.)* I don't . . .

LYDIA: *(Overlap.)* It worked out for *you.*

JILL: That's true . . .

MR. GONZALES: Dog, I love your daughter. She is everything I want. Try to understand.

DOG: Understand. UNDERSTAND! She's my baby.

JILL: She's not a baby anymore.

MR. GONZALES: That's right.

JILL: Well thank God Michelle left *you!*

MR. GONZALES: I know. It could have been uncomfortable.

(Tableau: think the Walton's family photo.)

LYDIA: *(To us.)* This is how I imagine it.

(Jill, Dog, and Mr. Gonzales all hug, laughing and chattering.)

LYDIA: But it's probably unrealistic. They'd be mad. . . .

DOG: *(Sudden, lunging at Mr. Gonzales.)* I'M GOING TO KILL YOU, YOU CHILD-MOLESTING TWENTY-FOUR-YEAR-OLD ASSWIPE!!

AND AFTER I KILL YOU, I'M GOING TO SUE YOU! AND AFTER
. . . I SUE YOU, I'M GOING TO MAKE SURE FOR GOD'S SAKE!
YOU GO TO PRISON AND THAT YOU ARE THERE FOR A VERY!
LONG! TIME! HERE, JACK! AFTER YOU'RE DEAD!

MR. GONZALES: (*Holding Lydia's hands, speaking intensely.*) Lydia. You have to
hold on for a few years. You can do anything when you're eighteen. I did.
I'll leave Michelle, and the time will fly. We'll be together, I promise! *Just
hold on.*

DOG: YOU'RE MEAT, GONZALES! AHH!

(*A puff of smoke; he's gone. A pair of shoes rests forlornly where Dog stood,
tiny yellow flames dancing, smoke rising from the shows. Jill stares at the empty
shoes in horror, turning slowly to Lydia.*)

JILL: You killed your father.

(*She drops to her knees over the shoes and sobs.*)

LYDIA: Maybe telling them isn't such a good idea after all.

(*Dog appears again.*)

DOG: You aren't in love with my daughter, Jack. It's me you're in love with.

(*He kisses Mr. Gonzales.*)

JILL: Bastard! You know you want me.

(*She kisses Mr. Gonzales. Gopal appears.*)

GOPAL: You are all seriously misled. Jack and I have been lovers since we were
freshmen together at Cal.

MR. GONZALES: I didn't go to Cal.

GOPAL: Shut up you fool.

(*He kisses Mr. Gonzales.*)

LYDIA: Hold it!

(*Mr. Gonzales approaches Lydia, looks into her eyes.*)

MR. GONZALES: We were meant for each other.

(*Lydia dips Mr. Gonzales in a swoony embrace. Swing music blares suddenly,
loudly, but strange and warped. Dog, Jill, Gopal, and Mr. Gonzales begin a
wonky dance — swing gone terribly awry. Each of them swirls off, dancing
wildly, jerkily. Lydia is alone. Jill walks through the smoke.*)

JILL: What is it Lydia?

LYDIA: Nothing. Nothing.

(*Jill begins to exit.*)

LYDIA: — Jill.

JILL: Mm hm?

LYDIA: Did you have a nice dance class this afternoon?

JILL: Very nice. You going to try West Coast Swing later?

LYDIA: No. Scuba.

JILL: Well, great. See, swing camp hasn't been so bad, has it?

LYDIA: It's okay.

JILL: Okay, sweetie. I'll see you in the dining hall at dinner. Oh, your dad just
called — he sends hugs. He'll be back before the big costume ball, and
he said for you to save him a dance.

(Jill departs.)

LYDIA: I want to say something out loud and I don't. I don't. But it's with me
all the time, this amazing secret, pumping through my blood. I keep thinking it shows on my skin.

Scene Twenty-nine

Underwater. Blue/green light. Ocean shimmer.
    *The Lead and Follow dancers lindy through in wondrous underwater
fashion, very slowly.*
    Lydia and Mr. Gonzales dance through, intimately.
    Jill moves through the water, dragging a school of fish behind her.

Scene Thirty: The Spit Scene/Bubble of Love

*Lydia and Mr. Gonzales play cards. They kneel across from one another.
Each holds half a deck of cards. Lydia is euphoric.*

LYDIA: One.

MR. GONZALES: Two.

LYDIA: Three. SPIT.

    *(They proceed to play Spit, a mind-bogglingly fast card game that involves
each person slapping his or her cards down on the pile. Lydia finishes her cards.)*

LYDIA: SPIT!

MR. GONZALES: Cheater.

LYDIA: It's sad when a person can't deal with his inadequacy. Very sad.

    (Lydia kisses him. He kisses back. They neck.)

MR. GONZALES: Again.

    (Lydia kisses him again.)

MR. GONZALES: The *game.*

LYDIA: I can't deal the cards if you don't give me my hands.

272 Bridget Carpenter

(He releases her hands.)

MR. GONZALES: I'm winning this time.

LYDIA: Yeah, right.

(Lydia deals cards.)

LYDIA: Ask me a question.

MR. GONZALES: Okay. . . . Where's your dream place to scuba dive?

LYDIA: Australia. The Great Barrier Reef. I'm going there once I get certified.

MR. GONZALES: And then you'll take me into the deep.

LYDIA: Maybe.

MR. GONZALES: Why do you like being underwater.

(Rest.)

LYDIA: You can't hear anything but your breath. You're somewhere you've never been before, ever, and there's nothing but you and your heart.

MR. GONZALES: Sounds pretty good.

LYDIA: Yeah.

MR. GONZALES: Ask me a question.

LYDIA: Okay. Did you get in trouble a lot when you were younger.

MR. GONZALES: No; I read all the time. I was a bookworm. I liked to be alone. When I was around other people I would get very quiet. I remember always being terribly, terribly nervous that I would somehow say something wrong. So I wouldn't talk at all. I'd just observe.

LYDIA: Huh.

MR. GONZALES: I was a strange kid. I got so good at being quiet, people would forget I was in the room. Sometimes *I* would forget I was in the room. Here's the difference between you and me, Lydia: no one will ever, ever forget you're in the room.

(Mr. Gonzales kisses her palm.)

LYDIA: What do you think about when we're. When you touch me.

(Rest.)

MR. GONZALES: I worry that I'm ruining your life.

LYDIA: That's *depressing.*

MR. GONZALES: It's complicated.

LYDIA: I don't think it's complicated.

(She smiles uncomplicatedly into his eyes.)

MR. GONZALES: I worry that I won't let go.

(Lydia sees someone in the distance.)

LYDIA: Look it's Attilla from class. Hey Attilla!

(They both wave.)

LYDIA: You are not ruining my life. Okay?

MR. GONZALES: Okay.

LYDIA: Tonight's the last night. There's a costume ball tonight. Are you going to the costume ball.

MR. GONZALES: Are you.

LYDIA: I wanted to know if you'd go with me. To the costume ball. Never mind. That was stupid. Never mind.

MR. GONZALES: I would like to go. With you. But. . . .

LYDIA: *(Quickly.)* I know.

(Rest. She smiles at him.)

MR. GONZALES: Will you dance with me when we're there?

LYDIA: Okay. Okay.

MR. GONZALES: Okay.

Scene Thirty-one

LYDIA: Last day of class. Certification dive.

Because of rain, the ocean's murky and dark.

But we do the dive anyway.

I get underwater and

something happens.

My breath is coming short and fast. My heart pounds like crazy. I look at my depth gauge and it's *okay,* I've been deeper than this. I've gone deeper than this. I have.

My instructor is signaling me. "Breathe slowly."

I try to make the sign with my hand that I am okay.

Because I am. Okay.

And I imagine myself turning blue, about disappearing right into the water, into nothing. And my heart beats even faster and I try to breathe deeper but no and I release my weight so that I fly straight to the surface.

I can't catch my breath.

You can try again next year, my instructor tells me.

I wish I could go under again, just once more.

Scene Thirty-two: The Costume Ball

Lead and Follow move seamlessly across the ballroom floor. Lead is dressed like 1940s doctor; Follow is dressed as a World War II nurse.

Gopal and Jill stand outside the ballroom at the railing, leaning, looking out at the sea.

They are in costume: Gopal wears a bright zoot suit and matching wide brim hat. Jill wears a glamorous forties dress. She looks picture-perfect, a war bride.

Gopal and Jill turn and watch inside the ballroom.

JILL: Your parents are wonderful dancers.

GOPAL: They are. They've been partners a long time.

JILL: I never saw my parents dance together. They were very happy — I'm sure they were happy — but, that's what I remember most about them: that they didn't dance. So when I met Dog, when he asked me out, I told him very sternly that I wanted to take lessons, that I wanted us to *dance* together. It was like a test.

And he said "fine" so easily. And when we had our first lesson together — which was also our first date — he tried so hard. He really did. I felt guilty. And after that lesson, I said, okay, you don't have to come with me anymore. But he just looked at me and said, well if I keep coming with you, by the time you marry me, I'll be really good. And he was.

GOPAL: Have you talked with Lydia?

JILL: Oh, she's heard this story a million times.

GOPAL: No. About . . .

JILL: Is something wrong?

GOPAL: No. No.

JILL: You're very sweet to her.

GOPAL: She's a friend.

JILL: She's this wonderful thing, my daughter.

GOPAL: She is. Lydia makes me sad, a little —

JILL: She makes you *sad?* Why?

GOPAL: Because — she is so much *herself,* so undiluted, I just — remember what it was like to be fourteen. That age. Awful and wonderful. Riddled with doubt and knowledge. She's so, raw — and. It makes me glad not to be that age anymore.

And her age also makes me remember the sexual affair I had fallen into. When I was that age. An affair with someone older. Old enough to know better.

(Silence. Jill looks at Gopal. Dog enters wearing a sailor suit. He looks remarkably like the kid on the Crackerjack box. Dog opens his arms.)

DOG: Hey! Hey! Give a sailor a dance? Who's going to dance with me first?

(*Jill runs into the ballroom.*)

DOG: Um. What'd I miss? (*Calling.*) Good to see you too, honey! Look at me. I wore this over on the goddamn ferry.

GOPAL: You look good.

DOG: For Christ's sake, Gopal, I look like a refugee from *On The Town.*

(*Jill drags Lydia outside. Lydia is also in costume, wearing a forties skirt with a flare and a very tight, low cut top — perhaps a mink stole.*)

LYDIA: Mom what is your *problem!* Jesus Fucking Christ!

JILL: Don't talk to me that way, Lydia!

LYDIA: You just dragged me *outside!* God! That is so embarrassing! — Dad!

(*Lydia runs to Dog and hugs him.*)

DOG: Look at you, gorgeous!

(*Lydia truly is remarkable — her face is made up and she looks much older.*)

JILL: I did not want to have a scene with you on the dance floor.

LYDIA: So why have a scene at all.

DOG: Honey —

JILL: Dog, be quiet! (*To Lydia.*) What are you wearing? Is that mine?

LYDIA: I just borrowed it.

JILL: That top is too old for you. Take it off.

DOG: Jill —

JILL: I mean it! Now.

LYDIA: Fine!

(*Lydia takes off the top (or stole) and throws it down. She still looks lovely; sexy.*)

DOG: Lids —

JILL: You're grounded.

LYDIA: Why are you doing this? Why do you always do this!

JILL: I am not doing anything.

LYDIA: Yeah it's always me, *I'm* the problem. You know I was *dancing.* I would never grab *you* while *you* were dancing!

(*Mr. Gonzales has come outside — he's also in a dashing costume, wearing an Army captain's World War II uniform.*)

JILL: I want to know what is going on with you.

LYDIA: Nothing!

JILL: Are you having sex? You heard me. Are you having sex?

(*Lydia looks at Gopal.*)

LYDIA: Yeah, Mom, I am. You know Attilla. Seen him in class? That's who I'm fucking.

(Jill slaps Lydia.)

DOG: *Jesus,* Jill! That's enough!

LYDIA: *(At Gopal.)* WHAT DID YOU SAY TO HER! WHAT!

GOPAL: Lydia, I told you I needed to say something.

DOG: Hold on a second. *(To Gopal.)* Have you touched my daughter?

    (Dog has moved toward Gopal.)

GOPAL: Absolutely not. No!

LYDIA: *(Overlap.)* Dad!

JILL: *(Overlap.)* Dog!

DOG: Has everyone gone crazy? What is going on here!

MR. GONZALES: I should probably say something about now.

    (Everyone stares.)

LYDIA: Yeah.

JILL: Jack, this isn't your concern.

MR. GONZALES: But it is. This is something I should have said earlier. I should
    have done something . . . it's my fault. All of it.

LYDIA: No it's not.

    (Lydia begins to move toward Mr. Gonzales.)

MR. GONZALES: *(To Lydia.)* Hold on. What I'm trying to say, not very suc-
    cessfully, is that Lydia's had, a, a, a kind of crush on me. And I was flat-
    tered — and I encouraged it. A little. Which was wrong. But —
    (Lydia is frozen. She cannot believe what she has just heard.)

GOPAL: *(Interrupting.)* What did you just say?

MR. GONZALES: Excuse me, I wasn't talking to you.

GOPAL: I want to understand what you just said. Are you *blaming* Lydia? I mean,
    who's the adult here?

MR. GONZALES: I don't think this is any of your business.

    (The following lines (*) all overlap and rise in volume.)

* GOPAL: I don't give a care ** what you think, I'm asking you to clarify exactly
    what it is you're saying. Repeat it, no, really, repeat it —

* MR. GONZALES: Look — why don't you cool down *** and back off—
    None of this has anything to do with you — I said BACK OFF —

** JILL: Both of you, stop it — I don't understand what you're trying to say
    — STOP IT — what do you mean, a crush, what's that supposed to —
    STOP IT, BOTH OF YOU!

*** DOG: Hey, hey — easy now Gopal, what is going on here — HEY! Cut
    it out — WHOA! Back off — I'm telling you BOTH RIGHT NOW to
    back off —

During the above, Gopal is getting in Mr. Gonzales's face. Mr. Gonzales has given Gopal a shove. Gopal swings hard at Mr. Gonzales, connecting with his jaw.

A fracas. We might see the Lead and the Follow dancing in the ballroom, but slowly, as though underwater.

Lydia, shivering, climbs high atop the wall and stands above and apart from the fray. Music from far away.

LYDIA: At school there was this book everybody was passing around, it was called the Magic Eye.

There are no words, only pictures. You stare at this picture, it's a picture of nothing, just a thousand dots, nothing. And then something clicks, and your eyes fall into the picture that's been there all along.

"People make mistakes."

And I see it clearly, like I never saw it before: I am his mistake.

You can't force your eyes to see the Magic Eye Picture. You just have to wait. Wait and see.

(She raises her hands above her head, looking like a professional diver. Jill sees her daughter.)

JILL: LYDIA!!

(Lydia dives. Everything goes blue. The only sound is of a faraway beating heart. The Lead and Follow dance through in their doctor/nurse costumes.)

Scene Thirty-three

Outside an infirmary. Jill sits. Mr. Gonzales sits beside her. His uniform has been torn, and he has a black eye.

JILL: You should go. We're not going to hear anything more until morning.

MR. GONZALES: I want to be sure she's going to be okay.

JILL: You should *go*.

MR. GONZALES: I'll go when Dog comes back.

JILL: Jack — fine. Never mind.

MR. GONZALES: Listen. You heard the doctor. Lydia's going to be okay. It's a miracle that it was high tide. The worst thing that'll happen is that she'll have a cold.

JILL: And a crush.

MR. GONZALES: Right.

JILL: Why didn't you say something to me.

MR. GONZALES: It felt. I felt — awkward.

JILL: Because of *us.*

MR. GONZALES: Yes.

JILL: Jesus. You know, that was a long time ago, and it's long over.

MR. GONZALES: I know, and I'm telling you that I still felt awkward.

JILL: *(Burning.)* This, this situation infuriates me.
I don't even know how to talk to you.
You *knew* she had a crush on you?

That is crazy!	MR. GONZALES:
What kind of behavior is that!	It's not any *kind* —
And why *wouldn't* you feel awkward —	
I mean, God! What were you thinking?	

MR. GONZALES: I wasn't thinking. I wasn't — thinking anything. I just *left;* I told you. And what was I supposed to say?

JILL: You were supposed to say, Jill I think your daughter has a crush on me. — Why am I telling you what you should have said!

MR. GONZALES: I didn't say anything to you because it felt like a betrayal.

JILL: Of whom?

MR. GONZALES: I would have felt as though I was betraying Lydia. If I had said something to you.

JILL: So you thought that quietly watching my daughter fall for you was a prudent way to handle the situation.

MR. GONZALES: I don't know what I thought! Obviously, I thought wrong. I thought: she seemed like she needed a friend. I liked to listen to her. I care about her. I never planned to hurt anyone.

JILL: Tonight I watched my daughter fall five stories, staring at you. And. If she had died. Do you know what my last words to her would have been? "That's not yours. Take it off."
(Rest.)

MR. GONZALES: *(Gently.)* She didn't die. You have to believe that everything is going to be okay.

JILL: Go away.

MR. GONZALES: Don't sit here and imagine the worst — why would you do that.

JILL: Because I'm her mother.

MR. GONZALES: It's not your fault.

JILL: It's my *responsibility.* You're responsible for the people you love.

MR. GONZALES: Lydia's at that age — you said as much.

JILL: *(Quiet.)* I did.

    (Rest.)

JILL: Go. Away. Which part don't you understand?

MR. GONZALES: I'll see you in the morning. I'm on the morning ferry. Tell Lydia — tell Lydia I know she's going to be okay.

    (Mr. Gonzales leaves. Dog comes out from the infirmary. His cheek is bandaged. He sits next to her. He takes her hand and holds it. They both look straight ahead, holding hands.)

Scene Thirty-four

Dog stands with a suitcase; Gopal stands with clipboard and sign-out stuff.

GOPAL: It's good you're avoiding the rush. On the ferry.

DOG: Sure.

GOPAL: You guys are on the five thirty, right?

DOG: Right.

GOPAL: That's a nice time to be on the boat. Afternoon sun.

DOG: Great, great.

GOPAL: You got all your bags okay?

DOG: Oh, sure. Yeah, we're okay.

GOPAL: I saw Lydia this morning. She looks fine.

DOG: She does. She is. I'm sorry. For my behavior.

GOPAL: You don't owe me an —

DOG: I do, I'm saying I'm sorry. You're a good teacher. You're a good young man and I made a serious misjudgment. I apologize. Just let me. I'm sorry.

    (Gopal nods. He hums the same music from Scene Twenty-four to highlight a break. They break together. And hold . . . for eight beats, then start up on the same beat. Dog smiles, takes the suitcases, and walks away.)

Scene Thirty-five

Lydia sits alone on a bench. Her face is puffy as though she's been crying. Jill enters.

JILL: I packed for you. So we're ready to go. Next ferry.

LYDIA: Where's Dad.

JILL: He's down at the boat.

LYDIA: Where's Mr. Gonzales.

JILL: I don't know.

LYDIA: Did he say good-bye to you?

JILL: No.

LYDIA: He probably left already.

JILL: Probably.

LYDIA: Just you and me, huh.

JILL: Yes. I'm sorry.

LYDIA: Why.

JILL: I'm sorry because . . . I have had crushes before. And I remember. What it was like.

LYDIA: It wasn't a "crush."

JILL: I didn't pay attention. I didn't see. And you were hurt. And it's my fault.

LYDIA: No it's not.

JILL: Did he. Did Mr. Gonzales. "Encourage" you. Did he ever —
     (Silence.)

JILL: Because if I thought, If you tell me he *did something* — Lydia. Because you can tell me. Please. I don't think that I could live with myself. If that were true. Because it would be my fault. It would be my fault entirely. You're the thing I love most.
     (Rest.)
     (Lydia speaks to us.)

LYDIA: I know — in that moment, I will never tell her. Because it will change everything. Because she'll hate herself. Mostly because when you tell people things, those things — they're not yours anymore. And this will always be mine. I'll never say anything. It becomes my secret. Mr. Gonzales sinks down, submerges somewhere inside me.
     (Rest.)

LYDIA: Mommy. I just liked him. And it was embarrassing when he didn't like me. That's all. It sucks though. Are you and Dad going to —

JILL: No.
     (Silence.)

JILL: You know when you were born, when I felt you coming out of my body I couldn't believe how much it hurt. That fierce pain. That endless pushing. And it made me *happy,* I was so happy because I felt you kicking, and then I saw you, so perfect, and holding you, I knew that I would take any amount of pain for you. I would. Labor was just a fraction. I wanted it always to be that easy.

(Faint music from the ballroom.)

JILL: You are so beautiful. What a silly thing that seems like to say right now. But it's true.

(Jill stands up and holds out her hand.)

JILL: Want to dance.

LYDIA: Mommm. Gah.

JILL: I mean it.

(Jill continues to hold out her hand.
Slowly, Lydia gets up.
Music.
Lydia and Jill dance smoothly together.
Fade to blue.)

END OF PLAY

LAST TRAIN TO NIBROC
by Arlene Hutton

For my parents,
Arlie and Mary Elizabeth Lincks,
with love and thanks

ORIGINAL PRODUCTION

Last Train to Nibroc was produced by Leonard Soloway, Chase Mishkin, and Steven M. Levy at the Douglas Fairbanks Theatre, November 21, 1999. It was directed by Michael Montel; the costume design was by Shelley Norton, the lighting design was by Christopher Gorzelnik, the set design was by Si Joong Yoon; the sound design was by Peter J. Fitzgerald, and the stage manager was Tamara K. Heeschen. The cast was as follows:

RALEIGH . . . . .Benim Foster
MAY . . . . .Alexandra Geis

Last Train to Nibroc received its premiere at the 78th Street Theatre Lab February 11, 1999, coproduced by the 78th Street Theatre Lab (Eric Nightengale, Artistic Director.) and The Journey Company (Beth Lincks, Producing Artistic Director.). It was directed by Michael Montel; the costume design was by Shelley Norton, the lighting design was by Christopher Gorzelnik and the stage manager was Julie Kessler. The cast was as follows:

RALEIGH . . . . .Benim Foster
MAY . . . . .Alexandra Geis

Last Train to Nibroc was presented at the Assembly Rooms for the Edinburgh Festival Fringe 1999 and at the Piccolo Spoleto Theatre Festival 2000, produced by The Journey Company and the 78th Street Theatre Lab. It was directed by Michael Montel; the costume design was by Shelley Norton, the lighting design was by Eric Nightengale and the stage manager was Eric Nightengale. The cast was as follows:

RALEIGH . . . . .Benim Foster
MAY . . . . .Alexandra Geis

Last Train to Nibroc was originally workshopped at The Players through a development grant from Loyola Marymount, with Benim Foster and Alexandra Geis, under the direction of Judith Royer. A showcase production with Benim Foster and Alexandra Geis, under the direction of Michael Montel, was presented at the Henry Street Settlement for the New York International Fringe Festival 1998, a presentation of The Present Company.

BIOGRAPHY

Arlene Hutton is a member of New Dramatists, the Dramatists Guild, The Journey Company and Circle East. Born in Louisiana and raised in Florida, she lives in New York City where she began writing plays at Alice's Fourth Floor under the direction of Susann Brinkley. Hutton is the author of *I Dream Before I Take the Stand* and many other one acts, including two Samuel French Short Play Festival winners, *Studio Portrait,* and *The Price You Pay.* Her short piece *Pushing Buttons* was a finalist for the 2000 Heineman Award. Credits include off-Broadway, off-off Broadway, regional and university theaters. *Last Train to Nibroc*, her first full-length work, was a finalist for the Francesca Primus prize and received the New York Drama League nomination for Best Play.

CHARACTERS

Note: for alternative casting purposes, the two characters could be played by minorities, but they should be of the same ethnicity.

MAY: Twenty-one or twenty-two. From a small town in Kentucky. She is sincere and honest in her beliefs.

RALEIGH: About the same age. From a nearby town. Just a good guy, slow to anger and quick to chuckle.

TIME AND PLACE

Scene One: December 28, 1940
    A train, somewhere west of Chicago
Scene Two: Summer, 1942
    A park bench near a woods.
Scene Three: Spring, 1943
    May's front porch.
(A park bench could be used for all three scenes with covers placed on it for Scenes One and Three, creating a train seat and a porch settee or swing.)

The play is to be performed without intermission. If that is not possible, the interval break should occur between Scene One and Scene Two.

GLOSSARY

Buggytop Shelton: a well-known bootlegger in Corbin, Kentucky, who made and sold moonshine up through the 1940s.

Moonshine: illicitly distilled liquor, especially whiskey.

Prohibition: the period from 1920 to 1933 when the sale of alcoholic beverages in the United States was forbidden by an amendment to the Constitution.

Jake leg: a sometimes permanent paralysis caused by drinking Jamaica Gin, a tainted gin from Jamaica sold by Skinny Eaton at his pharmacy in Corbin, Kentucky, during prohibition.

Dixie Dog: a restaurant on Main Street in Corbin, famous for its hot dogs with chili. As of late 1999 it was still there, still serving chili-dogs. You have to ask for ketchup.

Tent meeting: the summer revival meetings held in tents.

"Lamb of God": a hymn sung at revival meetings during the call to the altar, also known as "Just as I Am."

Asbury College: a Methodist church school in Wilmore, Kentucky.

Sharecrop: a rented farm.

Switch: a thin, pliable limb from a bush or small tree, used for spanking.

Nathanael West: author of *Day of the Locusts,* died in a car accident in California on December 22, 1940. His body was brought to New York on the Santa Fe Super Chief, which left Los Angeles at 8:00 P.M. December 26. Also on board was Sheila Graham — her companion F. Scott Fitzgerald, author of *The Great Gatsby,* had died of a heart attack on December 21. Both bodies were cared for at Pierce Brothers Mortuaries, and Fitzgerald's was also sent east, to Baltimore, most likely on the same train as West.

AUTHOR'S NOTE

People ask me why I wrote *Last Train to Nibroc,* which at first seems to be a rather old-fashioned story. Well, it was originally a one-act that took place entirely on a train. The idea for that scene came to me while reading a biography of S. J. Perelmann, who was a brother-in-law to the author Nathanael West. West died in a car accident in December, 1940, and his body was shipped east by train. Also on the same train was Sheila Graham, for her companion F. Scott Fitzgerald had also just passed away, and it is very likely that she was accompanying his body across the country to Maryland.

I put two young people from Kentucky on that train, basing them very loosely on my parents, who in real life had been falling in love at just about that time. Although this one-act version was very well received, the actors and director and I felt that there was a bigger story to tell. A year later, with the assistance of a development grant, and curious to find out more about May and Raleigh, I wrote two more scenes — finishing the play in six days. I've been revising it ever since at New Dramatists. I just made a couple more changes for this edition.

Last Train to Nibroc is a patchwork quilt of family lore and stories I heard as a child, all stitched together to tell the fictional tale of May and Raleigh. When I wrote the one-act version, which is the first scene of the full-length, I had no idea how the details about Raleigh and May would pay off later. Indeed, May was originally called Mary, after my mother. An early typo amended it to May and I liked that better, not realizing that it would be important in Scene Three. When setting up Raleigh's epilepsy in the first scene, I also had no idea, until I read it on my computer screen, that Raleigh would become ill at the end of Scene Two, or that May would misunderstand his sickness in the way she does. Moments like these were as much a surprise to me when I wrote them as they are for the audience seeing the play.

It has been extremely rewarding to see the audience response to this little play. The senior theatergoers are delighted to revisit their past, of course, but I have especially enjoyed the enthusiasm of teens and young adults who gain insight into the lives of their parents or grandparents, discovering that the "good old days" were not so simple and that stories of love and forgiveness are universal to all ages.

Arlene Hutton
December 1, 2000

LAST TRAIN TO NIBROC

Scene One

December 27, 1940. Two train seats on a train bound from California to Chicago. May, twenty-one or twenty-two, is seated by the window, reading a book. Raleigh, close in age, is standing next to her, in the aisle. He wears a flyer's uniform. They both have slight Kentucky accents. He looks at her, as though expecting her to say something. She is very shy with strangers.

RALEIGH: Mind if I . . .
    (May keeps reading her book.)
RALEIGH: *(Continued.)* Mind if I set a spell?
    (Raleigh gestures to the empty seat beside her.)
MAY: *(After beat.)* Don't make no nevermind to me.
    (May keeps reading her book. A pause.)
RALEIGH: This train —
MAY: Yes?
RALEIGH: This train's very —
MAY: Yes, it's —
RALEIGH: Full. Crowded.
MAY: Yes.
RALEIGH: *(Smiling at her.)* I was lucky to get a seat.
MAY: Yes. *(Looking around.)* But —
RALEIGH: Do you mind me sitting here?
MAY: I don't know you.
RALEIGH: I was standing all night.
MAY: Standing?
RALEIGH: Until the train stopped at this station.
MAY: Yes, it was full —
RALEIGH: It was packed leaving California. I got on in Los Angeleese. *(Pause.)*
    What'ya reading?
MAY: Pardon?
RALEIGH: Your book.
MAY: Oh.
    (May looks at the cover of the book.)
MAY: *(Continued.)* It's *Magnificent Obsession.*
RALEIGH: *(Gently teasing.)* Sounds pretty racy.

MAY: *(Taking him seriously.)* No. Not at all.

RALEIGH: A romance.

MAY: It's more religious . . .

RALEIGH: *(Still teasing.)* There's no romance in it?

MAY: It's not about that.

RALEIGH: There's not a girl and a guy?

MAY: Well, there is, but —

RALEIGH: It must be a love story.

MAY: It's not. I don't read —

RALEIGH: It's a love story. Has to be.

MAY: *(Flustered.)* Why?

RALEIGH: With a title like that. *Magnificent Obsession.*

MAY: That's not what the title is about.

RALEIGH: Not what?

MAY: Not about.

RALEIGH: Not about what?

MAY: Romance. A love story. What you — It's not about —
    (She pauses.)

RALEIGH: *(Simply.)* What is it about? Your book. What's it about?

MAY: This man — *(She stops.)*

RALEIGH: Do they kiss?

MAY: What?

RALEIGH: In the book?

MAY: *(Simply.)* I haven't finished it yet.

RALEIGH: Oh.

MAY: But it's religious.

RALEIGH: Uh-huh.

MAY: It is. It's from the church library. The library at church. It's religious.
    (May goes back to her book. A pause.)

RALEIGH: Are you?

MAY: What?

RALEIGH: Religious?

MAY: Well, yes.

RALEIGH: *(Pause.)* It's about a doctor. *(Pause.)* Your book.

MAY: You've read it!

RALEIGH: A couple years ago. I read everything.

MAY: Don't tell me the ending.

RALEIGH: It's a romance.

MAY: No, it's —

RALEIGH: Religious?

MAY: Well, inspirational.

    (A pause.)

RALEIGH: You like to read?

MAY: Well, yes.

RALEIGH: I like to write.

MAY: *(Interested.)* Really? You're a writer?

RALEIGH: Gonna be. *(Pause.)* There's writers on this train.

MAY: How do you know?

RALEIGH: Porter over yonder told me. He let me sit in the men's room for a
    while.

MAY: I thought you didn't have a seat.

RALEIGH: That's good.

MAY: What is?

RALEIGH: That's funny.

MAY: It's not funny that you had to sit in the —

RALEIGH: I thought it was lucky. Like having a private room.

MAY: A private room with running water.

RALEIGH: With hot and cold running water.

MAY: *(Laughs.)* You're funny.

RALEIGH: So're you.

    (They smile at each other. A pause. May picks up her book again.)

RALEIGH: The porter told me there's writers on the train.

MAY: Well, there's lots of people on the train.

RALEIGH: Guess who's riding this train with us.

MAY: I don't like to guess.

RALEIGH: No, just guess. You can't.

MAY: I know I can't guess, so I won't even try.

RALEIGH: Two of them.

MAY: Two what?

RALEIGH: Authors. Famous ones.

MAY: Who?

RALEIGH: Guess!

MAY: I don't — *(May reads from the spine of her book.)* Lloyd C. Douglas?

RALEIGH: Nope.

MAY: William Shakespeare?

RALEIGH: You're not even trying.

MAY: I don't care.

RALEIGH: Very famous writers.

MAY: Who, then?

RALEIGH: Nathanael West!

MAY: Who's that?

RALEIGH: You don't know who Nathanael West is?

MAY: No.

RALEIGH: He's a great novelist. *The Day of the Locust. Miss Lonelyhearts.*

MAY: I don't read books like that.

RALEIGH: Books like what?

MAY: Lonely heart books. Romances.

RALEIGH: They're not — What do you read? Besides. . . .

(Raleigh indicates her book.)

MAY: Inspirational stories.

RALEIGH: F. Scott Fitzgerald.

MAY: No.

RALEIGH: He inspired me.

MAY: That's not what I meant.

RALEIGH: He's on this train, too.

MAY: Is not.

RALEIGH: Is so. F. Scott Fitzgerald is riding on this train. Going to New York City.

MAY: You're making it up.

RALEIGH: Do you even know who he is?

MAY: Of course.

RALEIGH: Have you read his books?

MAY: No.

RALEIGH: Well, he's on this train. F. Scott Fitzgerald.

MAY: But he's dead, silly. He died. He died a few days ago. I read about it in the newspaper.

RALEIGH: He's on the train.

MAY: He's dead.

RALEIGH: He's in the baggage car.

(A pause.)

MAY: You're crazy.

RALEIGH: His coffin.

MAY: Pardon?

RALEIGH: His coffin is riding in the baggage car. F. Scott Fitzgerald is on this train. He's riding the same train we are.

MAY: Oh. *(Pause.)* How do you know?

RALEIGH: Porter told me.

MAY: Oh.

RALEIGH: With Nathanael West.

MAY: He's with him?

RALEIGH: His coffin, too. We're riding with two of the greatest authors of the century. We're all on this train together.

MAY: That's morbid.

RALEIGH: It's funny, what puts people on trains together.

MAY: Mmmm. *(May looks out the window.)* Where are we?

RALEIGH: Don't know. *(Raleigh tries to look out her window.)* Can't tell. But the sun's about to come up.

MAY: It's black as pitch.

RALEIGH: Little light over yonder. See? Just a glimpse of the sunrise.

(He leans over her even more to see out.)

MAY: You can't have this seat.

RALEIGH: *(Surprised.)* I don't want it.

MAY: Well, you can't have it!

RALEIGH: I never said —

MAY: You just want the window seat so you can sleep. Lean your head against the window.

RALEIGH: No, it's yours.

MAY: You're right. It's mine. And I'm not giving it up.

RALEIGH: Look, miss.

MAY: *(Starting to cry.)* I came all the way out here sitting on the aisle seat. People bumping me and I never got to sleep at all and I couldn't look out the window most of the time and there were small children running around. I like children —

RALEIGH: — of course you do —

MAY: — but not when they're running up and down the aisles a' screaming. And bumping my arm so I couldn't sleep for the life of me, not even doze, and there was this man —

RALEIGH: — a man?

MAY: — for hours, just hours, in the window seat here, and I couldn't find another seat, and I had to sit up straight and he —

RALEIGH: — what?

MAY: *(Really crying now.)* — he smelled. He just smelled bad. And the train and the smell made me sick and I had to —

RALEIGH: Oh, that's too bad.

MAY: Well, I almost had to, well, be sick. But I wasn't. And so I'm not giving up this seat to anyone, not my window seat, not to anyone, especially not to a soldier!

(A pause.)

RALEIGH: Would you like my handkerchief?

MAY: I have my own, thank you very much.

RALEIGH: May I get it for you? Your handkerchief.

MAY: *(Sobbing.)* It's in my suitcase.

RALEIGH: Here's mine, then. Take it. You need a handkerchief.

MAY: I'm just so tired. I don't know what to do.

RALEIGH: *(At a loss.)* Uh-huh.

MAY: It's been so awful.

RALEIGH: It will get better.

MAY: I don't see how. *(Pause.)* I have to go home.

RALEIGH: Well, that's good, isn't it?

MAY: I don't know how I can face them. My family.

RALEIGH: Please don't mind my asking this.

MAY: You're being very nice. And you don't even know me.

RALEIGH: You're afraid to go home to your family.

MAY: Not afraid. Ashamed.

RALEIGH: Is there? . . . . Are you? . . . . You felt ill.

MAY: No.

RALEIGH: On the trip out. You said . . . .

MAY: You think I'm . . . delicate?

RALEIGH: You said that you —

MAY: Oh, no. I'd never. How can you think that of me?

RALEIGH: I don't.

MAY: They'll think that.

RALEIGH: Your family.

MAY: They'll think that we . . . that I.

(May starts to sob again.)

RALEIGH: But you're not.

MAY: Of course not!

RALEIGH: Well, that's good then.

MAY: We were engaged.

RALEIGH: A soldier.

MAY: Well, he's training. To fly. Yes.

RALEIGH: You went out to see him. Before he went to England.

MAY: Yes. For Christmas.

RALEIGH: That was a nice thing for you to do.

MAY: No. He was different. He's changed.

    (A pause.)

RALEIGH: And now you're going home.

MAY: Yes.

RALEIGH: Home, where? Where's home?

MAY: Kentucky. Corbin. Corbin, Kentucky.

RALEIGH: No.

MAY: Yes. Corbin.

RALEIGH: I'm from Woodbine, Kentucky.

MAY: You're not.

RALEIGH: Yes, I am.

MAY: Well, how about that.

RALEIGH: How about that. Just a few miles apart.

MAY: So you're going to Woodbine?

RALEIGH: No, I'm just from there. I'm going to New York City.

MAY: You're not changing trains?

RALEIGH: No, I was. In the beginning. Almost. But I want to go to New York City.

MAY: You out of the service.

RALEIGH: Um, well, yeah.

MAY: Aren't you itching to go? Go overseas?

RALEIGH: I was.

MAY: Most people volunteering. Going into the service. I don't know anybody leaving the service.

RALEIGH: Medical.

    (A pause.)

MAY: I'm sorry.

    (An awkward pause.)

RALEIGH: It was hard to leave my buddies.

MAY: I would imagine it was. But don't you want to see your family?

RALEIGH: They'll be ashamed I'm not off flying like I said I was gonna do.

MAY: They'd be glad to see you.

RALEIGH: They'll think I gave up.

MAY: No. They'll be glad you didn't go fight. They'll be real glad to see you.

RALEIGH: Later. After I've been in New York City for a while.

MAY: Don't you miss Kentucky? I missed Corbin. When I was in California.

RALEIGH: Corbin's a nice town. The Nibroc Festival.

MAY: I've never been.

RALEIGH: You've never been to the Nibroc Festival?

MAY: No.

RALEIGH: And you grew up in Corbin.

MAY: Yes.

RALEIGH: Lived in Corbin all your life?

MAY: Yes.

RALEIGH: And you've never been to the Nibroc Festival?

MAY: No. Have you?

RALEIGH: Sure.

MAY: I haven't.

RALEIGH: Why not?

MAY: I always went to the tent meeting. It's the same time of year. I went to the tent meetings at the campgrounds. To hear all the preachers.

RALEIGH: You "saved"?

MAY: Of course. You?

RALEIGH: Baptist. I've been baptized. Don't have to keep being saved.

MAY: It's not exactly like that.

RALEIGH: A person doesn't have to stand up every time they hear the call, every time they hear "Lamb of God."

MAY: I don't.

RALEIGH: I never understood why people get saved all over again every summer.

MAY: I guess they have to, after the Nibroc festival. They go to the Nibroc Festival, then they have to be saved again.

RALEIGH: You're wrong about that.

MAY: It just seems to me.

RALEIGH: The festival's not like that. Some people, some boys get a little moonshine, maybe, but mostly it's just to get people together. And elect the queen. The queen of the festival. It's like a fair.

MAY: I know what it's like.

RALEIGH: No, you don't. You haven't been.

MAY: I'm from Corbin. I know what the Nibroc Festival is. You're not from Corbin. You don't know.

RALEIGH: I've been, though. I've been to the festival. And I'm going to take you to the festival.

MAY: No, you're not.

RALEIGH: Yes, I am. Next year I am going to take you to the Nibroc Festival.

MAY: I thought you were going to New York City.

(A pause.)

RALEIGH: I'm going to New York City and then I'm going to take you to the Nibroc Festival.

MAY: If you go to New York City, you won't be coming home to take me anywhere. People who go away, change. They're not like from home anymore.

RALEIGH: Like your fiancé.

MAY: Like him. Yes, like him.

RALEIGH: I was in California, too.

MAY: Well, I didn't know you before.

RALEIGH: You're starting to know me now.

MAY: We're just riding this train together. That's all.

(May starts reading her book. A pause.)

RALEIGH: There aren't any other seats that I can see, but if I catch sight of anyone getting off at the next station I'll try to move.

MAY: You don't have to.

RALEIGH: I don't like to sit where I'm not welcome. I'll move just as soon as I can, and some woman with a wailing baby will take my place. Well, I'm going to go ride back with the coffins. With F. Scott and Nathanael West.

MAY: Don't be silly.

RALEIGH: Is that a smile? No, couldn't be. Yep, I'd better go ride back there with the writers. The dead writers.

MAY: Stop.

RALEIGH: Old F. Scott and young Nat.

MAY: That's morbid.

RALEIGH: Scotty and Natty.

MAY: *(Suppressing a giggle in spite of herself.)* Scotty and Natty?

RALEIGH: Well, now. You're going home. See, you should be happy. Another few hours and you can change trains for Kentucky.

MAY: You, too.

RALEIGH: Nope. I'm staying. On the train. Going to New York City. Funny, when I got on, boarded the train, back in Los Angeleese, I was going home. Not happy about it, but going home. I got on this train. Thought, I can go anywhere. Chicago, anywhere. No one's expecting me. No one knows I'm coming. Got a uniform still on, got a pass. Anywhere I want to go.

MAY: Well, I could go anywhere, too.

RALEIGH: You wanting to?

MAY: I don't know. Hadn't thought about it.

RALEIGH: Well, I have. I can go anywhere. Thought about Detroit, lots of work in the factories, my brother-in-law says, but I can go do that any time.

MAY: You don't want to go home?

RALEIGH: Nope. Home'll always be there. I got on this train, and the conductor told me that the coffins were being loaded in. That Nathaniel West and

F. Scott Fitzgerald were riding the same train I was. So, don't you see, I
   can't let that go by. When would something like that ever happen again?

MAY: You didn't know them.

RALEIGH: I didn't know you, either, but now we're riding the same train. And
   no matter what happens, there will always have been a time that we rode
   the train together. Things are affected by other things. And I can't let it
   go by. That I'm on the train with the two greatest writers of this century.
   And I thought I've just got to stay on this train. Follow those men. This
   is my chance, my time, and if I don't take it now, don't move right now,
   not later, now, while I'm supposed to, it'll never happen again.

MAY: But you didn't know them.

RALEIGH: Sure I know them! I know everything they've written. Feels like I
   know them better than I know myself, even. And something real deep
   inside — I don't usually just spill everything out like this. *(A pause.)* I
   know your feller. Your fiancé.

   (May stares at him.)

RALEIGH: Not well, but I know him. I've seen your picture. He didn't get leave.
   I had to stay. To get ready to be discharged. Buddies got leave. For
   Christmas. I had to stay for processing.

MAY: They got time off?

RALEIGH: They got leave.

MAY: And he didn't?

RALEIGH: Reckon not.

MAY: How come?

RALEIGH: Must not've earned it. Must not've worked hard enough.

MAY: So I had to miss Christmas with my family? So I had to come all the
   way out here because he's lazy?

RALEIGH: I really don't know. Maybe he wanted you to come because he thought
   you'd have a good time.

MAY: Well, he was wrong. I had a terrible time. He was different and he smoked
   and he didn't have any place for me to stay.

RALEIGH: Housing is getting tight, hard to —

MAY: Why'd he have me come out?

RALEIGH: Don't know. I don't know him very well.

MAY: And I slept on this porch, this woman's porch. Didn't really sleep, couldn't
   sleep, it was a porch. A porch in a strange place.

RALEIGH: Were you cold?

MAY: No, but it was just a porch.

RALEIGH: Don't you sleep on the porch back home? When it's hot?

MAY: Well, yes.

RALEIGH: A porch is a porch.

MAY: This was in a stranger's house. Not even the house. The porch. This woman I didn't know.

RALEIGH: Well, where did you want to sleep? A hotel?

MAY: Of course not! Not unless we, if we were —

RALEIGH: Were you planning to get married? Out there?

MAY: I don't know! It seemed — I just went because he — I don't know. And then it just wasn't the same. He's different.

RALEIGH: Everyone's different. Everyone's changing. The world's changed. You've changed.

MAY: You never knew me.

RALEIGH: No, but I'll just bet you've changed. Going all the way across the country on a train. Something's got to be different when you get back. *(A pause.)*

RALEIGH: You going to need my handkerchief again?

MAY: No, I'm not.

RALEIGH: It's here if you need it.

MAY: I don't.

RALEIGH: Well, just in case, it's here.

MAY: I wouldn't take your hanky if this train went through the Johnstown flood.

RALEIGH: Little missy, this trip of yours has sure made you feisty. Bet they won't even know you back in Corbin. You'll march into the Dixie Dog and they'll hand you the catsup without you even asking.

MAY: He's the one changed.

RALEIGH: Think so?

MAY: Know so.

RALEIGH: So.

(An uncomfortable pause.)

MAY: I'm going to read now. If you don't mind.

RALEIGH: Be my guest. Back to your *Magnificent Obsession*.

MAY: Don't tell me the ending.

RALEIGH: You'll have to find out for yourself.

(Raleigh starts to stand up.)

MAY: Going to the smoking car?

RALEIGH: That's right.

MAY: Don't come back smelling of smoke.

RALEIGH: I don't smoke.

MAY: In that case maybe I'll save your seat.

298 Arlene Hutton

RALEIGH: Thanks. I'd like that.

(Raleigh turns to go up the aisle.)

MAY: Wait. What did he say about me?

RALEIGH: Your feller? He said you were a goody two-shoes.

MAY: (Pause.) You think I'm a goody two-shoes?

RALEIGH: I think you think you are.

MAY: That's the same thing.

RALEIGH: Nope. I think deep down inside you have an adventurous spirit. Not every girl from Corbin, Kentucky, would get on a train and ride all the way to California not knowing what she was going to find there. Not many girls would talk to a soldier she didn't even know and cry in his handkerchief.

MAY: I'm going to be a missionary.

RALEIGH: Excuse me?

MAY: I told him. I've always wanted to be a missionary. He knew that. I wanted us to be missionaries.

RALEIGH: I said you had an adventurous spirit.

MAY: That's not adventurous.

RALEIGH: You don't like sleeping on a porch. Think you're going to like living in a hut?

MAY: I won't sleep in a hut.

RALEIGH: You sure will. Missionaries live in huts.

MAY: I hadn't thought about it.

RALEIGH: I reckon you hadn't thought about it. Well, you better be thinking about it. Think you were going to live on a plantation with native servants?

MAY: Not exactly.

RALEIGH: Doesn't your church pack up barrels with used clothes for the missionaries?

MAY: Well, yes.

RALEIGH: You'd be getting a barrel full of old clothes to hang up in your hut. It's a hard life for a woman.

MAY: I live on a farm. I can hoe a row, shuck corn, milk a cow, and wring a chicken's neck.

RALEIGH: And I had you pegged for a town girl.

MAY: Just outside of town. Off highway twenty-five.

RALEIGH: North or south?

MAY: North.

RALEIGH: T'ward London.

MAY: Yes. Off twenty-five.

RALEIGH: You know the Logans?

MAY: Live across the road. They're neighbors.

RALEIGH: Cousins. I'm cousins with them. I know your farm. Nice piece of land.

MAY: It's —

RALEIGH: Not bottom land, like Raccoon Creek, but not too hilly.

MAY: We've got lots of blackberries.

RALEIGH: I love blackberries.

MAY: Me, too.

RALEIGH: I'll come pick blackberries on your farm and we'll go to the Nibroc Festival. Unless you're off in some jungle converting the natives.

MAY: That will be a while. I just finished school. In Wilmore.

RALEIGH: Asbury College. Church school. So you're serious about this missionary work.

MAY: Of course I am.

RALEIGH: I thought you were just making it up.

MAY: Oh, no. I've been serious about it for a long time. I'm serious. I think.

RALEIGH: You think? You'd better think. It must be a hard life. Lonely. No one you know around. Nobody to speak your language with. Except a husband. *(A pause.)* You have to be married to be a missionary, don't you?

MAY: I think so.

RALEIGH: So, it'll be a while before you go away.

MAY: I suspect so.

RALEIGH: Why don't you come with me to New York City?

MAY: Excuse me?

RALEIGH: Come to New York City.

MAY: I don't know anyone in New York City.

RALEIGH: You know me. There's women's boarding houses. I've read about them.

MAY: Maybe you read too much.

RALEIGH: Maybe.

MAY: I could never live in a city.

RALEIGH: Have you ever been to one?

MAY: Silly. I just came from Los Angelees.

RALEIGH: That's not a real city.

MAY: I've been to Louisville. *(Pronounced* L'LL-v'lle.*)* I don't like Louisville.

RALEIGH: I wanted to go to Paris. With the war. And London. That's why I volunteered. London, England, not Kentucky. So if I can't go to Europe I'll go to New York City.

MAY: Well, I'm going home to Kentucky. And so should you.

RALEIGH: I'm going to New York City. Going to be a writer. When I'm a writer then I can go back home.

MAY: It won't be the same.

RALEIGH: It's not the same now. We're all changing. We're all riding this country's future like this train's a'rollin' along the track, just hoping we get somewhere and don't run off the tracks somewhere along the way. Trusting that the engineer and the brakeman and the signalman are all on the job, trusting that they'll get us there in one piece.

MAY: That's very poetic.

RALEIGH: Told you I was a writer.

MAY: So you did.

RALEIGH: Now prove to me that you're a missionary. Pray something for us. Pray that we get to where we're supposed to go. Pray that we don't go to war.

MAY: I'm having a hard time praying these days.

RALEIGH: Okay. I'll leave you alone.

(A pause.)

MAY: I'm sorry I said those things.

RALEIGH: Which things are you sorry you said?

MAY: Well, about the porch. It wasn't so bad.

RALEIGH: Those things.

MAY: You keep teasing me.

RALEIGH: Just looking for the brighter side. *(A pause.)* Come to New York City.

MAY: With you? I don't do things like that.

RALEIGH: There's lady's boarding houses in New York City. Lots of jobs.

MAY: No. I'm not . . . brave.

RALEIGH: You're very brave.

MAY: I'm not at all brave. I'm a scaredy cat. I'm a whipped pup, going home with my tail between my legs. I'm silly. I'm timid. I'm not at all brave.

RALEIGH: I think you're brave.

MAY: 'Cause I want to be a missionary?

RALEIGH: Wanting something's not brave. If you become a missionary, I reckon that would be brave, but giving it up is brave, too. Giving up one dream for another is brave. Oh, you gotta read Nathanael West. Everydayordinary things are brave sometimes. Talking to strangers like me is brave. Going to California took courage, and leaving it took even more.

MAY: I hadn't thought about it. I've mostly just been feeling bad.

RALEIGH: You should feel good about, well, about escaping that fate.

MAY: Is going to New York City brave?

RALEIGH: Of course it is!

MAY: Being a soldier is brave.

RALEIGH: Not being a soldier, flyer, is braver.

MAY: Why aren't you gonna be a flyer any more?

RALEIGH: Discharge. Medical discharge.

MAY: Why?

RALEIGH: I started getting the fits out there.

> (May stares at him.)

> Something sort of like the fits. Just a little bit. Once or twice only. But they're discharging me.

MAY: That's why you don't want to go home.

> (A very long pause as May doesn't quite know what to say.)

> You can always go to New York City later, if you really want to.

RALEIGH: But now's my opportunity.

MAY: Following dead men. Going to New York City because there's some dead men going there?

RALEIGH: They're famous writers.

MAY: They *were* famous writers, or so you say. I've never heard of one of them.

RALEIGH: He's famous.

MAY: But they're dead.

RALEIGH: They're famous writers.

MAY: But they're dead. It's over for them. Not you. Having a couple of little fits won't kill you. So why're you following dead men? Can't visit them in New York City. And are those coffins even going to New York City? Isn't your friend Mr. Fitzgerald going to Virginia or Delaware or someplace?

RALEIGH: Maryland.

MAY: See? What'd he write about, anyway?

RALEIGH: Rich people, flappers.

MAY: Rich people where?

RALEIGH: The Riviera and New York City and —

MAY: He wrote about New York City.

RALEIGH: Yep.

MAY: So what are you going to write about?

RALEIGH: Stories.

MAY: About what?

RALEIGH: People.

MAY: People where?

RALEIGH: In the mountains.

MAY: In Kentucky.

RALEIGH: Yep.

MAY: So why are you going to New York City if you're going to write about Kentucky?

(Raleigh is taken aback. A pause.)

RALEIGH: That's where writers go. New York City.

MAY: Are they happy there? You think Mr. Fitzgerald was happy in New York City?

RALEIGH: No.

MAY: Were you happy in Kentucky? You miss it?

RALEIGH: Yes, of course.

MAY: I don't have to say any more.

RALEIGH: No, I reckon you don't, little miss.

MAY: Excuse me, mister.

RALEIGH: My mistake. Taking this seat.

MAY: You can tease the dog, but you don't like its bark.

(A long pause. Raleigh looks at May for a moment.)

RALEIGH: Yes, I do. Like its bark. *(A pause.)* My name's Raleigh. Nice to meet you.

MAY: *(Offering her hand.)* Oh. I'm May. Nice to meet you.

RALEIGH: Well, May, I've got a question for you.

MAY: What is it?

RALEIGH: Well, if I come back to Kentucky —

MAY: When?

RALEIGH: Now. If I change trains with you, when you do —

MAY: You thinking about it?

RALEIGH: I'm thinking about it.

MAY: *(Teasing.)* It'd be a brave thing to do. Going to Kentucky. Brave.

RALEIGH: That's enough.

MAY: Sorry.

RALEIGH: As I was saying, May —

MAY: Yes, Raleigh.

RALEIGH: You got a mouth on you, you know.

MAY: Never had before. Guess I got too much sun in California.

RALEIGH: Well, anyway, if I go to Kentucky.

MAY: Yes.

RALEIGH: Hush, now, I want to say this.

MAY: All right.

RALEIGH: No, hush. *(A pause.)* I know you're just getting over, that you don't know. I mean about the missionary work — that you'll be, well, I reckon, do you — if I come home, haven't decided yet, mind you, but if I do, or when — Could I take you to the Nibroc Festival?

MAY: Ask me when you're home.

RALEIGH: No, now, say I'm going home. I mean, that's home, say I'm going there. Will you go to the Nibroc Festival with me?

MAY: *(Pause.)* No.
(A long pause.)

RALEIGH: Why not?

MAY: It's heathen.

RALEIGH: What? What do you mean?

MAY: People probably drinking. And dances. And beauty contests.

RALEIGH: That's heathen?

MAY: Well, no, but its name.

RALEIGH: Nibroc?

MAY: After some heathen God or something.

RALEIGH: What do you mean? It's not named after —

MAY: Or something heathen.

RALEIGH: Nibroc is Corbin spellt backwards.

MAY: No.

RALEIGH: Spell it out.

MAY: I never knew that. I never thought about it before. I never went.

RALEIGH: It's just a big party, May.

MAY: Funny how you grow up with things —

RALEIGH: Yeah. Funny.

MAY: You come back to Kentucky and I'll go to the Nibroc Festival with you.

RALEIGH: Really?

MAY: Yes, I'll go. But I won't go alone.

RALEIGH: I should think not. Well, then, maybe I'll just have to take you.

MAY: What about your friends in the coffins back there?

RALEIGH: They're "different from you and me."
(Blackout.)

Scene Two

Late summer, just over a year and a half later — August, 1942. At the edge of a large park. The cover on the train seat has been removed, revealing a park bench. A church bell chimes eight o'clock. Music is heard from a distance. May enters quickly and angrily, looking back over her shoulder. She sees the bench, starts to leave the other way, looks behind her again, and finally sits. She pulls a small bank bag out of her purse; the coins contained make a noise. She looks over her shoulder, then puts the bank bag under the bench, thinks better of it and retrieves it, getting up to try to find another hiding place. Out of frustration she finally throws it off stage as hard as she can. She listens for a bit and then sits on the bench, staring out. She folds her hands and bows her head, praying simply, as she does every night. This comforts her. Raleigh enters carrying the bag. He is wearing a plaid shirt and overalls, worn but clean and pressed. He stares at her praying for a moment. She finishes and looks out again, not seeing Raleigh. He jingles the bag of coins. She looks at him, startled.

RALEIGH: Not much of a festival this year.

MAY: You!

RALEIGH: Expecting somebody else?

    (Raleigh and May just look at each other.)

MAY: *(Shaken.)* Haven't seen you in over a year and you just appear like a ghost!

RALEIGH: Didn't mean to scare you.

MAY: Where'd you come from?

RALEIGH: *(Simply.)* Woodbine.

MAY: Where'd you come from just now?

RALEIGH: The judging tent. Them jellies not much good. Not much good with so little sugar. Not much to taste. Not much to judge. No, sir, not much of a Nibroc Festival this year. It's a real disappointment so far.

MAY: Is it?

RALEIGH: Seen you at the judging tent. Did you taste them pickles?

MAY: You following me?

RALEIGH: Yep. Reckon we both are. Me and the preacher feller. You and the preacher fellow taste them pickles at the judging tent? Sure made me pucker up.

MAY: He's not following me.

RALEIGH: Never minded rationing before. Never missed the sugar 'til I tried them pickles just now.

MAY: I didn't try them.

RALEIGH: That was a wise decision.

MAY: I've got to get back.

    (May takes the bag from Raleigh. A pause.)

RALEIGH: Gonna be a nice twilight.

MAY: Could be.

RALEIGH: Yep, would've been nice weather for the big festival. If they'd held it. Not this rinky-dink little git-together.

MAY: You must have great expectations since you've been in the big city. Looking down on all us hillbillies back here.

RALEIGH: I just know what the festival used to be.

MAY: I wouldn't know.

RALEIGH: Didn't you go last year?

MAY: You know I didn't.

RALEIGH: I don't know anything. You mad at me?

MAY: I was.

RALEIGH: I figured you was.

MAY: Were.

RALEIGH: I figured you were. You didn't write back.

MAY: I didn't respond to one pitiful little postcard from Woodbine at Christmas time is what I didn't do. What I did do is start teaching school last fall in Lily, and keep on teaching Sunday School at Felt's Chapel, and learning to drive. I've been doing lots of things.

RALEIGH: You driving a car now?

MAY: How d'ya think I get to school?

RALEIGH: You got yourself a car?

MAY: Use my brother's. Got my own ration card for gasoline. He taught me to drive. I'm pretty good.

RALEIGH: I just bet you are.

(He looks at the bag and then off in the woods.)

MAY: You see something? Somebody coming?

RALEIGH: Just a firefly.

MAY: Oh. Good.

RALEIGH: Why're you hiding from the preacher?

MAY: I'm not hiding. I'm just . . . I'm just taking a moment to myself.

RALEIGH: A moment to yourself.

MAY: To collect my thoughts a bit.

RALEIGH: To collect your thoughts.

MAY: And you're keeping me from doing just that.

RALEIGH: And I thought I was helping you.

MAY: Helping me? You helping me what?

RALEIGH: I told the preacher I seen you go the other way.

MAY: You did what?

RALEIGH: Told the preacher I seen you go the other way.

(May puts the money bag on the bench.)

MAY: *Saw. Saw* me go the other way.

RALEIGH: *(Patiently.)* I told the preacher . . . .

306 Arlene Hutton

MAY: Why did you do that?

RALEIGH: Looked to me like you was trying to get away from him.

MAY: *Were* trying.

RALEIGH: *(Teasing her.)* Looked like you had an argument and you was trying to lose him. So when I seen you go this way, and he asked if I'd seen you, I said you went the other way.

(He smiles at her and shifts the bank bag on the bench.)

MAY: *Saw.* It's *saw*, not *seen.*

RALEIGH: *(Playing with her.)* When he asked if I'd *saw* you . . . . . .

MAY: *(Playing back at him.)* Seen.

RALEIGH: *(Feigning ignorance.)* You just said it was *saw.*

MAY: When you *saw* me.

RALEIGH: When I *saw* you.

MAY: He asked if you'd *seen.*

RALEIGH: He asked if I'd *seen* you. And I said I seen you go off the other way.

MAY: Saw. *(Trying not to laugh.)*

RALEIGH: *(Tongue-in-cheek.)* I said you were gone.

MAY: *(Laughing.)* Why would you do that?

RALEIGH: Looked like you wanted to be gone. So I helped you out.

MAY: I don't need any help from you. What time is it?

RALEIGH: Little after eight.

(May stands up quickly, as if to go.)

RALEIGH: Want me to go fetch him for you?

MAY: No.

RALEIGH: Want me to deliver anything to him? *(Raleigh glances down at the bank bag.)* Something I might've found over yonder in the woods?

MAY: No.

RALEIGH: Want me to leave?

MAY: Yes.

RALEIGH: Need my handkerchief?

MAY: *(Emphatically.)* I don't need anybody's handkerchief.

(A pause.)

RALEIGH: Reckon I'll be going then. Nice to *see* you. Glad I *saw* you.

MAY: Why'd you follow me?

RALEIGH: Wanted to *see* you again.

MAY: Why?

RALEIGH: Just wanted to, that's all.

MAY: Well, you have.

RALEIGH: Yep, I sure have. That's right. I sure have. I have *seen* you. You have *seen* me. We have *seen* each other. *(A slight pause.)* And you, you've been seeing the preacher. So what'ja running from the preacher for?

MAY: I reckon I don't know no more. *Any* more.

RALEIGH: You sure have turned into a school teacher.

MAY: I just hate to hear bad grammar. Especially from you. You were going to be a writer. You read lots of books. I liked hearing about all the books you read.

RALEIGH: I don't read much now. Not even the paper. Too much going on. Too much I'm missing out on. Can't join up, won't be drafted, can't even work on the line in the factory. Not much use reading books if I can't do anything. Can't afford them, anyway.

MAY: There's the library.

RALEIGH: I reckon.

MAY: You used to read big books and talk about ideas.

RALEIGH: Thought you didn't like them ol' ideas of mine.

MAY: Your grammar's gotten awful.

RALEIGH: Must be teaching school has made you listen to it different. Differently.

MAY: Must be. *(A pause.)* How was Detroit? I heard from somebody you went off to Detroit.

RALEIGH: Now don't tell me you've been asking around about me.

MAY: Sometimes people tell you things whether you care to hear it or not.

RALEIGH: Yep, sometimes people say things you don't want to hear.

MAY: You just up and left town.

RALEIGH: Figured you didn't want to see me.

MAY: You had dinner with my family. And then you up and left town.

RALEIGH: Now wait a minute. You was supposed to have dinner with my family.

MAY: You *were* supposed to have . . . Supper. It was going to be supper. So why aren't you in Detroit? I think you should be in Detroit. You belong in a city. Don't you like Detroit? What's the matter? Couldn't you keep a job?

RALEIGH: That's right.

MAY: I was just joking.

RALEIGH: No joke. I couldn't keep a job.

MAY: But there's lots of jobs there. Lots of factories. My brother says. Lots of jobs now.

RALEIGH: Not for me.

MAY: You must be pretty lazy not to keep a job. Why, they just hire anybody. From anywhere — there's foreigners there. They hire all kinds of people.

RALEIGH: Not me.

MAY: Couldn't work with the foreigners?

RALEIGH: People 'r' people.

MAY: They're foreigners.

RALEIGH: What would you know about foreigners?

MAY: Seen one down t' the lumberyard. There's one working at the lumberyard. A foreigner. I said hello to him just last week. A foreigner.

RALEIGH: *(Amused.)* You'd 'ave made a good missionary, that's for sure! It's a good thing you haven't gone off into the world and become a missionary. The whole world may go to war, but at least it'll be safe from you.

MAY: That's a mean thing to say.

RALEIGH: Sorry. Just made me laugh for a minute.

MAY: Glad it's funny to you. 'Cause it's serious to me. There's plenty of missionary work to do right here.

RALEIGH: I just bet there is. Lots of missionary work. You gonna help out your preacher friend with his mission work?

(He looks at May, who doesn't answer.)

RALEIGH: I heard you and the preacher feller were getting serious. Heard he was walking you home from the revival meetings.

MAY: You hear a lot.

RALEIGH: Not enough. Tell me, how does he keep so slick looking if he's always kneeling in the sawdust saving people?

MAY: He's a good dresser. Sets an example.

RALEIGH: Snappy-looking, all right.

MAY: He keeps himself tidy.

RALEIGH: Summer's almost over. Festival's over. Tent meeting's over. He's off to someplace else tomorrow.

MAY: I reckon so.

RALEIGH: He ask you to go with him?

MAY: You think you know everything, don't you?

RALEIGH: He ask you to go with him?

MAY: Yes, he did.

RALEIGH: You going?

MAY: I don't know what I'm going to do. He wants us to be missionaries.

RALEIGH: Well, that's what you always wanted. I don't see any difficulties here.

MAY: He's leaving on the train tonight. I'm supposed to meet him at the train station.

RALEIGH: Never know what'll happen on a train. Might as well go. Sounds like a pretty good offer to me.

MAY: Things aren't always as easy as you make 'em out to be.

RALEIGH: I never said things were easy. I'm back in town now. You think that's easy?

MAY: What's so hard about it? It's where you're from. You keep coming and going so much how can a'body keep track of you?

RALEIGH: You better get going if you're going to catch the evening train.

MAY: I reckon so.

RALEIGH: Is he your "magnificent obsession," May? You in love with the preacher?

(A pause. May looks away as if she's about to cry.)

RALEIGH: *(Tenderly.)* What's the matter, Maisy? Did he make advances to you? Did he try to hurt you?

MAY: No, he never, he'd never do a thing like that. You just don't know anything, do you?

RALEIGH: Not if you don't tell me.

MAY: I don't want to talk about it.

RALEIGH: May, what'd he do?

(May doesn't answer.)

RALEIGH: Just tell me. You should tell me.

MAY: I was helping him count the offering.

RALEIGH: He's stealing the offering?

MAY: No. I don't know. Every night I've been helping him. Count the money. It goes to the church. And for the use of the campground.

RALEIGH: Sounds reasonable.

MAY: But every night he puts away a few dollars for "his expenses."

RALEIGH: Still sounds reasonable.

MAY: But if he's a true missionary, all that money should go back to the church. Not to him.

RALEIGH: He's got to have some traveling money.

MAY: And then tonight he kept all of the money. For his expenses. If he were a true man of God he'd just trust that God was feeding him and looking out for him. That's what I would do. If he'd been a true man of God, he'd have trusted that God was providing for him.

RALEIGH: God did provide for him. He provided a lot of people and a big offering at the last meeting so the preacher would have enough money to get to the next town.

MAY: You've changed.

RALEIGH: So've you.

MAY: If I may say so, you have become very narrow-minded.

RALEIGH: *(Laughs.)* You may not say so, and you are even more narrow-minded.

You'll make quite a missionary. *(A pause.)* May, why didn't you come over and have supper with my family last year?

MAY: I just changed my mind, that's all. Person's allowed to change their mind.

RALEIGH: Person's allowed. Person's gotta have a reason, though.

MAY: Just changed my mind.

RALEIGH: 'Cause I whooped your brother for hiding in the back seat of the Studebaker?

MAY: You were just playing.

RALEIGH: 'Cause I argued with your daddy about Roosevelt?

MAY: He loves talk, to debate current issues, as he calls it.

RALEIGH: Must've been you and me then. Must've been me and you. And I thought we were getting along so well.

MAY: We were. Wasn't you.

RALEIGH: What, then? You hadn't met the preacher then.

MAY: That why you followed me just now? To ask me why I didn't have supper with you over a year ago? Over a year ago, before you went off to Detroit and never wrote me.

RALEIGH: I sent you a postcard.

MAY: Not much of a writer, are you?

RALEIGH: *(After a beat.)* I reckon I'm not. Not anymore, anyway.

MAY: I'm sorry I said that. My mouth just seems run away from me sometimes these days.

(A pause.)

RALEIGH: Mind if I set a spell?

MAY: Don't make no nevermind to me.

RALEIGH: Don't want to intrude.

MAY: Sure you got better places to be. With your friends.

RALEIGH: Tired of them. All they talk about is when they'll go to war. When they'll be drafted. Should they join up. They're not much fun. Rather be settin' here with you.

MAY: I'm not much fun.

RALEIGH: Maybe not. But you're prettier. Why didn't you come to supper at our place last year?

(May doesn't answer.)

RALEIGH: I had dinner with your family. Went to Felt's Chapel and then Sunday dinner.

MAY: I remember.

RALEIGH: Your mom's a good cook.

MAY: I helped with the soup beans. Snapped the beans.

Last Train to Nibroc 311

RALEIGH: It was a real good dinner.

MAY: Wasn't anything special.

RALEIGH: Your family's real nice.

MAY: They were on good behavior. For the most part. They were on their best behavior. Except for my brother Charlie. And my Daddy liked talking with you. Thought you were real bright.

RALEIGH: But I wanted to be with you.

MAY: I had to help clean up.

RALEIGH: Wanted to take a drive with you. Had my uncle's Studebaker that night.

MAY: Well, we tried.

RALEIGH: That son-of-a-gun brother of yours.

MAY: Charlie thought it was funny. Won't let me live it down yet. The family's still talking about it.

RALEIGH: Him a'hiding. Hiding in the back seat of the Studebaker

MAY: You sure scared him on the turns.

RALEIGH: No.

MAY: Don't you remember?

RALEIGH: He got carsick. Don't you remember? That's why he had to get off the back floor.

MAY: He got carsick because of those turns. Up the mountain.

RALEIGH: That's when he popped his head up.

MAY: You liked to run off the road when you saw his face in the mirror.

RALEIGH: I knew he was there. That's why I was taking the turns so fast.

MAY: You didn't know anything of the kind.

RALEIGH: Did, too. That's why I was driving up the mountain.

MAY: You were driving up the mountain to get me alone.

RALEIGH: I was driving up the mountain to shake up your little brother.

MAY: You were driving too fast. You still drive that fast?

RALEIGH: I don't drive any more.

MAY: Shouldn't use gasoline if you don't have to.

RALEIGH: Sure did scare your brother, though. He was really carsick.

MAY: I was so mad at him.

RALEIGH: I was, too.

MAY: I bet you were. He ruined all your plans.

RALEIGH: What plans you talking 'bout, May?

MAY: To get me alone top the mountain, that's what.

RALEIGH: What makes you think I had plans like that?

MAY: Why else'd you be driving me up there?

RALEIGH: See the moon, maybe.

MAY: And the stars. Don't forget the stars.

RALEIGH: That's right.

MAY: I recollect it was cloudy.

RALEIGH: All I recollect is how pretty you looked.

(They look at each other for a while.)

RALEIGH: Come have supper with my folks. Won't you?

MAY: Can't. I can't. Charlie says. . . . Did I tell you? He just joined up.

(A pause.)

RALEIGH: No. He's not old enough.

MAY: Just barely. He joined up. Not the infantry. He's going to fly. He wants to learn to fly. So he joined up.

RALEIGH: Well, good for him. Hope he doesn't get carsick in the airplanes. Hope flying don't give him the fits.

MAY: You still get the fits?

RALEIGH: Sometimes.

MAY: I thought that was over. In California.

RALEIGH: It started in California. I thought it would go away. Came back in Detroit.

MAY: Working gives you the fits?

RALEIGH: Farm work doesn't. But seems like lights make the fits come on. The airplanes have lights on them. Assembly line at the factories. Blinking lights. Seems like them lights is what makes the fits happen.

MAY: *Those* lights.

RALEIGH: What lights?

MAY: It's *those* lights, not *them* lights.

RALEIGH: You mad at me? Or you just fussin' at me right now because your preacher friend isn't here for you to be mad at.

MAY: Did you follow me out here to ask me about the preacher?

RALEIGH: Nope. My buddy made me a bet. He bet me a dollar that you wouldn't even talk to me any more 'cause you were going with the preacher.

MAY: You followed me because you made a bet?

RALEIGH: Reckon I won it, too.

MAY: You started gambling now?

RALEIGH: It was just in fun.

MAY: You make bets a lot, do you?

RALEIGH: It was just a game.

MAY: Lose all your money in Detroit making bets?

RALEIGH: Sorry I mentioned it.

MAY: Guess it runs in the family.

RALEIGH: Guess what does?

MAY: Gambling, smoking, drinking.

RALEIGH: What are you talking about?

MAY: Gambling, smoking, and drinking. What don't you understand about that? Seems to me you understand it pretty well.

RALEIGH: You think I run around fast?

MAY: Your daddy does.

RALEIGH: My daddy's a cripple. He walks with two canes. He's a cripple.

MAY: From drinking. Your daddy's got Jake leg.

RALEIGH: He got that more'n ten years ago.

MAY: He's got Jake leg. My brother Charlie told me your daddy's got Jake leg. He got it drinking Jamaica gin. Everybody knows what causes Jake leg.

RALEIGH: So you won't come and sit down with my family because my daddy's a cripple?

MAY: That's not it. . . .

RALEIGH: You won't eat supper with my daddy?

MAY: Your daddy's a drinker.

RALEIGH: Just because he didn't stick to moonshine like everyone else was doing back then.

MAY: My daddy didn't drink moonshine.

RALEIGH: Bet he did. Bet he made it, too. Just ask him for the recipe some day. Bet your daddy didn't have to use an old radiator, either. Bet he had real copper pipes. Your daddy didn't get paralyzed 'cause he was making moonshine himself or buying it from Buggytop Shelton.

MAY: How would you know about Buggytop Shelton?

RALEIGH: Same as you. Folks talk about things. Most are just not as mean about it as you are.

MAY: I'm not mean. I'm religious. D'you drink? D'you buy moonshine from Buggytop Shelton?

RALEIGH: No. But I bet if I'd been in Paris and London I'd been drinking wine and gin and all the stuff they drink there. When there's a war you gotta drink.

MAY: There wasn't any war going on when your daddy got Jake leg. It was prohibition, not a war.

RALEIGH: You're just judging everybody in sight, aren't you? Ought to be over yonder at the judging tent, judging those sour pickles. People make mistakes. Careful you don't make any mistakes. *(A pause.)* You going to cry?

MAY: I don't cry any more.

RALEIGH: Reckon you don't have feelings any more.

MAY: Reckon I don't. You going to have a fit?

RALEIGH: *(A slight pause.)* Reckon you don't have any feelings any more. Reckon it's better that way. One thing we can agree on, anyway. Not to have any feelings.

MAY: There's a war on.

RALEIGH: Reckon that's what's happened to our feelings.

(They sit in silence for a minute.)

MAY: Charlie's going any week now. My momma just can't stop crying. Seems like if she cries I can't.

RALEIGH: I'm sorry, May. *(Pause.)* I wish I was going. Wish I could go in Charlie's place. In anybody's place. *(Pause.)* Just going to stay here and take care of my folks. Everybody wondering why I'm not going.

MAY: Everybody knows farmers get to stay. The preacher's going to raise onions so he doesn't have to go.

RALEIGH: Maybe you should just go help him. Raise some onions. Raise some pigs, too. Wring some chickens' necks. Maybe you should do some hard work.

MAY: I work hard. I work very hard.

RALEIGH: Teaching school.

MAY: I have fifty-one children in my classroom. Fifty-one. And don't think I don't use the paddle when I have to.

RALEIGH: I just bet you do.

MAY: I do.

RALEIGH: Glad I'm not in your class.

MAY: I'd use it on you.

RALEIGH: I bet you would.

MAY: Whenever you'd mouth off.

RALEIGH: I'd mouth off a lot with you.

MAY: Not in my class you wouldn't.

RALEIGH: Bet I would.

MAY: Bet I wouldn't let you.

RALEIGH: Bet you couldn't stop me.

MAY: Bet I could.

RALEIGH: Tell me how.

MAY: I'd paddle you.

RALEIGH: You wouldn't.

MAY: If I had to, I would. I'd paddle you.

RALEIGH: How you gonna catch me to paddle me?

MAY: I'd use a switch. Switch's longer. I'd use a switch on you.

RALEIGH: Where're you gonna get a switch?

MAY: Bushes back by the outhouse.

RALEIGH: You gonna go run out and cut a switch.

MAY: Switch'd reach you better'n a paddle would. Hurt more, too.

RALEIGH: By the time you'd cut a switch I'd be gone. Think I'm gonna sit on a milkin' stool in the corner waiting for you to go out to the outhouse and cut a switch?

MAY: I can run fast as you.

RALEIGH: What would you do when you catch up with me? What would you do, then? I'm too big for you to paddle. What would you do?

MAY: I'd tell you off.

RALEIGH: I can mouth off good as you.

MAY: I'd make you behave.

RALEIGH: What would you do? Can't paddle me, can't outtalk me, what're you gonna do, May? Take away my toys? Take my belongings out of my book bag? Or out of my valise?

(A pause.)

MAY: I wouldn't take your things.

RALEIGH: Wouldn't have thought a fine religious woman like you would take anything from anybody.

MAY: I wouldn't. *(May picks up the bank bag.)* I'm giving it back to the church.

RALEIGH: May, the man's gotta make a living. How's you two gonna live?

MAY: People take care of him. He lives in people's houses. They feed him.

RALEIGH: In the summer. What do you think he does when he's not making the tent circuit? How do you think you're gonna live?

MAY: Is he a friend of yours? One of your buddies? You sure are standing up for him an awful lot.

RALEIGH: I just see both sides of it.

MAY: You must like him. You must think he's a good person.

RALEIGH: Well, I don't think he's a bad person. Just a man trying to make a living, that's all. And, no, I don't like him. I don't like the way he dresses in that white suit, and I don't like the way he talks so kind and quiet-like, and I don't like the way he guided your elbow when you walked through the crowd together at the judging tent. No, I don't like him. I don't like him at'll.

MAY: You watched us?

RALEIGH: Seen you.

MAY/RALEIGH: *(Together.)* Saw.

RALEIGH: *Saw* you.

(They just look at each other.)

RALEIGH: How'd you get so prickly, May? Don't remember you being so prickly. A little feisty, maybe, but not prickly.

MAY: I'm just more grown up now.

RALEIGH: You're just more prickly now. Like a blackberry bush. Or a rose bush. You used to be a, a weeping willow, that's what you used to be, a weeping willow, but now you're just a prickly old blackberry bush. Gotta watch out for you. Don't want to get blackberry stains all over me. No, sir, blackberry stains're hard to wash out.

MAY: You can leave now.

RALEIGH: Think maybe I will.

MAY: You're just an old. . . .

RALEIGH: An old what, May?

MAY: An old, an old tree. Won't move. An old tree. That won't move.

RALEIGH: Like one of those old trees yonder that rises so majestically from the ground?

MAY: Just an old tree.

RALEIGH: That shades and protects us? That awes us in the fall and takes our breath away in the spring?

MAY: You're always laughing at me.

RALEIGH: Not anymore, May.

MAY: You're just an old tree.

RALEIGH: Like those big old trees over t' the cemetery? Big old trees that stand over the graves. Shading and protecting dead people? Yep, you're right. I feel just like one of those big old trees over t' the cemetery.

MAY: You're an old dead tree.

RALEIGH: Or maybe I'm an old tree that's been uprooted by a big tornado, lying on its side with all its roots exposed to the howling wind and the pouring rain. Yep, reckon you're right about something, May. I'm just an old dead tree. Reckon I'm gonna be a stump soon. Just a stump in the ground, so you can sit on me. When you teach them fifty screaming kids of yours about trees you can tell them what a stump I am. Just a blackberry-stained stump with you a'sittin' on me.

(A pause.)

MAY: You trying to be poetical? I'd give that a low mark in my class.

RALEIGH: You don't have to grade me, May. I can do it myself. Give myself the low marks. Don't need you to do it for me.

MAY: Then I don't have to bother with you, then.

RALEIGH: You got that right. You sure got that right, missy. You don't have to bother with me no more, any more, missy. Missy Maisy. And I'm sorry I followed you here. Sorry I told the preacher you went the other way. Sorry you've become so prickly. Sorry I ever rode a train with you.

MAY: I'm sorry, too.

RALEIGH: Then we're both pretty sorry.

MAY: I'm leaving now.

RALEIGH: I'm leaving now, too. Want me to walk you to the train station?

MAY: No. And don't follow me again, neither.

RALEIGH: Wouldn't dream of it.

MAY: I'm leaving.

RALEIGH: So'm I. *(A pause.)* You're not leaving very fast.

MAY: I reckon I'm just not a very nice person sometimes.

RALEIGH: If you're wanting me to agree with you, it's not all that hard right now.

MAY: I'm sorry about your daddy. And I'm sorry I took the preacher's money. I feel sort of ashamed.

RALEIGH: You don't know what being ashamed is.

MAY: I feel very ashamed.

RALEIGH: Ashamed is when you can't go off to war with your buddies. When you're going to be the only one left in town.

MAY: *(Almost overlapping.)* I know that.

RALEIGH: Ashamed is when you have the fits in front of your sergeant.

MAY: *(Almost overlapping.)* I'm sure it is.

RALEIGH: Ashamed is when you give up your own dreams to chase after something in a skirt and find out she's not worth running after.

MAY: You're not talking about me.

RALEIGH: Ashamed is when your new girl won't come to supper at your house because your daddy is a cripple.

MAY: I said I was sorry —

RALEIGH: Ashamed is when you run into that girl a year and half later and you realize what a stupid mule-headed old rooster you've been for ever seeing something in her in the first place. Ashamed is having to come home to a dirt-poor farm and feeling guilty about taking care of your momma and your daddy. And instead of going off to war having to go to Detroit to stand fifteen hours a day on the line in a loud, sweaty dark factory. Ashamed is when the factory doctor tells you you got ep'lepsy.

MAY: You preaching at me?

(He is having the very beginnings of very mild convulsions.)

RALEIGH: You better leave now. Better catch your train.

MAY: Are you all right? You need a handkerchief? Raleigh, you all right? I'll get someone to help.

RALEIGH: It's just a fit. It's the ep'lepsy.

MAY: *(Scared.)* They put people away for having fits.

RALEIGH: The factory doctor said it was ep'lepsy.

MAY: I'm so sorry, Raleigh. Really I am. Forgive me.

(He doesn't hear her. The clock strikes the half hour and May runs off. Raleigh's petit mal convulsions continue into the blackout.)

Scene Three

The following spring — May, 1943. Early evening. The park bench has now become a chintz-covered porch settee or a swing. Perhaps a flag hangs from the window behind it, with a star on it. Raleigh enters from the house, looking older and a little sad. He pulls a brown paper bag out from under the porch seat and and holds it, staring out. He changes his mind and puts it back on the floor under the settee. May enters from the house. She looks tired and more mature. They stare out in silence for a moment.

MAY: Sure is bright down there. Never seen the sky so bright at night. Not even with a full moon. *(Pause.)* Why's it so bright?

RALEIGH: Lumberyard. Lumberyard's burning.

MAY: I know. But why does it burn so bright? Seems like it shoulda burned itself out by now.

RALEIGH: It's a lumberyard.

MAY: Seems the wood 'a burn itself out quickly.

RALEIGH: Big storehouse at the lumberyard.

MAY: Seems it would burn quickly, then. All that wood.

RALEIGH: Lots of paint. And glue.

MAY: I forgot about that.

RALEIGH: Those kinda things real flammable.

MAY: Oh, of course.

RALEIGH: Just gotta burn itself out.

MAY: Seems like they shoulda put it out by now. Everybody down there helping. Can't they put out the fire?

RALEIGH: Not with all that paint and glue a' burning.

MAY: They're just gonna watch it burn?

RALEIGH: Just keep it from spreading. Just contain the fire. It's too hot to fight.

MAY: I wish it would rain. That would put it out.

RALEIGH: Gotta burn itself out. Nothing anybody can do. It's too hot.

MAY: Sure makes the sky real bright.

RALEIGH: Sure does.

MAY: Sure is bright.

RALEIGH: Sure is.

MAY: It's kinda pretty.

(Raleigh doesn't answer.)

MAY: Reckon that's what the war looks like? The sky all lit up like that?

RALEIGH: Could be.

MAY: Never thought the war could look pretty.

RALEIGH: Reckon sometimes it seems to.

MAY: Wonder if that's what the sky looked like to Charlie. When he was parachuting down. Wonder if it was all lit up like that.

RALEIGH: Probably even brighter.

MAY: Sure is burning bright.

(A long pause, while they watch the sky.)

RALEIGH: If you want to drive down and see it, go ahead.

MAY: I don't like to drive at night.

RALEIGH: I'm on a bicycle.

MAY: I know. You want to go down there?

RALEIGH: Too many people. I don't like being around people much these days.

MAY: I don't want to go down there, anyway.

(Raleigh sits beside her on the swing.)

RALEIGH: That was a good dinner.

MAY: Not bad with the rationing goin' on.

RALEIGH: Wouldn't even know it.

MAY: I'm so tired of cornbread, aren't you? Wish we could have had biscuits.

RALEIGH: I thought it was a real good dinner. I appreciate it.

MAY: Least I could do.

RALEIGH: Didn't have to do anything.

MAY: Well, actually, Mama made most of the dinner. I just helped with some of the vegetables.

RALEIGH: It was real nice.

MAY: I'm not much of a cook. Never learned to cook much.

RALEIGH: I thought it was all real tasty. It was a real nice dinner. Good of you to invite me.

(A pause.)

MAY: I am so sorry about my daddy running on so. He always does after a glass of sherry.

(They share a look.)

MAY: He just loves to talk about all the news. I'm surprised he had the radio off during supper. Just talk, talk, talk. Talk about the battles. Talk about Europe. Talk about the Pacific. He can't talk about anything but the war. Can't seem to get enough of it.

RALEIGH: Nice to see him again.

MAY: He sure likes arguing with you. But he does run on. Especially during supper time.

RALEIGH: Well, I sure appreciated the fine meal. And the good company.

MAY: Hard to cook with the rationing on.

RALEIGH: I'm not much for sweets.

MAY: Thanks for bringing the strawberries.

RALEIGH: They're good this year.

MAY: Yes, they are.

(Silence.)

RALEIGH: Reckon I should be leaving, then. Got a train to catch tomorrow.

(A pause.)

MAY: You're leaving town?

RALEIGH: That's right.

MAY: When?

RALEIGH: Tomorrow.

(A pause.)

MAY: Going back to Detroit?

RALEIGH: New York City.

MAY: Why?

RALEIGH: Nothing for me here.

MAY: You're going to New York City? On the train? Tomorrow?

RALEIGH: That's right. Came to say good-bye.

(Raleigh stands up. May is speechless.)

RALEIGH: Don't want to keep you. I reckon you have t'get up pretty early.

MAY: You gotta go so soon? We haven't had a chance to catch up.

RALEIGH: Not much to catch up on. You still teaching, I reckon.

(A pause.)

MAY: Oh, I didn't get to tell you. I didn't get to tell you a thing. I'm principal now. Over t' Paint Lick High School. I'm principal now.

RALEIGH: Is that right?

MAY: They made me the principal. Funny times we're living in. I just barely got outa school and they made me the principal.

RALEIGH: Must be hard.

MAY: I thought it would be. But it was more money. More money'n teaching at Lilly. I thought it would be harder. But nothin's harder than fifty screaming children in one classroom.

RALEIGH: Teaching high school must be hard.

MAY: I thought it would be. But the boys, the really bad ones, they just join up in the service quick as they get old enough. Or even before if they can get away with it. One nice thing about the war. The boys get to go fight, so they don't have to do it at the school. Hard on the younger ones, though. Their brothers all sent off, sometimes their daddies, even. But the big boys, the bad ones are all gone. And the girls aren't much trouble. Always sewing, and writing letters and sending packages. We encourage them to write to the soldiers.

RALEIGH: So the girls aren't much trouble.

MAY: Never are. It's always the boys that are the trouble.

RALEIGH: *(With a twinkle in his eye.)* I beg to differ.

MAY: You're wrong. It's the boys that cause the problems. It's always the boys that are trouble.

RALEIGH: *(Laughing at her.)* I would have to differ with that statement.

MAY: Are you laughing at me? You always. . . . I'm telling you, it's the boys that make all the problems. It's the boys that fight. It's the boys that cause wars. It's the boys that go crazy. *(A pause.)* I'm sorry. I'm sorry I said crazy. I meant they get mean. I didn't mean to say crazy.

RALEIGH: It's all right, May.

(An uncomfortable pause.)

MAY: I've been wanting to apologize.

RALEIGH: What for, May?

MAY: For things I said. Last time I saw you. For leaving you when the ambulance came.

RALEIGH: You already apologized for that.

MAY: In the letters.

RALEIGH: Apology's an apology.

MAY: I wanted to apologize in person.

RALEIGH: Apology already accepted, May.

MAY: You got all my letters? I wanted to make sure I wrote to you every week. Did you get one every week? While you were in the hospital?

RALEIGH: I recollect I did. I haven't gotten any since, though.

MAY: I wrote you every week.

RALEIGH: I've been home for three weeks. Haven't gotten a letter.

MAY: I kept meaning to write after I heard you were home.

RALEIGH: It was nice to get the letters.

MAY: I didn't know if anyone else would write you.

RALEIGH: My daddy can't hold a pen for long. Just to sign his name.

MAY: Your mama wrote you, didn't she? She told me she did.

RALEIGH: She's not much for writing. She appreciated your bringing the corn and the apples.

MAY: Nice that your sister's moved back.

RALEIGH: It's a real help. She and my mama came to visit. Took the bus every week.

MAY: I didn't know you could have visitors.

RALEIGH: You never asked.

MAY: You could've told me you could have visitors.

RALEIGH: It wasn't prison, May.

MAY: Don't they have bars on the windows?

RALEIGH: It's not a prison. Just a state hospital.

MAY: But they've got bars on the windows.

RALEIGH: Yes, May, they've got bars on the windows.
    (A pause.)

MAY: You want to talk about it?

RALEIGH: Nope.

MAY: It might be good to talk about it. With a friend.

RALEIGH: You my friend, May?

MAY: Well, of course, I am.

RALEIGH: I'm glad to know that.

MAY: And you're looking really good. I didn't expect you to look this good.

RALEIGH: I'm doing all right.

MAY: Your, well, your skin looks real good. Good color.

RALEIGH: My skin is fine.

MAY: Well, I'm so glad to hear that. So glad to hear that your skin is fine. *(A pause.)* I know I wasn't much of a friend. When you got sick at the festival. Not much of a friend to anybody. I was scared that night. He's overseas now. The preacher is. Army chaplain.

RALEIGH: Well, good for him.

MAY: He joined up.

RALEIGH: You write to him?

MAY: No. I don't.

RALEIGH: He write to you?

MAY: No. He doesn't.

RALEIGH: Well, good for him. Joining up, that is. Good for him. You write your other feller?

MAY: I don't have a boyfriend. I wrote to Charlie.

RALEIGH: Your feller you were engaged to. You write to him?

MAY: I never wrote to him after I came home.

RALEIGH: You never did?

MAY: No, I never did.

RALEIGH: He ever write to you?

MAY: When he got to England, he did. But I never wrote back.

RALEIGH: He still writing you?

MAY: He got killed.

RALEIGH: Shot down?

MAY: No. He was in an automobile accident. Goes to war to fly, but gets killed in a car.

RALEIGH: Sorry to hear that. He was a lot of fun.

MAY: He got killed. Glad I didn't marry him. I'd be a widow. That's a mean thing to say, isn't it.

RALEIGH: It's an honest thing to say.

MAY: *(A pause.)* I'm sorry I ran away from you that night.

RALEIGH: Reckon you got home all righty. In the dark and all.

MAY: I felt bad leaving you.

RALEIGH: I know.

MAY: I didn't know they'd keep you in the hospital.

RALEIGH: Wasn't anything you could have done.

MAY: You want to talk about it? Being in the crazy hospital?

RALEIGH: You want me to talk about it, May?

MAY: If you want to.

RALEIGH: I don't want to.

MAY: It helps to talk about things.

RALEIGH: I know it does.

MAY: To tell all about it.

RALEIGH: Yes, it helps to tell all about it.

MAY: I'm willing to listen.

(Raleigh doesn't answer.)

MAY: It helps to talk about it. Why, when Charlie was captured, when they brought the telegram, telling us he'd been shot down and captured, I just couldn't stop thinking about it, and praying for him, and couldn't, well, couldn't think about anything at school and at all. Mama just kept crying, and I couldn't talk to her, 'cause she'd just cry, and everybody at school had people missing or dead or something, so I didn't want to burden them. So I just wrote everything to you, like I was talking to you and it helped. It helped an awful lot.

RALEIGH: I liked getting your letters.

MAY: So you see, it really helps to talk about it. Or write about it.

RALEIGH: I did write about it.

MAY: I didn't get any letters. Just a couple of postcards.

RALEIGH: I wrote about it for the newspapers. Sold it, too.

MAY: Sold what?

RALEIGH: The article I wrote.

(He pulls a newspaper clipping out of his shirt pocket and hands it to May.)

MAY: *(Reading the title.)* "A Prisoner in My Own War." You wrote this?

RALEIGH: Wrote it.

MAY: Well, if that doesn't beat anything.

RALEIGH: Sold it. To the *Journal*.

MAY: My, that sure is something.

RALEIGH: I thought so. Wrote it in the hospital.

MAY: That's something to be proud of.

RALEIGH: I am. I'm right proud of that.

MAY: I should think so. What's it about?

RALEIGH: About being in the hospital. About being in a crazy hospital when you're not crazy.

MAY: Will you have to go back to the hospital?

RALEIGH: Not that hospital.

MAY: No, of course you wouldn't.

RALEIGH: 'nother hospital maybe sometime. Regular hospital.

MAY: I'm sorry I didn't come visit. Was it awful?

RALEIGH: It was pretty bad.

MAY: I'm just so sorry.

RALEIGH: You keep saying that.

MAY: I don't know what else to say.

RALEIGH: There's nothing to say.

MAY: I guess not. *(A long, uncomfortable pause.)* You must've been glad to be home. For a while, anyway.

RALEIGH: I was.

MAY: What have you been doing with yourself?

RALEIGH: Reading and writing.

MAY: Glad to hear you've been reading again. F. Scott Fitzgerald?

RALEIGH: Nope. Lloyd C. Douglas.

MAY: You're making fun of me.

RALEIGH: Nope. I've been reading Lloyd C. Douglas. Brought you something. *(Raleigh gets the brown paper bag and a business-size envelope from underneath the seat and hands both to her.)*

MAY: What's this all about?

RALEIGH: Happy birthday, May.

MAY: You remembered my birthday!

RALEIGH: It's hard not to, *May*. Don't recollect the date, though.

MAY: It's next week. My birthday's next week. What is it?

RALEIGH: Open it.

MAY: The envelope or the package?

RALEIGH: Look in the envelope first. That's just to show you. Then you can keep the package.

MAY: It's a book. In the bag. I can feel it.

RALEIGH: You're a clever girl.

MAY: You're laughing at me. *(May opens the unsealed envelope and pulls out a piece of paper.)* It's a letter to you.

RALEIGH: From the *Saturday Evening Post*.

MAY: You get me a subscription?

RALEIGH: Read the letter.

MAY: *Charlie in the Back Seat.* What's this about?

RALEIGH: I sold them a story. *The Saturday Evening Post* bought my story.

MAY: This story's about you and me. And Charlie.

RALEIGH: That's right.

MAY: They're gonna print a story about you and me?

RALEIGH: It's changed a little. It's a story.

MAY: That's really something. You writing for the *Saturday Evening Post*.

RALEIGH: Just like F. Scott Fitzgerald.

MAY: My word.

RALEIGH: Open the bag.

MAY: It's a book. Did you write a book?

RALEIGH: Not yet. But I've been reading this one. And I wanted you to have it.

MAY: *The Robe* by Lloyd C. Douglas. This is the new one.

RALEIGH: I hope you haven't read it.

MAY: I've been wanting to.

RALEIGH: It's real good. Slow to get into, but then it really gets interesting. Hope you don't mind that I read it first.

MAY: I don't mind. I'm glad you read it.

RALEIGH: It's a good book. Made me think a lot. It's religious.

MAY: Glad you liked it.

RALEIGH: I did.

(*A pause.*)

MAY: I don't know what to say.

RALEIGH: You don't have to say anything. Just enjoy the book.

MAY: Thank you.

RALEIGH: You're welcome.

(*A pause.*)

MAY: You're really leaving.

RALEIGH: Reckon I am.

MAY: Well, you always wanted to go to New York.

RALEIGH: Reckon I did.

MAY: And you're all better? Well enough to go?

RALEIGH: Reckon so.

MAY: You just look so good. I can't believe it.

RALEIGH: You look pretty good yourself, May.

MAY: But you've been sick.

RALEIGH: Not that sick. Might not be again. Hard to tell.

MAY: It's just inside, then. Not on the outside? Doesn't that make it worse?

RALEIGH: We're all sick on the inside, May. I think we all are.

MAY: But yours doesn't show on the outside.

RALEIGH: Eventually it all shows on the outside. Take you, for instance. Your eyes are a little duller, 'cause you've been hurt inside. And your daddy. Your daddy's gotten grayer. Your mama looks like she's been tired for a long time. Eventually it all shows on the outside. Everything we've been through.

MAY: I mean your sickness. It doesn't show on the outside yet.

RALEIGH: May, whatever are you talking about?

MAY: It doesn't show on your skin. Not where I can see, anyway. Your skin is perfectly clear.

RALEIGH: I honestly don't have the foggiest notion of what you are referring to.

MAY: Your sickness. You said you had that disease. But it doesn't show on the outside. Is that a good thing? Will it just progress faster on the inside?

RALEIGH: It might not progress at all. It might never come back.

MAY: I didn't know that.

RALEIGH: That's what the doctor said. Might come tomorrow and might never come again.

MAY: So you did have it on your skin, then. And it healed?

Last Train to Nibroc 327

RALEIGH: It's not on my skin. It's in the nerves, they think.

MAY: Then that's worse, then.

RALEIGH: Worse than what?

MAY: If it's already in the nerves it's worse than on the skin. I read about it. When I was preparing to be a missionary. It moves faster if it's inside.

RALEIGH: May, just tell me what you are talking about.

MAY: Your leprosy.

RALEIGH: My what?

MAY: Your leprosy. I've been reading all about it.

RALEIGH: You've been reading too much.

MAY: I wanted to know how to take care of you.

RALEIGH: To take care of me?

MAY: After you told me, told me at the festival, that night when you told me. The night I ran off when you got sick? After that, well, a while after, sometime after I started to write you. After you were in the hospital.

RALEIGH: May, I don't . . .

MAY: I thought about after you were out. You'd need someone to take care of you. To look after you when you were sick.

RALEIGH: You decided to take care — of me.

MAY: Yes.

RALEIGH: Where?

MAY: I don't know.

RALEIGH: You were going to move to our farm? To a sharecrop?

MAY: No, well, no, that's too far out. And I have to keep my job.

RALEIGH: You were going to care for me here at your house?

MAY: No, I thought, I thought. . . .

RALEIGH: Just where were you going to take care of me?

MAY: Some place in town, maybe. Off Main Street.

RALEIGH: You had this all thought out, didn't you? When did you figure this all out? Didn't write it in your letters.

MAY: On my drives. To school. It's a long drive, and I'd be thinking a lot. And I sorta figured it all out. But I didn't know you were leaving.

RALEIGH: You were going to get us rooms in town.

MAY: Lots of places to rent here now.

RALEIGH: And we're just going to live there, you and me?

MAY: I'd look after you.

RALEIGH: We're going to live alone?

MAY: Well, we'd have to. . . .

RALEIGH: We'd have to what, May?

MAY: We'd have to be. . . .

RALEIGH: We'd have to be what, May? What would we have to be?

MAY: You know.

(A long pause.)

RALEIGH: Are you asking me to marry you?

MAY: No.

RALEIGH: But we'd have to be married.

MAY: Yes.

RALEIGH: But you're not asking.

MAY: No.

RALEIGH: Why not?

MAY: You have to do the asking.

RALEIGH: You've got that part figured out, too.

MAY: Not really.

RALEIGH: You invited me over to dinner so I'd propose to you.

MAY: To get reacquainted.

RALEIGH: Now, let me get this straight. You are going to make a mission out of me? I am going to be your new mission. You think I need taking care of. You are going to rent a room and marry me and take care of me.

MAY: You're laughing at me.

RALEIGH: Will you marry me, May?

MAY: What?

RALEIGH: Will you marry me, May? Now, just how did you think this part out? Am I supposed to get down on my knees or am I on my deathbed and you are Florence Nightingale? Should I lie down so I can gaze up into those pretty eyes and ask you to marry me as I breathe my last breath? How was this scene supposed to go, May? Here, look, I'm down on my knees. I'm down on my knees and proposing to you, May. Will you marry me?

MAY: You're laughing at me.

RALEIGH: Will you marry me, May?

MAY: I — are you serious? You said you were leaving town.

RALEIGH: Haven't left yet.

MAY: Are you serious?

RALEIGH: This is your story, May. Do you think I'm serious?

MAY: I don't know what to think.

RALEIGH: I wrote my story, May. Got my story published. This is your story.

MAY: You're just making fun of me.

RALEIGH: You're wrong. I'm just overwhelmed. Overwhelmed that you would. . . . Leprosy's contagious.

MAY: I know that.

RALEIGH: It can spread pretty fast, sometimes.

MAY: Sometimes.

RALEIGH: People care for a leper are apt to get it themselves. Even if they are careful.

MAY: I know that.

RALEIGH: We couldn't live in town long. Leprosy starts to show.

MAY: I know.

RALEIGH: They usually put lepers in a colony. A leper colony.

MAY: I've read about it.

RALEIGH: You willing to go away?

MAY: If I have to.

RALEIGH: You willing to go to a leper colony?

MAY: It might not be for a long while.

RALEIGH: You willing to go live in a leper colony? With me.

MAY: Yes, I am.

RALEIGH: You willing to leave town to take care of me.

MAY: I reckon so.

RALEIGH: To leave your family.

MAY: If I have to.

RALEIGH: That's really something. So you'd go wherever I have to go. California, Detroit, New York City.

MAY: Yes.

RALEIGH: Even go live in a leper colony.

MAY: Yes.

RALEIGH: Watching people's skin falling off. Their noses falling off. Must smell pretty bad, too. All that rotting skin. And people dying. Watching people die. You'd do that for me?

MAY: Yes.

RALEIGH: You'd go with me to a leper colony anywhere in the world, knowing that you might catch it.

MAY: Yes, I would.

(A pause.)

RALEIGH: You're really something, May. How'd you come up with all this?

MAY: When I started writing to you. Even though you didn't write much back. I, I just figured out that you were the only one I wanted to talk to. And when you said you were leaving . . .

RALEIGH: You figured out you couldn't live without me.

MAY: I don't know. I reckon.

RALEIGH: Even though I have . . . leprosy.

330 Arlene Hutton

(Raleigh bursts out laughing.)

MAY: Don't laugh at me. It's not funny.

RALEIGH: You think I have leprosy?

MAY: That's what you called it.

RALEIGH: I never said I had leprosy.

MAY: At the festival. Last year at the Nibroc Festival. You said the factory doctor in Detroit told you that you had leprosy.

RALEIGH: Epilepsy.

MAY: What's that?

RALEIGH: It's epilepsy, May, not leprosy. Epilepsy's the name they give to having the fits. The doctor said I have epilepsy. That's having the fits.

MAY: And that's why you were in the hospital.

RALEIGH: With the crazies. Shouldn't been in the hospital.

MAY: I thought you said leprosy.

RALEIGH: No wonder you thought I looked so good!

MAY: I thought your skin would be falling off!

RALEIGH: You sure are something, May. You sure are something.

MAY: I feel so stupid.

RALEIGH: Marry me.

MAY: You're making fun of me. You've been making fun of me.

RALEIGH: Marry me, May. Marry me now.

MAY: What do you mean?

RALEIGH: You got gasoline in the car?

MAY: Yes.

RALEIGH: Let's go right now.

MAY: To New York City?

RALEIGH: Down to Tennessee. Down to Jellico. Get married.

MAY: Right now?

RALEIGH: Right now.

MAY: I don't like to drive at night.

RALEIGH: I'll watch the road. I'll watch the road for you.

MAY: I have to teach school tomorrow. I can't miss school. I'm the principal.

RALEIGH: I'll get you back in time. Marry me tonight. Be brave.

MAY: I will. I'll marry you.

RALEIGH: Let's go.

(They start to go but she suddenly stops.)

MAY: Oh, Raleigh!

RALEIGH: What?

MAY: Look at it now. Look at the fire now.

RALEIGH: What about it, May?

MAY: It's burning brighter than ever.

RALEIGH: You're right. It sure is bright. Sure is burning bright.

MAY: Looks like a sunrise.

(They hold hands, staring out as the lights fade.)

END OF PLAY

334